THE ROAD TO JERUSALEM

Presented To The
BARON HIRSCH LIBRARY

By

MR. & MRS. BEN LEACH

In

MEMORY of

DAVID, ELIZABETH & SAM SHAINBERG

DATE NOVEMBER, 1968

THE

Road to Jerusalem

THE ORIGINS OF THE
ARAB-ISRAELI CONFLICT
1967

BY

Walter Laqueur

THE MACMILLAN COMPANY

NEW YORK

Library of Congress Catalog Card Number: 68–17517

FIRST AMERICAN EDITION

First published in Great Britain in 1968 by Weidenfeld
& Nicolson Ltd., London

The Macmillan Company, New York

Printed in the United States of America

Contents

Glossary

Ahdut Avoda	Left-wing Israeli party with its stronghold in the Kibbutzim.
Asifa	(Storm); military branch of Fatah.
Fatah	Anti-Israeli movement of Palestinian Arabs mainly in Syria.
Fidayeen	Arab guerrillas.
Gahal	Coalition of the Israeli Liberal party and the right-wing Herut.
Hagana	Jewish defence organisation before 1948.
Knesset	Israeli parliament.
Konenut (*Hebrew*)	Preparedness, alertness, battle readiness.
Maki	Israeli Communist party (mainly Jewish).
Mapai	Israeli Labour party.
Mapam	Left-wing Israeli party, much of its support in Kibbutzim.
Mitun (*Hebrew*)	Literally: moderation. Economic depression.
Palmah	Elite corps, part of Hagana; established in the Kibbutzim during the Second World War.
PLA	Palestine Liberation Army – the military branch of the PLO.
PLO	Palestine Liberation Organisation; sponsored by Egypt, headed by Ahmed Shukairy.
Rafi	Israeli political group, formerly part of Mapai – led by Ben Gurion, Dayan and Peres.
Rais (*Arabic*)	The head, leader – often used in connection with Nasser.
Rakah	Israeli Communist party (pro-Arab).

(Documents included as appendices are usually given in official translation. The spelling of Arab and Hebrew names is not therefore always identical with the *transliteration* in the body of the book.)

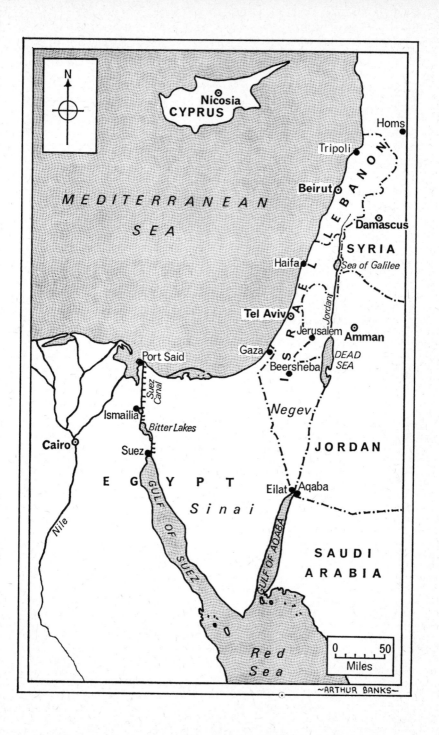

THE ROAD TO JERUSALEM

Introduction

The fact is, we have all been a good deal puzzled,
because the affair is so simple and yet baffles us
altogether.

E. A. POE: *The Purloined Letter*

The war between Israel and the Arab countries was one of the
shortest, and, everything considered, least destructive in modern
history. On the world situation it had only an indirect impact; it
is too early to say whether it was a turning point in the history of
the Middle East. But it certainly was one of the most dramatic
confrontations of our time. It had all the necessary ingredients;
unexpected turns, intrigue, confusion, triumph and tragedy.
There was high tension throughout. Not only those directly
involved, many millions of people all over the world followed
the news from the capitals of the Middle East with bated breath.
Never before has such a small war been so widely reported,
hardly ever have so many felt a deep concern about a conflict in
a distant country.

My work on the prehistory of the war began almost immediately after the armistice. The present study opens with a brief
historical account of the character of the conflict. I then deal in
greater detail with developments in the Middle East during the
year preceding the outbreak of hostilities. The book focuses
mainly on events during the three weeks between 15 May and
5 June 1967. For the student of politics these three weeks are of
even greater interest than the war itself. Lastly, I am dealing with
the repercussions of the conflict in various parts of the globe, its
impact on public opinion, and, of course, the policies of the
powers.

It is generally assumed that a writer on events which happened, so to speak, only yesterday, faces almost insurmountable
difficulties. Most of the source material is usually not accessible.
Nor is there the necessary distance to view the course of events

1

in a wider perspective. While engaged in research for this book I realised, somewhat to my surprise, that while a great many questions of detail remain unsolved, open to more than one interpretation, there are few, if any, real mysteries. (And these, I fear, are unlikely to be cleared up in the near future.) Most of the answers can be found in newspapers and radio broadcasts; one only has to know where to look as the late Sir Lewis Namier used to say.

The problem of detachment and objectivity is more intricate. If 'objective' is defined as equidistant from both camps, this book lays no claim to such an approach. The Red Cross is a great blessing to everyone but I doubt whether history could or should be written from the point of view of the Red Cross. The Arab-Israeli conflict is the kind of issue which leaves few people unmoved or uncommitted. Passions may calm down in coming decades, but, basically, this will continue to be a most controversial subject until the current problems have ceased to be live issues. But to realise that there is no 'scientific objectivity' is one thing, to write a partisan history with an untroubled conscience, another. There are certain rules: one is not for instance permitted to suppress evidence however inconvenient it may be. I have tried to the best of my ability to write a truthful history. It could not possibly be objective in the sense of the definition mentioned before. Every writer has his point of view, his sympathies and antipathies which will not necessarily be accepted and shared by others. With all this, I do not think the facts in this book can be seriously disputed.

There is an Arab as well as an Israeli case; I have tried to state this fairly throughout the book. At the same time, it has been necessary from time to time to call a spade a spade. The Arab world is in the throes of a major crisis; beyond the 'military setback' the events of June 1967 have revealed a much deeper malaise. The field of publicity and expression (to quote Cecil Hourani) has been left in the hands of professional demagogues, blackmailers and semi-educated fanatics; it has led the Arab nation 'not merely to disaster, but to the brink of disintegration'. Vital aspects of Arab policy and public opinion remain inexplicable unless they are viewed against the background of this deeper crisis. From the Arab point of view, this is a painful subject; any discussion of it is bound to provoke much emotional heat. A truthful account of Israeli policy during the crisis has to register shade as well as light. It has to record confusion, panic, individual and collective mistakes as well as manifestations of courage and a spirit of sacrifice. The biblical injunction to tell it not in Gath and publish it not in the streets of Ashkelon ought to be ignored by the historian.

The crisis of May/June 1967 can be approached in various ways. There is the popular account which, if successful, gives one the feel of these days; the reader accompanies the milkman (or the postman) on his rounds and relives the drama as witnessed by them – as well as seen through the eyes of generals, politicians, and other public figures. Such books are often of considerable value; the story of the crisis, after all, is not only a series of speeches, cabinet meetings and diplomatic notes. Books of this kind will no doubt be published and have the success they deserve. Something can also be said in favour of the monographs written by political scientists who are more interested in generalisations than in concrete historical situations; the Middle Eastern crisis will provide them with models for their theories. My own interest was in the crisis *per se*. I could think of several theories which are clearly disproved by the events of summer 1967, but of no fresh, revolutionary insight that has emerged. Probably it is just too early to theorise. I have aimed at an anatomy of the crisis that is neither reportage nor a theoretical treatise. It seemed to me the only way to deal with the subject so soon after the event.

Lastly, there is the crucial question, when and where to start. History is a seamless web, the decision to choose a starting point is always arbitrary. A good case could be made to begin on 15 May when the news about the Egyptian troop concentrations reached Jerusalem. But an equally good case could be made in favour of 7 April 1967 (the air battle between Israel and Syria) or the Israeli retaliatory action at Samu, in Jordan, in November 1966. These incidents contributed greatly to the escalation of the conflict. There would, however, have been no Israeli raids but for the activities of the Arab guerrilla units and of the Syrian Government which gave them full support. If so, January 1965 (when the Syrian-based guerrillas began their forays into Israel) or February 1966 (when the new Ba'ath government came to power in Syria) provide logical starting points. On the other hand, it can be persuasively argued that the escalation in 1967 was the direct sequel to the Suez war in 1956 or, indeed, to 1948, the establishment of the Jewish state and the military intervention of the Arab armies. 1948 and 1956 in their turn were merely the culmination of historical processes that had begun long before. It seems to follow that one ought to go back to the beginnings of the Zionist movement and the first stirrings of the Arab national movement. If so, 1882 is the obvious date when the Biluim, fourteen young men and one woman, landed at the port of Yaffa, the beginning of the first *Aliyah*, the first of successive waves of immigration which preceded the establishment of the Jewish state. Equally, it could be the story of the five young men at the Syrian Protestant College in Beirut who formed a secret society in 1875; many historians regard this as the cradle of Arab nationalism. The various literary societies in Beirut and Constantinople in 1912 could be the starting point or the Congress of al Fatat in Paris in 1913. These were the most important landmarks in the early history of the Arab national movement. There is a curious and in some ways tragic chronological parallelism: Moses Hess had published *Rome and Jerusalem* some years before the first Arab secret society came into being and Pinsker was then writing *Autoemancipation*. The Biluim were just about to leave for Palestine. In the year of the first Arab meeting in Paris, the eleventh Zionist Congress in Vienna decided to establish a Hebrew university in Jerusalem. No survey of recent events will be complete without a discussion, however brief, of the Jewish and Arab case for Palestine.

Throughout the ages there had been an historical connection between the Jews in their European dispersion and the country in which their ancestors had once lived. This link played a vital part in their religion, in their prayers ('if I forget thee O Jerusalem') and in their consciousness as a community. Yet the ritual Passover blessing *Le Shana haba be Yerushalayim* – Next Year in Jerusalem – had remained a phrase without much meaning for all but a handful of Jews. For, if their thoughts lingered in the East, to quote their medieval poet, physically they were clearly inhabitants of Europe. As the walls of the ghettos fell, as after the French Revolution Jews received almost equal rights in most of west and central Europe, assimilation made rapid strides. Jews attained important positions in many walks of life, and

4

with each generation the links with tradition became weaker. It seemed only a question of time before the Jews in the West would disappear, absorbed in French, German or British culture and society.

The great majority of Jews in Russia, Poland and Rumania were less fortunate. Cramped in the darkness of the ghettos, they just managed to survive. Latter day sociologists have discovered redeeming aspects of life in the *shtetl* – the small towns of eastern Europe. They have told us about the warmth and the spontaneity of human relations there; but even if the life of the ghetto was not one of undiluted misery, no one could doubt the intellectual atrophy and moral degradation of the inhabitants. The ghetto Jew was despised by his gentile neighbour; the experience of centuries had taught him that he had to bow in order to survive and the lesson had left him with little self-respect. There were Jewish masses who maintained a biological existence, like ants, Joseph Brenner wrote, but a living Jewish people, in any sociological sense, no longer existed.

During the second half of the nineteenth century a generation of young Jews grew up who realised more fully and felt more acutely the pain and the anomaly of Jewish life: wherever Jews lived they were strangers, at best tolerated, more often hated and persecuted. 'For the living, the Jew is a dead man; for the natives an alien and a vagrant; for property holders a beggar; for the poor an exploiter and a millionaire; for patriots a man without a country; for all classes a hated rival' (Leo Pinsker). Complete assimilation, discarding for good and all the mantle of Jewishness, seemed one way of escape. But assimilation did not work even in western Europe. 'The Germans,' Moses Hess wrote, 'hate the religion of the Jews less than their race – they hate the peculiar faith of the Jews less than their noses.' The forces of light and reason were not as strong as the liberals had thought; the anti-semitic movement made rapid progress even in countries where Jews constituted a small minority. There was no cause to assume that assimilation could ever work in eastern Europe.

The alternative to assimilation was projected in the movement that later became known under the name of Zionism. Most of the precursors of political Zionism were not Jewish traditionalists but men like Herzl who had been estranged from Judaism and were firmly convinced that total assimilation was both desirable and inevitable. Only with considerable reluctance had they come to realise that even the most assimilated of Jews lived in an invisible ghetto in a gentile world. In this world, in which the principle of nationality was coming to play an ever greater part, there was only one road to salvation: the restoration of the Jewish state.

Only in this way, they contended, would it be possible to restore to the Jewish people their elementary human dignity (*aus Judenjungen, junge Juden machen* – to make young Jews out of Jewboys, as Herzl put it). Their own state was necessary, furthermore, if the Jews were to be saved from physical destruction. Unlike the liberal assimilationists, the Zionists were not at all optimistic about the future of the Jewish people in the Diaspora. They were convinced that the anomaly of Jewish existence would produce steadily growing tension and widening persecution.

The first Zionist congress met in Basel in 1898 and the so-called second wave of immigration brought thousands of young east European Jews to Palestine. The first Kibbutzim, the co-operative agricultural settlements, came into being, and Tel Aviv was founded as a suburb of Arab Jaffa. But the Turkish authorities did not favour Jewish immigration and the idea of an autonomous Jewish state was anathema to them. The realisation of the Zionist dream became a practical possibility only with the end of the First World War and the breakdown of Ottoman rule. In the Balfour Declaration His Majesty's Government had expressed itself in favour of the establishment in Palestine of a national home for the Jewish people, under a mandate held by Britain, which was to be responsible for the country for an indefinite period. The Allies had also promised Palestine to the Arabs, though in a less solemn way. These declarations (like many other pronouncements about war aims) were made while the fighting was still going on; it is not at all certain whether those who made them were aware of their full implications.

From the Zionist point of view the Balfour Declaration was a towering milestone; it was Britain's historical merit to make the development of a Jewish national home possible.

But the enthusiasm of the British authorities rapidly waned. There has been much speculation whether the Balfour Declaration was motivated by genuine sympathy with the fate of the

Jews, or was simply a means to help the war effort and to promote British imperial interests in the Near East. Certainly there had been considerable support in Britain as in other European countries and in America, for the national aspirations of the Jews, but there was strong anti-Zionist feeling too, among both Jews and non-Jews. Could the promise be honoured? Britain had emerged from the First World War weaker than before: there was a growing opinion in London that the promise to the Jews had been rashly given and was a nuisance (to put it bluntly) from the point of view of British interests. The Arabs resisted Jewish immigration; there were riots in 1921, again in 1929, and most seriously in 1936–9. British military units had to be stationed in the Holy Land, and public opinion in other Arab countries was becoming more hostile, while Nazi and fascist propaganda fully exploited the British dilemma. Nor did the Jews show much gratitude as the mandatory government began to whittle away at the spirit and the letter of the Balfour Declaration. Immigration was restricted; it was announced that it would soon be prohibited – and this at a time when the rise of Hitler had made the state of European Jewry more desperate. There were various proposals for a long-term solution, such as the establishment of cantons in Palestine and the partition of the country. But Jewish opinion was divided and the Arabs rejected all these plans without qualification.

With the outbreak of the Second World War disaster overtook the Jewish communities of continental Europe. During the war only a few thousand succeeded in reaching the shores of Palestine, and many of them were turned away. By the time the war ended the urge to create an independent Jewish state had become overwhelming. Where else would the survivors of the death camps find a shelter but in their own state? And where would the 600,000 Jews of Palestine find security? The British mandatory authorities faced increasing illegal immigration and acts of sabotage inside Palestine. At the same time there was growing political support for a Jewish state throughout Europe and above all in the United States. In 1947, after some more rounds of inconclusive talks between the three parties concerned, Britain informed the United Nations that it was faced with an irreconcilable conflict of principles. The essential principle for the Jews was the creation of a sovereign state: for the

Arabs it was implacable resistance to any establishment of Jewish sovereignty in any part of Palestine. The United Nations accepted the challenge and after due enquiries and deliberations passed in November of the same year a resolution in favour of the establishment of a Jewish and an Arab state in Palestine. The case for the Jewish state seemed strong, almost incontestable. After a massacre of unprecedented extent and brutality, no one could in good conscience deny the survivors the right to live their own lives in their own country. A world that had been unable to save the Jews from the death camps could hardly force them to remain in a continent that had become the graveyard of the third of the Jewish people. Since the Arabs were irrevocably opposed to any further Jewish immigration and the British were unwilling to impose a solution, what alternative was there but to give their blessing to a small Jewish state?

Like the Balfour Declaration, the United Nations' resolution of 1947 was little more than a statement of intent. No major power was likely to gain from the establishment of an independent Jewish state. In terms of the *realpolitik* of the powers it was not a prudent decision; quite a few observers said so at the time. The Arabs were many and the Jews few; the Arabs had oil and their lands were strategically important. There were bound to be second thoughts about the wisdom of the resolution of 1947 – just as British foreign secretaries had come to regret the Balfour Declaration.

And then, of course, there was the Arab case: Palestine had been an Arab country up to the end of the First World War. Soon after it began the British had given a pledge that the Arabs would gain their independence when it ended. The Jewish community was intruded from the outside by Britain. In the 'twenties the Zionists had bought up the best Arab lands and had established their settlements and after 1942 the creation of a Jewish state became the main plank of their programme. The Palestinian Arabs were thus being asked to atone for the sins of the Nazis and of the other European peoples who wanted to get rid of the Jews. Was it the Arabs' fault that so many Jews had been killed? Had not Arabs and Jews, up to the rise of political Zionism lived together in peace and friendship throughout the ages? Hundreds of thousands of Arabs were now expelled from their homes following Zionist invasion and aggression, lost most of their belongings, became refugees; the Jewish refugee problem was solved by creating an Arab refugee problem. The Zionist invaders, moreover, were not satisfied by the areas assigned to them by the United Nations in 1947. The establishment of Israel was thus a crying injustice: if there had to be a Jewish state, why not in Europe or North America? Was it not the collective guilt that the European peoples felt concerning the Jews which made them ignore the fact that morally, and in every other respect, right was on the side of the Arabs in the conflict over Palestine?

Such, in briefest outline, is the Arab case. Palestine was a part of the Turkish dominions when the British took over, then inhabited by about 700,000 people, a mixture of nationalities and religions. Arabs usually overstate the cordiality and good relations between the two peoples in periods more recent than the 'Golden Age'. There were notable exceptions, but by and large the Jews were second-class citizens under Islamic rule. The advocates of the Arab case also forget that the concept of a Jewish state gathered so much momentum precisely because the Arab leaders were so unwilling at the time to take up the idea of a binational state. If Israel expanded beyond the borders of the 1947 resolution, if the Palestinian Arab state that had been envisaged did not come into being, was it not because the Arab governments had refused to accept the United Nations decision and had invaded Palestine in 1947? It is one of the ironies of history that but for Arab resistance a Jewish state might never have come into being; or have remained a small strip of land between Tel Aviv and Haifa.

That the Arabs lost the war of 1948 was a misfortune but not a moral argument. There has been traditionally, and still is, much loose thinking on both sides on the Arab-Jewish problem. Zionism more or less ignored the Arab problem for decades – it did not figure in the writings of the early Zionist movement. Later on it was argued that, since the Arabs inhabited such vast territories that had never been cultivated and developed, and since Zionism wanted only a tiny part, was it not in their own interest to make room for a small Jewish state? This was a little naïve; there was no reason to assume that Arab nationalism would ever give up any part of its homeland. But then the history of the Islamic peoples has also been one of conquests. Nations have not usually come into being in accordance with the moral law, but as a result of migrations, invasion, military conquest, and similar acts of violence. This was the way the Israelites originally came into their Promised Land, and, later on, the Arabs. After a while the right of conquest becomes a moral right – sometimes after a few decades, sometimes after a few centuries. The Jewish national movement had the misfortune to be a late-comer among the nations, and what would have passed as the most natural thing in the world in the nineteenth century was to be rejected in the twentieth. It has also been argued that in our day and age only big powers, or countries that have at least big-power support, have the right to annex territories. But these are political explanations, not moral arguments. In Palestine there was a clash between the aspirations of Jews and Arabs; on both sides the aspirations were natural and legitimate.

1

Israel and the Arab World, 1948–66

The UN General Assembly passed the resolution on Palestine on 29 November 1947. Mr Truman was then the occupant of the White House and Stalin of the Kremlin, the cold war was under way, but had not yet reached its climax; Czechoslovakia was not yet communist, Mr Jan Masaryk had not yet fallen from his room on the Hradcin. From the Zionist point of view, it was a unique constellation, perhaps the last opportunity; Russia and the United States could still agree on some topics; it was extremely doubtful whether the resolution would have been passed twelve months later. But the General Assembly could only express certain wishes and desires; it was neither willing nor able to help any people establish a state of their own. And since the Jews of Palestine were few and very weak – since they had no regular army, no air force, no artillery, it seemed doubtful whether they would ever get their state. On the very day the UN resolution was passed, the Arabs of Palestine rose against it and received help from other Arab countries; they attacked individual Jews and Jewish settlements, closed the road to Jerusalem and other places. Their aim was to get a stranglehold on communications and they very nearly succeeded. True, whenever they engaged in more ambitious military operations they fared less well. But they regarded this merely as a prelude, for it had been agreed that with the end of the British Mandate, the neighbouring Arab states would enter the country and throw the Jews into the sea.

The invasion took place, as expected, on 15 May 1948. The Jordanians sent their British-officered Arab Legion, and King Abdallah expected to enter Jerusalem on 25 May. The Egyptians had two brigade groups, including armoured units, on the way to Tel Aviv. An Iraqi contingent attacked on the central front and a Syrian mechanised brigade in the north. The Arab forces were relatively small and ill-equipped and there was no co-ordination between them; even so they were far superior to the hastily created Jewish army which got its first guns only after the invasion. Yet the Israelis managed somehow to hold on to Jewish Palestine during the first phase of the fighting, and passed to the offensive during the ten days in July 1948 when fighting again flared up. On 18 July, following the intervention of the UN, the war virtually ended, but for three brief Israeli operations, two against the Egyptians in the south, and one against the Syrian-sponsored army of irregulars in western Galilee.

The next scene in the conflict was enacted in Rhodes, where a series of armistice agreements was worked out between Israel and Egypt, Syria, Jordan and the Lebanon. The other Arab countries (including Iraq) refused to have an armistice agreement. At the time it was widely thought in Israel that the armistice would soon give way to real peace; but the hostility of the Arab states towards Israel had by no means diminished as a result of their military failure; they had not the slightest intention of recognising the 'gangster state' (as they came to call it), which had usurped Palestine and expelled its Arab inhabitants. The outcome of their invasion had been disappointing, for Israel now held more territory than the UN resolution had assigned to it – above all, Jerusalem and western Galilee. But the Arabs confidently expected that this first round would soon be followed by a second which would restore Palestine to its rightful owners.

The armistice agreements were not an unmixed blessing for the Israelis. Only in the north, with Lebanon, did the new border follow the old international frontier. Elsewhere, villages were divided, demilitarised zones and small corridors established and, of course, Jerusalem was partitioned. From a military point of view, the borders of the new state were a nightmare.

The Arab leaders, confident that time was on their side, rejected all Israeli proposals after 1949 for a partial repatriation of the Arab refugees (between 600,000 and 750,000 had left their homes in 1948), for border revisions, for economic cooperation, for a hundred years' peace treaty on the basis of the existing frontiers. The Arab leaders simply refused to accept the *status quo*, which in their eyes perpetuated a crying injustice: they wanted the repatriation of all Arab refugees, in line with the UN resolution of December 1948, which has been often quoted since. (Israel usually counters by drawing attention to that part of the resolution which refers to peace; could Israel be expected to take the refugees back before peace was restored?) The Arab governments also wanted compensation for Arab property seized in Palestine. Above all, they wanted a return to the original partition plan of 1947. But Israel was now totally opposed to the revival of a scheme which the Arabs had so emphatically rejected at the time, and which, it argued, had been nullified by the invasion of May 1948.

So the uneasy truce lingered on for years, interrupted only by Arab guerrilla forays into Israel and Israeli acts of retaliation. The Arab governments imposed an economic boycott against Israel, which became more and more stringent with the years; they closed both the Suez Canal and the Gulf of Aqaba to Israeli shipping. If the Israelis flouted the UN refugees resolution, they contended they were entitled to ignore the United Nations resolution about freedom of shipping. UN observer teams were established along the borders, but these unhappy men were to act only as accountants: their task was to register incidents and complaints and to transmit them to UN headquarters. In Arab attacks between 1949 and 1956 some 1,237 Israelis were killed or wounded; the number of Arabs killed or wounded was probably even higher. Israel was at a double disadvantage, for the part played by the Arab governments themselves in the guerrilla attacks could never be established, whereas the Israeli Government always took responsibility for the retaliatory actions. As a result Israel was condemned by the UN far more often than its opponents; in later years the Soviet veto in the Security Council effectively blocked any decision unfavourable to the Arabs. All this caused much bitterness in Israel. The vicious circle of infiltration, guerrilla attacks, and retaliation was after all always initiated by the Arabs; no one in Israel had any intention of infiltrating the Arab countries. And yet the umpire's decision usually went against Israel. By 1953 there was little gratitude or respect left for the organisation which had acted as the midwife of the new state six years earlier.

The situation on Israel's borders was dangerous, but it was not the main problem facing the Jewish state in the years immediately after the war of independence. Between 1948 and 1954 some 750,000 new immigrants reached the shores of Israel, the survivors of the concentration camps, Jews from south-east

Europe, the Middle East, and North Africa. Within a few years the number of newcomers exceeded that of the old settlers; the whole ethnic and social character of the state was changing. These were the years of austerity, of rationing and of the *ma'abarot*, the camps of wooden huts and tents in which the new immigrants were housed. Jewish Palestine had been a country of pioneers; immigration had always been selective, but now it had to absorb elderly and chronically sick people; most newcomers were, of course, unskilled. It was a tremendous strain; only the generous help of Jewish communities abroad, above all in the United States, made it possible to develop the economic resources of the country to increase its absorptive capacity. Subsequently, German restitution payments played a very important part in this respect. These were critical years. The situation gradually improved only after 1954 and in the late 'fifties steady growth turned into prosperity. But economic absorption was only one aspect of the crisis, albeit a very important one. Israel in 1955 was very different from what it had been ten years previously, and it was not at all clear whether some of the pioneering spirit would be preserved and whether it would be possible to integrate the newcomers in such a way as to make them conscious and active members of the new nation. The War of Independence had been the first challenge to the new state, but the Ingathering of the Exiles (as the mass immigration was officially called) was, if less dramatic, not less difficult. The early fifties in brief were not a happy period in the history of Israel. In a setting of drab poverty, morale was low, grave mistakes were committed by the Government and the political parties, and among the population not much was left of the civic spirit and the enthusiasm of 1948. These were anti-climactic years, shadowed by disappointment and occasionally by despair. But there was no alternative; encircled by hostile countries, the new state could not turn back, nor could it relax. The Israelis hung on, and step by step the country turned the corner. By 1955 there was no longer any doubt that Israel was a going concern.

Great changes took place in the Arab world after the unsuccessful war against Israel. The frustration of the lost war accelerated political and social developments. In 1948 Jordan and Iraq were ruled by the traditionally pro-British Hashemites, while King Faruk was the undisputed ruler of Egypt. The Palestinian war undermined these regimes, creating a condition of instability throughout the Arab world. King Abdallah of Jordan was assassinated; his relations in Baghdad and their faithful and powerful adviser Nuri Said hung on for a few years, but their ultimate fate was the same. Abdallah was the embodiment of the old school of Arab politicians; a conservative authoritarian ruler and a traditionalist, he had no use for new-fangled democratic ideas which, in his view, could only have disastrous consequences in a country like Jordan. He combined the virtues and the weaknesses of the old school of Arab statesmen. Neither an extremist nor a popular leader, he (and those like him) were totally out of step with the mood of the younger generation. There was no place for them in an age of radical policies in which the masses wanted to take an active part in the political process. The generation of Abdallah and Nuri Said was replaced by the generation of Nasser, Kassem and Arif, far more nationalist and radical in outlook, far more dynamic – but also far more irresponsible, ambitious and often more mendacious and hysterical. Western statesmen had easily found a common language with the conservative Arab leaders in the nineteen twenties; they found communication with the populist leaders of the fifties and sixties almost impossible.

Syria was shaken by a series of military *coups d'état*, the first occurring almost immediately the Palestinian war was over; these lasted to 1953, when the traditional party politicians again provided for a number of years a not very stable civilian government. The most radical changes took place in Egypt, which had been rent by internal strife for years. Religious fanatics of the Muslim Brotherhood and other movements, para-fascist and para-communist, sprouted and gained adherents not only among the intelligentsia, and especially the students, but among the middle classes as a whole and particularly the younger officers. The defeat in Palestine had shown up all the weaknesses of the regime and it triggered off the revolt. It was by no means the only cause, perhaps not even the deepest reason: there was the British occupation of the Suez area and the British presence in general – a disgrace in the eyes of every Egyptian patriot. There was the rule of a profligate king, a corrupt administration, abject poverty and quasi-feudal conditions in the countryside. There was no prospect of reform and revolution

15

thus became inevitable. The coup in the summer of 1952 was by no means extremist in character; its leaders wanted to get rid of Faruk and of a regime that was universally despised. It wanted to supervise the transition to a more honest and effective government. It had no philosophy of its own (*pace* Nasser's pamphlet), and was welcomed at the time by the United States and denounced by the Soviet Union as 'fascist' in character. But the honeymoon with America lasted only two years; Nasser's ambitions were different from those of Kemal Ataturk. In 1954 Egypt was at the crossroads, but it was already obvious that its policies would in future be influenced to a large extent by radical Arab nationalism. Arab nationalism as propagated by Nasser and his followers throughout the Middle East is ill defined as a political doctrine, but this did not necessarily make it any less effective as a political movement. It is the key to the understanding of the state of mind of the Arab world, and it is to the origins and the character of Arab nationalism that we have next to turn.

The Ottoman Empire was inhabited by millions of people who spoke Arabic, but up to the end of the nineteenth century there was no specific feeling of community between them; the Turkish overlords hardly had cause to worry about Arab separatism. Where such stirrings occurred, as in Egypt or on the Arabian peninsula, they were usually motivated by local nationalism or religious dissension. An Arabic consciousness developed only in the eighteen-eighties, partly under the impact of the revolt of Araby Pasha and Britain's occupation of Egypt, partly as the result of the spread of western ideas of progress, democracy and nationalism among Syrian and Egyptian intellectuals. The idea of a national revival fell on fertile ground and found a sympathetic response among the Allied powers who redrew the map of the Middle East at the end of the First World War. Nevertheless the Arab parts of the Ottoman Empire did not gain full independence – Egypt and Iraq remained under British tutelage, Syria and Lebanon became French, Palestine was ruled under a British mandate. (Hardly anyone at the time thought of the Maghreb as part of the Arab world.) There was no real independence; certainly there was no unity. Egyptians thought of themselves above all as Egyptians, not Arab patriots; Egypt had its specific traditions and interests, many of them on the African continent. The main advocates of Arab unity in these years were the conservatives – King Saud on the one hand, and his enemies, the Hashemites of Transjordan and Iraq, on the other. A League of Arab States was formed only much later, towards the end of the Second World War, with British blessing; but it has never been more than a loose working group.

The frustrations of a young Arab nationalist who reached political consciousness in the thirties and forties were manifold and deep, and were often intensified by the impact of radical ideologies imported from Europe. The radical Arab nationalist found the Arab homeland dominated by the imperialists and their stooges. Nowhere was there a truly popular government, nowhere any real attempt to bring about Arab unity and social justice. In his eyes British colonialism still reigned supreme in Egypt. There were the memoirs of Denshawi fifty years earlier; the scuffle between British officers, hunting pigeons and local peasants. One British officer died, probably from heat stroke, but the tribunal sentenced four fellaheen to death and others to severe floggings. King Faruk himself had been humiliated by a British ambassador who imposed his will by bringing up a few tanks to the Royal Palace. Wherever the Arab patriot looked, he saw foreigners in control: the British and the Americans exploited the rich oil wells of Arabia and Iraq. The older generation of Arab leaders had believed in close collaboration with the West, because they had genuinely believed that the Arabs needed its help. The younger generation of radical leaders regarded the West as (at best) an obstacle. They were aware that Arab society had to be reformed, but they saw no chance for social reform under semi-colonial rule, or the even more insidious neo-colonialism. Nor did they expect any advance on the road to Arab unity so long as the power of imperialism remained unbroken in the Middle East. For western imperialism, they said, has a vested interest in perpetuating the artificial divisions in the Arab world.

The Second World War brought full independence to most Arab countries, but this did not give much comfort to the radical nationalists. The old gang was still in power. A real change would come only after the conservatives and the stooges of western imperialism had been replaced by popular forces. But the 'old gang' was supported by the imperialist powers, among whom the Americans now played a central role. You must move cautiously, the Americans advised them, do one thing at a time, put your house in order before you engage in more ambitious schemes. Only the communists are likely to benefit from hasty and sweeping changes. But, given the urgency of the problems of the Arab world, how could anything but radical change be effective? The young Arab nationalist of the fifties was not likely to be impressed by the menace of communism; Russia was far away and western imperialism still very much in evidence nearer home. Arab nationalism was on the move, it wanted to achieve things, but everywhere it came up against walls erected by western imperialism. There was a growing conviction that the supreme aim of the West was to stifle and humiliate Arab nationism, to retard the development of the Arab world, in order to keep it in permanent bondage. Smouldering resentment against the West now turned to hatred. In part this was the after-effect of colonial rule, with its humiliations and indignities. It was an unfortunate reaction but hardly unnatural and certainly not the Arab's fault. But why did anti-western feeling become so much more intense after the West had begun to withdraw from the Middle East? Was it simply a conditioned reflex? The colonial relationship does not explain it. Above all, it was a mixture of envy and impotence. Arab nationalism differed from other national movements both by its vast ambitions and its tremendous internal difficulties. The West became the obvious scapegoat, the alibi for the failure to solve the internal problems. The Arabs are heirs to a proud cultural tradition, their ancestors had kept the flame of civilisation burning in the dark ages. But since then the Arab world had gone through centuries of sad decline; modern European political structures had been imported into the Arab world, republicanism was tried and parliamentary democracy; fascism had many adherents in the nineteen-thirties, and later on, socialism and communism.

Arab expectations had been revolutionised to such an extent by their own propaganda that the failure to realise them was bound to result in deep frustration and often in anarchy. In some ways the Arab reaction in its irrationality resembled the Chinese Cultural Revolution. China's attitude to the West, like that of the Muslim world, had been for centuries one of superiority and self-contained complacency, until in the nineteenth century it was suddenly realised that the despised West was far more powerful, and that it was getting richer and more powerful every day, whereas the East continued to stagnate. The mood of the Easterner changed (to quote Bernard Lewis) to anxious emulation. It was thought that by study and imitation, it would be possible to discover and apply the elusive secret of the strength of the West: 'Generations of eager students and reformers toiled in the search. They may not have loved us, or even understood us, but they did admire and respect us. Today they usually do neither. The mood of admiration and imitation has given way to envious rancour.'

The Cultural Revolution in China, like the crisis in the Arab world, is the result of the continuing gap between ambition and performance. The frustration of the Arab world is aggravated by the fact that it has neither 700 million inhabitants, nor a hydrogen bomb. Nor has the Arab world been able to develop its industry without foreign help; the work ethos of the Muslim world is not that of China – communist or pre-communist. This backwardness exemplifies a failure of the Arab élite which naïvely believed (and largely still believes) that political and economic doctrines can by themselves work miracles, that radical socialist phraseology rather than hard work is the key to economic progress. It was never fully realised that there could be no advance towards the socialist goals proclaimed by radical Arab nationalism without integrity and patience and a sense of moral responsibility on the part of the elite. In the eyes of many new leaders socialism and social justice were, so to speak, a public issue, a matter for speeches and articles, which had little bearing on human relations – let alone on their private lives. In the Arab world in the nineteen-fifties the belief gained ground that the standard of living of the population could be dramatically raised by a mixture of pan-Arabic propaganda, the import of armaments, and over-ambitious plans based on the hope that either the United States or the Soviet Union, or both, would pay for them.

All this refers mainly to Egypt, and it may be argued that such criticism is basically unfair. For Egypt is so desperately poor and overpopulated that no social or political system could in the long run be successful. It has been said that Nasser's desire to raise living standards was subordinate to his chief aim: to advance

19

Egypt's prestige. But would he have received loans and gifts but for the fact that he showed that Egypt had a considerable nuisance value for both West and East? And since it seemed impossible to solve Egypt's economic problems inside Egypt, were the armaments not a means to an economic end: to expand, to gain control of the oilfields of Arabia – or at least of Libya? The Egyptian plans could not succeed because the fellaheen were too poor to make primitive capital accumulation possible. At the same time the Amir of Kuwait and the Saudian Government received $600–700 million each year from the oil companies. However intense their feelings of pan-Arab solidarity, they had not the slightest intention to share their wealth with their poor brethren. There were and are many reasons for the failures and frustrations of radical Arab nationalism. At bottom many may be traced to natural human shortcomings, but it would be unfair to ignore the circumstances which have impeded the social, economic and political development of the Arab world, quite independently of the quality of its leaders and its élites.

Israel in the Arab Mirror

The hostility of radical Arab nationalism towards Zionism and the Jewish state hardly needs an explanation. The establishment of a Jewish ('racialist') state is felt as a grave injustice and there can be no compromise with Israel. Occasionally Arab spokesmen have threatened a war of extermination ('a momentous massacre which will be spoken of like the Mongolian massacres and the Crusades' – Azam Pasha, secretary of the Arab League, on 15 May 1948). Ahmad Shukairy, head of the Arab Liberation Organisation, said at a press conference in Amman almost exactly nineteen years later that hardly any Jews would survive in Israel after the invasion of the Arab armies (*Daily Telegraph*, 2 June 1967). On other occasions – in conversation with western statesmen and journalists – Nasser and other Arab leaders have argued that their only aim was to destroy the state, not its inhabitants, and that 'extermination' should not therefore be taken literally. Arab nationalism considers Zionism and Israel as an enemy both in themselves and at the same time as the spearhead of western imperialism. Israel's temporary survival is compared with the vain attempts of the crusaders to gain a foothold in Palestine; despite their initial achievements they lost in the end. According to the official Arab image, the Jew is a weak being and a coward, but at the same time omnipotent. (The standard lines of traditional anti-Jewish propaganda are used in this context; the argument that Arabs cannot possibly be anti-semitic since they are themselves 'Semites' can safely be ignored.) These themes of propaganda are of some importance, for they misled both Arab leaders and the masses about their enemy. To give but one illustration: the weekly organ of the Egyptian army, *Al Kuwat al Muslaha* wrote on 16 November 1964:

the Jew in his very soul and character does not possess the qualities of a man who bears arms. He is not naturally prepared to sacrifice his life for anything, not even for his son or wife. If there is today a man in Israel who bears arms he does so because he is sure that there is another man who will precede him, who will stand in front of him, not behind him, in order to defend him when the time comes.

But the Jew is also all-powerful, pulling the wires all over the western world in virtue of his immense cunning, his wide connections, and his vast resources. The Jew was behind both Kennedy and Kennedy's murder; he is behind all the scandal and corruption throughout the world.

In conversation with westerners Nasser and others have argued that Arab nationalism is not against the Jews and Judaism *per se*, only against Zionism. This contention is not, however, borne out by the domestic policies of the Arab countries; the Jewish communities all over the Arab world are subject to discriminatory legislation. When Prime Minister Bourguiba of Tunisia appointed a Jewish member to his cabinet, he was bitterly attacked by the Egyptian press for this betrayal. When the Ecumenical Council undertook certain revisions with regard to the responsibility of the Jews for the Crucifixion, all Arab governments were up in arms. They claimed in their protest notes that the Jews – not the Zionists! – bore 'total and perpetual guilt' for Christ's death. ('What Hitler did to them was simply revenge for what they did to Christ' – *Al Mussawar*, 6 December 1963.) The line taken *vis-à-vis* Nazi Germany and Nazi anti-semitism is inconsistent. Nasser and other leaders of Arab nationalism have stressed their opposition to Nazism and Fasc-ism; there is no reason why they should like Hitler, for would a

Jewish state ever have come into existence but for the Nazi persecution of the Jews? Yet Nasser also said in an interview with the neo-Nazi *Nationalzeitung* (1 May 1964) that during the Second World War 'our sympathies were with the Germans', and that the 'lie of the six million murdered Jews is not believed by anybody'. On another occasion Nasser emphasised the great relevance of the 'Protocols of the Elders of Zion' for an understanding of the key issues of our time (in an interview with the Indian journalist Karanja, *Al Ahram*, 29 September 1958).

After the war of 1967 the Egyptian leaders realised that their anti-Jewish propaganda had been a tactical mistake, and that their Russian and Spanish friends had been embarrassed by the threats to exterminate the Israeli Jews. But it is doubtful whether there will be a basic change. Israel is the enemy, the Israelis are Jews, and most Jews support the Jewish state. The essence of effective propaganda is simplicity; even if they really meant it, the Egyptian leaders would find it almost impossible to differentiate between Jews and Israelis in their propaganda. So far, the war of 1967 has not caused any basic change in the Arab approach; the propaganda organs continued to devote time and space to the 'Protocols' and ritual murder (see, for instance, *Akher Sa'a*, 21 June 1967).

The Soviet Union

The Soviet Union first entered the Middle East in 1955; it did so with a bang and its influence has grown ever since. Its success cannot be ascribed to any single cause; Russia had not been involved in Middle Eastern affairs for forty years and it could not be tarred with the brush of imperialism in the Arab world. The western powers throughout the forties and fifties sought to gain the support of the Arabs, for sundry military pacts, whereas the Russians advocated a neutrality which coincided with the desires of the Arab leaders. Western interests clashed almost everywhere with the rising tide of Arab nationalism, whereas Russia appeared as a disinterested and benevolent onlooker. Capitalism and democratic socialism seemed tired doctrines while the Soviet Union evoked dazzling dreams of speedy modernisation and industrialisation for the peoples of under-developed countries. Above all, Russia became so popular because it was anti-western. What had begun as a tactical manœuvre – the arms deal of 1955 – to counter western plans to align Iraq in its pact system, gradually became a basic reorientation in the policy of Egypt and other Arab countries. An alliance with the Soviet Union, formal or informal, corresponded to the general anti-western mood, the wish to spite the West, and, if possible, to humiliate it. This was the overriding cause; the growing influence of some aspects of communist doctrine happened almost imperceptibly and was a by-product.

Up to the middle fifties the appeal of communist ideas in Asia and Africa was strictly limited; their doctrinaire essence, their heavy emphasis on the class struggle, their hostility to religion impeded their growth. With the change in world communism that took place after Stalin's death, and particularly the gradual spread of polycentrism, communism gained many new friends, even though the monolithic character of the world movement had gone. The ill-digested mixture of communist doctrine and Arab nationalism that now became fashionable would have been anathema in Stalin's day, but was now welcomed as progressive achievement. The countries that embraced this new ideology were welcomed as friends and allies in the struggle against western imperialism.

During the first stage of this reorientation of Arab politics, the stress was still on 'positive neutralism'. With the erosion of the 'third world' bloc, neutralism gave way to anti-western commitment. While the 'national revolutionary' regimes continued to receive massive western economic help, their stand in world affairs became in most cases downright hostile to the West. In its anti-western ardour, public opinion began to outdo the Soviet bloc; some of it veered towards China, for it was felt that with the growing prosperity in the Soviet Union the distance between Moscow and the wretched of the earth had widened. Its foreign policy had become more cautious and the national-revolutionary struggle had suffered as a result. While political and military leaders in Washington and Moscow developed a new feeling of responsibility befitting their position as super powers, there was not much concern in the Arab capitals about the possible consequences of a third world war. The idea of an International of the Have nots, an alliance of the poor agricultural regions of the world against the metropolitan countries, would have won even greater sympathy in the Arab world but for the geographical distance between Cairo and Peking, and China's inability to give the Arab world, for the time being, much more than verbal support. Soviet policy in the Arab world did not proceed in accordance with a well thought out master plan prepared in minute detail. The Soviet Union was drawn into the Middle East not exactly against its will, but in response to a sudden challenge. It has been its policy ever since to fortify and extend its positions. In pursuance of this policy it has been willing to cooperate with any Arab government and political party; if communist or near-communist groups came to power in Arab countries they did so by their own momentum, without the benefit of substantial Soviet help. If Soviet policy was pro-Israel in 1948 and became bitterly hostile later, this had nothing to do with anything Israel did or refrained from doing. It was simply that in 1948 there was no scope for Soviet initiative in the Arab countries, whereas in the nineteen-fifties the opportunities became far more promising. Israel was small, the Arab countries far more populous; the Arab states had oil, Israel merely potash. The Soviet Union greatly overestimated the strength of Egypt and Syria, in the naïve belief that countries engaged in what were thought to be popular revolutions were invincible – the wave of the future. But western observers were equally naïve in their belief that it was inconsistent on the part of the Soviet Union to support Arab regimes which imprisoned their communists, and to oppose Israel which had the only legal communist movement in the Middle East. As if Soviet foreign policy had ever been influenced by considerations of this kind; even a communist Israel would not have made the Soviet leaders swerve from their support for the Arabs, it would merely have embarrassed them. Israel's mistake in Soviet eyes was not its social character and its foreign policy, but the fact that it had only 2·5, not 25 million inhabitants.

Suez

In October 1956 Britain and France tried to regain control of the Suez Canal; previously an agreement had been reached with Israel to coordinate military action between the three countries.

The attempt badly planned and indifferently executed encountered much opposition all over the world (including Britain), it aligned Washington together with Moscow with the great majority at the United Nations. The decision to invade the Canal Zone (which had been given up by Britain only a short time before) followed the nationalisation of the Suez Canal by Nasser. This was in retaliation against the American withdrawal of an earlier offer of substantial financial help. These are the bare essentials; in fact, the motives on both sides were, as usual, more complicated. Nasser's decision was not merely retaliation for one specific western slight. It was an act of defiance, demonstrating in a most dramatic way that Egypt was at last truly independent, that it had grown in stature and strength, that it was no more to be pushed around by the big powers. Financial considerations may also have crossed his mind: if the West was not willing to contribute to Egypt's industrial development, the revenues accruing from the Suez Canal Company would replace the loan that had been cancelled. Nasser's action alone would not have induced London and Paris to attack Egypt. But there was a general fear, both among British Tories and French Socialists, that Nasser was a fascist dictator, that his appetite was insatiable and that, in cooperation with the Soviet Union, he would do his utmost to damage western interests all over Africa and the Middle East. These fears were not altogether groundless: Fascist features in Nasser's Egypt are as pronounced as the communist influences, his ambitions are very wide, and they clashed almost everywhere with the West. But Eden and Mollet erred on three basic points: they exaggerated the danger – a new Hitler was most unlikely to arise on a foundation so shaky as Egypt. They also overrated their own ability to defeat Nasser. They mistakenly believed that the lessons of the 'thirties ('appeasement does not pay', 'fascist dictators have to be opposed immediately'), sound enough in themselves, were applicable to very different circumstances. Nasser was not defeated. On the contrary, his prestige grew enormously; having successfully defied the British and the French, he became the undisputed leader of Arab nationalism and one of the elder statesmen of the third world. It is not at all certain how Nasser's political fortunes would have fared but for the Suez war; he faced enormous domestic difficulties and much resistance in the Arab world.

Suez gave him almost unlimited credit in his own country and throughout the Arab world.

Was the Israel decision to attack Egypt prudent and did it achieve its aim? For Israel several issues were involved: Nasser had repeatedly threatened to destroy the Jewish state; for the Israeli leaders it was not a question of *whether* to fight, but when and where. The alliance with Britain and France seemed at the time a unique opportunity; the air umbrella certainly made Israel's task easier. But, politically, the whole undertaking was distorted to Israel's detriment, by this link; what had been a straight issue between Israel and Egypt now became 'collusion' in an 'imperialist plot'. The war was fought by Israel to stop guerrilla attacks from across the Egyptian border which had risen to an alarming degree since 1955, and to open the Straits of Tiran, which had been closed by Nasser to Israeli shipping. These limited objectives were achieved. There was no infiltration from the south into Israel for ten years after Suez, and the Straits were reopened. Other territorial gains had to be surrendered by Israel. Militarily, the Israeli victory was impressive, but since it was achieved in collaboration with France and England, Nasser could plausibly argue that Egypt would easily have defeated Israel but for Anglo-French intervention. The military lesson was therefore not as clear cut as the Israelis had hoped. Some observers have argued that Israel's decision to wage war was a grave mistake, because, whatever its short-term gains, it fatally impaired its long-term chances to coexist with the Arabs. Arab hatred of Israel increased and the collaboration with Britain and France 'persuaded every Arab that Israel was indeed a tool of the western imperialism'. There is some truth in this; the tie with Britain and France did harm Israel. Whether it really affected the prospects for a lasting peace is doubtful; the available evidence shows no significant changes in Arab attitudes; the Arab leaders were as hostile, as unwilling to put up with its existence in 1955 as after the Suez war.

Israel between the Wars

In 1956 Israel gained a respite, not more. But the years were put to good use; a visitor who had known Israel in 1950 would hardly have recognised the country ten years later. Many new settlements and factories were established, whole new suburbs had come into being. There was a new prosperity; houses had become more modern, flats more roomy; shops were full of luxury goods, the many private cars caused congestion in the streets, and the restaurants offered better fare than ever before. A trip abroad every two or three years had become almost *de rigueur* for many Israelis, despite a prohibitive travel tax. Rates of economic growth were high; industry in 1962 (to give but one example) was 13 per cent higher than in the previous year, and even in agriculture, where progress is notoriously slow, there was an advance of 8 per cent. Nor was this a flash in the pan; similar progress was made for about eight years. Most startling perhaps was the advance in agriculture, which in some respects was now the most highly developed and intensive in the world. There was an abundance of fruit and vegetables; egg production had risen so sharply that there was now a substantial export to Europe. No one ten years before had expected this in his wildest dreams. There was an unprecedented building boom; foreign construction workers had to be enlisted to cope with the demand.

The picture was not altogether rosy. Living standards had risen even faster than productivity; the country was living beyond its means. Economic progress was by no means uniform; there were serious miscalculations in some fields, and towards the middle sixties the boom had petered out, rates of growth had dwindled to insignificance, and there were between 50,000 and 100,000 unemployed, a very high percentage of the total labour force. It was a crisis of growth. Serious as this was, political and social problems caused even more concern. In Israeli politics the tendency towards division and fragmentation progressed at an alarming rate; the old saying 'three Jews – four political parties', became very nearly true. Mapai split, so did the liberals, Herut, and even the communists. Among the younger generation there was growing impatience and scorn for the older generation of leaders – old fashioned, east European Jews with their Zionist and socialist phraseology which, as the younger people saw it, no longer had any bearing on present realities. The politicians of the old school, on the other hand, were in no hurry to make room for the new generation; they were alarmed by its lack of ideals and principles, which often bordered on downright cynicism. The old elite itself was a house divided; a number of incidents,

27

such as the Lavon affair, had poisoned public life and caused many old friendships to break up. Ben Gurion, Prime Minister since 1948 and the architect of the new state, stepped down; Levi Eshkol succeeded him only to be attacked by his predecessor (and party comrade) as totally unfit for the job. A decent man, far more amenable and reasonable than Ben Gurion, he lacked his predecessor's drive and charisma; a competent administrator and committee chairman, it was not at all clear whether he had the qualities of leadership and quick decision needed at a time of crisis.

There was the problem of organised religion; a minority of orthodox Jews found themselves in a strong bargaining position as a result of the precarious internal balance of power. Their attempt to impose the traditional Rabbinical Law on the majority caused growing friction. The Government and the political parties procrastinated, trying to postpone what seemed an inevitable *Kulturkampf*. Few people opposed religion as such, but the medieval (or pre-medieval) restrictions of traditional religious laws were increasingly incompatible with the exigencies of industrial society – not to mention the prevailing concepts of moral law (equality of women, for instance). There was also the great, unresolved problem of integrating the 'second Israel' – the new immigrants mainly from Middle Eastern countries and North Africa. Israel was proud of its democratic regime, but it was not at all clear how deeply rooted Israeli democracy really was. Nor, some individual achievements apart, was the cultural scene encouraging. The Hebrew University was on the whole a less impressive institution than the Israeli army, and not only for want of money. Provincialism and mediocrity were perhaps to be expected, given the country's size and its limited resources, but they came as an anti-climax after the immense contribution that had been made to European culture in the course of more than a century by so many outstanding Jews. There was a feeling of self-importance, largely unwarranted, the belief that Israel still had a vital message of universal validity to deliver to the world. Despite the growth of the last decade, Israel's place in the world was now only too clear: it was not a spiritual power, nor was anyone but fellow Jews looking to Israel for moral inspiration. Palestine in 1938 had been even more confined, but there was continuous immigration – the limit was not yet in sight.

By 1960 it was clear that the millions of American and Russian Jews would not settle in the country, that Israel would remain essentially what it then was.

The list of shortcomings and disappointments could be prolonged. But in an imperfect world it would be unjust to overstress them. Israel's achievements and failures should be measured against the performance of other new countries. Since its foundation, the traditional Jewish weaknesses had reappeared: impatience, intolerance, lack of discipline, abnormal excitability with a touch of hysteria. But there was also the traditional inventiveness, dynamism and sense of solidarity. These were reinforced by characteristics acquired in the process of building a new nation: toughness and the ability to improvise. Altogether there was reason for some pride.

Jews have traditionally been a self-conscious people. This was not so marked among the younger generation, but Israeli attitudes to other peoples and nations continued to be a subject of much discussion and introspection. The Arabs were not hated; there was a genuine, though naïve inability to understand the Arab point of view: how could the Arabs be so foolish as to attack the Jews, since they could benefit so much from cooperation with them? The attitude to the Arabs was on the whole a mixture of goodwill, suspicion and amused contempt, generated by the discrepancy between Arab claims and Arab performance. There was a great reservoir of goodwill and admiration for Russia. Many Jews were traditionally left wing and even the liberals' sympathies could easily be enlisted for 'progressive causes' even after these causes had become suspect. But, communism apart, an entire generation of Israeli leaders had grown up in eastern Europe, was steeped in Russian literature, had come to regard the Russian intelligentsia as the torchbearer of justice and humanity. In fact they had often modelled themselves, consciously or unconsciously, on the Russian intelligentsia. In other circles there was considerable admiration for Soviet achievements, much of it admittedly ideological in character, based on hopes rather than actual achievements. It was therefore only gradually that many Israelis took cognisance of the implications of Soviet hostility towards Israel after 1955. Many thought it was a misunderstanding which could be cleared up, that the Russians could be influenced by gestures of goodwill and friendly persuasion. The awakening was painful and took a long time.

Britain had many friends in Israel despite the friction of the Mandatory era; Jews admired in Englishmen some of the qualities they themselves lacked. France had many sympathisers not only among the new immigrants from the Maghreb, but again there was more than a little naïveté in the assumption that de Gaulle was a real friend and that he would continue to support Israel indefinitely. Israeli attitudes to America were complicated; it was largely a love-hate relationship. Culturally and in many other respects, America became the main formative influence in Israel. At the same time there was awareness of American weaknesses, among Babbits and intellectuals alike, and there were even occasional feelings of superiority *vis-à-vis* America. By and large the conviction grew that in a time of crisis, to put it crudely, only the Israeli army stood between survival and extermination. Perhaps this isolationist despair, the result of Israel's precarious position in the world, was carried too far. But it is difficult to blame anyone. Jewish experience in recent decades had not strengthened the belief in humanity.

Egypt between the Two Wars

In 1960 Gamal Abdul Nasser, the son of the people, was at the height of his power. He had made Cairo the capital of the Arab world, the focal point of Arab politics, and it seemed only a question of time before it would become one of the main centres of world politics. Under his leadership miserable, backward Egypt had not only regained its independence, it had engaged on a vast programme of rebuilding the country. Its prestige grew; West and East competed with each other in wooing Egypt which had suddenly emerged as the leading force in one of the world's key areas.

Egypt was having its social revolution. The ruling stratum, the pashas and their hangers-on, disappeared; their place was taken by the new class, the young officers and the technocrats. Most of the officers received civilian appointments and they constituted a majority in the Government and held the key positions in the administration. Nasser was the undisputed leader: he displayed virtues infrequent among Arab statesmen – great daring coupled with caution and persistence, fortitude at a time when things went against him – and there were quite a few setbacks in the Arab world and elsewhere. He displayed supreme tactical skill, time and again outsmarting his opponents in Egypt and the Arab countries. Not an effective speaker himself, he provided his country with a most impressive propaganda apparatus. The 'Voice of the Arabs' became a major political factor all over the Middle East. An excellent diplomat, he gained many friends and sympathisers: Soviet communists and German neo-Nazis, British liberals and General Franco. With Khrushchev he was a non-party Bolshevik; with Mayhew and Nutting, a reasonable, moderate, responsible statesman; with Dr Frey of the *Nationalzeitung*, a pupil and admirer of national-socialism. For years he was almost all things to almost all people. Hard working, incorruptible, dynamic, he symbolised for many foreigners the spirit of the new Egypt. Only a few close observers were aware of the reverse of the coin: the irrational streak in his behaviour, the indifference to moral principle, the absence of a sense of moderation, his overweening ambitions.

The new class was no doubt sincere in its desire for a national revival and social reform. Some of its members were capable men, others turned out failures; but, the individual record apart, the new class gradually lost its idealism and the common touch. It supported Nasser with all its heart – so long as its privileges in the new order were not touched. It ruled with the help of the propaganda apparatus and the secret police – both enormously inflated – states within the state. This was the essence of 'military socialism' – not any clear ideology or doctrine or socialist ideal. Nasser himself, a reader of many newspapers and few books, was a pragmatist in politics, not a political thinker. But a pragmatist who tended increasingly to be carried away by emotion, with only a slight understanding either of the outside world, or of Egypt's most vital economic and social problems. He was a leader of immense shrewdness and little wisdom. Above all, he shared with many of his compatriots the capacity for self-delusion. He did not want to understand what was possible for Egypt and what exceeded its potential. Nasser was impatient – understandably so in the light of the many urgent tasks facing him. He tackled all at the same time: social reform, industrial expansion, the Aswan Dam, Arab unity, rockets, construction of

jet planes, space travel, a not-so-little war on the Arabian peninsula, a campaign against other Arab rulers. There were highly
ambitious five-year plans, very impressive on paper, but the
economic experts were not at all happy with the real state of
affairs hidden behind the figures and the triumphant announce-
ments about new victories on the economic front. The country
was simply too small and too poor for Nasser's ambitions.

All this became evident, admittedly, only as the years passed.
1960 was the high tide of Nasserism; with Nehru and Tito he
appeared as the head of the Third World at the UN General
Assembly in New York – his only visit to the West. Economically these had been good years for Egypt: he had just received
$100 million from America, and the Russians were building the
Aswan Dam. Cotton sales were high, the adverse balance of
trade was eliminated, earnings from the Suez Canal traffic
reached a record high. Nasser was President, not merely of
Egypt, but of the new United Arab Republic – the union of
Egypt, Syria and the Yemen. Courted by the world's leaders as
an equal, he had become a world statesman in his own right – or
so it seemed. And for a little while it even seemed that in his new
role he would not bother to deal with small problems, such as
Israel; it would have been beneath his dignity.

But the very next year, 1961, the tide turned. In September
Syria seceded from the UAR; the year after, civil war broke out
in the Yemen. Nasser intervened and eventually some 60,000
of his troops were involved in a cruel and inconclusive war,
detrimental to Egypt's prestige. The Third World began to
disintegrate; Nehru died, Ben Bella, Nkrumah, and Sukarno
disappeared. There was growing opposition to Nasser and
Nasserism even within the Arab world, from Tunis to Baghdad.
Nasser's African ventures did not go well, and there were more
and more difficulties in the economic field. The population
explosion continued, the lot of the fellaheen had not improved,
there was substantial unemployment, the country was approaching bankruptcy as it became more and more difficult to repay
the many debts that had been incurred. For Egypt had lived all
these years on credit; most of Nasser's prestige operations had
been undertaken with borrowed money. Great leaders are not as
a rule interested in economics, and act regardless of financial
considerations. But great people have financial wizards. Nasser

32

had no such wizard, and even a Dr Schacht would not have been able to extract money from a country as poor as Egypt.

Nasser reacted to the setbacks with characteristic vigour: in 1961 the new socialist course was launched: banks, insurance companies, factories, the merchant fleet, were nationalised. A new agrarian reform made 100 feddan the new upper limit of landholding. There were many arrests, and the property of some 700 leading capitalists (many of them foreigners and Jews) were seized. Some 90 per cent of the country's industry was now in the hands of the state, but this did not make it any more productive; Charles Issawi wrote that at best Egypt's economy would now develop on Titoist lines. But there was another possibility: the economics of neo-barbarism.

The Arab Socialist Union had an aggregate membership of more than seven millions; practically every literate Egyptian between the age of twenty and fifty belonged to it – it meant precisely nothing. There was much talk about creating within the Union a 'vanguard party' consisting of the real elite. An Institute for the Study of Socialism was created, supporting 'scientific socialism' (Leninism) and opposing Arab socialism, which had been the fashionable trend hitherto. In his foreign policy Nasser had been neutralist throughout the fifties; if his propaganda had been far more hostile to the West than to the Soviet Union, he had not refrained from attacking the communist parties in Iraq and Syria when these had challenged his leadership. His relations with Moscow gradually became very close; Khrushchev even made him a 'Hero of the Soviet Union' against the protest of some of his colleagues in the Moscow Presidium. But there were still normal, though not cordial, relations with the United States. The turning point came in 1964; there was not one single, dramatic cause for this deterioration, nor did it happen suddenly. The war in the Yemen was one of the reasons; though America had been one of the first countries to recognise the pro-Nasserist regime there, it also supported the Saudian backers of the Yemen royalists. And Saudia with its rich oilfields, not poor Yemen, was Nasser's real target on the Arabian peninsula. There were several little incidents which suggested that the Egyptians had decided to annoy America as much as possible; the American Library in Cairo was burned down by a mob, and the fire brigade from across the street was very slow to act. An

American civil plane was shot down, and the Egyptian authorities were slow to make even the most perfunctory apologies. There was growing reluctance in America to extend or continue economic aid to Egypt; agricultural surplus stocks were running low and, anyway, India was in an even more critical situation. All this gave much offence in Cairo; the planners had counted on American assistance: it was also a political insult, because it showed that Cairo's nuisance value had decreased in Washington's eyes. There were probably other reasons, some perhaps fortuitous. Nasser's close confidant, Hassanein Haykal, in a long series of articles on Egyptian-American relations, tells how Ambassador Byroade (an admirer of Nasser) once offended the *Rais* at a cocktail party by complaining that the American labour attaché had been beaten up by a group of Egyptians: 'Your men behaved in an uncivilised way.' 'We have the oldest civilisation on earth', Nasser retorted, and stormed out of the party. This incident, according to Haykal, was one of the turning points in the relations between Cairo and Washington. If so we move into the field of micro-history; the quest of the historian for cause and effect becomes very difficult indeed, if not totally unrewarding. But other factors cannot be so easily dismissed – Nasser's growing dependence on the Soviet Union as a supplier of arms, and in many other vital fields. By 1967 the Russians had become 'our true and selfless friends'; the Americans the 'bloodsuckers of people, the arch criminals of the twentieth century, the savage barbarians'; in the words of the head of Cairo radio: 'Here we shall bury American international gangsterism. Arabs, dig graves everywhere, dig them for every US presence. Dig up all the homeland. Dig it, Arabs, Dig it, Arabs. Dig it, Arabs.' This reflected the patriotic elation of midsummer 1967; the excesses will possibly be explained away at some future date by reference to the rhetorics of the Arab language. After all, no one expected the Egyptians to dig up the desert. But Nasser and his regime had travelled a long way from the early days of the struggle for Egyptian independence and the policy of neutralism. It was one of the ironies of history, the sad end to a chapter in Egyptian history that had begun not without promise. There had at first been much goodwill and idealism, a sincere wish to build a freer and more prosperous Egypt. But the goodwill was quickly eroded, the idealism degenerated into the self-perpetuation of the new class. The feverish, ever expanding ambitions could lead only to bankruptcy – military, political, economic. It may not be the end of the road, but it was a discouraging interim balance.

Ferment in the Arab World

The decade between the Suez war and the new Arab-Israeli conflict saw many changes in the Arab world. The Iraqi monarchy was overthrown in July 1958 and replaced by a military dictatorship under General Kassem – radical nationalist and populist in inspiration. The Government veered sharply to the left and collaborated with the communists against Nasser's partisans and other left-wing groups. Later it turned to the right, dissolved the special revolutionary courts and the popular militia, and launched a military campaign against the Kurdish minority. Kassem was a man of limited mental capacity, and, at best, unstable character; his regime soon became a personal dictatorship. He managed to hang on for five years before he was overthrown by a revolt led by the left-wing nationalist Ba'ath party. In 1958 the communists had persecuted, arrested, and often killed their left-wing rivals; now the Ba'ath retaliated in kind. But it remained in power for only about nine months and was replaced by yet another military dictatorship under General Aref.

These governments carried out agrarian reforms and about 75 per cent of the country's industrial production (excepting the oil industry) was nationalised. They claimed to be inspired by left-wing principles, all waged war against the Kurds. Some were closer to Nasser than others, none really wanted union with Egypt. The economic situation deteriorated and internal instability was fed by popular discontent and unsuccessful *coups d'état*. The Iraqis have been called the Prussians of the Arab world; as a collective they did little to justify their reputation. The ideological differences between the various groups fighting each other were small, sometimes non-existent. But there was a great deal of personal and group antagonism, traditional enmities played a certain role, and to a considerable extent it was simply a struggle for power.

Syria

Syria is the heartland of the Arab world, the cradle of Arab patriotism. It has always been the most extreme country – radically pan-Arab, anti-Israeli, and most recently, fanatically anti-western. Political passions in Syria run higher than in the other Arab countries. There is more fanaticism and viciousness in Syrian politics; Syrians, unlike Egyptians, are not famous for their sense of detachment and of humour. Syria is an unhappy country; it has experienced more military coups in its brief history than any other Arab state. Friction between religious and ethnic groups still has a considerable impact on Syrian life, even though the old divisions now appear under new labels. For the most part the army has dominated Syrian political life, but since it is not able to rule alone, it has had to look for an alliance with like-minded civilians. In these coalitions there is no doubt where real power lies. Basically a rich country, Syria has experienced an almost permanent economic crisis for the last seven or eight years; the 'capitalist' 'fifties were a period of considerable prosperity, unlike the 'socialist' 'sixties. The Government explanation is bad harvests; the opposition put the blame on the Government's mismanagement.

The political struggle in recent years has been mainly between Ba'athists (split into a right and left wing), Nasserists, and communists. After the dissolution of the union with Egypt, power passed into the hands of the Ba'ath and its supporters in the army. About 80 per cent of the industry, the banks and insurance companies were nationalised after 1964 and foreign trade is now controlled by the Government. These measures were opposed by the middle class, but the Government succeeded in overcoming resistance by drastic measures such as shooting merchants who refused to cooperate. The communists also began to take a prominent part in Syrian politics, though they were critical of certain ultra-leftist, Maoist trends among their allies.

Other Arab Countries

Developments in other Arab countries can be quickly recapitulated: Ibn Saud, an incompetent and reactionary king, was gradually forced to hand over power to Faisal, the crown prince, and in 1964 he left his country. He established himself in Cairo with his vast entourage and harem, proclaimed himself an ardent Arab patriot, supported Nasser, and bitterly attacked Faisal and his policy. Faisal, on the other hand, carried out a number of modest but long overdue reforms and pursued, on the whole, an anti-Egyptian policy. He also became very much involved in the Yemen civil war. The Yemen was, and still is, the most backward Arab country; about one quarter of the usable land was the private property of the old Imam Ahmed, who died in September 1962. His son was overthrown almost immediately by a group of pro-Nasserist officers under Abdalla al Salal. However, Salal proved to be even less popular than the deposed Imam and he had to call on Nasser for military assistance to combat the royalists who put up a stubborn resistance. Nasser sent in several divisions; ultimately some 60,000 Egyptian troops were concentrated in the Yemen. This army was not however very successful, and even the occasional application of poison gas by the Egyptians failed to bring a quick decision. An armistice between Nasser and King Faisal in August 1965 did not last; fighting flared up again and has been in progress ever since. Nasser-inspired nationalism has been more successful in Aden; Britain was gradually forced to give up its own crown colony. But there, too, rivalries between opposing factions took a heavy toll among the Arab population.

Mention ought lastly to be made of developments in North Africa – the Maghreb. Tunisia, Algeria and Morocco had gained independence, all after a struggle – Algeria, after long and bloody fighting. Morocco and Tunisia followed a relatively moderate and unexciting policy and displayed no major foreign political ambitions. There was plenty of excitement in Algeria under Ben Bella. In some respects it reminded one of Nasserism, above all in its thirst for prestige. Despite the ravages of the long guerrilla war, there were promising prospects in Algeria when it became independent. Much of its agriculture, formerly in the hands of French settlers, was modern and well equipped; the infrastructure of a modern industry had been built. Most of these advantages were quickly lost in hasty and ruinous economic experiments which brought the country to the verge of bankruptcy. It was Ben Bella's ambition to expand the Algerian economy at a faster rate than any other country, and at the same time to make it more socialist than the communist bloc countries. Most of his former comrades, the leaders of the Algerian rebellion (the 'Band of Brothers') were exiled, imprisoned, or executed. Ben Bella cooperated with Nasser; at the same time he felt some contempt for the relatively unsophisticated, unideological character of Nasserism and its leader. Ben Bella had far-reaching political ambitions of his own; he threatened Morocco and Tunisia, and tried, with some success, to play an active role in third world politics and in its relations with the communist bloc. His regime was overthrown by an army rebellion under Colonel Boumedienne, who promised to repair the damage that had been done under his predecessor. In this he was not particularly successful, but he managed to get Soviet and French military and economic assistance. Boumedienne, a man of limited abilities, continued in broad outline the foreign policy of Ben Bella. After some initial hesitation on the part of Egypt, there was again close collaboration with Nasser. Islamic and traditional xenophobic elements played a greater role in Boumedienne's government, for he lacked Ben Bella's veneer of western sophistication (Marxist ideology, etc.). Not that it greatly mattered, as far as his relations to Russia and China were concerned.

The countries of the Maghreb joined the Arab League, and all three, but particularly Algeria, were drawn more and more into Arab affairs, including the conflict with Israel, which in the past had been outside their frame of active interest. Bourguiba took a moderate line on Israel and the Jews, only to be rebuked by the other Arab leaders; the attitude of the Algerians was intransigently hostile towards Israel. Not only were the films of Simone Signoret banned, but even the books of Jean-Paul Sartre, who, though no Zionist sympathiser, had declared that Israel, too, had a right to live. There was some common interest between the three countries of the Maghreb, and between them and the Arab states, but these bonds did not, on the whole, go very deep. Nor was the urge for closer unity strongly felt; even a modest scheme, like the Arab Common Market, failed to make any significant progress.

2
Escalation

The world in the spring of 1967 was a slightly more dangerous place than a year or two earlier. The escalation in Vietnam had continued; there were now 460,000 American soldiers in that country and the generals were asking for more. American opinion was violently divided about a war no one had wanted, and that had arisen out of a commitment that many now regretted. The race problem had also grown more menacing and there were fears for an even hotter summer than the one before. America was not in good shape; many of its intellectuals thought it was in fact the sickest, most sinful, and most reactionary country in the world. We do not know what Chinese intellectuals thought about the state of their country; it is unlikely that they were satisfied with Mao's little red book. The cultural revolution had now been on for many months, it had dislocated much of the country's economy and social life, discredited its party and political institutions. It was difficult to explain this strange eruption by rational argument; parallels with Stalinist Russia and with the Middle Ages were misleading. The Soviet Union, too, had its worries. Economic progress was steady, but the rate of growth was far less dramatic than had been once imagined. The idea of catching up with America and overtaking it was still a dream. Some countries, such as Japan, had in fact been making quicker progress. Internally, there were some rumblings among the intelligentsia and rumours about dissension among the collective leadership: Kosygin the technocrat against Brezhnev the party bureaucrat. Probably there were differences, there always are. Whether they ran along these lines no one knew, not even the Kremlinologists. Nor had Soviet foreign policy been outstandingly successful; there had been reverses for the progressive cause in Indonesia, Ghana, and other countries; more recently, a right-wing military clique had taken over in Greece. True, Moscow had established a fairly close relationship with France.

But Chinese attacks on Soviet revisionism continued with un-diminished vigour. Continuing American intervention in Viet-nam made it difficult, if not impossible, to make progress on any issue at all. Some former satellites, such as Rumania, had become very independent indeed; the monolithic character of the communist camp was by now a fond memory of bygone days.

The rest of the world was deeply preoccupied with its own problems: Biafra split away from Nigeria, Germany was worried about a possible resurgence of right-wing nationalism, and, like most European countries, about an economic recession: Volks-wagen that symbol of post-war prosperity was no longer work-ing at full capacity. Britain was overwhelmed by the exploits of Sir Francis Chichester, who had just sailed to Australia and back. De Gaulle had just thrown another spanner into British attempts to join the Common Market. The General continued to rule France, majestically impervious to public opinion, seem-ingly the only statesman with a grand design; he showed increas-ing signs of spleen and old age. And Jean-Paul Sartre had just published a special issue of his journal, *Temps Modernes*, one thousand pages devoted to one subject – Arabs and Jews.

The interests of the major powers in the Middle East were not shrouded in mystery. China wanted revolution at any price, and in any place, but it was totally absorbed in its own problems, and, despite the H-bomb, just about to be exploded, could do little to help foment revolution. America wanted the preserva-tion of the *status quo* at almost any price. Most people in Wash-ington thought that one world crisis at a time was about all America could handle. Mr Richard Nolte, a scholar, had just been appointed ambassador to Cairo. His writings showed sympathy with the Arab cause.

The Soviet attitude was somewhat less clear. For some time past the attitude towards America (and the West in general, except for de Gaulle) had been hardening. There were some dis-quieting incidents, none of any consequence in itself, but taken together they constituted something like a new trend, a tougher line, which gave rise to speculation about the possibility of a 'second front' somewhere in the world to compensate for Soviet inability to do much about Vietnam, and to meet the growing pressure on Moscow to regain the initiative. Perhaps this was the way to exert pressure on America to bring the war in Vietnam to an end? During the last week of March Mr Gromyko had paid an unexpected visit to Cairo. He may have discussed economic assistance, but for this the presence of the Soviet Foreign Minister was hardly necessary. What other outstanding political problems of major importance were on the agenda? We can only guess. At a conference of European communist parties in Karlovy Vary (24 April), Mr Brezhnev demanded the withdrawal of the American Sixth Fleet from the Mediterranean. It was not the first time this demand had been made; perhaps it showed growing Soviet preoccupation with the area particularly because of the concern in Moscow over the right-wing coup in Greece. Did Moscow have much to gain from a crisis in those parts? It certainly had little to lose from a war fought by proxy. In a book published in 1959 I expressed the view that the decision to supply arms to Nasser and other Arab countries in 1955 did not involve great risks: if Nasser lost his next war he would be tied to the Soviet Union in order to replenish his arsenal; if he won, the prestige of the Soviet Union in the Arab world was bound to increase. This does not mean that the Soviet Union actually wanted a war fought by proxy; such a war has its risks of escalation, and even though the Soviet Union was under pressure to do something to give a fillip to the progressive cause in Asia, Africa and Latin America the stake may have been too high for such a risky scheme.

Moreover, if it was one of the main Soviet aims to get rid of the Sixth Fleet in the Mediterranean, a war between Egypt and Israel was hardly the best way to achieve this. For such a war was bound sooner or later to involve the Soviet Union, if only indirectly, and this would almost certainly strengthen the ties between the NATO countries, which would put an end to the chances for a policy of disengagement in Europe. All this does not, of course, prove anything beyond the question of interest and intent; countries, like individuals, do not always act rationally, and even if they do, there is a wide margin of miscalculation. Perhaps the Soviet Union favoured a minor test of strength in the Middle East that would benefit its clients and in which the risk of war would be minimal? We shall have to return to this question when dealing with the May crisis.

Up to 15 May 1967, there were no signs pointing to a dramatic conflict in the Middle East. There was, of course, the latent and potentially dangerous permanent crisis, but over the past few years there had been little difficulty in bringing the various flare-ups under control. There seemed to be no immediate reason for a clash. Nasser had a good deal to occupy him and was hardly in a state to attack Israel with a large section of his army tied down in the Yemen. Israel had its most un-warlike government ever and was immersed in its economic crisis. For years the world press had devoted little attention to the Middle East, rightly perhaps, since the Middle East's monopoly of crises and instability, which had lasted, broadly speaking, from 1948 to 1958, had been decisively broken. There was reason to assume that the Middle East would stay out of the headlines for a long time to come.

Syria again

The history of a revolution does not start with the masses shouting 'To the barricades'; the first shot in a war is sometimes fired only at the opening of the third or fourth act of the drama. In 1967, as so often before in history, the junior partner in an alliance, Syria, involved the senior partner in a war. Its motives and actions will have to be closely scrutinised.

When the crisis came Syria had the most bellicose government in its entire history. These were the leaders of the left-wing Ba'ath who had come to power in February 1966 on the coat-tails of the generals Salah Jadid and Hafiz al Asad. The Ba'ath (Renaissance) party had been founded by two Syrian intellectuals in the nineteen-forties, Michel Aflaq and Salah al Din al Bitar; their ideology was a mixture of Marxist and nationalist elements, their slogan 'One Arab nation with an Eternal Mission'. The party was not confined to Syria but had members in Iraq, Jordan and elsewhere; it was the only Arab party not limited to one single country. Originally, the Ba'ath leaders had been close to the communists, but Aflaq and Bitar gradually became convinced that communism was incompatible with Arab nationalism and Arab unity, and the two movements entered into bitter rivalry. When Syria decided to join Egypt and form the United Arab Republic, it was mainly because the Ba'ath was extremely worried by the growth of communism in Syria, especially in the higher ranks of the army, and escaped, so to speak, into Nasser's embrace. But the marriage with Egypt was not a happy one. It was not so much a matter of ideological disagreement; in that respect little divided the partners. Nasser after all had no clear political programme. The Ba'ath was slightly to the left of Nasser, though this did not prevent the *Rais* later on from denouncing the Ba'ath as 'fascist adventurers'. ('Fascism' became a bad word in the Arab world in the 'fifties.) The Ba'ath disliked Nasser's personal dictatorship, the undemocratic character of his regime, the fact that his word was the supreme law of the Egyptian revolution. That the Egyptian representatives in Syria behaved like colonial administrators, and that the Syrians were notoriously ungovernable, only added to the enmity. The union broke up in 1961; since 1963 the Ba'ath has been in power, not owing to a popular mandate (15 per cent was the most it ever polled in free elections) but on the strength of its alliance with politically ambitious colonels.

The Ba'ath leadership justified this in terms of 'ideologisation of the army' – but the army had always intervened in politics since the beginning of Syrian independence. What the coup of 1963 really achieved was the militarisation of Syrian public life; the government and the Ba'ath itself were gradually taken over by a group of officers who had joined the party only after the coup. First Colonel Amin al Hafez ruled through the old Ba'ath leadership (Michel Aflaq and Salah Bitar). These men advocated a relatively moderate line – in world affairs, in relations to Nasser and *vis-à-vis* Israel. The moderation was only relative; for Syria was traditionally the most anti-Israeli of all countries, and no Syrian politician really wanted full cooperation with Egypt. But Amin al Hafez and his civilian friends realised that Syria needed some accommodation with Egypt, and they also believed that there was no chance for a successful war against Israel in the near future. They had no particularly friendly feeling towards the West, but neither did they want too close a rapprochement with the Soviet Union or with China, and they regarded the Syrian communists as their main political enemies. This group was challenged by another section of the army, headed by Colonels Salah Jadid and Hafiz al Asad, which had civilian frontmen of its own (Yusef Zuayen and Dr Nuredin Atassi) who demanded a more radical policy all along the line: a more activist policy against Israel, independence *vis-à-vis* Egypt, closer collaboration with Russia, China and the local communists. The conflict was not only ideological in character: it was a rivalry between two generations, and also (though they were both denying this) between military commanders from rival ethnic and religious groups. (Amin al Hafez was a Sunni Muslim, his antagonists were Alawites; later on the conflict between Alawites and Druze also played a considerable role.) Amin al Hafez, though himself a high ranking army officer, wanted to limit the army's influence in Syrian political life – and especially the role of officers who hailed from minority groups. In this he was not too successful: during 1965 there was a prolonged tug-of-war between the two sides; eventually the old leadership was deposed.

The radicalism of the new masters was basically emotional; it was a general mood that did not necessarily follow a consistent, political pattern. Originally bitterly hostile to Nasser, they came eventually to cooperate closely with Egypt. While their manifestoes proclaimed deep attachment to the party, they ruled in fact through the army; the Ba'ath became a mere transmission belt of political instructions: it certainly had little in common with the old Ba'ath. This was an interesting case of take-over of a political party by forces diametrically opposed to its aims; it may not be a unique happening, but only in a country where political programmes and ideologies counted ultimately for very little could there have been such a complete right-about-turn.

Not that ideology could be discarded altogether under such a regime. The Ba'ath always put great stress on doctrine, and the new leadership borrowed from Boumedienne the concept of the 'Ideological Army'. The ideological commitment was vociferous, it was violent – but it was not deep; hence the sudden political changes that appear incomprehensible to observers accustomed to think in terms of party loyalty and ideological consistency.

The old leadership was purged, either imprisoned or exiled, and the new masters embarked on a political course that was in most respects quite different from the line of the old Ba'ath. They proceeded with their decrees of nationalisation so quickly that even Khaled Bagdash, Syria's leading communist, felt compelled to protest: such hasty, infantile pseudo-communism, he said, could only ruin the country and bring about the downfall of the government. But Bagdash was a Muscovite, whereas the leaders of the Ba'ath took some of their inspiration from Peking, from Havana, and from Frantz Fanon. They modelled their party on the communist pattern; in their propaganda they proclaimed not only their undying devotion to the cause of world revolution, their unflinching hostility to America and other western countries, but also their belief in the leading role of Syria's small working class. In this respect they went beyond Nasser, who always thought of his regime as representing the interests of several classes. Once he had broken the power of the old pashas, and the upper middle class Nasser, unlike the Syrians, did not think that the class struggle was his most urgent assignment.

In its manifestoes the Syrian regime was no doubt the most extreme in the Middle East; its leaders were full of self-praise for their great progressive achievements. There were constant warnings that American imperialism, the Zionist gangster state and the other forces of world reaction were out to overthrow socialist Syria. World reaction, alas, did not take Syria very seriously. The leaders of the Ba'ath with all their Marxist phraseology were, in fact, populists, unbalanced and quite irresponsible; this type of leadership has also been seen at work in other parts of Asia and Africa. In Syria it emerged in its purest form. Their progressive achievements were largely mythical, they had little popular support. Only owing to the help of the army did the left Ba'ath survive the attempts to overthrow it in September 1966, and again on 2 February 1967. But its leaders continued to feel very insecure.

The Soviet Union was fully aware of the weakness of its Syrian protégés. Throughout the winter of 1966/7 there was a steady stream of reports and broadcasts in the Soviet press and radio about impending plots against the Damascus government. On 8 January, *Pravda* announced that a Syrian government-in-exile was to be established, ships of the American Sixth Fleet were to stand off the coast of Syria, and after the Israeli armed forces invaded the country a new regime was to take power. On 18 and 19 January there were similar broadcasts; Israel wanted to create an atmosphere of unrest in order to overthrow the progressive regime in Damascus: in the service of its allies 'Israel was prepared to ignite the fire in this part of the world'. Why then did Moscow not counsel Damascus to discontinue the guerrilla activities which gave Israel a pretext for an attack? This was apparently out of the question. On 7 November 1966 *Izvestia* wrote following Syrian attacks and an Israeli complaint to the Security Council: 'All the babble about troops of the Fatah . . . will deceive no one . . . Are the Israeli diplomats so lacking in imagination that they must play the same record over and over again?'

It was not the strength of the Syrian regime which frightened outside observers but its weakness. For it was clear from the beginning that this very weakness would impel the regime to take a militant line on the one issue that was universally popular – Palestine. Syrian politicians had traditionally been the most bellicose towards Israel; they had always been in the forefront of those clamouring for immediate war against the Jewish state. At the time of the first Arab summit in January 1964 they had called Nasser a traitor because he said the Arabs were not yet ready to attack Israel. To appear 'more anti-Israel than thou', as one observer put it, had been a familiar game among Arab politicians for a long time; it had almost become a conditioned reflex. However revolutionary their manifestoes, in this respect the new Syrian leaders followed a time-honoured tradition. But there were new elements: Maoism, Algeria, Cuba. The Syrian leaders had read Mao and Che Guevara on revolutionary war and decided to apply their principles (as they understood them) to the Middle East. Israel was to become Vietnam, the *Fidayeen* (Palestine guerrillas) were to be the Viet Cong, who would strike terror into the hearts of the usurpers. The Palestine Viet Cong would eventually be joined by 'China' (i.e. Syria, Egypt and the other Arab revolutionary peoples) who would give the dwarf gangster state the *coup de grâce*. America would try to intervene but its intention would be as ineffectual as in Vietnam. The Viet Cong has shot down half of America's airforce, we shall finish off the rest, Damascus radio announced. 'The Ba'ath party has advanced the slogan of the popular liberation war', Prime Minister Zuayen said in his May Day speech (1967): 'through such a war the Arabs can expel the Zionists from Palestine ... We should take the Algerian liberation war as an example.' Later on that month he said 'The situation in Israel is deteriorating. Eshkol and his government are at their last gasp and are in a state of confusion and division.' (Damascus Radio, 17 May, address to officers at the front.) A week later there was an open call for war: 'Arab masses, this is your day. Rush to the battle-field. The time has come to fight. Fight, Arabs. Let them know that we shall hang the last imperialist soldier with the entrails of the last Zionist...' (Damascus Radio, 23 May 1967.) The violence in these Syrian outbursts was great, the confusion even greater.

The new Ba'ath leadership announced that in the battle for the liberation of Palestine it would break the shackles – 'the shackles of hesitation and laggardness which inhibited our thoughts'. The Arabs would pass to the attack, never again would they complain to the UN – 'Israel will be the one on the defensive and the one to complain'. (Damascus Radio, 15 August 1966.) 'We have decided to drench this land with our blood, to oust you, aggressors, and throw you into the sea for good.' (Radio Damascus, 24 May 1966.) This was to be achieved by the strategy of a war of liberation that was not based on classical methods. Suydani the new Syrian Commander-in-Chief explained that traditional war, based on superiority of the quantity of arms, 'will lead us up a blind alley'. (Damascus Radio, 22 May 1966.) The Algerian war and Vietnam would serve as an example. But what were the regular armies to do meanwhile? Would they merely provide an umbrella from behind which the guerrilla forces would launch their attacks against Israel? The Syrian leaders never clarified their ideas on this vital point; while rejecting 'classical' methods of warfare in principle, they called at the same time for armed intervention as the way to regain Palestine. (Salah Jadid, Syrian Chief of Staff, Damascus Radio, 23 August 1966.) These conflicting statements did not reflect any deep differences of opinion in the military and political leadership – the very same people who advocated revolutionary popular war demanded old-fashioned military intervention. No one had a clear conception to offer – there was simply much impatience.

The armed attacks followed a standard pattern and during the winter of 1966/7 became almost a daily occurrence: Syrian border posts opened fire on Israeli settlements or tractors working in the fields; frequently the gun batteries joined in. At the same time the Fatah attacks became more professional and there was deeper infiltration into Israel. On 7 October 1966, demolition charges exploded underneath two buildings in the Romema quarter of Jerusalem – a few hundred yards from the Knesset and Eshkol's office. On the next day, a mine blew up an Israeli police car, killing four. On 14 January 1967, an anti-personnel mine went off at a football game in Dishon, a little village in Northern Israel, killing a spectator and wounding several others. These and other exploits of the Fatah were broadcast in the form of official communiqués over Damascus Radio.

The damage done and the number of casualties was larger than in any year during the last decade – but it was still considerably smaller than in 1955. In Israel, behind closed doors, there ensued a major controversy on the most effective way to combat this new strategy. Some argued that the only way to stop the guerrillas and the Syrian shelling of border settlements was to let the army to do the job, hit back with tanks and aircraft against Fatah bases. This of course meant escalating the conflict. Others argued that such major acts of retaliation were not effective – and, in addition, they would play into the hands of Fatah and the Syrians. Was it not more logical to respond to Arab guerrilla activities by Israeli commando raids on a similar scale? If Israel had survived the attacks in 1955, would it not also overcome the new wave of guerrilla activities? There were, however, two considerations that made such a policy difficult to pursue. The Israeli government and the military staff were not overawed by the Fatah raids on the present scale, but they assumed that unless drastic action was taken immediately, these attacks would become more numerous and dangerous. They thought that Israeli moderation would be interpreted as a sign of weakness and thus invite aggression on a larger scale. It is not certain, in retrospect, that this was a correct assumption; Fatah was a small group of guerrillas, it could not easily enlist new members, there was a limit to the damage it could inflict. From the military point of view the case for retaliation on a major scale – such as Samu in November 1966, and the battle with the Syrians on 7 April 1967 – was therefore not quite conclusive. But there were disquieting signs in the border settlements in the North; some members announced that they would leave unless something was done against the almost constant Syrian shelling. After the incident in Dishon only the presence of a police patrol stopped the crowd in its fury from crossing the border into a nearby Arab village to take revenge. There was mounting tension among the civilian population, nerves were on edge. The Israeli Government was under growing pressure to do something. To that extent Fatah and the Syrians had achieved their aim. But their real target was, of course, far more ambitious. Their idea of a popular liberation war presupposed the existence of large-scale guerrilla activities in the enemy country, and eventually the emergence of a guerrilla-dominated liberated territory. These were, of course, sheer fantasies, and the Syrian leaders apparently lost patience with their own predictions: if there was no Viet Cong, if the Israelis refused to behave like Marshal Ky, an old fashioned frontal attack was called for. And since Syria by itself was too weak for such an attack, the help of the senior partner would be needed.

We do not know what the Soviet leaders made of all the revolutionary talk about a popular liberation war; by 1967 no one in Moscow felt enthusiastic about Maoist ideas. There was, however, a special relationship with Syria; after Zuayen had come to power, his first visit was to Moscow, and he was followed by Syria's generals. Moscow no doubt felt uneasy about the excess of revolutionary enthusiasm on the part of the Syrian firebrands, their wild and irresponsible talk. There seemed to be no better way to control them than bringing about a rapprochement between Syria and Egypt. Kosygin himself took a hand; during his visit to Cairo in May 1966 he persuaded the *Rais* that a mutual defence pact between Cairo and Damascus (to be guaranteed by Moscow) would be in the best interests of all those concerned. The defence pact was duly signed in November 1966. Nasser no doubt felt that this was a clever stratagem, one way to re-establish his hegemony in the Arab world. It was, in fact, a fatal mistake. For far from restraining the Syrians, the pact gave them added self-confidence; they became even more aggressive in their speeches and actions, secure in the knowledge that however much they provoked Israel, they now had an effective guarantee against retaliation. The Serbians (and Montenegrins) many years ago used to say, 'We are two hundred millions – together with Russia'; the Syrians now took a similar line; their Big Brother would always get them out of trouble.

There were three main bones of contention between Syria and Israel: The demilitarised zone in the north, the Jordan water dispute, and the guerrilla activities of Syria-based Arab refugees. The demilitarised zone was a constant source of irritation but it played no major role in the 1967 crisis nor is it basically of great importance; we shall ignore it in the present context. The water dispute was more serious; more than once during the last ten years war between Israel and the Arabs over the diversion of the river Jordan had seemed a distinct possibility. There had been several schemes to divide the water among the riparian states, the most famous the Johnston Plan in 1955. The Arab governments had refused as a matter of principle to share the water with Israel, whereupon Israel drew up its own scheme based on the Johnston Plan. The Arab states declared that this would be an act of aggression and that they would fight. However, when Israel concluded the preparatory work and began pumping Jordan water from Lake Tiberias through the national water carrier to the Negev, there was no armed resistance by the Arab states. A summit conference was convened in Alexandria (September 1964) to organise immediate work on diversion projects. This rapidly developed into a farce; for though the Arab governments very much wanted to deny the water to Israel, they had no realistic plans of their own to put it to good use. Eventually, pressure was brought to bear on Lebanon to establish a diversionary pumping station, and the Syrians too began to work, albeit in a desultory fashion, on a canal near the Israeli border. Work on the Lebanese pumping station was eventually discontinued for lack of funds, and the Arab states lost their enthusiasm for the Syrian scheme. Nasser told a meeting in Cairo in May 1964 that he would not be provoked into a war with Israel 'just because Israel committed an act of aggression against Syria and destroyed one or two tractors' (at the proposed diversion canal). 'If we are not able to divert the Jordan river today, then we must postpone it until we are ready to defend ourselves.' The Jordan water dispute may again flare up at some future date; in 1967 it was not among the major causes of Arab-Israeli conflict, certainly not one of the immediate reasons for hostilities.

The Fatah and the refugees

The recurrent terrorist raids from across the borders constituted a serious security problem for Israel. For the Arabs, the continued existence of Arab refugee camps with their hundreds of thousands of inhabitants was a constant reminder of the injustice that had been done to Palestinian Arabs, making it a moral obligation never to give up the fight. The refugee question, more than any other, poisoned Arab-Israeli relations. There would have been plenty of Arab hostility to Israel even if this problem had been solved; the fact that so many refugees continued to vegetate in conditions of abject poverty and despair prevented any lasting reconciliation.

The exact number of Arab refugees is unknown. Arab estimates (before the new wave of refugees in June 1967) varied between 1 and 1·3 million. According to Israeli sources only 587,000 Arabs had left Palestine in 1948 (in 1947 there were roughly 747,000 Arabs in what a year later became Israel). Slightly more than 150,000 remained; the rest fled – partly following the advice of the Arab leaders, partly under the impact of the Israeli victory, which was not free from acts of terrorism and murder (Deir Yassin) *vis-à-vis* the Arab population. By 1967 UNRWA, the UN Relief and Work Agency was taking care of 1·3 million refugees, including by now third generation refugees, children of refugee children born in the camps. About 700,000 lived in what was then Jordan (400,000 on the West Bank, the rest in Jordan proper). There were 300,000 refugees in the Gaza strip, about 160,000 in the Lebanon, and 136,000 in Syria. How can one explain the discrepancy between these figures? The birth rate among the refugees was high, deaths were usually not reported (because it meant the loss of a ration card for the family). There were false and duplicate registrations, and indigent Arabs in Jordan, Syria, and the Gaza strip, attracted by the free distribution of food and clothing, smuggled themselves on to the refugee lists.

But politically and psychologically, did it really matter whether there were 1·3 million refugees or only 900,000? The Jews knew better than any other people what it meant to be a refugee; should they not have shown more compassion and a greater readiness to solve this problem? Was it not a tragic irony that the Jewish refugee problem had been solved by creating an Arab refugee problem? Was it not callous of the Israeli Government to resist a solution of the refugee problem, inhuman not to restore them to their homes, or at least to pay compensation? And was it not, in the last resort, self-defeating because the refugee issue became the most effective political weapon in the hands of the Arab governments?

Israel's position was not easy. The country was small and densely populated. Many of the inhabitants were refugees from Arab lands: 125,000 from Iraq, 50,000 from the Yemen, 60,000 from Egypt, 240,000 from other Arab League countries, mainly North Africa. Israel had taken back some Arab refugees, 48,000 to be precise, in a scheme designed to reunite divided families. At the Lausanne conference in 1949 it had offered to take back another 100,000. The Arab states rejected the offer – it was all or nothing. In 1953 Israel had released accounts held by Arabs in Israeli banks, freeing some 10 million dollars.

The Arab countries did little to help the refugees; some of them because they were poor (like Jordan), others, like Egypt, because they were both poor and overpopulated. The oil-rich Arab countries could have provided the money and Syria and Iraq could have absorbed them; Iraq's Foreign Minister said in April 1957: 'Iraq alone is capable of absorbing all the Arab refugees.' Millions of refugees had been resettled all over the world: in Greece after the First World War, in Germany, India, Pakistan and many other countries. The objection of the Arabs to the integration of the refugees was political in character, not economic. Was not a resettlement tantamount to renouncing the Arab claims to Palestine? How could an Arab patriot advocate such a concession; was he not compelled to say 'No, no never' – as the Hungarians did in protesting against the peace treaty of 1919.

The Arab governments were, of course, aware of the fact that Israel was a small country; the return of a million refugees would totally upset its balance. 'If the Arabs return to Israel, Israel will cease to exist', Nasser told a Swiss correspondent (*Zürcher Woche*, 1 September 1961). More recently the Lebanese Prime Minister Abdulla al Yaffi had said: 'The day of the realisation of the Arab hope for the return of the refugees to Palestine means the liquidation of Israel.' (*Al Hayat*, 29 April 1966.) As an Arab refugee conference at Homs in Syria put it in July 1957: 'Any discussion aimed at a solution of the Palestine problem which is not based on ensuring the refugees' right to annihilate Israel will be regarded as an act of treason.' 'Let us try to make the refugees our fifth column for the day of revenge and reckoning', a Lebanese paper, *Al Sayad*, wrote in April 1950. And so the Arab leaders went on, adamant in their refusal to rehabilitate the refugees and to undertake large-scale development projects. They rejected all absorption and employment, they prevented any integration, because their aim was to maintain an *irredenta*, to have an effective political weapon against Israel. Not everyone in the Arab world agreed with this policy: King Hussain, whose country suffered most from the mass influx, said on 17 January 1960 that the Arab leaders had approached the Palestine problem in an irresponsible manner: 'They have not looked into the future. They have no plan or approach. They have used the Palestine people for selfish political purposes. This is ridiculous, and I could say, even criminal.' The West, through the United Nations, continued to pay for the upkeep of the refugees – $580 million on relief alone. UNRWA was involved in delicate political problems, even though it tried to stay out of politics. Since 1964 there had been a Palestine Liberation Army in the Gaza strip, forming an integral part of the Egyptian army command. This army drew United Nations rations, and the UN thus, indirectly, contributed to the Egyptian war effort.

What could Israel do in face of the intransigent attitude of the Arab governments, and their declared policy to use the refugees to destroy Israel? A more imaginative approach might have had results, it would not have worked a miracle. True, there was the talk about using the refugees as a fifth column – but how many refugees would have played that role? Was not Israel strong enough to absorb all the refugees who would have actually chosen to return? An Israeli declaration to take back by stages all refugees willing to return would have been a risk, but not perhaps so great a risk as most Israeli leaders thought. It is unlikely that most refugees would have come back, and such a declaration would have taken the wind out of the sails of the Arab governments and compelled them to face their responsibilities.

Lastly, there were the refugees themselves in the Gaza camps – resembling a concentration camp, in their miserable huts and tents in Cis – and Trans-Jordan – vegetating year after year on subsistence level rations that just kept them alive. It was an inhuman sight, and few visitors failed to be deeply touched. The older refugees had given up hope of returning to their homes and lands which they could see across the border. But the younger refugees, those who had been small children in 1948, or those born in the camps felt differently: they were resolved to fight to return to the homeland, to kill the usurpers, to destroy their property. All they needed was leadership and weapons. A new generation of young Arabs grew up in the belief that a holy war was inevitable and that Arab might was invincible. What were the Arab governments waiting for?

Against this background there developed a new militancy. Refugee politics date back to 1948 and are exceedingly intricate; there were many abortive meetings, initiatives, and decisions. The old leadership – the Mufti of Jerusalem and the Arab Higher Executive – had long been discredited; most of its members had withdrawn from active politics. But the attempts to play refugee politics continued in the Arab capitals; from 1960 onwards there was much talk about the 'Arab entity'; Palestinian military units were established in Egypt, Iraq and elsewhere. In 1964 the Arab League decided upon Egyptian initiative to establish a Palestine Liberation Organisation (PLO) with a little army of its own (the Palestine Liberation Army – PLA), to 'serve as a vanguard for the liberation of the usurped part of Palestine'. The young refugees in the Gaza strip and in Syria were given military training and formed, under Egyptian officers, special military units with artillery and tanks; they lacked only aircraft. On the eve of the war, the headquarters of the PLA were transferred from Cairo to Gaza. The PLA was to participate in the coming war for the liberation of the Palestinian homeland, but it had also two other perhaps even more important assignments. One was to harass the Zionist enemy by constant raids from across the border, which were gradually to turn into full scale partisan warfare. 'We will continue guerrilla attacks in Palestine. We expect our actions will lead to reactions from Israel – a chain reaction. This will definitely lead to war; we know it, we accept it.' This was the strategy of the PLA as outlined by its leader Ahmad Shukairy in an interview with an American correspondent (*Wall Street Journal*, 2 June 1967). Shukairy, a Cambridge-trained lawyer from Acre, had begun his political career as a young man in Mandatory Palestine. He represented Syria in the United Nations, and later Saudi Arabia; eventually he began to work for the Egyptians. An excellent speaker and indefatigable traveller, he was one of the first Arab leaders to look for support to China. During a visit to Peking in 1965 he received a promise of light arms; a PLO office was opened in the Chinese capital and members of the PLA were sent there for training and, it is said, also to Hanoi. It is doubtful whether these Chinese ties made any great difference as far as the fortunes of the PLA are concerned. Shukairy, at any rate, does not remind one of the popular image of the Chinese-style militant leader. In conversation with an American journalist he spoke with nostalgia of his property in Palestine. ('I had a $25,000 home in Acre, and about $200,000 worth of land.') Not the kind of attitude of which Lenin would have approved.

Arab refugee politics and military activities were made more complicated by the existence of yet another group in Syria, the *Fatah* (Harakat al tahrir al Falishtine – Arab Liberation Movement), with the storm troops (Kuwat al Asifa) as its military branch. The leaders of Fatah talked much less than Shukairy – but in the context of the war of 1967, Fatah was more important than the PLO because it was more radical and more active.

The Fatah had been in existence for a number of years, a group of militant young Palestinian Arabs who had the support of Haj Amin al Hussaini, the ex-Mufti of Jerusalem and other Palestinian Arab personalities. They talked about the necessity of regaining the lost homeland by direct action; they were disillusioned with the official Arab leadership and the ritual resolutions about Palestine that were passed by the governments and the Arab League. The official line of the governments was that time was working for the Arabs, that the Zionist state would collapse just as the Crusaders had been expelled in the end. The Fatah and the radicals of the Syrian Ba'ath did not share this official optimism; 'The Fatah movement believes that time works in favour of the enemy' (*Al Thawra*, 15 March 1966).

During the early years of the existence of the Fatah these ideas found expression in brochures and newspaper articles in Syria and Lebanon – but the group was small, it had no substantial financial support and it was in no way prepared to engage in military action. This changed during the winter of 1964/5; from January 1965 on the Fatah received some assistance from the Syrian intelligence. From documents that fell subsequently into Israeli hands it appeared that the Israeli desk of the Syrian Deuxième Bureau under Muhammad Araka (himself a Palestinian) began to sponsor Fatah activities; 'Asifa' was founded, its members received specialised military training, they were given explosives and arms for their raids into Israel. This assistance was in the beginning on a small scale, and so was the extent of their military activities. The Syrian Government did not yet officially associate itself with the Fatah, and the other Arab governments were hostile. A pro-Nasser paper in Beirut wrote that there was reason to believe that the Fatah was tied to CENTO and to Israel. (*Al Anwar*, 3 January 1965.) The governments of Jordan and Lebanon announced that in their view the Asifa caused much damage to the cause of Palestine. They were unwilling to tolerate such activities on their territory. On various occasions Lebanese and Jordan police and military forces intercepted Asifa units on their forays from Syria to Israel through Lebanese and Jordanian territory. The Asifa usually refused to be identified and to surrender their arms when challenged; there were pitched battles, one in July 1966, when four members of a commando unit were killed. (*Al Ba'ath*, 25 July 1966.) The publications of the Fatah bitterly attacked the Jordanian and Lebanese authorities for putting these obstacles in their way (cf. *Al Asifa*, May 1967) and making operations from bases outside Syria more and more difficult.

With the advent to power of a new Syrian Government in February 1966 the decision was taken to support the Fatah in a much bigger way than before, and from July 1966 the organisation came entirely under Syrian control. Their raids became more ambitious; in the past, their main targets had been water pumping stations, and irrigation networks which were not usually closely watched; beginning with summer 1966 the attacks showed greater daring and competence, and the equipment used was of much higher sophistication. The Fatah was not the only guerrilla organisation operating in Syria – there were smaller groups such as the 'Heroes of the return to the homeland', the Abd el Kader al Hussaini commando unit, etc. Ahmed Shukairy's PLO, which was sponsored by the Egyptians, kept initially aloof from Fatah activities, though it had close ties with one of the smaller groups – the 'Heroes of the return'. This reluctance reflected fairly accurately the Egyptian attitude to the Fatah; meetings in early 1966 between leading members of the various Palestinian groups did not bring unity between them any nearer. Only towards the end of 1966 Shukairy's attitude and that of the Egyptian Government became much warmer. There were a number of reasons for this: The growing number of Fatah exploits – and as a result the growing popularity of that organisation – made Shukairy fear that he would be outflanked by the extremists. Already it was being said in these circles that the PLO, like the Arab governments, was more interested in talk than in action. At the same time, relations between Shukairy and the Jordanian authorities had gone from bad to worse, while the chief of the PLO saw the Fatah as a welcome ally in his fight against Amman. Shukairy went to Damascus in December 1966 and an agreement was reached with the Syrian Government providing for full coordination between the PLO and the Fatah. The Egyptians now began to give great publicity to the Fatah raids in their newspapers and broadcasts and also assisted them in other ways. But they still had one important reservation. Although enthusiastic about the Fatah raids from Syria, Lebanon or Jordan, they strictly opposed the establishment of Fatah bases in Egypt or the Gaza strip. The raids might involve them in a major clash with Israel at a time and at a place which was not of their own choice, and, perhaps even more important, they were potentially dangerous from the point of view of internal security. Nasser's intelligence service was not in principle averse to terrorist activities – but these were to be steered by their own people – not by the Syrian Deuxième Bureau.

Every day Damascus Radio and the 'Voice of Palestine' broadcast their military communiqués: Palestine Fidayeen had again inflicted heavy losses on the enemy in the north and central areas; many vehicles had been destroyed and their occupants killed; mines had been laid and water pumps blown up; army patrols had been ambushed.

Frequently these were mere fantasies such as the following report on Fidayeen operations:

A statement published by the Palestine Liberation Front says that the unit of Martyr Izza ad-Din al Quassam did the following: On 13 May 1967 it planted a bomb in the Cinema Royal hall in Haifa. The explosion wrecked the hall killing or wounding over a hundred people. On 13 May it planted a time bomb in a bus on its way from Haifa to Tel Aviv. The explosion killed or wounded forty people ('Voice of Palestine' on 19 May 1967).

Some damage certainly was done; the terrorists mined railway lines and destroyed property in outlying settlements. There were also some cases of murder each month. The communiqué already quoted continues:

it swears by the blood of the martyrs that it will make your life hell. Zionists, before you depart from our country once and for all ... We will have no mercy on women and children ... (19 May 1967, 16.30 GMT, published in 'Summary of World Broadcasts', 22 May 1967).

The strategy was, in brief, to apply Algerian methods to Israel. There was one flaw in the scheme however; the Israelis were not French settlers, they had nowhere to go. Israel could not be defeated by such small-scale attacks, which could do no more than provoke a war in which the regular forces of the Arab armies would become involved. The Fidayeen raids, despite their limited effect, created a sense of insecurity in Israel, especially among the settlers of the more remote settlements in the north. Eshkol, on a visit to Galilee Kibbutzim, was told that 'we want to be as safe as the inhabitants of Tel Aviv'. This was an unrealistic demand; the Israeli Government and the army could not provide absolute security. Israeli policy was to retaliate every now and then, when warnings had been of no avail, attacking Fidayeen bases, as well as public property in Arab villages and towns across the border. The wisdom of such actions was sometimes doubtful; the targets were sometimes ill chosen and the raids yielded diminishing returns. In October 1965, for instance, Israeli forces had attacked two Lebanese villages, and Israeli army units had crossed into Jordan in May and September of that year, and again in one of the biggest raids, at Samu in November, 1966. The Samu raid had been planned as a punitive action of limited scale against a local terrorist base. It developed against all planning into a full scale battle with the Arab Legion which lasted four hours and which caused many deaths. These retaliatory actions were criticised not only at the UN but also within Israel. Neither Lebanon nor Jordan had collaborated with the guerrillas. The Beirut government had in fact apologised for their raids. The Israelis thought, no doubt, that both Amman and Beirut should have taken stricter measures against the terrorists, but the governments were, in all probability, not strong enough to do this. The Samu raid provoked violent demonstrations against King Hussain and his relatively moderate government. For a while his regime was in real danger, and the possibility of a Syria-style coup in Jordan became greater. The Israeli raid had been a mistake; the impression was created that Israel was afraid to strike at Syria, the real base of the Fidayeen operations (perhaps because it had Soviet backing), and chose instead a less risky target. Many thought that this was not the way to deter the guerrillas; it was the misguided action of a weak government under constant pressure from public opinion to do something against the growing menace. Samu, at any rate, was one of the turning points on the road to war in 1967.

The PLO and the Fatah had yet another task – to fight, and eventually to overthrow the 'reactionary' Arab governments. The Syrians in particular always made it clear that Palestine could be liberated only *after* the liberation of Amman, Ryad, and Tunis. The PLO and the Fatah became weapons in the hands of the 'revolutionary' Arab states in their offensive against the 'reactionaries', after June 1966, when Nasser announced that 'peaceful coexistence' between all Arab states irrespective of social and political differences had come to an end. To be active in Jordan, with its big concentration of refugees, was of course essential for the PLO. King Hussain had originally permitted the organisation to establish its headquarters in the Old City of Jerusalem. But when Shukairy imposed 'taxes' on the refugees, established training camps, and built up a private army, the King protested. After the PLO had taken a leading part in the riots following the Samu raid (November 1966) the committees of the PLO throughout Jordan were closed and hundreds of its militants arrested. Shukairy countered by setting up an 'underground revolutionary Council' and calling for a holy war against the 'tyrant of Amman' who had betrayed God, the Prophet and Palestine. (Hussain had called Shukairy a 'tool of international communism' – hence the appeal to religion.) Relations between Hussain and Syria were even more strained. The Fatah sent small terrorist groups to Jordan to commit acts of sabotage there, explosions were set off near Jordanian government buildings, and one group confessed that they had orders to kill King Hussain and Wasfi Tal, his Prime Minister. Its activities culminated in the dispatch of a truckload of explosives which exploded (or was exploded) in Jordan, claiming many victims, and caused Jordan to break off relations with Syria, just before the outbreak of war in June 1967.

For the communists PLA and the Fatah constituted something of a problem. Basically, communists were in favour of their struggle, and the fight against the 'reactionaries' endeared them even more to the party. Fuad Nasar, the head of the Jordanian Communist Party, complained bitterly in a long article written for a Soviet periodical about the cruel repression of the PLO by King Hussain. The Israeli communists were less happy about them. Meir Vilner, leader of their pro-Arab wing thought their activities were as much responsible for the growing tension as the bellicose attitudes of the 'Israeli reactionary circles'. Mikunis and Sneh, leaders of the (Jewish) Israeli communists, were even more outraged and attacked the Arab communists for their identification with an organisation whose avowed aim it was to show no mercy to women and children. Moscow opted for a division of labour: sometimes the Soviet press included the pro-PLA statements of the Arab communists in its reports, on other occasions it censored them. Foreign communists looking to Moscow for guidance could therefore find ideological support for either version in the Soviet press.

Militarily the PLA was not a serious force. It did not distinguish itself during the defence of Gaza. A few days earlier the world TV stations had carried pictures showing rallies in Gaza with thousands of young refugees gesticulating wildly and shouting 'We shall return' and 'Death to the Jews' – determined, fanatical, seemingly an irresistible force. To many it was a frightening spectacle. But frustration, hatred, and wild enthusiasm do not necessarily make good soldiers. Shukairy just evaded capture in the Old City of Jerusalem where he had stayed on the evening of June the fifth. Arab politicians felt bitter about him once the fighting was over; his activities and wild statements had cost the Arab cause much sympathy. But the irrepressible Shukairy was not to be silenced for very long. By early July he was at it again, advising the Arab states to leave the United Nations. The Fatah announced after the war that its headquarters had been transferred to occupied Palestine: in future the Zionists would have no pretext to attack another Arab country in retaliation. Shukairy's group and the Fatah played a baneful role in Arab politics in the nineteen-sixties. On the whole they did far more damage to Arabs than to the Jews. To Nasser and the Syrians it may have seemed a clever move to organise and arm these groups. In fact, their activities precipitated the disastrous war. They were also potentially dangerous to their sponsors. If the campaign against Israel went badly it would not be the first time in history that members of such irredentist groups, feeling betrayed, would in their rage turn against their patrons.

Egypt in Crisis

Egypt in early 1967 had made little advance towards the goals President Nasser had so often outlined in his speeches. The economy was in very poor shape; in addition to the enduring troubles of over-population and under-employment, consumption had risen much faster than production; above all, the country was heavily in the red and could not repay its debts. Egypt had received about $2·3 billion in loans from abroad; of this about 1·3 billion from the East. Most pressing were the debts that had to be repaid in foreign currency: about $340 million to the Soviet Union, $112 million each to the USA and West Germany, $90 million to Italy. (These figures do not include the vast debt for arms, the greater part of which were to be met by half or more of the yearly cotton harvest.) For a number of years Egypt had successfully stalled its creditors, either by taking up new loans or by repaying debts on condition that the credit was extended and enlarged. This 'repayment' had largely become farcical but it was quite effective for a number of years. West Germany and Italy were reluctant to break off trade relations with Egypt for both commercial and political reasons.

But now Egypt's credit was running out. Even the most lenient creditors had become impatient; they were not going to throw good money after bad indefinitely. The International Bank refused to give a loan, since its recommendations for financial reforms had been disregarded. The Americans had discontinued the wheat shipments. Egyptian reserves were down to $46 million in foreign valuta and $40 million in gold. Nasser himself realised how desperate the situation was: with the financial year in July the new three year fulfilment plan was to begin. But, as he asked listeners in his May Day speech:

Where shall I get the money to set up factories and reclaim land?

... How can we provide work for people seeking it? Without new factories we can not provide work ... It will come from savings. We are using Suez Canal revenue and factory reserve funds in addition to savings. At present our savings amount to 10–12 per cent of our national income ... Were we to reach 20 per cent we could then increase our investments. We want to save 25 per cent of our national income. Without investment and work we can not attain our ends ...

There was no reason whatever to assume that the new plan would be financed by Egyptian savings – 25 per cent of the national income cannot be saved in a country as poor as Egypt. It would have meant more than bleeding white the peasants and the workers and the new class; such a policy could perhaps be carried out by a government that combined Stalin's ruthlessness with American efficiency and German (or Chinese) industry. But Egypt was neither America nor China. Did Nasser really have such illusions? It cannot be entirely ruled out that he thought there was some hope left. After all, the revolution had established new factories, the Aswan Dam would soon be completed; social services and education had been improved, and the Suez Canal functioned more efficiently and more profitably than most foreigners had expected. We do not know how Nasser's mind was working in the early months of 1967. He clearly was under considerable pressure. Relations with the other Arab countries were not good. In 1964 there had been two Arab summit conferences, another show of Arab solidarity, an *ad hoc* attempt at a common front. But the divisions were too deep. The war in the Yemen continued. King Faisal initiated a new 'Islamic Alignment' to counter Nasser's influence in the Arab world. Visiting most Arab and North African countries, he found some support in Iran and Jordan, in Tunisia and Kuwait. Nasser reacted violently; Faisal was an 'agent of western imperialism', Hussain a 'CIA agent'. ('King Hussain works for the CIA. If King Hussain works for the CIA, obviously his radio does too.' Nasser's May Day speech 1967.) A new Arab summit had been convened for September 1966, but Syria and Egypt had declared well before that date that peaceful coexistence in the Arab world had ended. The forces of socialism and progress could no longer march together with the reactionaries who constituted a danger even greater than Israel itself. First the reactionary Arab regimes had to be liquidated, only then would it be possible to tackle the

Palestine problem. About Saudia Nasser said: 'Faisal's rule has no foundation. His rule is based on a dynasty. It has no constitutional rules. They kill the people. Every Friday they execute them by chopping off their heads in the public square.' (May Day speech 1967.)

During the winter this Homeric battle of words and notes reached its climax: Tunis broke off diplomatic relations with Egypt in October 1966, Jordan recalled its ambassador from Cairo in February 1967. There were the familiar accusations that President Nasser wanted to dominate the Arab world, that he used the Arab League as a tool for personal aggrandisement and for Egypt's ambitions. Nasser's only consolation was a visit by Boumedienne in December at which a meeting of all Arab 'progressive' parties was discussed. The rise to power of the left-wing Ba'ath in Damascus may have gladdened Nasser's heart, but the Syrian comrades had ambitions of their own; they were undisciplined and unruly; they wanted to outflank him from the left in the struggle for leadership in the Arab world.

What irked Nasser particularly were the attacks on him emanating from Amman and Riyad, that he was a coward, afraid of the Israelis, unwilling to honour his promises to the Syrians to go to their help if they were attacked. There had been similar criticism for years, part of the 'more anti-Israel than thou' game, and he had ignored them. But his patience was now wearing thin; he devoted more and more time to angry refutations. In early April there had been a clash between Israeli and Syrian troops and an air battle that extended from the skies of Damascus to Jordan. The Syrians put out fantastic claims, but when the dust had settled it appeared that the Israelis had shot down six Syrian MiG for no loss of their own. And now Amman and Riyad began to rub salt in Nasser's wounds attempting to goad him into action. Cairo and Damascus had a defence treaty: why had it not been invoked? Why was the Egyptian-Israeli border so quiet? And why had it been so quiet for years? Why did Nasser tolerate the presence of UN soldiers on his territory? Why did he not close the Straits of Tiran? Nasser replied:

King Hussain was very angry, and he and his mother were weeping because the agreement had not been implemented ... Fighter planes have a limited range. Our fighter planes cannot reach the Syrian border. Their limited range does not enable them to get to Syria and back ... Our Syrian brothers said they had an adequate number of planes. (May Day speech 1967.)

For all the sarcasm, he was stung by the criticism of his Arab foes. He could no longer afford to sit by idly. Something had to be done when the Israelis next retaliated. What was it to be?

America had made Nasser even more angry. In the early days of the revolution he had thought America was on his side – as indeed it was. But much water had flowed down the Nile since. At one time Nasser had been the blue-eyed boy of the CIA. Now, in 1967 (he said) America wants to dominate the world, it leads the counter revolution all over the globe.

> Brothers, the battle we are fighting is not an easy one. It is a big battle headed by America. Actually we are not fighting Faisal, Hussain, the Shah or the imbecile Bourguiba. Never. They are all tools in the hands of the United States. These tools are nothing to us. (May Day speech 1967.)

There was, of course, much demagogy in this; Nasser knew that the State Department had followed over many years a pro-Arab, pro-Nasser line. He knew better than anyone else about the immense economic aid America had provided. He knew that the conflict had erupted only after his own priorities had changed. Even then the Americans had leaned backward not to spoil relations; they had closed their eyes and ears to all the insults hurled at them. But he was correct in one assumption: America did have other interests in the Middle East, and if he were to challenge them, he was bound to clash with Washington. The State Department might regard Israel as a nuisance which gravely undermined America's position in the Arab world, but if Nasser was going to carry out his threat to destroy Israel, he would at one stage or another encounter American opposition. Nasser had lasted far longer than any Arab military ruler because he combined daring and caution. Most of his successes were the result of playing the East against the West, of cleverly manœuvring in a world in which small and weak countries could successfully blackmail the big powers, whether friendly or hostile. He had been very lucky for a long time, and he was now about to push his luck too far. The logic of events, the critical situation in Egypt, were forcing him on to a more and more radical line. He needed some dramatic new triumph and this could be achieved not with America, but only against it. There may have been a personal element; he had always been a proud man and over the years had become vain. The Russians and their allies exploited this weakness, referring to his selfless patriotism, his farsighted statesmanship, his genius in leading Egypt. The Americans were sober, matter-of-fact, not very cordial, not very tactful. They lacked the flair to deal with him. The Russians were accomplished flatterers, the Americans talked about the balance of payment. Then there were the CIA people in Cairo who in the privacy of their homes had made offensive remarks about the leader of the Egyptian revolution; but Nasser's agents had listened in, and the *Rais* had a long memory. Nasser in the spring of 1967 showed all the signs of a man under pressure whose patience had grown very thin indeed.

The Military Balance

The military balance in early 1967 was in favour of the United Arab Republic. It had two armoured divisions (a third was about to be formed), four infantry divisions, one parachute brigade, twelve artillery regiments. Its strength in armour was 1,200 tanks and assault guns, including 350 Russian T-34, at least 450 T-54, a sprinkling of British Centurions and French AMX tanks. Its navy consisted of six destroyers, nine submarines, escort vessels, minesweepers, submarine chasers, etc. Its air force had been quickly built up – it included at least 70 bombers, 130 MiG-21 interceptors with air-to-air missiles, 80 MiG-19 all-weather fighters, as well as fighter bombers and transport aircraft. Then there was the Missile Command, separate from both the army and the air force. At its disposal were *Al Zafir*, carrying a 1,000 lb. warhead some 235 miles, *Al Kahir*, carrying an even larger warhead up to 375 miles, and *Al Ared*, the biggest of the three.

The Egyptian army, like the other Arab armies had been very much improved since 1956: 'We are ready for war,' Nasser said in his speech at UAR Advanced Air Headquarters on 23 May, 'our armed forces and all our people are ready for war.' Most military commentators were inclined to believe him. United Arab Command had been established in Cairo in 1964. The

Arabs had received from the Soviet Union the most sophisticated weapons, they had missiles (which Israel had not), the Nile Delta and Aswan were protected by a highly efficient radar network. This time Nasser's tanks and artillery did not have to meet Israel half way; the logistic weaknesses of 1956 had been eliminated. Above all, as the (Manchester) *Guardian* said on 6 June 1967, 'the element of surprise is absent, the Israelis cannot this time catch the Egyptians on the wrong foot'. The other Arab armies were by no means negligible: Syria with 8 armoured and motorised brigades, complete with T-54 and T-34 tanks, about 160 planes, including the most modern MiGs. Iraq had several divisions (including two motorised and one armoured), with more than 500 tanks, and an air force including not only MiG but also TU-16 medium bombers. Jordan had a smaller, but well equipped and trained army, with American M-48 Patton and British Centurion tanks.

It was a most impressive line up, the result of an arms race that began in 1955 with the Egyptian-Soviet (or, as it was then called, Czechoslovak) arms deal. There had been small Soviet arms shipments to the Middle East before, but Britain had been the main supplier of tanks and jet aircraft. Since the recipients had to pay in hard cash there were narrow limits to their purchases. This western monopoly was broken by the Soviet Union, which established itself in the middle fifties as one of the world's main arms suppliers. The original deal with Egypt was not big; it included about 150 MiG-15s and 17s, as well as some 40 Ilyushin tactical bombers, several hundred tanks, two destroyers and three submarines. But it was far in excess of anything Israel had at the time. And since Israel thought that an arms balance was the only guarantee of peace in the Middle East it made an immediate effort to acquire arms of similar quality. In the race that ensued the Soviet Union supplied some 2,500–3,000 tanks to the Arab countries, more than a thousand aircraft, thousands of guns as well as missiles (and missile-firing vessels) of all kinds, an investment of at least 1–2 billion dollars altogether. These are substantial figures: total world annual arms sales were estimated at $1 billion in 1965 – of which the Soviet Union provided some 40 per cent, France 20 per cent, Britain and America 15 per cent each. In the Middle East the Soviet Union had become the chief arms supplier. Soviet aims in supplying these arms were mainly political, partly economic. The 1955 deal was a unique opportunity to effect a political breakthrough. Egypt wanted arms, it could not obtain them from the western powers, and Moscow provided an alternative on advantageous conditions. (Egypt and most other Arab countries paid for the Soviet arms with raw materials or other local products.) In the course of time this business relationship led to closer collaboration in many fields (such as training schemes covering hundreds of officers) and it fitted admirably into the general pattern of Soviet-Arab rapprochement; ultimately it made the recipient dependent on the supplier in many respects.

All this posed a grave threat to Israel. In 1948 and again in 1956 the numerical superiority of the Arabs had been offset by the better quality of Israeli arms, and the superior technical level of the country. But as the years passed the balance changed: Egypt and the other Arab countries were receiving not only far larger quantities but also more developed and sophisticated arms. The Soviet Union was eager to supply them, whereas the United States was reluctant for political reasons to give arms to Israel; it took two years, for instance, to negotiate and deliver tactical jet bombers. The sale of Hawk anti-aircraft missiles was authorised by President Kennedy in 1962, but only after Cairo had received TU-16 bombers. Israel received some 200 Patton M-48 tanks from America via Germany – a cumbersome deal negotiated in secret which, when revealed in the end, caused embarrassment to all concerned. But Patton tanks had also been sent to Jordan, which received in addition F-104 supersonic fighter-bombers, Saudi Arabia also received substantial arms shipments from America. Russia supported only the Arabs, America both Arabs and Israelis. As seen from Tel Aviv it was not a very encouraging state of affairs. France was willing to supply tanks and aircraft to Israel, but these had to be paid for in hard currency, not in oranges and grapefruits.

The Israeli economy had developed rapidly since 1956. With its 2·7 million inhabitants, the country's GNP (Gross National Product) in 1966–7 was within striking distance of Egypt's, with its population of 30 million. But the arms purchases were an enormous drain on the economy. Israel's defence budget for 1966–7 amounted to $447 million, more than 11 per cent of the GNP, one of the highest in the world. Israel made a great effort to keep up with the Arab states, but more and more people in Cairo and Damascus persuaded themselves that Israel had fallen behind, that it was now militarily inferior. Typical of this new contempt for Israel was a broadcast by the director of Cairo Radio, Ahmad Said, in May 1967:

Arabs, here are full and accurate details of Israeli military power obtained from sources which know the whole truth about Israel ... Israel has a number of old Sherman tanks which have been repaired and fitted with diesel engines and French 105 mm. guns ... In war Israel could mobilise within 48 hours 250,000 soldiers who could undertake home guard duties but who do not take part in battles involving regular armies ... ('Lies exposed by facts', Cairo, 'Voice of the Arabs', 16 May.)

In conclusion, Ahmad Said said that the Israeli forces would be incapable of facing even the small UAR contingent remaining in the Yemen or the Syrian army, let alone the full force of the Egyptian army: 'We challenge you, Eshkol, to try all your weapons. Put them to the test; they will spell Israel's death and annihilation.'

Three weeks later the Israeli home guard was bathing in the Suez Canal and Ahmad Said and his friends were sadder and wiser men. Some of them talked about Pearl Harbor and *Blitzkrieg*, others about massive American and British intervention; the more realistic among them admitted that they had underrated Israel. The Jordan Prime Minister said that in some respects Arab intelligence had been very faulty indeed; the 'Zionists' were four times as strong as had been expected.

Israel at the time had some 800 tanks (including 200 M-48 Patton and 150 AMX 13), compared with some 1,200 on the Egyptian side; it had about 350 aircraft (including Vautour light bombers, Mirage 3 CJ, and Super Mystère – there also had been some last minute shopping in Paris). But though the Israeli army was stronger than the Arab military leaders estimated, it was still inferior on paper to the Egyptian army, not to mention the combined strength of all Arab armies. The overall balance did not look too good in May 1967; the Arab leaders were confident of victory, Jews and their wellwishers were worried; in some of the appeals circulated in those days in London and Paris there was talk of annihilation and Auschwitz. Almost all military correspondents agreed that the Arab armies were far stronger than in 1956. But such calculations ignored the most essential, the human factor. Israel was fighting for survival, the Arab countries to get revenge. It is a well established fact that human beings will fight back with unexpected strength if threatened with annihilation even if they are not born and experienced fighters; this was ignored by the Arabs and their Russian suppliers, who never had a high opinion of the Jew as a fighting man. But the Israelis were not merely fighting back with the strength of desperation, they had over the years developed a military spirit and a discipline which came as a surprise to the world at large. By a strange mutation they had shed in their new homeland what were believed to be pronounced racial characteristics. Trade and finance in Israel were in an unholy mess, and the quality of Israel's cultural life was somewhat disappointing. But the country had made enormous progress in those two fields which were traditionally the least Jewish of all – agriculture and the armed forces. The experience of the Second World War also had a lasting impact: never again were Jews to be killed like sheep, there was a determination not only to hit back at any cost, but to hit back five minutes too early rather than too late.

Israel had not become a militaristic society; Jews by nature are far too disputatious to obey orders at any time but a national crisis. It was a citizens' army of shopkeepers, building workers, students, in which rank counted for little. Somehow it had managed to preserve the pioneering spirit of the early days, though the human material was now very different from what it had been in the pre-historic age of the *Palmach*. There were other factors that contributed to its success: Israelis are excellent improvisers and the combination of impatience and quickness made for startling performances, individually and collectively, in the air as well as on the ground. Egyptian equipment was every bit as good as the Israeli – the automatic Stormovich rifles were certainly the equal of the Israeli FN. The new Russian T-55 tanks were superior with their infra-red equipment for night fighting and their heavy long range guns. But the superior equipment was not altogether an advantage; sometimes these prestige weapons, ill-suited for the desert, were difficult to handle.

It was not the element of surprise that explains the Arab defeat in June 1967. Every Arab leader from Nasser down had declared that he was most eager to fight in a war that would break out any day. It was not the 'air umbrella' nor any mystery weapon or intelligence gimmick. According to the Russians and the Yugoslavs it was poor leadership, the fact that 'the sons of the pashas and beys' commanded the Egyptian armies rather than the sons of the working people. Such an explanation has much to recommend it from an ideological angle; with the facts it has nothing in common. The army in Egypt had never been considered a fit occupation for the sons of pashas; like Nasser, most officers came from poor, or, at most, lower middle-class families. (Dayan's father was a farmer, Rabin's a worker – not that it made them necessarily better military leaders than Yadin, whose father had been a professor of archaeology.) In fact, the Russians were concerned not so much about the social background of the officers, which was perfectly respectable from a Marxist point of view, but about their 'ideological weakness', the fact that they had constituted themselves as a new class, that they had taken far better care of themselves than of the soldiers under their command. This was all too true, but it was unfair to blame Egypt for manifestations of a trend that is not altogether unknown in communist societies.

The reasons for the Arab defeat are manifold. We are concerned here with the military balance in May 1967, a balance in which missiles, aircraft, and guns counted for much more than the fighting spirit. Tanks and aircraft can be measured, the human factor is an unknown quantity. The Egyptians had not made a good showing in 1956, but who could say whether eleven years of the national revolution had not made a great difference? The Israelis had given a better account of themselves in 1948 and again in 1956; but the Israeli army was no longer the same; there had been a great influx of Jews from backward societies. Who could guarantee that these new soldiers and sergeants would be equally good? It is all very well to talk in retrospect about Nasser's folly; at the time his appraisal of the military balance was shared by most military observers. And even in Israel there were voices giving warning that this time the odds were heavily against the Jews.

3

Confrontation

In May 1967 all the ingredients existed for a major flare-up in the Middle East: the arms race had continued for twelve years. Arab guerrilla activities against Israel had reached a new climax in the past few months; there was more tension than ever before between Israel and the Arab countries. But these ingredients had existed all along, and yet war had not broken out on past occasions.

War broke out in June as the result of a series of events that had started three weeks earlier. It was a textbook case of escalation; one event led to another with almost iron consequence. Yet calculation looms larger in retrospect than it was, improvisation and accident played a great role. There is as so often a temptation to read too much purpose and premeditation and far-reaching planning into the course of events.

The crisis began in Syria – as most Middle East crises have in recent years. 'All of us know how the crisis started', Nasser said in his resignation speech on 9 June. 'At the beginning of last May there was an enemy plan for the invasion of Syria and the statements by his politicians and his military leaders openly said so. Sources of our Syrian brothers were categorical on this and our own reliable information confirmed it. Add to this the fact that our friends in the Soviet Union warned the parliamentary delegation which was on a visit to Moscow that there was a premeditated plan against Syria. We considered it our duty not to accept this silently. This was the duty of Arab brotherhood, it was also the duty of national security.' The explanation seems straightforward enough and other details that were published amplified it. On 13 May, Marshal Amer had received a message from his colleague, the Syrian Defence Minister Hafiz al Asad, that there were disquieting reports about Israeli troop concentrations on the Syrian border: 11–13 Israeli brigades were massed on two fronts, north and south of Lake Tiberias; they were to attack on the night of 16/17 May between 4 and 5 in the morning.[1] According to one report the news had reached Cairo through the Lebanese intelligence; according to another, two Syrian emissaries had arrived in Cairo who claimed they had proof of a forthcoming attack.[2] On another occasion, in a speech on 26 May, Nasser said, 'We sent reconnaissance aircraft over Israel. Not a single brigade was stationed opposite us ... all Israeli brigades were opposite Syria.'* We shall have to devote some attention to these reports, because, according to Nasser, they sparked off the decision which, less than four weeks later, led to war. If the news was substantially correct, it does not really matter very much who warned Nasser and when the warning was received. But if it was not, the question who misled Nasser – if he was misled – is of paramount importance. Already at the beginning of the crisis there were rumours that the Syrians had been warned by Moscow of an Israeli attack.[4] Nasser's declaration tends to confirm this, at least in part, but the circumstances seem unusual. An Israeli invasion of Syria with the aim of overthrowing the Damascus regime was certainly no small matter; would the Soviet Union have chosen an Egyptian parliamentary delegation visiting Russia to convey to Cairo information of such vital and urgent importance? It seems unlikely; there are other channels of information in such cases. Why then was the attempt made to cover up the origins of the warning?

Perhaps the warning was given in vague terms, the Russians simply drawing Egyptian attention to certain speeches by Israeli leaders. But Nasser could read the newspapers himself. Ten days later he said he had been angered by a 'very impertinent statement' made on 12 May. 'Anyone reading this statement must believe that these people (the Jews) are so boastful and deceitful that one simply cannot remain silent. The statement said that the Israeli commanders announced they would carry out military operations against Syria in order to occupy Damascus and overthrow the

---

*Subsequently the story of the plot was further embellished; it became part of a conspiracy of truly giant extent. According to the *Unità* correspondent in Cairo the aim was not merely to overthrow the Socialist government of Syria, but also to bring down the Egyptian Government, to promote a coup in Cyprus, to counter the revolutionary struggle in Yemen, and to reinforce fascism in Greece. All this on the authority of a 'highly qualified person closely connected with the Egyptian Government, whose name I am not permitted to disclose ...'[3] It was exactly the kind of story likely to appeal to both Soviet and Arab politicians. Eric Rouleau (*Israel et les Arabes*, pp 53–4), reports the same story.

Syrian Government. On the same day the Israeli Premier, Eshkol, made a very threatening statement against Syria, and, the commentaries said, that 'Israel believed that Egypt could not make a move because it was bogged down in Yemen'. It is surprising that Nasser should think such a statement 'very impertinent'; after all, he and other Arab leaders had more than once threatened war against Israel and the annihilation of the state – not just the overthrow of the regime. Was it not natural that in this war of words the Israelis should retaliate in kind?

Who made the 'impertinent' statement? This was the weekend of Friday, 12 May, and just about every Israeli politician was engaged in that national sport, speechmaking. The Chief of Staff, Rabin, spoke at the Habimah Theatre in Tel Aviv; reminiscing about 1948, he said that the central lesson of the War of Independence was that if Israel was engaged in battle once again it should not be in conditions of unpreparedness. Mrs Golda Meir spoke at the same meeting; she recalled her meetings with King Abdallah and said that the Fatah saboteurs were not an anonymous group but linked to the Syrian High Command. The Minister of Transport, Moshe Carmel, spoke in Kiryat Gat and regretted that there was still no prospect of peace. The Minister of Justice, Shapiro, spoke in Natanya, and the Foreign Minister, Eban, in Holon; there were no startling revelations. But there were also two speeches by the Prime Minister, Levy Eshkol. At a closed meeting of Mapai leaders at the Yahdav Club in Tel Aviv he said that 'In view of the 14 incidents in the past month alone, we may have to adopt measures not less drastic than those of 7 April.' And in a Remembrance Day broadcast he said: 'Any border which is tranquil on their side will be tranquil on our side as well. And if they try to sow unrest on our border, unrest will come to theirs.' The answer to Syrian sabotage activities would come when, where, and in a manner which Israel would decide. No one made a statement about overthrowing the Syrian Government.

What Israel did in mid-May was according to Nasser unprecedented: threatening troop concentrations and impertinent statements made it imperative for him to act. But the record shows that between May 1966 and May 1967, there was hardly a week without news in the Syrian and Egyptian press about major Israeli troop concentrations on the Syrian border. The Soviet press frequently commented on it: 'Israel extremists plan war on Syria', 'Israeli reactionary plot against Syria', 'Israel threatening Syria' were standard headlines in the Soviet press, and there were also official notes by the Soviet Government. One, on 12 October 1966, stated that, 'According to information in our possession, concentration of Israeli troops can again be discerned along the Syrian frontier'. And even the item about the planned overthrow of the Syrian Government attributed to General Rabin was not new – *Pravda* had featured it at least once a month (13 October, 17 November, 18 December 1966, etc.). On 3 February 1967 *Izvestiya* reported that 'War psychosis is mounting in the state of Israel. The country's armed forces are being alerted. All leave has been cancelled and more reservists have been called up. Large armed forces have been concentrated on the northern border.' It was the same story all over again. It cannot have possibly come as a surprise to Nasser and the question remains: What induced him to react differently when the story about troop concentrations and the planned overthrow of the Ba'ath government came up again in early May? Was it simply the cumulative effect, or were other considerations involved?

There had been since April a rise in guerrilla activities from Syria; Israel had complained to the UN and U Thant, in a special statement, regretted this increase in Fatah type activities: the incidents were 'very deplorable', he said at a luncheon of the UN Correspondents' Association, especially because in their nature they seemed to indicate that the individuals involved had had more specialised training than was usually evident in such incidents. 'This type of activity is insidious' U Thant added and, 'menaces the peace in the area.'

Arab spokesmen were aggrieved; after all, the Palestinians had the right to attack those who had stolen their country. The Israeli authorities made it clear that they were not willing to put up with this; there was talk in Tel Aviv – no official statement – about a major act of retaliation. The warnings by the Prime Minister were regarded by authoritative sources as an ultimatum – if the Syrians would not stop their attacks, there would be Israeli counteraction: 'The anticipated clash is not thought likely to assume the dimensions of a full scale campaign, but to be in the nature of a military expedition intended to take the wind out of the Syrian sails once and for all.'[5] Tough talk – but not half as tough as the speeches of the Arab leaders. We do not know where these reports originated; perhaps it was an anonymous defence spokesman. A United Press dispatch datelined Jerusalem, 12 May, reported that 'a highly placed Israeli source said here today that if Syria continued the campaign of sabotage in Israel it would immediately provoke military action aimed at overthrowing the Syrian regime'. The dispatch added that Israeli action would fall short of all-out hostilities, and that Israel was ready to risk possible Egyptian intervention, although Cairo was too deeply committed elsewhere to take on additional obligations.[6] It was apparently a garbled account of Eshkol's Tel Aviv speech. But it was sufficient to create 'serious concern' (U Thant) at the United Nations; the Paris press and the *New York Times* (14 May) reported it at length. The first reaction in the Arab capitals was that though Israeli warnings against Syrian attacks had become almost 'routine' in recent months, the risk of war had grown 'slightly more dangerous'.[7] The same report mentioned the 'novel tactics of mortar bombardments from the Lebanon' and a speech by Mr Shukairy: 'We all believe in armed struggle as the only road to the liberation of Palestine.' There had been to repeat again no Israeli threat to overthrow the Damascus government – but merely a series of reports from the Middle Eastern capitals to the effect that Israel would soon react against the intensification of guerrilla warfare; such news was not sensational. One day before the United Press dispatch a Lebanese nespaper – to give but one example – quoted Eshkol's interview with the Israeli army weekly *Bamahane* to the effect that Israel took a grave view of the recent minings of roads by the guerrillas.[8]

The Israeli warning made it clear that there would be a major act of reprisal – unless the Syrians stopped guerrilla activities. No immediate action was planned – whenever Israel envisaged a large-scale raid there was, for obvious reasons, no advance warning. There were no troop concentrations in the north – there were a few companies stationed in the north, not a brigade, let alone eleven or thirteen. Mr Eshkol gave instructions to ask the Soviet ambassador to see for himself; Mr Chuvakhin did not avail himself of the invitation. The UN observers reported from the Syrian border that there were no significant troop movements. (U Thant's report to the Security Council, 19 May 1967.)

Nor were the Arab leaders alarmed, as some claimed later, by the fact that the Israeli Independence Day parade was smaller than usual, that much of the heavy equipment was not shown – and that some Arab spy had therefore reached the conclusion that the missing troops and their equipment were on the way north. An interesting theory, but it does not stand the test; for the Independence Day parade was held on 15 May, whereas Nasser claims that the information about the Israeli attack had reached him two days earlier, when he decided to give marching orders to his army. And Syria had already previously informed the chairman of the Security Council that Israel was preparing a 'new Suez' as part of a plot sponsored by the CIA.

Nasser is very emphatic that information about the Israeli invasion reached him only on 13 May. He rejected reports that the subsequent military movements must have been the result of a well laid plan worked out in advance. 'I say that the sequence of events determined the plan. We had no plan before 13 May because we believed that Israel would not have dared to make such an impertinent statement.'[9] Nasser attributed a great deal of importance to the chronology of events to explain his decision. Already on the day before, 12 May, and on 13 May, the Syrian Foreign Ministry had published a statement on 'planned Israeli aggression'. It argued that the details of the Israeli plot were 'known to all', and had apparently been known for a long time. 'Using the Palestinian Arab People's struggle as a pretext for launching aggression against Syria cannot hide the Imperialist-Zionist-reactionary plot against our homeland. The details of the plot have been revealed to the Arab people and to the whole world. It hinges on a large Israeli attack by mercenaries and agents of Jordanian intelligence with imperialist weapons. This is to be accompanied by the efforts of reaction and the remnants of agents (inside Syria) who were affected by the revolution.'[10] The Syrians said at the end of their long communiqué that the aggression prepared by the Zionist circles would not be confronted by Syria alone; joint defence agreements would be put into effect. Did they make this declaration without consulting their senior partner?

There is some reason to assume that the decision to concentrate several divisions in Sinai was in fact taken at a four-hour meeting at the general staff on 11 May – before the Israeli warnings. (S. Segev, *Sadin Adom*, Tel Aviv, 1967, p. 37.)

Al Ahram, Nasser's own newspaper, said in an article published on 13 May and written, one would assume, before that date, that 'an attack is definitely about to take place'. But there was no CIA-Israel-Jordan plot to overthrow the Damascus government; if it did not exist, who invented it and why? Was it a genuine mistake, or a deliberate attempt to find a pretext for a political and/or military offensive? If so, who misled whom?

The crisis began in effect not on 13 May but during the second half of April. Ever since the Israeli retaliatory action on 7 April the Syrian Government and the army command had shown signs of nervousness. There were frequent reports about an impending big Israeli attack. *Gumhuriya* was most emphatic: 'Israel prepares aggression on a broad front in the North'.[11] A left-wing Lebanese newspaper predicted an Israeli attack in the very near future which would make it dossible for the Western powers to intervene directly against Syria.[12] To consider immediate counteraction several high ranking officers had been sent to Damascus – among them the commanders-in-chief of the army and the air force and Sidqi Suleyman, an Egyptian Minister. Well before the Israeli 'impertinent statement', the executive of the ruling Ba'ath party published a declaration in which the whole Arab world was told that an Israeli attack against Syria was imminent.[13] This coincided with a major internal crisis.

On 25 April the Syrian army newspaper *Jaysh al Sha'ab* published an article, strongly atheist in flavour, ridiculing Islam, the Prophet, and, incidentally, the other world religions. Such an article was something of a novelty: the Syrian regime was very radical but, like Egypt, it had never dared to touch certain taboos.

It had never made great efforts to achieve the equality of the sexes, it had never accepted proletarian internationalism (a Jewish communist too was an enemy), and it had never challenged Islam. The publication of the article caused much indignation in Damascus and other Syrian cities.* The Ulema, the religious dignitaries, called protest meetings and there were speeches in the mosques against godless communism. The Government reacted sharply: Shaikh Hassan Habanakah, the head of the League of

---

*There was also an economic crisis: a Soviet journal had noted already in April the 'growth of discontent among the middle class and the lower middle class in Syria and Egypt which are numerically quite significant'.[14]

77

Ulema, and many others were arrested, their property seized.[15] But unrest continued in the Al Maydan quarter of Damascus (Shaikh Habanakah's stronghold) and spread throughout Syria. There were clashes in Homs and Hama, explosions in Damascus. Strict controls were imposed on Syria's borders. The Ba'ath party supreme command was in constant session for three days. Armed clashes occurred between security forces and citizens protesting against the Government and its policy. Khaled Bagdash and several other Syrian communist leaders in a cable to the Government demanded strong action against the conspirators but suggested at the same time to help the small businessmen and shopkeepers against the big capitalists and blackmarketeers. The country seemed again on the verge of civil war. A Lebanese newspaper reported that the present crisis was unprecedented since the Ba'ath party had seized power four years previously.[16] There was a total blackout in Damascus: most information about events in Syria now came from outside Arab sources, but there was more than enough in the Syrian official statements to indicate that the Government was in a state of panic. *Humanité*, the French communist daily, reported on 9 May that soldiers and armed workers were patrolling the streets of Damascus. Armed guards had been posted in front of the mosques; many inhabitants of Damascus had been unable to buy bread and meat because the big merchants and the clergy had called for a strike against the Government. This agitation was to facilitate a Jordanian plot under the leadership of Colonel Hatoum and Major Badr Juma, Syrian army officers who had fled to Amman after the unsuccessful coup of September 1966. One of these officers had recently returned from Amman and had denounced the conspiracy on Damascus television: 'The religious leaders, the big merchants and the author of the (anti-religious) article have all been arrested.'

A major domestic crisis was on – and it had nothing to do with Israel. The Syrian leaders were afraid of the 'CIA agent – Colonel Hatoum', undoubtedly one of the key figures in the May crisis. As the officer commanding the parachute brigade, it was mainly owing to him that the left Ba'ath had come to power in February 1966. Hatoum was said to be the head of the ultra-left (pro-Chinese) faction in the Syrian leadership; there was a tug-of-war, not on ideological but on mainly personal grounds.

Ethnic factors also came into play: most left-wing Ba'athists were Alawite, Hatoum was a Druze. After a new coup in September 1966 had failed he escaped to Amman, to return to Damascus only in early June 1967. When he heard that Syrian political prisoners (of whom there were quite a few) were being released during the war against Israel, he returned to Syria in the belief that old quarrels would be forgotten and his services accepted in the fight against the common enemy. He was mistaken: arrested in Damascus, he was executed a few days after.

The military governor of Damascus, in a statement on 7 May, announced the 'sinful and insidious article' in the army newspaper had been written by a CIA agent who had 'squalidly infiltrated the army to create confusion among the citizens'. It was all part of a plot between Israel, the CIA, the escapees in Jordan. (Many Syrian officers had been purged in previous months; some had escaped to Jordan.) The Israeli attack on 7 April had been merely the beginning, the main plot was still to be executed. But the masses, led by the High Command of the Revolution, would crush all hostile forces. The army was out in force in Damascus and the streets of the other Syrian cities. There were mass arrests – 1,500 according to one report. Some demonstrators were killed and more were wounded. Shops closed down, and the Government, in reply, seized the businesses of 45 'leading exploiting capitalists after it had been established that they had conspired against the gains of the working masses and were involved in a reactionary – imperialist – Zionist plot' (9 May). More army officers were arrested as yet another plot to overthrow the regime was discovered; they included the former deputy commander of the internal security forces (5 May).

Syria, during the first week of May, was in turmoil, its leaders in a state of great agitation. The Government had little popular support; it reacted as desperate governments do – with severe repression. There had been other crises since its take-over in February 1966; but this seemed the most serious, or so it appeared to the leaders of the Ba'ath and their allies in the army, whose actions and speeches revealed more than a touch of hysteria. The situation was bad, their imagination made it appear even worse. The Israeli raid of 7 April, had been a serious blow to their prestige. Would they survive another such blow now that most of the army was fighting the 'internal enemy'? What happened next is a matter for surmise, but it is certain that the Russians were consulted, for, although relations with Cairo were now much better than in the past, the link with Moscow was even closer. Whether Moscow counselled a diversion or whether this was originally a Syrian proposal, we do not know. There is some reason to assume that the Russians were more acutely aware of the dangers facing the Syrian regime than the Ba'ath leadership itself. The obvious course of action for the Russians would have been to counsel moderation in Damascus; to stop the attacks against Israel and to solve the internal crisis by some concessions. But the Russians knew that the Syrians were not in a mood to accept such advice. It seemed far more promising to call in Nasser; after all, the defence treaty between Egypt and Syria had been signed a few months previously, *inter alia*, to bring the Syrian hotheads under control. It must have seemed a safe enough course. The story about an impending Israeli invasion of Syria could serve more than one purpose: it would give the harassed Syrian Government some respite on the domestic front; it might induce Nasser to come to Syria's help under the provisions of the new defence treaty; and it would compel even the 'reactionary' Arab countries to discontinue their attacks on Damascus. This then, as far as can be reconstructed, was the origin of the May crisis.

The Syrians could always argue that, at worst, their warning was premature. Even if there was no immediate Israeli danger, even if Israel did not want to attack on the morning of the 17th, sooner or later there would be a new retaliatory raid. For the Fatah would continue to attack Israel and it could be predicted with certainty that, sooner or later, Israel would hit back. The Fatah, and, to a lesser extent, the other guerrilla organisations also played an important part in unleashing the May crisis. Ever since the beginning of their military activities in January 1965 they had stressed that the 'people's war' (guerrilla activities) was merely the first phase of the struggle. Israel was to be provoked into major acts of retaliation which, in due course would make the intervention of the regular Arab armies, and thus all out war, inevitable. This policy had been outlined on many occasions; it was directed not only against Hussain but also against Nasser who had declared that the Arab armies were not ready, and would not be ready for a long time for the final showdown with Israel. The leaders of the Fatah were not willing to wait that long. They used other arguments as well: it was dangerous to wait too long because in the meantime Israel would obtain nuclear weapons and the chances of liberating Palestine would decrease even further. In a series of articles in a Lebanese newspaper[17] Salah Shabal the head of the 'Palestine Liberation Front' demanded that Egypt should bomb Dimona (the Israeli atomic reactor) as part of a preventive war to be launched immediately. The same suggestion was pressed on subsequent occasions.[18] The guerrilla organisations did all that was in their power, and not without success, to cause the escalation of the conflict. They provoked the big Israeli attack on Samu in November 1966 which considerably added to the existing tension and which became one of the landmarks in the road to the war that broke out the year after. Their hopes were rising; if they would only step up their activities the liberation of Palestine would be inevitable. In March 1967 they used for the first time minethrowers in an attack from Lebanese territory against an Israeli settlement – an experiment that was repeated the following month.[19] This policy had the full support of the Syrian Government. In May Israel made an attempt through the UN observers to reach a local compromise with the Syrians – but to no avail. There was (as a Jordan newspaper wrote) a suicidal element in the policy of the Syrian Government to step up the attacks despite its military weakness so as to invite another Israeli attack like that on 7 April (when Israel had inflicted a heavy defeat on the Syrian air force).[20] It was madness, but as far as the Fatah was concerned there was method in it: they could not wait for the outbreak of war. It is not certain whether these implications were clear to the Russians who at first did not attribute much significance to the guerrilla activities. But they realised that Syria was really in trouble – why not look for preventive medicine? Moscow itself could do little. An official declaration was published, a solemn warning against imperialist intrigues against Syria, and particularly the Israeli threats.[21] But Russia could not intervene at this stage; Nasser had to be called in. Did Nasser believe the story about the impending Israeli attack? Perhaps the Syrians told him the truth: after all, their troubles were no secret, and Nasser stood to lose much if the Ba'ath regime fell. For years he had refused to come to the help of the Syrians, who had managed to

provoke the Israelis and get themselves into trouble with mono-
tonous regularity at least once a year. But now, in May 1967, the
situation was different. Nasser was still smarting under the insults hurled at him by his Arab rivals after Samu and the raid of
7 April. He had suffered setback after setback in recent years;
his enemies thought Egypt was finished, what with the war in
Yemen and the economic crisis. Nasser must have been sorely
tempted to show friends and enemies alike that he was still a
major force, the leader of the Arab world, still able to regain the
initiative. It was in this mood that the Soviet-Syrian request
found him, and that he took his fateful decision.

Nasser takes the Plunge

Syria in early May faced an acute crisis and the Soviet Union
wanted to help. But only Nasser could help and he was nobody's
tool. The origins of a crisis are never easy to trace, involving as
they do multiple and often conflicting factors. Some moves in
that May crisis were planned, but most decisions were apparently taken on the spur of the moment. The Soviet leaders no
doubt wanted a show of Egyptian strength on Israel's southern
frontier; but did they want the closure of the Straits of Tiran?
The evidence is conflicting. Events soon acquired a momentum
of their own; once Nasser had taken the first step there was a
very strong temptation to advance further towards the brink.
And then, at a certain point, retreat became impossible.

Escalation in May proceeded in three stages. At first there
were troop movements towards the Israeli frontier and the UN
forces were asked to withdraw. But it was still widely believed
that this was a political demonstration, not a real military challenge. According to the Israeli version, based on the interroga-
tion of high ranking Egyptian officers who were captured, the
troop concentrations were in the beginning demonstrative; they
proceeded not in secret but were given great publicity.[21a] The
forces that were dispatched to Sinai were not sufficiently strong
for any major military operation. It is an interesting explanation
and it fits in neatly with the original Israeli intelligence appraisal
– that Nasser would not attack, and that the change came
suddenly between 18 and 22 May. But there remains some doubt.
Only at the second stage was it announced that the Tiran Straits

had been mined (which turned out not to be true) and that no Israeli ship would in future be permitted to sail through the Gulf of Aqaba. Even then it was thought that this was a local challenge, albeit a dangerous one, for Israel had declared that freedom of navigation was essential; the war in 1956 had been fought to open the Gulf. But it was still thought that war could be prevented. Yet a few days later Nasser asserted that it was a mistake to believe that the issue was Tiran or Suez. Egypt wanted a military confrontation with Israel. The intention was to undo not merely Israel's gains in 1956 but to remove the Israeli danger once and forever – to destroy the Jewish state. The hour of the liberation of Palestine had come.

What induced Nasser to take his original decision? He himself has provided two versions: in his 'resignation' speech and again on 23 July 1967, he described it as a purely defensive measure, necessary to help Syria under the new treaty; as well as being a matter of honour and solidarity, it was also a question of Egypt's own security. But earlier, on 26 May, in a speech to Arab trade unionists, when things seemed to be going his way, Nasser had described the sequence of events in a different light: there had been a plan, a series of calculated steps. He had always wanted to close the Straits of Tiran, but had had to wait for an occasion: the Israeli declarations warning Syria provided the pretext.

We were waiting for the day when we would be fully prepared ... I say nothing aimlessly. One day, two years ago, I stood up to say that we have no plan to liberate Palestine ... recently, we felt we are strong enough, that if we were to enter a battle, with God's help we could triumph ...

Taking over Sharm al Shaykh meant confrontation with Israel. Taking such action also meant that we were ready to enter a general war with Israel. It was not a separate question ... Actually, I was authorised by the Arab Socialist Union's Higher Executive to implement this plan at the right time. The right time came when Syria was threatened with aggression.

The action was 'one calculated and effective step after another' as Haykal put it. There had been a plan and the enemy had been taken by 'complete surprise'. Haykal was one of the two or three men closest to Nasser; he had known him since the very beginnings of the 'Free Officers Movement', when, as a military correspondent, he had been close to the 'free officers'. He accompanied

Nasser on his major trips, Nasser's home was open to him at all hours. He was the semi-official interpreter of Nasser's ideas. For more than ten years he had had the privilege of publishing those of Nasser's thoughts which the *Rais* for one reason or another could not express himself. Haykal was now most emphatic. Frustrating the Israeli plot to invade Syria and closing the door of the Gulf of Aqaba was not the end of the matter: 'the problem has not ended but rather has hardly begun ... I am confident that for many reasons, chiefly psychological, Israel cannot accept or remain indifferent to what has taken place.' Haykal continued: 'Israel has to reply now, it has to deal a blow. It has no alternative but to take up arms. Therefore I say that an armed clash between the UAR and the Israeli enemy is inevitable. Let Israel begin. Let our second blow then be ready. Let it be a knockout![22]

It seemed to be a clear case of premeditation, a deliberate attempt to provoke a war with Israel at a time and place chosen by Nasser. Certainly there was a strong element here of post hoc rationalisation: 'I say nothing aimlessly' – a reckless statement by any man, especially an emotional man like Nasser, whose aims have often changed, sometimes without advance notice. He had been authorised, he said, by the Arab Socialist Union's Higher Executive to implement the plan to close the Straits of Tiran at the right time. It does not sound very convincing, unless he refers to the meeting which took place at his home on 22 May in which the closure of the Gulf of Aqaba was discussed. (Speech on 23 July 1967.) But since the closure was decided upon the same day, and announced in the early hours of the next morning, the phrase about 'the right time to implement the plan' does not make sense. Nasser's decisions have usually been taken without benefit of formal consultation. Would he seek authorisation from the Arab Socialist Union, his (largely fictitious) state party which had never played a part in shaping Egypt's foreign policy? Was it not far more likely that Nasser had mentioned the idea to some friends and confidants, and that improvisation had played a far greater part than he was willing to admit? That, in fact, he had taken the decision on 22 May on the spur of the moment?

Emotions had usually played a big part in his major policy decisions: he had not really foreseen all the repercussions of the arms deal in 1955, and he had stumbled into the war in the

Yemen. He had been a very lucky man: often his improvisation had worked, but sometimes it didn't. He had never really understood Israel; he thought it was a very minor imperialist power. If pressed hard, it would retreat – like France and Britain after Suez. He did not understand that there was nowhere to retreat for Israel.

The first official news about Egyptian action had been given by Cairo on 16 May: Mahmud Riyad, the Foreign Minister, had informed the Soviet, Syrian, and Iraqi ambassadors that Egypt would take measures to repel Israeli aggression against Syria. General Muhammad Fawzi, chief of the Egyptian General Staff, had gone for a brief trip to Damascus to coordinate operations with the Syrians. Lt.-General Abdel Muhsin Murtagi had been appointed to take command on the Egyptian front with Israel 'in the event of an outbreak of miltary operations'; Air Marshal Sidqi Mahmud would personally command the Air Force; Admiral Suleiman Izzat would command the Navy. The state of alert of the Egyptian forces had been raised to a state of battle readiness as from 2.30 p.m. on 14 May. 'The formations and units specified in the operations plan will move from their present positions to predetermined concentration points';[23] this meant that an unspecified number of army units had moved into Sinai in the general direction of the Israeli border.

All these seemed to be routine military moves aimed at impressing Israel. There had been many troop concentrations during the previous decade and a state of battle readiness had been in force more than once. No one outside Cairo knew how many divisions were involved; by and large the announcement was regarded as just one more move in the unending Arab-Israeli conflict. The fact that the troop movements were made in an ostentatious way seemed to confirm this interpretation. But a novel element was introduced when the Egyptians demanded that the United Nations observers should withdraw. At 20.00 GMT (22.00 Gaza local time) on 16 May General Fawzi was received by the Indian Commander of UNEF, Maj.-General Rikhye, and asked for the withdrawal 'of all UN troops installing observer points along our border'. UN troops, he said, must be withdrawn immediately from Al Sabha and Sharm al Shaykh because it was imperative for the Egyptian forces to gain control of these two points that very night. Rikhye replied that he had no authority to comply with this request and would have to refer the whole matter to U Thant. The scene now moved to UN Headquarters: U Thant received the news at 21.30 GMT the same evening (17.30 New York time) and asked the Egyptian representative at the UN for immediate clarification. The next day there followed consultations between him and the representatives of the countries involved. The Canadians and Swedes expressed serious doubts about the consequences of agreeing to a peremptory request for the withdrawal of the UNEF. The Indian and Yugoslav representatives disagreed: Cairo, in their view, was entitled to request the removal of UNEF and the request would have to be met regardless of what the General Assembly had to say, for the original agreement about UNEF had been made between the then Secretary General, not the General Assembly, and the Egyptian Government. The diplomatic representatives, needless to say, were acting under instructions from their governments. Nasser had sent messages to Belgrade and Delhi the day before, and it can be taken for granted that he asked for, and received, the support of the Yugoslav and the Indian governments for his policy before he actually demanded the withdrawal of the UNEF. Meanwhile, more news continued to come in from UNEF headquarters in Gaza. The UN observers in Al Sabha had been prevented by the Egyptians from entering their observation posts on the international frontier at El Kuntilla camp. Egyptian officers had entered El Amr camp and asked the UNEF platoon there to withdraw within fifteen minutes. UAR officers went to Sharm al Shaykh and told the local commander that they had to take over within fifteen minutes. There had been a few incidents: two artillery shells had been fired at the UNEF camps at El Quseimah and Al Sabha. The official Egyptian request to withdraw UNEF did not arrive in New York until 16.00 GMT on Monday 18 May, U Thant was informed at his meeting with the Egyptian representatives that he should not make an appeal to Nasser to reconsider his decision; such an appeal would be firmly rejected. If he wanted to come to Cairo, by all means, he would be welcome. One hour later U Thant met UNEF Advisory Committee. There was no change in the position of the two sides: the Egyptian demand was unacceptable to the Canadians and the Scandinavians, who contended that ultimate responsibility lay with the UN, through the Security Council and the

General Assembly. No, said the Indians and Yugoslavs, the Secretary General had no choice but to comply. 'The moment the request will be known, my government will withdraw its contingent', one of them said (as if his government did not know already). The other said that his government had already informed Cairo that it would withdraw its contingent from UNEF.

Immediately after the meeting ended U Thant dictated a letter in which he said that the Egyptian Government's request would be complied with; he would be issuing instructions for the necessary arrangements for an orderly withdrawal. U Thant was bitterly attacked for this decision, which appeared doubtful from both the political and the legal point of view. Some Egyptian sources and some Western observers have argued that Nasser was not prepared for such quick acquiescence, that he wanted no more than a partial and temporary withdrawal of the UNEF; the Gaza strip had not figured in the original demand forwarded to General Rikhye. Nasser's hand was forced by U Thant's immediate surrender. The first Egyptian note was somewhat unclear, it must have been hastily prepared. Nasser wanted to oust the United Nations observers from some observation points – and to concentrate them in the Gaza strip. According to this explanation – which is also the version accepted by the Israelis[23a] – Nasser had no alternative but to insist on the total removal of the UNEF after U Thant told him that it was all or nothing. But this explanation is not altogether convincing; there is also the possibility that he wanted to effect the removal of the UNEF in two stages. Or perhaps he wanted to keep the observers in some places – but what really mattered was Sharm al Shaykh. And U Thant notes in his report to the UN[24] that the UNEF positions there were rendered ineffective by the Egyptians before the request for withdrawal was received in New York. Nasser said on 23 May that had the UNEF ignored the Egyptian request, 'we would have regarded it as a hostile force and disarmed it'. Of the 3,300 UN observers only 32 were stationed in Sharm al Shaykh and these had instructions not to resist. It wasn't really a fire brigade (as some argued); their presence would not have made any difference.

Fortunately, as Nasser said, there was no reason to apply force: 'The UNEF has honourably and faithfully carried out its duties. The UN Secretary General refused to succumb to pressure. He issued immediate orders to the UNEF to withdraw; consequently we praise UNEF which has stayed ten years in our country serving peace. And when they left at a time when we found that the neo-imperialist forces wanted to divert them from their basic task, we gave them a cheerful send off and saluted them.'

U Thant was sharply criticised in the West: 'overhasty', 'precipitate collapse', were some of the milder epithets used. His action was called high-handed and grossly irresponsible; he could have given his reply two days, perhaps a week later; perhaps he could have passed on the Egyptian demand to the Security Council. But there is no reason to assume that this would have prevented the subsequent course of events. The Egyptians would either have disarmed and expelled UNEF, or they would simply have by-passed it. The Straits of Tiran could have been closed even without occupying the Ras Nasrani observation post at Sharm al Shaykh. It is argued that by procrastinating U Thant might have gained time for the powers to solve the conflict by diplomatic means; but the powers had three weeks for negotiations after U Thant's surrender, and their talks and visits were futile and led nowhere. Two or seven more days would have made no difference. U Thant acted precipitately, but he is not the main villain – it was not his war.

There was also the legal aspect. Israel maintained that it would not have withdrawn its forces from Sinai and Sharm al Shaykh in February 1957 but for a pledge from the United States, Britain, and the Secretary General, Dag Hammarskjold, that President Nasser had a private commitment never again to make these areas a cause of belligerency. Hammarskjold had negotiated with Egypt in November 1956 on the entry of UNEF into Egypt. (Israel having refused consent to have these forces stationed on its territory.) When Israel mentioned a memorandum by Hammarskjold to that effect, which had been prepared at the time, U Thant denied all knowledge of its existence. A short time after, Mr Ernest Gross, a former legal adviser to the UN, made it known that he had a copy of the memorandum and published both the text and the interpretation (which bore out the Israeli point of view) in an American legal periodical. Mr Hammarskjold had made it clear that since UNEF had been set up by bilateral agreement, there were two parties to the bargain: 'The consequence of such a bilateral declaration is that were either side to act unilaterally in refusing continued pressure or deciding on withdrawal ... an exchange of views would be called for towards harmonising the position.'

This, of course, was embarrassing for U Thant who had wholeheartedly accepted the Egyptian version. He countered that the *aide-mémoire*, dated 5 August 1957, was not an official paper but a 'purely private memorandum of unknown purpose or value in which Secretary General Hammarskjold seems to record his own impressions and interpretations of his discussions with President Nasser'. U Thant said that this was not an official paper and had therefore no standing; it could not affect the basis for the presence of the UNEF in Egypt. Nasser, in other words, had been entitled to ask for the withdrawal of UNEF, and the UN was obliged to comply: U Thant had acted according to the spirit and the letter of the original agreement. For him this was the end of the discussion: others have disputed his view and the debate on whether he acted correctly will no doubt continue for a long time.

21 May 1967

Egyptian forces were now deployed in Sinai along the Israeli border and had taken over Sharm al Shaykh, but as yet there had been no incidents, no armed clashes. No Israeli ship had been stopped. For a few days – from 19 May, when UNEF received its marching orders, to 23 May – it was not quite clear what Egypt would do next. Nasser waited: the withdrawal of UNEF had been a prestige success; Nasser could claim that by concentrating his troops in Sinai he had compelled Israel to desist from invading Syria and to transfer its divisions to the south. Escalation could have been stopped: Nasser would have made his point, the military situation would not have changed and, after a decent interval, the troops could have been sent home. For several days, most observers thought that this was all that would happen. True, the propaganda campaign was intensified. Ahmad Said, head of the 'Voice of the Arabs', announced:

The Zionist barrack in Palestine is about to collapse and be destroyed. As for Israel, what can the Arabs prepare for it? Every one of the hundred million Arabs has been living for the past nineteen years on one hope – to live to see the day Israel is liquidated . . . There is no life, no peace nor hope for the gangs of Zionism to remain in the occupied land.[25]

The next day, he was even more emphatic:

It is our chance, Arabs, to direct a blow of death and annihilation to Israel and all its presence in our Holy Land. It is war for which we are waiting and in which we shall triumph. Allah akbar, Allah akbar, Allah akbar![26]

And, a day later:

Our army is on the frontiers in the biggest massing the region has known. Behind it is the people, the whole people, awaiting the first shot to blow up everything that is American in all the Arab towns. We will be waiting for you with death and with victory, we will raise banners for our generation. Allah akbar, Allah akbar, Allah akbar.[27]

Arab newspapers thought the prospects for victory were excellent. There was only one way to end the tension – to send the Arab armies to Tel Aviv in support of the guerrilla forces. The march on Tel Aviv would result not only in the downfall of the racialist rule of the Tel Aviv agents but also in the collapse of all reactionary regimes in the Arab world: 'This fateful battle will not lead to a third world war as some believe because the imperialist forces are not prepared to lose everything just for the sake of defending Israel.'[28]

This was strong stuff – death, destruction, annihilation, extermination. But the Voice of the Arabs had talked that way for many years and Arab newspapers had published articles in a similar vein. It was the secret of Nasser's appeal throughout the Arab world – the hysterical shrillness of the propaganda, the extreme statements, the relentless hostility to all enemies, and (let us not to mince words) the blatant lies. If the approach was successful it was not only because those who directed the Voice of the Arabs were unusually clever at their job; it succeeded because the listeners wanted to hear propaganda of this kind, which appealed so much more to their emotions than the western (or even Soviet) unemotional approach. A special study ought to be devoted to the responsibility of Cairo radio for the disaster which overtook Egypt in 1967; this sort of propaganda was both the source of Nasserism's strength and its weakness. Some of this was realised after the military defeat: 'We have been saying things,' *Al Mussawar* claimed, 'that we did not always mean, and thus antagonised even our well wishers and friends.' This is no doubt true, but an investigation into the effects of this propaganda should not be limited to its impact abroad. Its main influence was on the Arabs; it raised their expectations to a point where the promises had to be fulfilled. Day after day, year after year, it had been announced that the sword of Arabism would soon triumph over all its enemies; after this tremendous build-up it became increasingly difficult for Nasser and other Arab leaders to pursue a less extreme policy. Such propaganda strengthened the innate tendency of many Arabs towards self-delusion. Arabs have a great many engaging qualities (including some which Jews lack); they have also an almost unlimited capacity for believing what they want to believe. This streak in the Arab character cannot be too strongly stressed; it explains much about the coming of the war and its aftermath. The constant stream of propaganda emanating from Cairo, Damascus, and Baghdad about Arab cultural distinction, economic progress, and military might was so enthusiastically accepted because it corresponded to a deep emotional need of a proud people which had excelled in so many respects in past centuries but had not been able to come to terms with its place in the modern world, and felt resentful about it. Hence the necessity to create a fantasy world in which the enormous problems besetting the Arabs could all be solved. In this fantasy world industrial projects can be built in record time, battles won without losses, enemies destroyed. There is no resistance, there are no obstacles in this world of fantasy. This propaganda created illusions among the Arabs about their own power and reinforced the inclination, fairly strong anyway, to ignore unpleasant realities. It influenced not only the masses but also, in the long run, the leaders, whose judgment was likewise affected.

While the Voice of the Arabs was calling for a holy war, Israel was still in doubt about Nasser's intentions, and so was Jordan. According to Amman the return of Egyptian forces to Sharm al Shaykh was not by itself an heroic deed or a great victory, but simply an attempt to remedy the calamity of 1956. All the rest so far was histrionics:

We are used to hearing curses against America, and America's response to the curses by granting more loans, aid and wheat and surplus supplies.[29]

The real question was whether Egypt would close the Straits of Tiran:

Logic, wisdom and nationalism make it incumbent on Egypt to do so, because closure of the Gulf of Aqaba to Israeli navigation will destroy the Negev reconstruction plan and prevent the immigration of millions of Jews to Israel ... if Egypt fails to do so, what value would there be in military demonstrations? (ibid.)

Jordan had never accepted Nasser's argument that UNEF was merely a symbolic force and that it would not seriously hinder an Egyptian offensive against Israel. For a long time King Hussain had been under pressure to permit other Arab forces to move into Jordan; how could a real offensive against Israel be waged if there was no full coordination between Israel's Arab neighbours? But Hussain refused to give in to these demands; Egyptian or Syrian troops in Jordan would have constituted a greater danger to his rule than to Israel. And his main argument was that unless Egypt got rid of UNEF, there was no point in letting other Arab forces into Jordan. For while UNEF was stationed on Egypt's border a war against Israel could not be fought anyway.

Nasser was egged on by Jordan. Syria went one better: its Defence Minister Maj.-General Hafiz al Asad told a Damascus correspondent that 'since 23 February our air force has entered the occupied territory dozens of times on reconnaissance and other flights. On the latest such occasion our aircraft penetrated dozens of kilometers inside enemy territory. This was on 14 May, around noon'.[30] Threats by a radio station were one thing, an open admission by the head of the Syrian army that his planes had entered Israel dozens of times, another. Hafiz al Asad also said that the Syrian army, 'which had its finger on the trigger', demanded in one voice that battle be engaged. Of course, they had to wait for the signal from the military leadership. 'As a military man I feel that the time has come to wage the liberation battle. In my opinion it is necessary to adopt at least the minimum measures required to strike a disciplinary blow at Israel.'

Arab confidence was now very high: the Egyptian army had been transferred to Sinai, Israeli air space had been violated countless times, but Israel had not dared to retaliate. It was afraid because, in contrast to 1956, it could not count on Britain and France, while America was totally absorbed in Vietnam. Israel alone was no match for the Arab armies, which in the meantime had been fully mobilised. In Cairo on 21 May the reserves had been called up; the Iraqi forces were put in a state of readiness on the 20th; the Palestinian regiment was said to be ready for battle and an army delegation left for Damascus for military talks. Leave was cancelled in the Lebanon and the frontiers, according to news from Beirut, were reinforced. King Hussain sent his Chief of Staff to Cairo to coordinate his military plans with the United Arab command. And then, in the early hours of the morning of 23 May, Cairo Radio broadcast a speech made by President Nasser the previous day in which he said that 'under no circumstances will we allow the Israeli flag to pass through the Gulf of Aqaba'. Nasser had been with some of his closest advisers on a visit to Advanced Air Headquarters when he announced his decision: 'Our armed forces and all our people are ready for war, but under no circumstances will we abandon any of our rights. This water is ours.' The die had been cast.

Did Russia know beforehand about the blockade? Unofficially, Soviet sources have said that it came to them as a surprise. But Nasser met the Soviet ambassador a few hours before he made his statement, there had been close cooperation between Moscow and Cairo all along. Could Cairo afford not to consult Moscow on such an important step? There were during the last days of May several Soviet letters to Nasser – including one from the Central Committee of the Soviet party – that have not been published. Cairo broadcasts announced at the time that they expressed full support for Nasser's course of action. Perhaps the situation was more complicated than that; after the end of the war the Russians complained that information had been leaked in the Arab capitals that should not have been made public. Perhaps the Egyptians in their eagerness misunderstood the nature of the Soviet undertaking. But Nasser was very sure by that time that America would not intervene and he probably learned this from the Russians.

The Straits of Tiran, the access to the Israeli port of Eilat, had been closed once before by Egypt, in September 1955. It had been one of the reasons for the Israeli attack on Egypt one year later. Israel had made it clear that any interference with the freedom of shipping in the Gulf constituted in its eyes a violation of its sovereign rights, an act of aggression. Since 1956 there had been no such interference. Much of Israel's trade with Asia and East Africa went through the port of Eilat which had been greatly developed during the last decade. Hundreds of ships under dozens of flags had passed through the Straits on their way to and from Eilat. But they had no legal right to do so, said the Arabs, the right of passage had been imposed following the Suez attack; it was the last remaining iniquity of this act of imperialist aggression. And now, albeit with a delay of more than ten years, it was to be liquidated. The entrance to the Gulf was Egyptian territorial waters and, since Egypt was in a state of war with Israel, it was fully entitled to close it to all Israeli ships and to all others carrying goods of strategic importance to Eilat. The first part of this contention was indisputable: the entrance to the Straits was in Egyptian territorial waters. It ignored, however, two facts: the maximum breadth of the Gulf was more than three miles and it was therefore 'high seas' from a legal point of view. Secondly, all legal experts agreed that merchant vessels (and probably also warships) enjoyed the right of passage through territorial waters; a coastal state could regulate passage, it could not prevent it altogether.[31] The Egyptians and the other Arab states did not recognise the traditional three mile limit, but claimed twelve miles. If this claim was accepted, the Straits of Tiran could not be considered 'high seas'. Even so, Israel had the right of passage according to international law which says that a sea can be closed only if all the littoral states agree on this course of action. Jordan and Syria would agree with Egypt but Israel, of course, would not. Legally therefore everything pointed in Israel's favour. But Egypt's answer was simply that it did not recognise the existence of Israel. It was therefore, in the last resort, not a legal but a political issue. The Hague International Court, to whom some wanted to refer the dispute, would not have been able to decide a political question.

How vital were the Straits of Tiran for Israel? It was of course not true, as the Jordanians had argued, that closing the Straits would prevent development in the Negev, or the immigration of millions of Jews. Not that many ships had passed through the Straits each year, re-routing them via the Mediterranean would have been a major nuisance, and would have cost Israel millions of dollars but it would not have been a fatal blow. The economic aspect, however, was by no means the decisive one. The effect of the closure of the Straits was mainly political: Haykal was correct when he wrote that it was a major psychological defeat for Israel. For once Israel accepted a limitation of its sovereignty, it was only a question of time before it would be faced with fresh demands and renewed pressure. It was, or at least it appeared to be, the beginning of the end, the slow strangulation of the Jewish state. Could Israel, a small country surrounded by enemies, afford to give up one of the few lifelines to the outside world without a struggle? Israel's whole existence was based on the assumption that it was able to defend its rights and its territories – in other words on its credibility. Once it appeared that it was powerless to do so, its whole existence was put in question. One can only guess what the next step would have been – the cessation of immigration to Israel, or the interception of arms shipments via the Mediterranean, or large-scale guerrilla attacks in the 'triangle', culminating in the demand to cede part of its territory? The parallels with the nineteen-thirties were obvious. But Nasser, it is said, never intended to attack Israel: according to a Soviet interpretation 'President Nasser decisively rejected later on even the idea that the UAR might attack Israel'.[32] Later on, it is true, Nasser rejected the idea, but not before 5 June. It is impossible to say with any certainty what his intentions were on 18 May or on 28 May; he was not acting according to a detailed master plan, but improvised as he went along. Perhaps he did not want to attack, perhaps in his innermost heart he hoped that the crisis would not turn into a war, because he knew only too well that he was not ready for a military campaign. But neither his words nor his actions were that of a leader who did not want to attack. Perhaps Israel should have ignored the troop concentrations, the blockade, and the threats to 'undo 1948'. Perhaps – but that is a lot to ask.

If there was one historical lesson Jews had taken to heart, it was that appeasement does not pay. People in Tel Aviv and Jerusalem got gloomier and gloomier; Israel's friends, as one correspondent put it, were lapsing more and more into the circumlocutory oratory that is so often the prelude to surrender. 'The atmosphere in the UN had become grotesque: we were not exactly shunned in the UN corridors,' an Israeli delegate said later, 'we just got pitying smiles wherever we went.'[33] In the West, some commentators began to write Israel off: the Israelis had been out-manoeuvred, they were no longer arguing from a position of strength, they had to make concessions: 'President Nasser had to choose between being a local Bismarck and a statesman with a claim to world stature. The Israelis have the unhappier and lesser choice of seizing the ball of peace if and when it is thrown toward them.'[34]

Nasser's prestige in the Arab world had soared to new heights overnight. Only a few days before the Arab countries had been disunited, bitterly quarrelling among themselves; no one had been willing to follow Nasser's lead. The closure of the Straits of Tiran worked like magic – his leadership was at once re-established. Congratulations and messages of support poured in from all Arab capitals. Delegations began to arrive in Cairo from Iraq, Syria, Algeria, Kuwait and other countries: 'The states and peoples are closing their ranks for a new battle,' as *Al Ahram* put it, 'under the leadership of Nasser.' The expected disagreements between the western powers began to emerge. The Soviet Union announced that the aggressors would confront not only the UAR and the Arab peoples but all 'freedom and peace loving forces throughout the world'. China, India, Yugoslavia and other countries expressed fervent support and promised assistance. And even Nasser's enemies in the Arab world had to rally round him; King Hussain declared that he and his people were in the forefront of those ready to sacrifice themselves, enthusiasm stirred the blood of all Jordanian citizens and soldiers. Arabism was 'trembling, trembling with joy and happiness', as Amman Radio said.

Saudia fell into line and dispatched troops to Jordan; Tunisia buried the hatchet and expressed admiration for Nasser's resolute action. 'Victory appears on the horizon as the battle begins.'[35]

Arab political and military leaders worked overtime during these last days of May; the Egyptian War Minister went to Moscow, so did the Syrian Prime Minister and Foreign Minister.

There was a flurry of visits between the Arab capitals and a great traffic in telegrams. King Hassan II of Morocco congratulated Nasser, as did the Sudanese President. Libya announced that it would not permit foreign powers to use Libyan territory as a base for operations against an Arab country; there was the big American base at Wheelus Field and Cairo was putting poor old King Idris under constant pressure: 'Statements alone are insufficient and passive attitudes are unacceptable.'

Among these activities, not all of them very purposeful, the sudden visit to Cairo of King Hussain of Jordan was the most dramatic and the most important. Late in the morning of 30 May, Hussain arrived in the Egyptian capital with his Prime Minister and several high army officers. A few hours later the text of a new defence agreement was announced and at 5 in the afternoon Hussain was already back in Amman – together with Ahmed Shukairy the head of the PLO and Hussain's pet aversion. Through streets fringed with jubilant crowds the King drove back to his palace. King Hussain was a man of quick decisions, but even so, his sudden reconciliation with Nasser, who only yesterday had been his bitterest enemy, came as a surprise. Only yesterday he had been 'the CIA dwarf from Amman' and Nasser 'the arch-villain, the sinister plotter, the man who, behind a cloak of demagogic oratory, had betrayed the cause of the Palestinian people'. Now it was all kisses and embraces, 'brother Nasser' and 'our sincere Hussain'. Egypt had become the dear 'homeland' and Jordan the 'home of the brave'. Even Shukairy, the 'champion charlatan' of yesterday, who had called for Hussain's assassination was now a 'valiant warrior'.

King Hussain, to do him justice, had been walking a tightrope for a long time. He had waited for a week assuming that Israel would attack immediately Nasser had imposed the blockade. But Israel did not attack; perhaps it was too weak to challenge Egypt? If so, there was no alternative for Hussain. His country was the most exposed; it had a common frontier of 530 km. with Israel, and most of its inhabitants were Palestinians who felt no particular loyalty to the young monarch such as the Jordanian tribes had felt for his grandfather, the Emir Abdallah. The sympathies of most Palestinians were on Nasser's side. When Hussain succeeded to the throne in Amman, more than a dozen years earlier, no one had rated his chances high. In 1956 and again in 1958, when Hashemite rule was overthrown in Iraq, his cause seemed pretty well lost. But he had weathered these storms and countless others since, and there was grudging respect for the little man to whom no one could deny personal courage. He was out of step with the general mood in the Arab world: the Jordanian monarchy seemed a relic of the past. Hussain's reluctance to cooperate closely with the Soviet Union did not endear him to Cairo and Damascus. His British wife, his playboy antics, had antagonised others. He was second to none in his hostility to Israel, but there was a greater sense of reality and responsibility in his speeches and actions. On more than one occasion he had blamed the other Arab states for their irresponsible attitude towards the refugees (of whom his country sheltered more than any other Arab state) and for making vain promises about destroying Israel which could not be fulfilled. All this had made him a welcome visitor in Western capitals, but it had not endeared him to Nasser and the Syrians. Only recently Jordan had left the Arab League meeting in protest and relations with Egypt had become, not for the first time, very strained indeed. But during that great surge of patriotism in the last week of May, Hussain felt that he had no alternative but to join a movement which, in the course of a few days, had gathered so much momentum. The decisive battle seemed at hand. His duty as a patriot was to let bygones be bygones and to join Egypt in its struggle. The idea no doubt must have crossed his mind that this was also an act of self-preservation, the only way to safeguard his rule; when he returned to Amman he is said to have told a confidant, 'Today I have taken out my life insurance'. And so agreement was reached: 'Tell the fraternal Jordanian people that we are united as one hand', Nasser said after the pact was signed. 'In past hard times we in the two countries have always been as one hand and one heart,' Hussain replied. And the faithful Shukairy added 'Amen'. The defence agreement had a preamble ('In response to the desire of the Arab people in both countries and proceeding from their absolute faith in the common destiny and the unity of the Arab nation, etc.'), and eleven points establishing, *inter alia*, a joint Defence Council. But the most important point was article seven: 'In the event of the commencement of military operations, the Chief of Staff of the UAR armed forces shall assume command of operations in both states.' Shortly before the Suez war there had been a similar pact when Nabulsi was Prime Minister in Amman. For Israel this was one of the reasons for the 1956 campaign. But in 1956 the Jordanian forces had not moved despite the orders of the Joint Defence Council to open operations against Israel. Could Israel take it for granted that the new pact was no more meaningful than the old agreement? There was no inclination in Jerusalem to play down its significance; Nasser had predicted that in the decisive hour all Arabs would rally and forget their past quarrels. The prediction was coming true. Israel was now completely surrounded by Arab armies, as a Cairo commentator said, in the full sense of the word.

The decisive hour was at hand: escalation had started with Egyptian troop concentrations, then the Straits of Tiran were closed. The third stage was reached when Nasser told the National Assembly on 29 May: 'Now that the time has come – and I have already said in the past that we will decide the time and place and not allow others to decide – we must be ready for triumph and not for a recurrence of the 1948 comedies. We shall triumph, God willing. Preparations have already been made, we are now ready to confront Israel ... we are now ready to deal with the entire Palestine question. The issue now at hand is not the Gulf of Aqaba, the Straits of Tiran or the withdrawal of the UNEF, but the rights of the Palestinian people. It is the aggression which took place in Palestine in 1948 with the collaboration of Britain and the United States. It is the expulsion of the Arabs from Palestine, the usurpation of their rights and the plunder of their property.' It was in the same speech that Nasser said that he had not requested the USSR to intervene, because 'we really want to avoid any confrontation which might lead to a world war'. Ten days later Nasser and all the other leaders were bitterly disappointed that the Soviet Union had not intervened.

The time had come. The issue was the existence of Israel. The call was echoed in all the Arab capitals. Dr Zuayen, the Syrian Prime Minister, said on the same day in a speech to a convention of Arab lawyers: 'We are now on the threshold of the battle for the destiny of all Arab people. Conditions today are most favourable for waging the battle of Arab destiny.' President Aref told the Iraqi soldiers who were leaving for Jordan a week before the outbreak of hostilities: 'This is the day of battle ... we are

determined and united to achieve our clear aim – to remove
Israel from the map. We shall, God willing, meet in Tel Aviv and
Haifa.'[36] Shukairy announced at a press conference on 28 May,
'Zero hour has come. This is the hour our people have been waiting for the last nineteen years. The UAR army alone is capable of
destroying the Israeli aggressor within a few hours.' Haykal had
predicted in his weekly article in *Al Ahram* on 28 May that war
with Israel was inevitable because it was not a matter of the
Gulf of Aqaba but something bigger. The week after[37] he still
thought war more than probable. But there was a chance that
Israel would collapse from within, overcome by terror in the face
of an unprecedented demonstration of Arab military might.
'Israel used to say in the past, and even just before Egypt took its
decision to close the Gulf of Aqaba, that the existence of a single
soldier in Sharm al Shaykh would mean war.' Powerful Egyptian
forces had entered the Gulf, not just one soldier – and Israel was
powerless to do anything about it. 'Israel is definitely heading
towards a final collapse from within or without. Israel has never
had, and never will have, a natural sovereign existence that can
easily and quickly adjust itself to the changing atmosphere.
Israel has been, and still is, an artificial state composed of poor-
quality, brittle material, something like plaster, which can only
change when it breaks up.'

The politicians in the Arab capitals and their spokesmen had
persuaded themselves by the last week of May that a military
confrontation with Israel was inevitable. The military leaders
believed that victory was certain. The Egyptian intelligence had
received news that the Israeli army would concentrate five divisions on the Egyptian border but the Egyptians were ready to face
up to any challenge. Israel had no defence in depth, El Mortagi,
the Egyptian C.-in-C. said, Egypt had superiority both in tanks
and in the air, the Egyptian missile system was safeguarding the
whole area: 'All the enemy knows, we know too, and we are prepared for quick and strong counter action.'[38] The general mood
of the masses was expressed in simple formulas: 'We want War',
and 'Kill the Jews'. Correspondents of the *Neue Zürcher Zeitung*
and of the *Frankfurter Allgemeine* reported from Beirut, not
normally a hotbed of fanaticism, that even solid, sober middle-
class citizens were now convinced that a war with Israel was the
commandment of the hour and that in this struggle the Arabs

should accept help from whatever quarter it was offered. Reports from Cairo stated that Egyptian public opinion wanted war and that some circles were impatient with Nasser's leadership as being unduly cautious. The *Observer* correspondent reported that tens of thousands of young people now believed that the time had arrived to fulfil the Arab destiny. This was the first generation to grow to manhood after Suez, it had been slogan-ised by the powerful propaganda machinery. 'They are dedicated to the philosophy of armed struggle against "Zionism, imperial-ism, and Arab reaction", they all believe that Nasser is the man of destiny and they see their role as forcing his hand.'[39] To that purpose they had banded together in secret societies whose watchwords were: 'Nasser's victory in the Gulf must be followed up. He must see that this is the time to strike,' whereas Nasser's message was 'Hold your fire. Don't precipitate events by rash and independent action.' Nasser, in other words, was riding a tiger: 'only if he manages to hold his ground in Aqaba will he have the faintest chance of controlling his fiery supporters – and then only for a measure of time'. A well informed French obser-ver, Eric Rouleau, has given an account which is almost iden-tical, 'We have waited long enough – this has lasted twenty years. It does not serve any useful purpose to wait any longer. Let's finish with Israel and be done with it. No more words, quick action is needed. Forward to Tel Aviv!'[40]

These were the slogans displayed on red banners, and the arguments advanced in public discussions. M. Rouleau describes a big public meeting at which Abdel Meguid Ferid, Secretary of the Presidency, was shouted down when explaining the need for 'Revolutionary self-discipline' in those critical days. His moder-ation only provoked the crowd to frequent interruptions. It was only partly reassured when the speaker announced that 'we are as much decided as you are to fight'. M. Rouleau also reports a meeting between Nasser and younger officers in Sinai, in which the cautious attitude of the *Rais* was criticised, respectfully and firmly. Nasser was told that whatever the political arguments, from a military point of view the best form of defence was always the offensive, and that they should not wait for an Israeli surprise attack.

A great deal of hate had accumulated over many years, and it had been assiduously fostered by the powerful propaganda machine. But it had not been created by it. The slogans of the anti-imperialist struggle were, as far as the masses are concerned, bloodless abstractions: the imperialists had withdrawn from the Arab world long ago, although they still held on to a few positions in distant places. Most Arab students had probably never seen an 'imperialist' in their life. The masses do not think in terms of political abstractions and even the elite needed a more concrete enemy to stir the passions and emotions. That the ideological neo-Leninist arguments were only skin-deep and carried little weight goes without saying. It appeared most clearly from the propaganda of the Syrian regime. Far more doctrinaire in character than Nasser's government, it referred on every occasion to 'Our ideological army'; its spokesman talked in terms of 'monopoly capitalism', Vietnam, the solidarity of all the oppressed classes and peoples. Yet when the real crisis came, all this changed abruptly: 'By God, if it is decreed that we have to wade through seven seas of blood and that the whole nation has to sink in blood to get revenge for its honour and dignity, then we will wade through the seas of blood.'[41]

Forgotten was the appeal to ideology, to proletarian internationalism; discarded the atheistic motives and the class struggle. Instead a series of totally different symbols and images was projected: God, blood, nation, nationalism, dignity, revenge; a fascinating picture emerges from a mere enumeration of the nouns.

The Arabs saw themselves as a brave, proud, and strong people, distinguished by all the manly virtues, ready for sacrifice, heroic in battle. The popular image of the Jew was, at best, that of a small minority dispersed among the Arab world and barely tolerated, leading a marginal existence, a sect of merchants, money-lenders, many poor people, and some intellectuals. The Jew was thought to be the very opposite of the Arab in his lack of pride and military qualities. That such a handful of people had been able to defy the Arab world in 1948 and had maintained their dwarf state ever since was intolerable, totally unacceptable: it was not a question of the borders of Israel, but its very existence; it was not the refugee problem but the humiliation to national pride that really mattered. One hundred million proud Arabs versus two million cowardly Jews: it was incredible, a blot to be erased as quickly as possible. Official propaganda constantly stressed the virtues of the Arabs and the vile character of the Jews, which made the existence of Israel even more inexplicable. This propaganda also emphasised that the Jews by themselves would never have been able to defy the Arabs. It had been the powers behind Israel – on this point there was full agreement between the few ideologists (who claimed that neo-imperialism was the enemy) and the masses to whom the idea that a small and despised enemy had prevailed over the great Arab people was anathema. There were different shades and degrees in the intensity of this feeling. The Syrians were by tradition the most militant; the Lebanese, again for historical and political reasons, the ones least eager to precipitate a fight. Egyptians are by nature not a bellicose people but the intense propaganda had made a considerable impact. There was also the fact that those shouting loudest for a war were firmly convinced that it would be a walkover; neither Egypt nor any of the other Arab countries had experienced a real war in recent history; 'blood', 'sacrifice', 'to die on the battlefield', were all abstractions. Unlike most European nations they had not the faintest idea of the horrors of modern war.

Since Israel alone could not possibly have resisted the Arabs, let alone prevailed over Arab power, a different explanation was needed. And so, by a general consensus, America became the chief culprit. 'With a typical display of Al Capone type gangsterism, Washington is brandishing the tripartite declaration,' Ahmed Said said on May 23; 'with hysterical frenzy America is emitting a hate-filled hissing ... the pirates, the bloodsuckers of the people, the criminals of the twentieth century have joined the band of outcasts, the scum of the earth.'[42] 'You enemies of the Arab nations, you savages, criminals, highwaymen ... '[43]

'Bury America' became one of the main propaganda slogans: 'We are stronger than you, we shall defeat you'. The whole history of the last twenty years was re-written in this fashion; the fact that America had opposed the establishment of a Jewish state in the spring of 1948, the fact that the Soviet Union had extended *de jure* recognition before Washington did, the enormous economic help extended to the Arab world over the decades, all were deleted from the annals. That the French had done far more than the Americans to equip the Israeli army was ignored, so was the fact that in the actual confrontation with 'imperialism' Britain was still the one real opponent (Aden and the Trucial Coast).

America was the real enemy, Israel did not count. It was partly (as one Cairo correspondent put it) the resentment of the poor and the weak against the powerful and the rich. It also reflected Nasser's own frustration – that his own ambitions for supremacy in the Middle East had so often encountered American resistance. This frustration had gradually turned into a paranoid attitude: America considered him its main enemy ('You do not know how dangerous they think I am', he said in a speech in early May). They were out to get him; very well, he was going to show them ... In this, he had the full support of the Syrian leaders, who were only waiting for the moment, as they had said, to shoot down that half of the American air force that had not been destroyed by the Vietcong.

This then was the atmosphere in the Arab capitals in late May. War will break out within the next week said one newspaper[44] – the Egyptian Foreign Ministry expects war any moment said another.[45] Moscow had promised to help the Arabs up to the very limit. This time Egypt intended not just to restrain Israel but to destroy it. The Egyptian people had entered the struggle under the leadership of a genius who had been victorious in all his campaigns.[46] Where would Egypt strike first? Would it be the atomic reactor at Dimona?[47] Or would it cut off Eilat first and then destroy Israel in a giant pincer movement? Or would masses of parachutists be dropped? The papers were full of speculation. Israel, at any rate, had no more hope to surprise the Arabs, but if it did not accept the Arab challenge it would lose anyway.[48] Mention has been made of the domestic difficulties which probably gave the initial impetus to a showdown with Israel. But it would be misleading to think of it as a mere diversion: the thirst for revenge was a very real factor. The propaganda machine had played so much on this theme over the years until it had assumed a momentum of its own. Once the Arab leaders had started to go through the motions of a confrontation with Israel in May, there was no turning back or controlling the tide. To wreak revenge on Israel had always been a popular cry in the Arab world; Cairo and Damascus had made it the most popular cause. Nasser forgot his own warnings, that the mistake of 1948 should not be repeated, that war should be waged only if the Arabs would be ready for it. During the first days of June Ahmad Shukairy went to Arab Jerusalem; after prayers in the mosque, there was a big demonstration from Al Aqsa. The chairman of the PLO was carried shoulder high; there were enthusiastic cheers and calls for struggle and the day of liberation. Iraq acceded to the UAR-Jordanian Defence Agreement. Nasser said in a brief speech after the treaty had been signed:

'Today we tell them: we are facing you in the battle and are burning with desire for it to start in order to obtain revenge for the 1956 treachery. This will make the world realise what the Arabs are and what Israel is.' (Cairo Radio, June 4.) Iraqi forces took up positions in Jordan. This did not make the Israelis any happier. In 1948 Iraq had refused to sign even the armistice. Formally, Iraq was already (or still) in a state of war with Israel.

All but the Syrians were happy about the reconciliation with Jordan. Damascus had constantly asserted that the overthrow of the Arab reactionaries was a prerequisite for victory. Unlike Nasser, the Syrians saw no reason to change their views now, and continued to attack 'the traitor Hussain', the imperialist hireling who was resisting commando activities, harrying and killing the fidayeen.

This dissonance apart, there was now full national harmony. Nasser was 'burning with desire' for the war to start and he had the support of all the Arab leaders who counted. Had there been a plan, or was the sequence of events accidental, a series of contingencies and improvisations? Did the Israeli attack come as a surprise? The speeches and articles by Arab leaders up to the outbreak of the war present one version, their utterances after the war another. Before 5 June Nasser argued that he had had a plan all along, that he used the Israeli threat to Syria to carry it out. Tahir Yihya, Iraqi deputy Prime Minister at the time also talked about a plan. On 4 June in Cairo, he said to Nasser: 'Circumstances stipulate that all Arab countries should take the sound road which you have personally planned. Otherwise, the consequences, God forbid, will not be good.'

The Syrians announced that the 'finger was on the trigger', the military campaign for the liberation of Palestine was about to start. Haykal had demonstrated that war was inevitable. When Israel attacked on the morning of 5 June, King Hussain in a broadcast said: 'Exactly as we expected, the enemy this morning carried out his aggression and attack on our Arab territory. We were expecting this.'[49]

Yet only a few days later, this version gave way to another: there had been a treacherous Israeli attack which had taken the Arabs unawares. Even the Syrians now argued that 'The Arabs adopted a position of self-defence but Israel launched a surprise air attack ...'[50] Nasser in his 'resignation' speech made no more mention of his plan for a general confrontation with Israel. He had merely wanted to come to the help of the Syrians who were threatened; it had been a purely defensive measure.

Which of these two conflicting versions should be given credence? The argument of self-defence does not stand up to scrutiny. No one would admit after a lost war that he had planned to attack but was forestalled by the enemy. To put the blame on the element of surprise in the enemy's attack was psychologically and politically far better policy. But this does not change the fact that all Arab leaders maintained right up to 5 June, that war was imminent, inevitable, inescapable – and that all had happened exactly as they had foreseen. To what extent was the Arab pre-war strategy really planned? A conclusive detailed answer to this question should not be expected for a long time. It all happened quickly; memory is notoriously selective, and the archives will not be accessible for many years – if ever. But there can be no dispute about the basic facts. That Nasser and the Syrians wanted to destroy Israel can be taken for granted; they never made a secret of their intentions. There were, of course, plans for military action against Israel, but there is no reason to assume that there was a master plan for a concerted campaign in May or June. The claims of Nasser and his spokesmen during the last week of May (that all the actions since 13 May proceeded according to a preconceived scheme) should not be accepted at face value. They stumbled into war without a plan, hoping that somehow Israel would crumble. In times of crisis statesmen and military leaders seldom adhere to previously prepared plans, no matter how carefully these have been rehearsed. The reaction of the enemy, and many other factors, make changes necessary almost from the beginning of a crisis. This applies with especial force to the Arab world, where improvisation has always played a far larger role than planning. That there existed a scheme to close the Straits of Tiran is very likely indeed, and Nasser no doubt calculated that this entailed the risk of war. As he said after the war: When we concentrated our forces I estimated the likelihood of war breaking out was 20 per cent. Before we closed the Gulf of Aqaba I told them that the possibility of war was 50 per cent. At another meeting I said it was 80 per cent. Then came the political changes in Israel and the probability of war became 100 per cent.[51] If Nasser really thought the situation in Syria was sufficiently serious to warrant intervention (and even this has not been established), it would have been sufficient to threaten Israel with an air strike. Nasser may have had a gambit, a plan to impose a blockade on Israel; the Israeli threats against Syria provided the opportunity to carry it out.

This would explain his behaviour and that of his allies up to 25 May. But then there came yet another stage in escalation: on 26 May, Haykal's famous article appeared which said that war was inevitable, on the 29th Nasser said Tiran was not the issue, but the existence of Israel. Then there was the long press conference. Did Nasser want a political victory or did he want a war? At this stage he seems to have been carried away by the general enthusiasm his moves had generated from Algiers to Baghdad. Once again he had become the leader of the Arab world – and the leader was called to lead. Always to keep the initiative was one of Nasser's basic rules of conduct. Imposing the blockade might have meant war; challenging the very existence of Israel made it certain. This last decision was spontaneous; when Nasser received all the messages of support, and when he heard about the confusion and the disarray in the enemy camp – he wanted to make certain of a great victory, not just of a political success. He was carried away by popular acclaim and by his initial success. Since he had won a first, partial victory, why not pursue it while the going was good? Yet he could not attack first; Russia had warned him against 'firing the first shot', and his own native caution made him oppose such action. 'Let the Jews make the first move, and let our counter blow be quick and decisive,' Haykal had written. To talk afterwards about a surprise attack is illogical; the Israeli attack was an essential part of Nasser's strategy – without it he could not move. Nasser's arguments are not consistent: he maintains that 'we were the victims of a diplomatic trick, of political deception' – by America.[52] Yet in the same breath he relates that on 2 June he went to the Armed Forces Supreme Command HQ and told the senior officers present that 'we must expect the enemy to strike a blow within 48 to 72 hours and no later ... ' (ibid.). If Nasser exactly predicted the attack he could not have been the victim of a trick. The attack came, and it upset all previous calculations; Egypt and Syria had not been prepared for the war they wanted.

There remain some speculative questions: what if Israel had refused to move first? Would Nasser have attacked anyway, and would an Arab offensive have been more successful? The Arab armies could not have waited indefinitely along Israel's border; sooner or later, probably sooner, they would have taken the initiative. From documents that fell into Israeli hands it is known that there was a plan for the destruction of the Israeli air force on the ground and for a tank offensive in the Southern Negev, with the intention to cut it off from Israel and to seize Eilat. Whether there were more ambitious plans we do not know; Nasser had always thought the main blow against Israel would have to come from north and east – not from south. Perhaps there was no plan; the assumption being that this would be a long war of attrition and that gradually during the battle some Arab strategy would evolve. Perhaps the Arab generals regarded operation 'Victory' (as it was called) as a police action rather than full-scale war. An offensive war entails even more preparation, co-ordination, and careful planning than a defensive one. Israel would no doubt have suffered more civilian losses and more material damage had it left the initiative to the Arabs. Short of a miracle, the result of the war would not have been different.

4

Konenut

The news about the Egyptian troop movements reached Jerusalem on 15 May – Israel's nineteenth Independence Day. Two hundred thousand people watched the parade on that late spring day in the streets of the capital and the Municipal Stadium; never had Independence Day been so gaily and widely celebrated. The decorations were bright, the lights well designed, the massed flags seemed a more intense blue, a clearer white; the bonfires in the Valley of Rehavia provided entertainment for the young.[1] There were as usual some minor incidents. A group of young right-wing extremists distributed leaflets protesting against the Government decision in compliance with the armistice regulations, not to put artillery and other heavy equipment on display; some derisively called it a mini-parade. Another leaflet lamented the loss of the Wailing Wall, to which for many years now Jews had not had access.[2] There was a military tattoo ('a sustained display of dramatic combinations of colour, light and sound', as one reporter put it), and a poem by Nathan Alterman, 'At the dawn of the Day', was read. Composed for Independence Day 1956, it was a warning to the Arabs as well as a call for peace. General Rabin, the Chief of Staff, had approved it two months earlier, but there were some last minute protests by the Prime Minister's Office, on the grounds that it was 'too aggressive' – after all, the situation was very different now. The offending sections were replaced by other stanzas from the same poem. Not every one liked the parade; a Soviet observer who was there as a guest of an Israeli group wrote later about the 'impertinent faces' of the parachutists which reminded him of the Hitlerite youngsters who had burned Poland in 1939 and attacked France the year after.[2a] Towards the end of the parade it was noticed that the Prime Minister leaned over to his saluting Chief of Staff and whispered something in his ear: News had just been received from Cairo about Egyptian troop concentrations

109

– the two should meet later in the day to discuss the situation.[3] They met in Mr Eshkol's office and later on the Prime Minister also saw his Foreign Minister and a few other advisers. Routine measures were taken: a state of alert was declared and some reinforcements were sent to the southern border. But while the Israeli ambassador in Washington in a special news conference at exactly the same time told those present that a serious situation had arisen on the border with Syria (adding that 'serious is a serious word'), no one was greatly alarmed about the Egyptian moves. Neither General Rabin nor Foreign Minister Eban thought that Egypt had any intention of starting hostilities at the present time. The army certainly was not in a state of alert: most of the ground-to-air missiles ordered from the United States had not yet been installed; of Israel's four submarines only one was available for immediate duty. It had been almost axiomatic among Israeli leaders that Nasser simply could not move against Israel while he had an expeditionary force of more than 60,000 in the Yemen. In an interview with an American journal Mr Eshkol had said in April that he did not think there would be full-scale war in the next few years.[4] Nor were Israeli newspapers worried by the Egyptian moves, which were thought to be 'demonstrative both in nature and aims'.[5] Nasser simply had to put on a show of solidarity with the Syrians; the stream of tanks and armoured cars through the central areas of Cairo in broad daylight was so ostentatious that this seemed the obvious assessment.

The Israeli leaders therefore returned unworried from their consultations to the social obligations awaiting them – the receptions, the International Youth Bible Quiz, the distribution of the annual Israeli prizes. The editorialists went back to their offices to write about the Kennedy Round, the Israeli film industry, and other current topics of interest and importance; visitors continued to arrive at Lydda airport, including Richard Tucker and Erich Leinsdorf and Edmund Wilson. No one suspected that the Egyptian troop concentrations were anything but a routine move; no special Israeli counter-measures were needed.

The next day the Israeli cabinet was called together. The cabinet usually met on Sundays; midweek sessions were unusual. But the date of the meeting had been arranged several days before, and though foreign politics and military developments

110

figured on the agenda, there was no sense of urgency. Eshkol reported about recent border incidents and the Egyptian troop movements; his assessment based on intelligence reports, was still that it was a demonstration of solidarity with Syria on Nasser's part, and also perhaps a prestige move to bring Egypt back into the Middle East limelight. The Foreign Minister reviewed the diplomatic moves that had been undertaken in the world's capitals; he welcomed U Thant's statement, in which the UN Secretary General had deplored the recent increase in acts of terrorism. Details of the meeting with the Soviet ambassador Chuvakhin a few days previously were made known; the Soviet Government had sent another warning to Israel two weeks earlier: Israel had been again accused of aggression against Syria and reprisals had been threatened. Mr Levavi, Director-General of the Israeli Foreign Ministry, had replied that peace in the area depended on the cessation of terrorist activities. But in the Soviet view the terrorist activities were unimportant, they merely served as a pretext for Israel's designs to bring down the Damascus government. Such exchanges were routine; there was no long discussion. The cabinet confirmed certain defence measures that had been agreed upon at a meeting earlier that day between Mr Eshkol and General Rabin, including a partial call up of reservists. But the army assessment on 16 May was still that there was no reason for concern: Egypt probably wanted to exert pressure on Israel; hence the demonstrative character of its mobilisation. There was a historical parallel: in 1960, after an Israeli retaliatory raid on Tawfiq in Syria, there had been similar troop concentrations on the Sinai border, and after a while the troops had been withdrawn. The real danger, in the view of the army, was that the Egyptian moves would induce the Syrians to step up their guerrilla activities. Mr Eban, too, was still optimistic when talking that day to a correspondent but added as an afterthought: 'One never knows what is going to happen ...' The army spokesman said that the defence forces 'were following developments closely and were alert to the situation'.[6]

On the morning of the next day, 17 May, there began that long series of meetings which continued almost without interruptions up to 5 June; the ministers with a special concern in security met; later on Eshkol saw the Chief of Staff again; and in the afternoon the Knesset Foreign Affairs and Security Committee heard the

Prime Minister and General Rabin on the 'dangerous implications' of the Egyptian moves. News had just been received that the Egyptian commander had demanded the immediate withdrawal of UNEF. General Rabin reported in detail on the troop concentrations and the steps Israel would have to take to meet the situation. His assessment was that the one Egyptian armoured division that had been dispatched to advanced positions and reinforced by MiG-21 fighters was far from being capable of launching a serious offensive. It was a war of nerves against Israel; the military balance was unchanged; Egypt was, as before, opposed to a military confrontation with Israel. Vigilance was needed, but the possibility of a war was ruled out. Some precautions had been taken. (An Egyptian newspaper reported that Israel had moved a tank regiment and three infantry units to its southern border.)[7] President Shazar, who was about to leave on a state visit to Canada and Iceland, enquired whether he should call off his trip; he was told that there was no reason to change his plans, the little storm would soon blow over, as so often in the past. The editorials in the press on that evening discussed the turmoil in Hong Kong and England's problems with the Common Market.

The next morning, Thursday, 18 May, Eshkol invited the Foreign Minister, the heads of the intelligence services, and high-ranking army officers to his Tel Aviv office and asked for a new appraisal of the situation. Did the Egyptian demand for the evacuation of UNEF signify a policy change on Egypt's part? Until then it had been assumed that Nasser wanted to postpone a war until the time was ripe. The army intelligence assessment began to change rapidly on that day; no one claimed to know what had induced Nasser to act as he did, but whatever his motives there was no longer any doubt that the continuing troop concentrations constituted a danger to Israel. General Rabin and his intelligence chiefs admitted that their extent had taken them by surprise.* Further measures were taken to strengthen the

* General Yariv, chief of army intelligence in a conversation with a visitor in autumn 1966, discussed the possibility that the junior partner (Syria) would in the not-too-distant future involve Nasser in a war with Israel, which Nasser did not yet want. General Yariv thought this unlikely, not only in view of Egypt's involvement in the Yemen but also in the light of Nasser's firm resolve, shown many times in the past, not to be provoked prematurely by the Syrians. The Israeli intelligence appraisal was substantially right: Egypt had no chance of winning a war in these circumstances. It was wrong in assuming that there would therefore be no

Israeli forces in the south. Mr Eban saw more ambassadors during the day and told them that in Israel's view the winding up of the UNEF could not be decided arbitrarily by one side – it was an international issue. Its presence had been part of a package settlement by the UN and the major powers concerning Israel's withdrawal after the Sinai campaign. There was the danger of a change in the *status quo*, and Israel had to take military counter-measures to be ready for any eventuality.

But the consensus of opinion in informed political quarters, in the army high command, and among the party leaders and the diplomats, still was that the danger of war was remote. A military correspondent wrote that Nasser was no doubt aware of the dangers and logistic difficulties involved in keeping his units in the desert for a long time. In 1960 the Egyptian troops had been kept in Sinai for two months. This time Nasser would probably withdraw them sooner, once he had gained his propaganda victory.[8] On Thursday afternoon, Eshkol met some of his colleagues from the 'Ma 'arakh' (Mapai and Ahdut Avoda). A few thought there might be a clash over Sharm al Shaykh, but Mrs Golda Meir, a former foreign minister, who argued that a war might be nearer than anyone had expected, found herself in a minority. In the evening, while the Prime Minister and General Rabin were again in session, news was received from the United Nations that U Thant was about to order the withdrawal of UNEF. This was unexpected. How would it affect the situation? What was Nasser really up to? It was decided to resume consultations the next day.

So far events have been related in their chronological order; at this point a digression becomes necessary. At the beginning of the crisis there had been full agreement, or, to be precise, equal confusion about Nasser's motives and aims among Israeli leaders. But as the crisis continued to unfold major differences of opinion developed: party politics, public opinion, the relations between the army and the Government, and the impact of personalities became increasingly important.

war, that because Nasser had not been provoked in the past he would continue to act in the same way in the future. In brief, the estimate was wrong because it erred on the side of rationality and logic. It left little room for emotional reactions and irrational behaviour. A high-ranking intelligence officer wrote later that only an astrologist could have foreseen that there would be war in 1967. But isn't there something to be said for the employment of astrologists in time of war, as the British realised in 1940?

113

When the crisis broke, Mr Eshkol, then seventy-two, had been Prime Minister for almost four years. Born Levi Shkolnik, he came to Palestine from Russia as a member of the second Aliyah – almost literally with the last ship before the outbreak of the First World War. A member of one of the earliest collective settlements (Degania B) and at first an agricultural worker, he had drifted, like so many of that generation, into public life in the nineteen-twenties. Secretary of the Zionist Settlement Department in Berlin (1933–6); Secretary of the Tel Aviv Labour Council (1944); Treasurer of the Jewish Agency (1950); Minister of Agriculture (1950) and then of Finance – these were the major stages in his political career. A popular, though not an inspiring figure, he lacked both Ben Gurion's charisma and his weaknesses. Most of his experience had been in the economic field; in foreign politics and in defence questions he had to rely far more than his predecessor on his advisers. His was the pragmatic, common-sense, down-to-earth approach; not for him the ideological visions and the doctrinal speeches. Relations between government and opposition were on the whole less acrimonious under his leadership than under Ben Gurion; he was more conciliatory, less stubborn. Eshkol's ideal Prime Minister was a good chairman, not an inspired leader. He had realised early on that Ben Gurion's 'orientation towards France' was not in the long run a sound basis for Israeli foreign policy; under Eshkol relations with Washington were improved, fewer risks were taken in offending the Americans. At the same time efforts were made to normalise relations with the Soviet Union and other East European countries.

During the last year or two Eshkol had come increasingly under fire from Ben Gurion and Rafi – the group that had split away from Mapai. It was probably more a question of style than policy; Eshkol, the critics said, was a national misfortune, he was the embodiment of irresolution and hesitation, a man who at the end of a session would say 'Well, children, what should we decide?' He was accused of grave sins in the field of security, as in the famous 'Machdal' affair, which everyone talked about but no one could mention in print. (This concerned the production of missiles in Israel; under Ben Gurion preparations had been made for building them locally. Eshkol, on calculating the cost, decided that it would be much cheaper to buy them abroad.)

Some of these accusations were justified. Eshkol was not in the best health, he showed indecision, was too eager to establish a consensus when initiative and leadership were needed. Perhaps he was too democratic, too decent for a politician in such a position, lacking in toughness. Above all, his style was not in line with the younger Israelis who were becoming increasingly impatient with the older generation of Labour-Zionists of the second and third Aliyah, their homely stories about the East European *shtetl*, their antiquated *Zionut*, their unending speeches. There were many jokes about Eshkol's great willingness to compromise. (In a coffee house: 'Tea or coffee, Sir? Oh – better give me half and half ... ') But was he really less resolute than his main critic? Ben Gurion, too, when faced with major decisions or a crisis had procrastinated; during the Sinai campaign he had fallen ill; his critics said that these had been psychosomatic illnesses. Eshkol's relations with the army command were excellent; he had always given them his full backing. Because he was less of an expert in this field, they had a freer hand under him than under his predecessor. Since late 1965 the Israeli economy had stagnated; there were signs of a major crisis (the 'Mitun', as it was euphemistically called), unemployment was rising. But this was thought to be more or less inevitable after so many years of uninterrupted growth. The Government could have shown greater firmness in tackling the crisis, but even his worst enemies did not contend that the 'Mitun' was Eshkol's fault.

In foreign affairs Eshkol relied above all on Abba Eban, who had played a prominent part in Israeli politics almost without interruption since the state was founded, as ambassador to the United States, and later as Foreign Minister. South African born, and a Cambridge graduate in Oriental languages, Eban had many admirers, and almost as many detractors, but hardly any real friend in the Israeli establishment; somehow he seemed not to belong; he was not what the younger Israeli called a 'Chevreman', a good mixer, a good man to have around at a party. His egocentrism and intellectual arrogance were proverbial; if he kept his position all these years it was by sheer merit; he was thought to be indispensable. An outstanding diplomat and brilliant speaker in many languages, he had most successfully represented Israel at the United Nations; many a television viewer in the United States came to regard him as a mixture of Shakespeare and Churchill.[9] In Israel the judgment had been harsher; he had offended too many people and had made it a practice to ignore the advice of his own ministry. His eloquence irritated some and made others impatient; the rhetorical cascades, the magnificent word pictures were no doubt very impressive; but what was the content, what was the *tachles* (brass tacks)? Did they contain any new ideas, any fresh approach? His critics said that Eban had no policy of his own, that his judgment could not be trusted; he was said to lack backbone, moral force, conviction. He could convincingly represent almost any policy; he was a linguist and lawyer of genius, and a good ambassador, but not a reliable Foreign Minister. Much of this criticism was unfair; there was much venom in it and perhaps also some envy; it reflected the intolerance of Israeli public life. Abba Eban became the most disputed figure of the *Konenut* period.

Like Ben Gurion before him, Eshkol was his own Defence Minister, which meant that he came to rely to a great extent on the advice of General Rabin and the other members of the army high command. Rabin, almost thirty years younger than the Prime Minister, was *primus inter pares* among that remarkable group of leaders, the fifteen Alufim who constituted the backbone of the high command. Their background was strikingly similar; they were all between 39 and 46 years of age, almost all had been born in Israel or had, at any rate, received their education in the country. Most, like Rabin himself, were former members of the *Palmach*, the small illegal élite corps that had been established in the Kibbutzim during the Second World War, spending much of their time in agricultural work. During the war of 1948 they commanded companies and battalions. Rabin, only 26, was then already a brigadier. Later they received formal military training in staff colleges. Most also decided to broaden their general education and spent a few years in European or American universities or at the Hebrew University.

Rabin, blue-eyed, broad shouldered, quietly spoken, was a remarkable Chief of Staff. Thorough, with a clear analytical mind, respected and universally beloved, he exuded calm and confidence. The army owed a great deal to his leadership. Three years is the normal tour of duty of the Chief of Staff in Israel.

Only twice had it been prolonged, in Dayan's case and in Rabin's. Other chiefs of staff such as Dayan, had left far more to improvisation; the methodical Rabin, while aware of the part improvisation would play in any war, had tried during his years at the helm to reduce the element of chance to the minimum. Under Rabin the army was completely modernised, learned to use the most up to date and sophisticated equipment. The war of 1967 was fought according to a blueprint that had been approved more than three years previously; there were some last minute changes introduced by General Bar Lev, but basically it was the plan of 1964 which Rabin had prepared.

To the army and the country at large he was a tower of strength. Only those nearest to him knew that behind the composed exterior there was a withdrawn sensitive man, acutely feeling the pressures which he never showed. More than anyone else, Rabin was aware of the responsibility he carried for the survival of the country. If a minister failed, there were ways and means to repair the damage; Rabin knew that any mistake he committed would be paid for by thousands of young officers and soldiers with their lives; the very existence of the state would be at stake. The Arab countries were out to destroy Israel, not merely to defeat it. He bore a responsibility more formidable than any military leader in our time, and he almost broke down under the superhuman burden. He had all the gifts of a great general but one: he was too sensitive to have that ultimate ruthlessness needed at a time of great stress. Exposed to civilian pressures and counter-pressures, he began to waver at one decisive stage. He fell ill – according to the official version it was a case of nicotine poisoning. This was true, but it was not the whole truth; a deeper conflict had caused the breakdown. But there was never a question of replacing him; his friends and fellow officers rallied around him. Soon he recovered, regained his confidence, and led his country to victory.

Eshkol's coalition government consisted of the three Labour parties (Mapai, Ahdut Avoda, and Mapam), the religious groups and a liberal faction. Mapai had been the leading force in Israeli politics since 1948; it had in fact been the strongest party in the Zionist movement for much longer. It had shown signs of fatigue for a long time but there was no alternative, no other party to replace it. Ahdut Avoda represented a section of the Kibbutz movement; ideologically to the left of Mapai, its leaders had always advocated a tough line in foreign and defence policy. They had provided the backbone of the *Palmach*; Rabin and many other military leaders were former members or sympathisers. The party was represented in the cabinet by three distinguished former military leaders – Yigal Allon, Moshe Carmel, and Israel Galili. Their line during the crisis was unequivocal. Mapam, also basically a Kibbutz movement, was the furthest to the left of the Zionist parties; it had originally advocated a binational state in Palestine and it had never given up the hope that the Arab-Israeli conflict would be resolved once the progressive forces in the Arab world took over. Its belief in the Soviet Union and the socialist world in general had hardly been shaken by the purges and trials by Stalin and the hostility of the communist parties to the state of Israel. Its leaders and members were the most decent of people, worthy of admiration in every respect but one – their political judgment was too often quite wrong; the crisis of 1967 came as a major shock to most of them and plunged them into a deep ideological crisis.

The religious groups and the liberals, few in numbers but influential in view of the multi-party system and the relatively small government majority, tended to follow a cautious line in foreign and military affairs; like Mapam, they were to be in the camp of the doves during the crisis.

The main opposition force was the *Gahal* – a coalition of right-wing groups among which Menahem Begin was the strongest personality. The two communist factions, formerly united, had split over the issue of Arab nationalism. The majority under Tawfiq Toubi supported Egyptian and Syrian policies towards Israel; the Arab cause, in their view, was just and progressive. The minority, under Mikunis and Dr Moshe Sneh, was outraged by this total acceptance of Arab nationalism, which they felt could not be justified in terms of Marxism and proletarian internationalism; Israel too, had the right to exist, and if necessary to defend itself. Almost all Arab communists belonged to the Toubi faction (Rakah), most Jews to the Mikunis group (Maki). The Soviet Union had not yet finally decided which group was more worthy of support, but it was already clear that it gravitated towards Rakah. Lastly, there was Rafi, the party that had split from Mapai; it was led by three men with special competence in the military field: David Ben Gurion, Moshe Dayan, and

Shimon Peres. Ben Gurion, now 82 and out of office, commuted between Sde Boker, the Kibbutz in the Negev, and his home in Tel Aviv; he had been Prime Minister in 1948, and in 1956 during the Suez war. With a short interruption he had been the leader of the country during the first fifteen years of its existence. He still enjoyed great prestige; his wild and often unjustified attacks on his former colleagues had antagonised many Israelis, but for most of them he still was the Grand Old Man of Israeli politics. During the crisis he was to play a major role behind the scenes; many went to consult him – General Rabin and General Dayan, Shapiro of the religious party, and Hazan of Mapam. To all he gave the same advice: once the immediate occasion to react had passed, there was no alternative for Israel but to dig in. It was too late for an offensive; only with the support of a major power could Israel regain the initiative. He had no doubt that Israel would win in the end, but he had also dark visions of death and destruction and of hecatombs of victims. Ben Gurion had the reputation of a hawk, and precisely for that reason his advice not to attack carried great weight.

There was no agreement on this point between him and Moshe Dayan, the victor of the Sinai campaign; Rafi, during the crisis, like most other parties, was a house divided. Mention ought to be made of Shimon Peres, who for many years had been Deputy Minister of Defence. A native of Poland now in his forties, he had come to Palestine as a young boy with the Youth Aliyah. A keen political mind, he had much experience in foreign affairs and defence, and was to play a key part in the negotiations between the parties during the crisis. Numerically Rafi was a small party, but its impact on public opinion, especially on the younger generation, was considerable. It had no daily newspaper of its own, but some of Israel's leading papers gave it substantial support throughout the crisis. Its line was, however, not unambiguous; early in the crisis Rafi argued that Israel had to choose between a Middle Eastern Munich and the smashing of Egyptian imperialism. Immediate action was therefore needed lest the country's survival was endangered. At the same time, the party argued that Israel should take the diplomatic initiative but keep Nasser guessing in the military sphere. Was Munich to be averted by a diplomatic initiative? It wasn't quite clear.[9a]

On Thursday evening, 18 May, the army command had first

discussed the possibility that Nasser would close the Straits of Tiran. The next morning consultations continued in the Ministry of Defence in Tel Aviv. The various heads of department were called in, defence planning was rapidly reviewed, army intelligence provided current information, and decisions were taken to speed up the delivery of equipment from Europe that had been on order. News came in about the violation of Israeli airspace by Egyptian planes coming from Jordan; some had apparently been near Dimona. This as Eshkol later related, induced him and Rabin to speed up mobilisation.[96] During Friday the mobilisation order came into effect; most reservists got the news by special messenger late on Friday night, others were notified by telephone or cable. The functioning of vital services which might have been affected by the call-up was ensured by special orders gazetted over the weekend. In Tel Aviv, Haifa, and Jerusalem reservists were seen walking or hitch-hiking to their collection points, usually accompanied by their wives and children. The older citizens were reminded of the scenes they had witnessed in Europe in July and August 1914. Some women wept, the children were, as usual, patriotic. There was neither great enthusiasm nor any marked dejection. The reservists greeted each other, as one correspondent reported, like members of a bowling club out for a day's sport.[10] No one as yet really believed there would be war.

This was the first warm weekend of the season, and thousands on that Sabbath went to the beaches and to popular excursion spots. Private cars and trucks had not yet been taken over by the authorities. In Western Galilee 4,000 participated in an annual twenty kilometre route march; at Zemah, on the Syrian border, thousands watched the local football match where Tel Katzir trounced Ha'om 6–2; there were many weekend bathers even on the faraway Eilat shore, which runs to the Egyptian border. But the call-up continued during the day, and by early evening Tel Aviv had the look of a deserted city. For the first night in many a home children were told to pray for the safe and speedy return of their fathers. Eshkol and General Rabin went to inspect the troops in the south during Saturday; they also visited some of the border settlements. Otto Klemperer conducted the Israeli Radio Orchestra that evening in Jerusalem; Tel Avivians could choose between 'Marat-Sade', 'Black Man's Burden', and 'The

Man from la Mancha'; residents of Haifa had the rare opportunity to see a Yiddish musical 'Di Koshere Almone'. But theatres and concert halls were half empty that night.

Sunday: 21 May. The cabinet meets in the morning for its weekly session. The newspapers report on U Thant's impending visit to Cairo. General Rabin informs the cabinet that about 80,000 Egyptians are now massed along Israel's borders, the largest such concentration ever. Eshkol reports on the notes sent to the powers, protesting against the guerrilla attacks as well as the Egyptian massing of troops. The powers have been asked to exert their influence in the Arab capitals to lessen the tension and to protect freedom of shipping in the Straits of Tiran. It is decided that in view of the critical situation only the Prime Minister and Mr Eban will from now on make political statements. Eshkol and Eban are still optimistic, so are most members of the cabinet; they believe that there has been a slight lessening of tension during the last twenty-four hours. Now that UNEF is withdrawn and the Egyptian army directly faces the Israeli defence forces across the border, the situation is frozen, no major developments are expected. From now on diplomacy will take over. The withdrawal of UNEF (some maintain) does not by itself constitute a danger to peace. But there are voices that dissent sharply: there has been only a momentary lessening of tension, the entire situation resembles the state of affairs in 1938-9; then too there was a slight lull after each of Hitler's conquests: Nasser cannot be pacified by Israeli concessions. No attempt should be made to enlist the powers. The Israeli army is stronger; Nasser has to be told in unmistakable terms that it will fight unless the freedom of shipping is maintained and the guerrilla attacks cease. But Nasser must be told now, no further time is to be lost.[11]

In Jerusalem the deliberations continue but Eshkol has to leave in the middle for Lydda airport: Paasio, the Finnish Prime Minister, arrives in the afternoon for a state visit. He had been invited a long time before, the situation is not considered sufficiently critical to cancel the visit. Eshkol and Paasio have no common language, the translation of the speeches of welcome takes a long time. Eshkol continues on his way to a memorial meeting in Avihail, a little place near Natanya; in his first speech during the crisis he talks about the defence measures taken so

far: 'We have full reason to assume that our forces will successfully meet any challenge at any time.' There is loud applause but
the speech is not reported in next day's papers.

On Monday, the Israeli Parliament meets for the first time for
its summer session. The house is full, the galleries overflowing.
In the front row, facing the Prime Minister, half a dozen high
ranking army officers are seated. Eshkol says in his opening
speech that Israel was not heading for any attack on the Arab
countries, did not desire to undermine their security, attack their
territory, or challenge their legitimate international rights. But
Israel demanded full reciprocity. Egypt now had 80,000 troops
on its border with Israel compared with 35,000 before the crisis
began; this was an unprecedented build-up, a direct threat to
peace. There was no shred of truth in Egypt's allegation that its
troops had been massed to prevent an Israeli attack on Syria.
Eshkol again calls on the great powers, especially on the Soviet
Union, to use their influence in Cairo and Damascus for peace.
He concludes with an appeal to 'all the peoples of the Middle
East for reciprocal respect for the sovereignty, integrity and
international rights of each of our countries'. Israel, for its part,
'expresses at this hour her readiness to participate in an effort to
reinforce stability and advance peace in our region'.[12] It is a
moderate, statesmanlike speech and it makes a good impression
in New York, London, and Paris; Israel clearly was not likely to
act rashly. The impression inside Israel is less favourable. Some
commentators claimed later that the speech may have encouraged Nasser to close the Straits.[13] In this grave situation, the
public expects a major statement of policy if not a rousing call to
action. Eshkol's speech contains neither, it simply repeats things
that had been said many times before. The Fatah has not the
slightest intention of respecting Israeli sovereignty and integrity;
to reinforce peace and stability in the Middle East is the last
thing the Syrian Government wants, and Nasser refuses to recognise Israel, let alone to respect its international rights. In these
circumstances, it is felt, a few blunt words would fit the occasion
better; the Arab leaders who had mobilised their armies are
clearly not to be impressed by measured statesmanlike declarations. There is a procedural wrangle whether the Knesset discussion should be in closed session; this is demanded by Rafi,
which is extremely critical of the Government's handling of the

situation. But Rafi does not want to air its criticism in public at a time of crisis. Gahal insists on holding the debate in public, precisely because forthright statements are needed and because Eshkol's statement has been too moderate. Begin, who opens the debate, calls on the Government to be as explicit as possible in making known the line across which it will not permit Nasser to proceed under threat of war. This includes immediate withdrawal of Egyptian troops from the borders, and the clear assurance of freedom for Israeli shipping to and from Eilat. He differs from Eshkol on the original interpretation of the crisis: the assessment that the troop movements are a mere propaganda show had not come from abroad (as Eshkol had argued): it had originated inside Israel. When Shimon Peres' turn comes to address the Knesset on behalf of Rafi, he waives his right to speak. He can not speak freely in open session. The debate goes on for a long time; there is a great deal of shouting, provoked mainly by the smaller factions; most ministers have meanwhile left the Knesset for urgent talks and Zerah Wahrhaftig, Minister of Religion, is left alone to hold the fort. Eshkol that night gives a dinner for the Finnish Prime Minister; the possibility of war is hardly discussed; Eshkol is in good humour and entertains his guest with old Jewish stories.

At 4 o'clock the next morning Eshkol was awakened by a call from General Rabin: news had just been received from Cairo that Nasser had announced the closure of the Straits of Tiran. In a speech at Advanced Air Headquarters he had said that no single Israeli vessel would from then on be permitted to cross the Gulf of Aqaba. He was aware that this could mean war. (Nasser did not use the word 'war', but 'military confrontation'. It is astonishing to what extent circumlocution was used by both Arab and Israeli leaders in those days. Instead of war they spoke about conflict or confrontation; instead of attack, they used 'action' or 'initiative' instead of defeat 'setback'; instead of America 'international factors', etc.) If General Rabin wanted it, by all means, 'ahlen ve sahlen' (welcome), the Egyptians were ready. Eshkol was immediately driven to army headquarters in Tel Aviv. The most critical day in that period of waiting had dawned: now the fat was really in the fire. So far Nasser's moves had been open to various interpretations; now it was clear how far he was prepared to go. There had been many in Israel who claimed that he would be satisfied with concentrating troops in Sinai and achieving a propaganda victory by claiming that he had deterred Israel from attacking Syria. The removal of UNEF was a serious matter, but hardly a *casus belli*; Nasser would not interfere with Israeli shipping, for it had been made abundantly clear that Israel would fight if the straits were closed. Now it suddenly appeared that they had misjudged Nasser.

On that morning Eshkol was told by the military that immediate action had become imperative. But Eshkol knew that most members of the Government would not be in favour of war at this stage; there had been no formal vote prior to 23 May, but everyone had already had his say in countless private discussions. Mapam, the religious parties, the Liberals, and also many Mapai leaders had argued that the threat to Israel was far greater than in 1956: Egypt was more strongly armed and there was no air umbrella to defend Israel's cities. True, Israel would win the war, but at what price? There would be tens of thousands of victims, Israel's cities would be in ruins. The military were confident; they had said in the closed sessions that it would be a short war, that there would be few civilian casualties. But how did they know? There were so many unpredictable factors in war. Perhaps the Egyptians would use some secret weapon? Perhaps the Israeli army did not, after all, have the superiority it had in 1956? Ten years of training and indoctrination had surely made the Egyptian army a more formidable opponent. Above all, what would America do, and how would Russia react? Soviet policy was the big question mark: if Nasser had been put up by the Russians to provoke Israel (as many now believed), if the whole affair had global implications, if Moscow wanted war in the Middle East, surely they would give Nasser more than verbal support once war broke out? This was the line taken by many Israeli political leaders, among them Ben Gurion, Mr Eban, and Arye Levavi, Director-General of the Foreign Ministry. The army commanders and the intelligence chiefs showed growing impatience: they vigorously criticised the over-anxious comments and the dire predictions, and some were openly contemptuous of the Cassandras of East European origin who were always overawed by Russia. Had not Mr Eshkol recently invoked the 'spirit of Tashkent' – as if Moscow had the slightest intention of working actively for peace in the Middle East. Had not Eban engaged in various futile manœuvres during the last year (such as the recognition of the Oder-Neisse line), to gain Soviet and East European support? Prominent among the activists were Brigadier Meir Amit, head of Israel's intelligence (which included the *Mossad* and the *Shin Bet*) and Brigadier Aharon Yariv, head of army intelligence. Amit, Israeli born and a predecessor of Yariv, had just gone on record (during the celebrations making the tenth anniversary of the Sinai campaign) that Israel's cardinal mistake ten years before had been to pay too much attention to the threats of the great powers, and in particular to those of the Soviet Union. The Russians, he said, had been bluffing. Their threats to intervene in force would not have been implemented if the bluff had been called.[14] Yariv also thought that the Russians had been watching with growing alarm the fortunes of their protégés in the Arab world; but while they had decided to encourage them to restore their prestige, they were by no means willing to be drawn into an armed conflict.

Torn between these conflicting approaches, Eshkol decided to call in the leaders of the opposition parties for consultation. Dayan and Begin were flown by helicopter to Tel Aviv, so were other leading members of Gahal and Rafi, and a few Mapai leaders, including Golda Meir, and David Hacohen (head of the Knesset Committee for Foreign and Security Affairs). Together with the cabinet they discussed the situation that had been created following the closure of the straits. Was it enough to tell the world that Israel would use the right of self-defence under paragraph 51 of the UN Charter if the blockade continued? If so, how long should they wait, and in what way exactly should Israel react? Should a ship be sent through the Straits of Tiran as a test case? The military refused to take this proposal seriously; it would leave the initiative in Nasser's hands. What if he gave orders for an all-out attack on Israel a few hours before the Israel ship reached Sharm al Shaykh? What if he let the ship pass unmolested but attacked the next ship several weeks later?

While these talks were going on an urgent request was received from Washington that no attempt should be made by Israel to force the blockade within the next forty-eight hours ('two to three days', according to another account). It was not at all clear

125

what Washington hoped to achieve in this period; it was already obvious that U Thant's mission to Cairo was doomed, and the Security Council session that had been called was bound to end in a stalemate. What other initiative could be taken to restore the *status quo ante*? But the majority of opinion in Tel Aviv that morning was that an attempt should be made to resolve the crisis by diplomatic means. Eban said that he had a letter from John Foster Dulles, dated 11 February 1957, that America regarded the Straits of Tiran as an international waterway, and that in cooperation with other maritime nations, it would act to safeguard freedom of shipping there for all. Both American presidents had since reaffirmed their support for Israel on that issue; surely they ought to be reminded now of their obligation. Eshkol wanted originally to send a special emissary (Yaakov Herzog, Director-General of the Prime Minister's Office or Golda Meir) with personal messages to President Johnson, Mr Wilson, and de Gaulle and to keep Eban in Jerusalem. But he accepted Eban's reasoning in the end. The Government decided, with the approval of Dayan, Begin, and the other opposition leaders, to send the Foreign Minister immediately to Washington; he left for Paris after midnight in a special El Al transport plane. On the same day General Rabin fell ill.

The military were unhappy about Eban's mission; they had no illusions about its outcome. Meanwhile valuable time was being lost. Some ministers, too, had agreed only reluctantly; Moshe Carmel, Minister of Transport, said at another meeting that day that every hour that passed without military action would strengthen the position of the Egyptian dictator. Golda Meir on the same occasion expressed the fear that Israel would, at best, receive vague promises from the Americans and that a long time would pass before it would finally emerge whether these promises were of any value. And in the meantime 'our hands would be tied'.

In the afternoon Eshkol mounted the Knesset rostrum to reply to the debate. He said that the Egyptian action was a gross violation of international law and an act of aggression against Israel. He called on the powers to act without delay to maintain the right of free passage. It was a very brief statement; Eshkol did not want to answer in detail all the criticism and the suggestions that had been aired in the debate. Nor did he make direct mention of what action Israel might take, confining himself to the remark that the Government would adhere to the policy which it had announced at the UN General Assembly on 1 March 1957. This referred to a statement by the then Foreign Minister Mrs Golda Meir that interference with her ships would be regarded by Israel as an attack entitling her to take under Article 51 of the UN Charter all such measures as were necessary to ensure free and innocent passage. At the close of Eshkol's statement a resolution was moved charging the Security and Foreign Affairs Committee with continuing and summing up the debate. The vote was 89 to 4, with only the communists opposing it. Veteran Knesset reporters said they had not seen such unanimity for ten years. On that day the idea of broadening the Government was first mooted; it came up in private discussions and in meetings between the various political parties. Ben Gurion's name, above all, was mentioned, so was Dayan's and Begin's. Eshkol's first reaction, and that of his party, was wholly negative; the Government was perfectly able to cope with the situation. Within two days the movement for a national government ('from wall to wall') gathered momentum and could no longer be shrugged off. Those who thought an all-party cabinet consisting of more than twenty members unworkable argued that it would never reach a decision. A war cabinet was needed to be appointed on a personal, not a party basis, to conduct the political and the military battle.[15]

Israel was on the eve of momentous decisions; almost hourly the international situation had become more tense, and now the domestic struggle was about to begin. The Finnish Prime Minister, who had already visited a few Kibbutzim, museums, and social institutions, decided that his hosts would not be offended if (with deep regret) he cut his visit short. Before leaving Jerusalem Mr Paasio laid a wreath on Herzl's tomb and lit a torch at the Yad va Shem Memorial crypt. At the airport he and his party received an honour guard of girl soldiers, and Mr Eshkol gave him a present of a silver chess set. There were brief speeches, and the guests boarded their plane. Mr Paasio had been a young man in 1939 when his own country was attacked by a vastly superior power, yet Finland had not hesitated for a moment; it had fought back against hopeless odds. And in the end it had survived while other, less fortunate neighbours had disappeared.

Finland was strictly neutral now, but is there any doubt what advice Mr Paasio would have given in a private capacity?

It is comparatively easy to describe the first week of the crisis; the general mood was still one of calm, even complacency. Only a few had been called up, life had not really changed for the great majority of Israelis. It is doubtful whether the general name that was given to the period after Independence Day 1967 – *Konenut* (Preparedness) – really fits that first week, for no one prepared for anything in particular. During the second week all this changed. Israel's citizens army of students, bank clerks, workers and salesmen streamed to the south in buses, taxis, and every other kind of conveyance. Within two days it was deployed in the empty spaces of the Negev. Many came who had not been called up; no one wanted to be a gentleman now a-bed in Tel Aviv. Once they had changed into uniform, the army routine got under way and the waiting game began. The oldtimers told their stories about 1956, about Gaza and Khan Yunis and the Mitla pass; the younger ones listened, half incredulous, half bored; fathers worried about their wives and children – whole pages in the newspapers, entire programmes on the broadcasting service were devoted to greetings from soldiers in the field; students worried about their studies – they had been called up just before the yearly examinations were about to start, would they lose a year or would they be able to sit the tests later on? There were, as in any army, a great many rumours: tomorrow there would be the great battle – no, Johnson would intervene and everyone would be sent home again. The army, the air force the navy began to publish their own newspapers, small and modest at first, more ambitious later on. The Israeli press was not very communicative about army life. Many of the reporters, too, had been called up: an increasing number of news stories was date-lined 'Somewhere in the South'. Actors, artists, and musicians volunteered for performances at army bases.

But not only the life of those who had become soldiers had changed. The bustling cities of Israel were curiously deserted for the greater part of the day; even the coffee houses of North Tel Aviv, where normally not a seat could be had in the afternoon or evening, were now virtually empty. For once there were no parking difficulties; most cars and trucks had been taken over by the army. School hours were cut to enable the pupils to work as mailmen. Scouts volunteered to make the rounds as milkmen and newspaper deliverers. Others were furiously digging shelters. The civil defence authorities published elaborate instructions on how to stock communal shelters, on first-aid kits, fire equipment, equipment for rescue work and shelter toilets. All over Israel householders dumped waste paper, abandoned ice-boxes and sundry rubbish along the sidewalks in a giant shelter-cleaning operation. For once they were encouraged by the local authorities to do so; and city workers cleared away the debris as fast as they could. School children from the upper grades filled hundreds of thousands of sandbags and dug trenches where there were no shelters. Schools were instructed in air raid drill, students who had not been called up signed up for first aid courses teaching assignments, blood donations, and driving jobs. Faculty members were asked to carry on normal teaching 'as long as conditions permitted'. Factories and public institutions, too, carried on their work as well as they could, but the enlistment of so many of their staff drastically reduced output in all but the most essential undertakings.

Israel was preparing for a siege. The signs were unmistakable: the first representatives of the International Red Cross arrived and offered their services. It was very generous and decent, but it was a bad omen; the Red Cross had an uncanny sixth sense as to where serious trouble was likely to start. Foreign correspondents, those harbingers of doom, began to arrive; by 23 May seventy new foreign correspondents had already registered in Tel Aviv, so had fifteen TV networks. One week later there were hundreds of them. On 23 May the American and British embassies advised their nationals to leave Israel unless they had essential business; the Canadians and the Australians did the same. The next day the Scandinavians, the West Germans and others followed suit. The British thought that the situation in Israel, the West Bank and the UAR, was critical; it was 'probably in the best interest of British nationals to leave'; in the other Arab countries, including Syria and the East Bank, they 'should make preparations to leave at short notice'. El Al cancelled group flights and the other airlines sent special planes to Lydda to evacuate foreign nationals; 3,000, mostly tourists, left on the 24th, 5,000 on the day after. The shipping companies, too, were besieged by tourists and foreign nationals.

There was no good reason why the tourists should stay; in an emergency they would only be in the way. The taxis and the buses were needed, and good use would be made of the big hotels. (The Accadia, for instance was to become an emergency hospital.) And yet, not only the hotel owners saw them leave with regret. The storm clouds were drawing nearer.

What was the general mood this last week of May? Many had criticised the lack of public spirit in Israel in years past – old-timers in particular had sadly compared the pioneering spirit, the selfless help of the early years of the Jewish national home, with the egotism, the rudeness, the every-one-for-himself-and-the-devil-take-the-hindmost attitudes prevailing in the fifties. They recalled with nostalgia the days when no one in Tel Aviv or Haifa thought of locking his door, and they concluded that those heroic early days had gone forever and with them the spirit of the frontier, the idealism of youth, the willingness to make sacrifices.

No one was more surprised than they were by the high morale, the readiness to volunteer and to help shown by every section of the population. It was unexpected and totally unprecedented. Children under military age and over age adults, disabled persons and foreign nationals, insisted on joining the army, and, upon being rejected, on performing other emergency assignments. Companies and private individuals hurried to the tax offices, paying income tax ahead of schedule. One Tel Aviv lawyer paid IL. 250,000 in advance; many followed his example. Workers and employers in every locality gave cash, or gave up their annual holiday and sent their earnings to the Ministry of Defence. Free rooms were offered to the soldiers in hotels, free food in restaurants, laundries washed their clothes free of charge. The shopkeepers gave credit to women whose husbands had been called up. The Kibbutzim sent fruit to the soldiers in the Negev and Jewish mothers dispatched so many cakes that the O.C. Southern Command had to ask them politely but firmly to desist. Motorists collected hitch-hikers – and there were many of them as fewer and fewer buses were seen in the streets – and delivered them at their place of work. Even the underworld did not stay aside; a group of Tel Aviv ex-convicts asked the police whether their driving licences could not be temporarily restored so that they could drive trucks for the army. An Israeli inventor offered the Ministry of Defence three of his patents – a cosmic death ray, an engineless aeroplane and an instant water desalination machine. At Lydda airport stewards, flight engineers, and clerks volunteered to fill in as porters. All over Israel neighbourhood aid committees were set up: women volunteered to visit at least once a day elderly people living alone, to help mothers with young children. It was widespread, it was spontaneous, it was efficient and often very moving. Even the pessimists were touched; why is it, they pondered, that the good qualities of our people emerge only at a time of supreme crisis?

The volunteer spirit was not limited to Israeli Jews. Young Druzes demonstrated in Tel Aviv; they too wanted to fight in the army. Volunteers started to arrive from abroad; first (around 24 May) it was a trickle, gradually it became a stream. Most were members of Jewish youth movements, but many had come on their own initiative and at their own expense. All were willing to help in whatever way they could best serve the country: to replace the young men in the Kibbutzim who had been called up, to drive ambulances, to man civil defence posts, many students and visitors from abroad who had been asked by their governments to leave ignored the advice and offered their services as volunteers. Some were famous men – musicians, artists, scientists – and others very ordinary people.

The spirit of *Konenut* became something of a legend among Israelis, and rightly so, for this was their finest hour. But alongside high morale and willingness to sacrifice there were also manifestations of panic and hysteria. A great many people rushed to foodshops and supermarkets and bought up staple foods as well as tinned meat and other non-perishable commodities. Some even stocked up on fresh fruit and vegetables. All this despite assurances by the Government and the supermarket managers that there were adequate stocks for many months. As a result there was a shortage of rice, and also of sugar, flour, and oil. On 24 May it was decided to keep the Government stores open all night so that fresh supplies could be rushed to the retailers. Even so shortages persisted in some fields; the reserves were not as impressive as the authorities maintained. Elsewhere there was no transport to dispatch the goods to the shops. Some shopkeepers started to hoard and a few raised their prices. By 26 May the run was tapering off, partly because some of the goods

131

were still in short supply – supermarkets limited the sale of sugar to two pounds per person – partly because the hoarders had reached saturation point.[16] The run had been started by housewives with memories of the Second World War and the war of independence, when food – especially in Jerusalem – had been very short indeed; the others simply followed their example. The Government briefly considered introducing rationing, but decided against it; the administrative effort was not worth it. Israel was not preparing for a long war.

It was a curious phenomenon: the very same housewives who fought for sugar and rice in the supermarket, baked cakes for the troops, donated blood, volunteered to work in the hospitals. Perhaps this ambivalence reflected the mood of the population in general; there were very few heroes *sans peur et sans reproche,* and relatively few cowards. The image of which Jewish sympathisers outside Israel are so fond, the tough, quietly confident Israeli who never hesitated, never looked back, is largely mythical. They behaved as all ordinary human beings would in such a situation: they were afraid; only fools and people devoid of all imagination would have reacted differently. A few talked about Auschwitz, Maidanek, and a new holocaust. Most were convinced that Israel would win the war but that there would be many victims. (The army, as usual, was far more optimistic than the civilians.) Many Israelis spent worried hours and sleepless nights during the crisis and some considered whether they should not make use of offers from relatives abroad to send their wives and children to Europe or America, but the great majority were not even willing to consider this step. This was the end of the line; Israel was their country, here they would live and if necessary die. No one, of course, talked in these terms; over the years Israelis have become impervious to fine phrases. With all their apprehensions they were resolved to sell their homes and their lives very dear. Memories of the Second World War, of the greatest disaster in Jewish history, were still fresh: never again were Jews to be conducted like sheep to the slaughter.

True, the Israel of 1967 differed in essential respects from the country that had fought in 1948. Even demographically it was totally different. A new generation had grown up; the majority of the new Israel hailed from Middle Eastern and Mediterranean countries; they were of a different outlook and heirs to a different cultural tradition. No one could know for sure how they would react in a crisis; perhaps they would be defeatists, perhaps they would panic.

There was no panic apart from the supermarkets. Once war was accepted as inevitable, the general mood became one of impatience. If thousands were to die and if whole cities were to go up in flames, why not get it over as quickly as possible? Public opinion became increasingly dissatisfied with the way Eshkol's government was handling the crisis. The situation grew steadily worse; the Government continued to waver, seeming always to trail after events. What was Mr Eshkol waiting for?

Mr Eshkol was waiting for Abba Eban. The Foreign Minister had left Israel after midnight on 24 May; it was still early morning when he reached Paris. Walter Eytan, the Israeli ambassador, awaited him at the airport; a meeting with de Gaulle was arranged at very short notice. De Gaulle was not unfriendly; he recalled that he had long been a friend of the state of Israel. But the moment Eban began to discuss the crisis, the General became more aloof: of course he would do all he could to help bring about a settlement, but Israel should realise that no solution was possible without consulting the Soviet Union. A four-power conference was probably the best way to reach an agreement. If Mr Eban wanted to put his trust in America, that was his own business. As for the blockade – it could not really be regarded as a declaration of war (as Eban had argued); it was up to the four powers to find an arrangement acceptable to all. Eban replied that his government would on no account be willing to put up with the blockade, and that any delay in calling it off would make war more likely. If it was a choice between surrender and resistance, Israel would choose resistance – just as de Gaulle had done in June 1940. But the General was not impressed; Eban's arguments did not fit into his general appraisal of world affairs, and of his concept of France's part in it. Above all, de Gaulle had apocalyptic visions: a third world war was much nearer than most people thought. If Israel started a shooting war the situation would become even more dangerous. After forty-five minutes Mr Eban was dismissed with a compliment on the quality of his French and a warning: 'Whatever you do – don't make war. Don't fire the first shot.'

A disappointed Mr Eban left the Elysée and boarded the plane for London. For a long time France's friendship and support had been taken for granted in Jerusalem. It was not so many years since de Gaulle had embraced Ben Gurion at a reception and had spoken in solemn words about the Franco-Israeli alliance. Some Israelis had attributed more importance than others to these ties, some had given warning that the French Government had recently shown great eagerness to come to terms with Nasser. Ambassador Roux in Cairo had impressed on the General that there was an excellent chance for a reconciliation with the Egyptians now that they had such a bitter quarrel with the Americans. But not even the greatest pessimist in Israel had been prepared for this letdown. It was bad enough to lose France's political support; the military implications were even more ominous in view of Israel's dependence on French arms deliveries.

In London, Eban went directly to Downing Street. If the meeting with de Gaulle had been bitterly disappointing, the conversation with Prime Minister Wilson gave him a little encouragement. Wilson was quite angry about Nasser's interference with Israeli shipping. Something clearly ought to be done. England together with the United States and other maritime nations was quite willing to help Israel to restore freedom of shipping for all. Consultations with Washington were already under way how best to effect this. Mr Eban could be assured that H.M. Government would take practical steps if necessary. Altogether it was slightly more than Eban had expected, but it was obvious that the key to solving the crisis was in Washington, where Eban went next.

Eban's trip had been decided upon at very short notice and it had not been well prepared. Many details had been left open and there were misunderstandings. Afterwards it was said that Eban should have gone straight to Washington; there had been no Government decision to visit Paris and London, and it was a waste of time; as the meeting with de Gaulle had shown, it was courting disaster. Eban had argued that this simply was not so, that it had been left to him whether to see de Gaulle and Wilson on his way. It was not his fault if de Gaulle was uncooperative. Above all, there was the case of the missing cable which later figured so prominently in the attacks on him. Eban had left Israel early on 24 May; later that day Yigal Allon, Minister of

Labour, returned to Israel from a visit to the Soviet Union. Allon, 48 years of age, a native born Israeli, was one of the central figures in Eshkol's government, and frequently mentioned as a future Prime Minister. He was a military leader of distinction; commander-in-chief of the Palmach up to its dissolution in 1948, his name had figured more prominently even than Dayan's during the war of independence. Immediately upon returning to Lydda, Allon went to the general staff, and was briefed by Rabin and the other generals. Most of these men had served under him and were his personal friends. In their eyes he was one of them, with whom they could talk openly. They told him how unhappy they were about Eban's mission: even if Eban did get some verbal promises, how would that effect the military danger created by the Egyptian troop concentrations? In the meantime, incidentally, another Egyptian armoured division had been identified in Sinai. Allon talked to Eshkol; on the 25th a cable was sent to Eban in London, instructing him to raise this as well as the Tiran question. It missed him in London and reached him only in Washington. The point has not yet been cleared; according to one source the cable had been hastily formulated by the head of the Prime Minister's office and was unduly alarmist; according to another version, Eban did raise the matter of troop concentrations with the Pentagon, but was told that his facts were at fault; the Israelis had exaggerated Egyptian strength. Eban was annoyed and his relations with the generals became even cooler, he was not altogether sure whether the ifnormation he had received from them was the whole truth and nothing but the truth. The cable was to figure prominently in the post mortem on Eban's failure of a mission.

Greatly fatigued, Eban arrived in Washington on 25 May, but there was to be no immediate meeting with the President; Mr Johnson was to see him only on the evening of the next day. This made it possible for him to get some sleep, and to pay a visit to the State Department and the Pentagon. President Johnson, to be sure, did not really know what to tell Eban – 'Operation Regatta', the move to break the blockade, was not going too well. The British and the Canadians had at first been eager to join, but Mr Lester Pearson later got cold feet. The Italians and the Scandinavians had been unenthusiastic, the French unwilling, only the Dutch and the Australians were ready to cooperate. Johnson was told by his advisers that a fresh effort was needed to get out of the stalemate, but they were not at all sure what exactly should be done.

As so often, there were different approaches to the crisis in the various Washington government departments and agencies. The President and some of his advisers were in favour of helping Israel, but it was all rather indefinite; if Israel waited long enough, it would somehow get through the Straits of Tiran. Johnson had stressed repeatedly that he needed substantial support in Congress, and many Congressmen, for all their sympathy with Israel, were reluctant to accept any further American commitment. This was the position taken by Dean Rusk and McNamara as well. The Pentagon was totally opposed to a second Vietnam in the Middle East; the US was simply not prepared for such a contingency. They were against American military intervention in an attempt to force a blockade. But precisely because the Pentagon was so strongly opposed to American intervention, and because it realised that something ought to be done, it took a more lenient view of any possible military action by Israel. According to their intelligence, Israel would win a war not only against Egypt, but against any alliance of Arab states. The CIA had once supported Nasser, but in recent years there had been little enthusiasm for Egypt among the leading members of that agency, while Nasser had singled out the CIA for bitter attacks in almost every speech. But the CIA, contrary to accepted folklore, had not made policy of late in the Middle East; if some favours had been done to Israel, they certainly amounted to a good deal less than the help that had been given over many years by Soviet intelligence to the Egyptians.

Eban's meeting with President Johnson was to be prepared by 'Eppy' Evron, the Israeli number two in Washington. On 22 May, Evron had been called in to transmit an important message to his government: Israel should not try to force the blockade for the next two or three days while Washington would work for a diplomatic solution. Now, on the afternoon of the 26th, he was again in the White House, preparing Eban's meeting. Suddenly the President called him in. President Johnson, with some time on his hands, talked for an hour about what America could and should do. Evron, a knowledgeable but comparatively junior diplomat, wanted to bring in Eban, who was waiting in the embassy, but could not interrupt the President, and so, with the time for the meeting approaching, Eban left for the White House accompanied by Avraham Harman, the ambassador, and arrived at the wrong gate. The confusion ended only when a guard phoned to say that 'some guy out here, by the name of Eban wanted to see the President'.[17] It was not an auspicious beginning.

Perhaps the confusion was deliberate. Johnson had been informed by his advisers that the Israelis were about to attack Egypt. At the same time Eban argued that he had news about an impending Egyptian attack. According to close observers of the Washington scene, the meeting with Eban took place only after the administration had reached the conclusion that war was not immediate.* Was there reason for such concern? Two days before, on 24 May, General Ezer Weizmann had submitted to Eshkol a detailed plan for immediate action but in view of the Government decision this had been ignored for the moment. Nevertheless, a state of alert was declared on 26 and 27 May; the army high command expected that they would be given the green light upon Eban's return, and they were making all the necessary preparations.

The meeting in Washington was friendly but indecisive. Johnson said that he would honour the undertakings given by his predecessors; the Straits of Tiran would not remain closed. He agreed that prolonged delay in taking action would strengthen Nasser's position and perhaps encourage him to make further aggressive moves against Israel. But the President also made it clear that, constitutionally, he was not a free agent; he needed the full support of Congress. He wanted to see first whether action could be taken by the Security Council. But what if that should not be possible, and if the western powers failed to agree on action to break the blockade? It was Mr Eban's impression, as he left the meeting, that the United States would then act unilaterally to open the Gulf of Aqaba. The protocol seemed, albeit in rather vague terms, to confirm this, but it had been a rambling and somewhat inconclusive discussion, and it could also be argued that the issue had been left open and that there would be further talks. Eban says that he mentioned

---

*T. Draper: *Israel and World Politics* (New York, 1968), gives an authoritative and detailed account of the negotiations in Washington.

the Egyptian troop concentrations, but that Johnson shrugged this off; Israel had no reason to be afraid, it was militarily strong and well prepared, and anyway, the United States had repeatedly guaranteed its territorial integrity. Later on there were differences of opinion; had Eban really raised the question forcefully, or had Johnson reason to assume that this was merely a side issue? It was understood that Mr Johnson had asked the Israelis to show restraint for about two weeks. It was not at all clear what would happen thereafter.

A few hours later Eban was on his way back to Israel. He carried with him a detailed report of some fifteen pages about his meeting with President Johnson, written by ambassador Harman. Eban had preferred not to cable Jerusalem about the outcome of the meeting. He knew how eagerly the Government was waiting, but thought that any message, however detailed, would leave too many questions open. He preferred to report in person. When he reached Tel Aviv on Saturday evening, 27 May, the cabinet had been in session for several hours the previous day. Those who strictly observed the Sabbath had been asked to spend the weekend in Tel Aviv to be on call for further emergency meetings. For it was generally assumed that the decision on war or peace might well be taken within the next twenty-four hours. There had been several false alarms; on 25 May it was generally believed that Nasser was about to attack Israel at once. Washington and Moscow decided on concerted action, and Johnson and Kosygin sent urgent messages to Cairo calling for restraint. The Soviet ambassador went to see the Egyptian leader during the early hours of 27 May, conveying Moscow's request that Egypt should not be the first to open fire.

Nasser was not the only one to have his night's rest interrupted. After yet another meeting with the military, Eshkol had retired, well after midnight, when the Soviet ambassador telephoned Aviad Yaffe, the Prime Minister's secretary and asked for an immediate interview. Yaffe stalled for a bit, but when Chuvakhin stressed that the matter was extremely urgent, Eshkol was wakened, put on jacket and trousers over his pyjamas, and at 2.40 in the morning the ambassador came in and handed over his note. The note was couched in comparatively moderate terms, but in substance accused Israel of collusion with imperialist powers and of aggressive designs against Syria and Egypt.

It warned Israel against any attack. It said in detail that 'according to the latest information reaching the Government of the USSR the tension on the borders of Israel, the UAR and Syria is mounting more and more, with the two sides increasing their forces and in Israel sharpening as though there was no alternative to acts of war. It would be a tremendous error if circles eager for battle, unrestrained by serious political thought, had the upper hand in such a situation, and arms were to begin talking ... We are convinced that however complicated the situation in the area of the borders of Israel, Syria and the UAR may be, it is necessary to find means to resolve the conflicts by non-military means, as it is easy to ignite a fire but putting out the flames may not be nearly as simple as those pushing Israel to the brink of war imagine.' (*Jerusalem Post*, 4 June 1967.) There was no reference in the note to the Arab threats which had caused the present crisis, nor was it made clear that a similar note was delivered at about the same time in Cairo.[18] People are usually not at their best when wakened from their sleep; Mr Eshkol, after studying the note, entered into a fruitless discussion with the ambassador. He said he was ready to fly to Moscow to explain the Israeli side of the conflict. Why was the Soviet Union so excessively helpful to Syria and so hostile to Israel? 'It is true that we are only a small nation,' Mr Eshkol is reported to have said 'but the contribution of our people to human civilisation is at least as substantial as that of Syria'[19] Chuvakhin, needless to say, had no instructions to discuss the Jewish contribution to world civilisation, nor was he empowered to invite the Prime Minister to Moscow. His only instruction was to deliver his note and to warn Israel. It was not the ideal moment for discussing the general nature of the conflict. Like some other Zionist leaders, Mr Eshkol assumed that Russia's hostile attitude to Israel was based at least in part on a misunderstanding that could be cleared up in direct talks. But was it? The Soviet leaders had firm views about the Middle East; they also had specific interests; no explanation by Eshkol or any other Israeli leader would make them revise their policy now. Chuvakhin took his leave; it was after 4 o'clock in the morning.

On Friday the cabinet had been in session for six hours. Saturday's meeting was unscheduled; it was also kept secret. Beginning in the afternoon, it was interrupted when Eban arrived; resumed at 11 p.m., it went on for another five hours. Eban reported in detail about his meetings in Paris, London and, above all, in Washington. As he had foreseen, there were many questions, and as the night wore on they became more searching and even acrimonious. What kind of action did the Americans contemplate? It had been suggested that an oil tanker flying say, a Liberian flag but carrying crude oil to Israel or a merchant ship flying the Israeli flag, should attempt the passage of the Tiran Straits. An international flotilla would escort the ship, and it was hoped that this show of stength would dissuade the Egyptians from interfering with it. These were not schemes that appealed to Eban's colleagues; how long would the flotilla stay around? What if Nasser preferred to play a waiting game, deciding to interfere with shipping not immediately, but, say, six months hence? The idea of sending a ship that did not fly the Israeli flag was rejected as an intolerable limitation of Israel's sovereign rights. Mr Eban had to provide answers to all these questions and objections as well as he could, assuming, as it were, part reponsibility for the various schemes, however half-baked, that had been advanced in Washington and other capitals. But the blockade had ceased to be the central issue; what about the military threat to Israel? Did America have any answer to that? Here, the Foreign Minister was not at his most convincing; to some of his listeners it never became quite clear whether this issue had been fully discussed in Washington. Mr Eban's speech is usually sophisticated, ornate, and at the same time, cautious, as befits an experienced diplomat. That night clear and straightforward answers were expected. But the situation was complicated and Eban's explanations failed to make it less so. His difficulties in communication were not made easier by the unmistakable fact that Eban belonged in any case to the doves in the Israeli cabinet. It was only natural that he should; it is the business of diplomats to work for peaceful solutions. They should not be expected to abdicate voluntarily, to declare that certain problems cannot be solved by diplomatic means. On 27 May Eban was against war for more than one reason: he thought that something might be achieved through diplomacy; he believed that since Israel had no naval force in the Gulf of Aqaba it could not engage in limited military action, but would have to attack in Sinai. This would be most unfortunate, for Israel

140

would again be branded the aggressor. Above all, he feared that an Israeli victory would be futile. The events of November 1956 had made an indelible impression on him; he was now reliving the experience of the Suez war.[20] At the time, Eban had been Israeli ambassador to Washington; no one had then bothered to tell him that Israel would go to war, and that he had to justify the attack with scarcely any preparation to a very angry administration. He remembered how Ben Gurion, faced with an American-Soviet ultimatum had decided on 7 November in less than three hours to give the order to retreat from all the positions newly occupied by the Israeli forces. A great effort had been made by the whole nation, soldiers had been killed – for what? Was not this likely to happen all over again? Israel would win the war, probably at much greater cost, and would in the end, again be compelled to retreat, giving up the fruits of victory.

Eban's arguments were rejected by the military, among whom there was growing distrust of the man and his politics. The intelligence chiefs disputed both Eban's reports and his recommendation to wait. According to their information, operation 'Regatta' was a non-starter; some even implied that Eban was misleading the Government. Brigadier Amit, the head of the Intelligence Services, left on a secret mission to Washington to find out for himself, and what he saw and heard was to confirm his suspicions. His report to the Government played an important part in the later stages of the debate on war or peace. There were acrimonious exchanges between Eban and the army chiefs, who argued that the world situation in 1967 was not the same as in 1956. While America would not help Israel, it would not do much either to discourage it from taking appropriate action. Above all, there would be no common American-Soviet front. Both America and Russia would stay out of the conflict. There was no danger of Soviet military intervention, contrary to what Eban and Levavi believed. They submitted a substantial body of evidence to strengthen their thesis. The struggle between Eban and the army was to go on and become even more bitter during the next few days. In a radio interview a few days later, the Foreign Minister went over to the attack: it was ridiculous to say, he claimed, that the Israeli people were not able if necessary to live with the tension over a period of time. It was a heavy burden, but they could shoulder it. Their qualities should not be underestimated. 'They are capable of the swift courage that strikes in time of need. They are also capable of what is, in a sense, the higher courage of a patient, tenacious effort so long as the patience is reasonable and so long as the tenacity is geared to a rational and specific purpose.'[21] But was it still geared to a rational purpose? A growing number of people were disputing this. After his return from America, Eban had given an off-the-record talk to a group of editors; after that meeting a signed article appeared in *Davar*, the paper controlled by Eban's own party Mapai, in which the writer, without mentioning any names, was sharply critical of Eban's policy: he said that it was natural for the powers to counsel moderation and patience; it was not natural for Israel to accept this advice. The *status quo ante* could be restored only if Nasser gave in all along the line, and this was not very likely to happen. No one would help Israel, unless Israel was willing to help herself. Above all, not the blockade was now the main danger, but the Egyptian troop concentrations.[22]

To return to Mr Eban's reporting on his mission to his colleagues. It was a long session, taking up again and again, Israeli military strength, America's policy, the possible Soviet reaction. At its conclusion, the cabinet had to decide for or against immediate military action. The military had had their say, so had Mr Eban; the American and Soviet notes counselling restraint had been received. Now it was up to the ministers to cast their vote. For some the choice was simple, for others agonising. Yigal Allon and his comrades of Ahdut Avoda, sharing the apprehension of the army command, were in favour of military action at once. War, in their view, was inevitable, any further delay would jeopardise the country's security and cost many victims. Most Mapai ministers were on the same side, including Eshkol. But Eshkol had not exerted all his powers to persuade the others to follow his lead. One minister said later that his impression was that Eshkol had not been too unhappy that the decision had gone against him. Nine were in favour of military action, nine were against. Among the opponents were Mapam, which had two representatives in the cabinet, the Independent Liberals, who had one minister and the religious bloc with three. The religious bloc leaders were afraid of the risk; Ben Gurion had advised them that military action was most dangerous; they also said they wanted a new Minister of Defence, and they continued to waver throughout the crisis. At one stage the military chiefs asked the army Chief Rabbi, Shlomo Goren, to reassure his friends of the religious bloc and give them fresh courage. Goren was given to understand that it would be a mission of historical importance if he succeeded in restoring their confidence. Mapai, too, was divided – three of their ministers, Abba Eban, Salman Aran and Pinhas Sapir (Minister of Finance) opposed military action. Nine were still in favour and nine against: stalemate and further waiting.

After the war, some of those who had voted against asserted that they had not opposed military action in principle, but believed that the right conditions for successful military action did not yet exist. Others said that they were not in favour of waiting indefinitely, but they were not ready to go to war unless there was a broader, national government and a new Minister of Defence. These considerations, no doubt, played an important part, but the differences were not merely tactical. Some ministers were full of confidence, others had doubts, and a few expected the worst. There was even doubt in the ability of the army; recalling later the atmosphere of those days, one minister talked about confusion and panic in the ranks of the Mapai leadership: 'Even some of our best people were not immune.'[23]

A personal letter from President Johnson to Eshkol played a decisive role at this juncture. Eshkol later said that he had regarded the vote of Saturday night as a trial vote: 'I know that if I would have pressed them I would have received the support of the majority ... had I banged the table and insisted no one would have resigned from the government. I did not do that and this could be quoted in evidence against me. But I don't regret it ... ' (interview in *Ma'ariv*, 4 October 1967). He said he did not want to have a final decision until all the issues involved had been fully discussed. During the night he decided to tell the cabinet the next day that the die had been cast. Yet at this very moment the Johnson cable reached him in his suite in the Dan hotel. The President emphatically advised Israel not to take military action; an accompanying note by Dean Rusk was said to be even stronger mentioning the catastrophic consequences such action could have. Johnson quoted a cable he had received from Kosygin that Russia would come to the help of the Arabs if they were attacked. But according to Eshkol it was not the Soviet warning which induced the cabinet to vote in favour of a further waiting period. (A similar note had been handed to the Israeli ambassador in Moscow four days earlier.) Eshkol says: 'When the Johnson letter arrived I said to myself I must not give him a pretext to say later on – " I told you so".' The cabinet met again on Sunday afternoon and discussed the American note. The great majority, some reluctantly, now favoured to wait; the one minister who rejected any further delay was Moshe Carmel.*

Sunday, 28 May was a black day for Levi Eshkol, who had to tell the army chiefs that the Government could not make up its mind whether to go to war or not, he also had to prepare a brief statement to the nation. For several days now there had been growing impatience among the public; all they knew was that the Government was almost permanently in session. Everyone expected an announcement. The man in the street knew little about the political and military considerations involved. He certainly was not aware at the time that Eshkol himself was in favour of military action but had been outvoted by his colleagues. All he knew was that his country was threatened with extinction and his Government kept on talking instead of making a decision. There was a breakdown in communication between the leadership and the people which, within a few days, created a real crisis of confidence. The first demands for broadening the Government, for appointing new ministers, and even for replacing Mr Eshkol, were made on 25 May. As the result of the events of 28 May, above all Eshkol's radio address that day, and his disastrous talk with the generals, the demand for Government changes became irresistible.

Eshkol's broadcast, live over *Kol Israel* on Sunday evening, was one of the turning points in the crisis. Studied in cold print, after the event, it is not easy to understand what agitated people

* The dramatic events of 27 and 28 May will probably remain for a long time a bone of contention between 'hawks' and 'doves'. Eshkol has given a detailed and on the whole convincing description of the events and the considerations that influenced him and the other ministers (*Ma'ariv*, 4 October 1967). A different interpretation from the army point of view, critical of Eshkol, and even more of Eban, has been provided by Ze'ev Shiff (*Ha'aretz*, 4 October 1967). Eban and other key figures will, no doubt, provide their versions in due course. All these accounts ought to be studied with critical sympathy; the motives involved were complex, there is a great temptation to rationalise them after the event.

so much, why it spread so great a degree of despondency and made them call for a new leadership. It was a brief and sober statement: the Government at its recent meetings had adopted several resolutions; it realised that the danger facing Israel continued unabated, and so long as the danger existed it was necessary to maintain military preparedness: 'The Government notes with satisfaction the valiant spirit of the people and the Israeli defence forces ... The Government of Israel expresses the opinion that the closing of the Tiran Straits to Israeli shipping is tantamount to an act of aggression against Israel. We shall defend ourselves against this in the hour of need, in virtue of the right of self-defence to which every state is entitled.' Eshkol also announced that the cabinet had heard Abba Eban's report: 'The Government has laid down guiding principles for the continuation of its political activities in the international sphere. These are designed to induce the international factors to adopt effective measures to safeguard the freedom of international shipping in the Tiran Straits. Lines of action have also been adopted for the removal of military considerations from Israel's southern border and for action to safeguard our sovereign rights, our security along our frontiers and for the prevention of aggression. The Government declares that the Israeli defence forces are strong enough to defeat any aggressor and to ensure Israel's sovereign rights. Tomorrow I shall have an opportunity to explain the Government's position in a speech before the plenary session of the Knesset.' And that was all.

Eshkol's policy during the *Konenut* period has been severely criticised and he, personally, much maligned; his political enemies have charged him with all the sins in the calendar – hesitation, lack of initiative and of leadership, the inability to take a decision. Some of this is factually untrue, other accusations are exaggerated. But neither his personality nor his style were a source of inspiration in a time of national crisis. Eshkol had much experience in economics and party politics; but the public called now for Churchillian gestures and speeches, for 'We shall not flag or fail' and 'blood, toil, tears, and sweat'. Instead of summoning his countrymen to fight and never surrender, instead of words of comfort about broader lands and better days ahead, Eshkol talked about 'international factors' and forthcoming speeches in the Knesset. Above all, the delivery was lamentable; Eshkol had apparently mislaid his glasses; he had to interrupt his speech several times and there were interjections which would have spoiled even one of Churchill's great speeches. Israel is a nation of passionate radio listeners; there is no television and on that particular evening hardly any one in the country had not turned on his receiver. The situation was grave; the headlines in the morning newspapers had reported a further deterioration. There was great uneasiness and a great desire for reassurance. Instead of encouragement, Israelis were treated to a speech whose very delivery seemed to symbolise the weakness and uncertainty of the Government. A reader's letter in next morning's *Ha'aretz* asked: 'The Prime Minister's speech last night was painful, perhaps he'll understand now that the burden is too heavy for him and he'll pass it on to someone else?'[24]

Eshkol had his defenders, one of them argued that a great leader was not necessarily a brilliant orator and vice versa; did not the Bible say that Israel's very first leader, Moses, stammered badly?[25] But, as far as public confidence was concerned, the damage had been done, more and more people talked the next day about the 'failing government', 'Munich' 'Neville Chamberlain'. Two days later Mr Eban's press conference was broadcast. Again there were ambiguities: 'Although there is of course some danger in action, there is also danger in inaction.' When asked whether Israel had set itself a deadline as to the reopening of the Straits, the Foreign Minister stalled: 'Well, if I said a limited period, instead of days or weeks it is really not because of a deficiency of vocabulary. This lack of definition is to some extent inherent in our position ... ' Eban, like everyone else, was overworked; the broadcast left an unfortunate impression on many listeners.

On 28 May, the day of his radio address, Eshkol summoned the generals to army headquarters for a heart-to-heart talk. He brought them bad news; he had to inform them that the cabinet had decided in favour of waiting. Explaining its position was not made any easier by the fact that he himself had been in favour of military action. Eshkol said at the outset that he welcomed the opportunity to meet all of them and to listen to their views; so far he had usually seen the Chief of Staff alone or with a few aides. But Eshkol hardly gave them an opportunity to have their say; he talked at great length and not always convincingly. Yigal

Allon, who was also present, felt embarrassed but did not interrupt the Prime Minister. Eshkol said that he could not accept the argument that the army had to attack immediately. The military would have to get accustomed to the idea that political considerations had to be taken into account. (Abba Eban had said at another meeting that of course they could wait a fortnight, or more if necessary. After all, during the Second World War as a British officer he had waited in the Western desert for nine months.) The generals listened to the Prime Minister with sinking hearts; Israel had a first class army, but the best army in the world was ineffective if its hands were tied by a government that was not up to its job. Someone later said: our main enemy is not Nasser, but the Second Aliyah – the generation of men who had reached Palestine before 1914 and still dominated Israeli politics. In many ways this was a clash not only between two concepts but between two generations; the six-day war was the swan song of the old generation of Zionist leaders: the names of Ben Gurion and Nahum Goldman were only seldom mentioned, those of Eshkol and Golda Meir often with bitterness. The people obviously wanted a leader who did not belong to the second or third Aliyah.

The generals had several complaints. It was difficult to sit and wait in the desert for very long. The mood of the army would deteriorate rapidly. There had been conflicting orders; many units had already prepared for an offensive, but at the last moment the orders had been revoked. It was impossible to keep the fighting spirit high in such conditions. At one place parachutists had refused to leave the aircraft after the third or fourth false alarm. Soldiers could not be kept in a state of tension indefinitely. There were individual cases of desertion. But, the psychological factor quite apart, the generals tried to impress on Eshkol that to wait was dangerous from a military point of view. Nasser's order of battle was offensive, not defensive. War was inevitable, but each additional day that passed would cost many additional victims – some said 200, others gave higher figures. The Egyptians would be able to dig in, the element of surprise would be completely lost. The generals clearly overrated the strength of the enemy, but then a good general usually does. It was most dangerous, they argued, to wait for the intervention of the powers; even if it came it would fatally affect Israeli credibility in Arab eyes and it would invite further Arab pressure. It was equally unacceptable to send Israeli ships through the Gulf of Aqaba under foreign protection. Nasser had thrown down the gauntlet; the challenge had to be accepted. The issue at stake was not Tiran but Israel's existence.[26] Yet Eshkol remained adamant, there was no meeting of minds and after bitter exchanges the generals left the meeting with heavy hearts and dire forebodings. Their dissatisfaction continued to grow during the next few days and there were even rumours about an impending 'march on Jerusalem' and a military coup. But Israel was not Egypt or Syria; the colonels had no ambitions to rule, nor did they want to play party politics. To make quite certain, care had been taken after Ben Gurion's resignation to appoint a Chief of Staff who was not one of his sympathisers. There was no military conspiracy; it is difficult to know what would have happened if the Government had waited many more weeks. Israel is a small country and news of Eshkol's meeting with the generals soon became known to hundreds of people. It gave fresh impetus to those who demanded a new government. We now reach the 'crisis within a crisis', the domestic conflict which had begun the week before and which led eventually, on 1 June, to the establishment of a national government. At first, there was just talk among politicians and in the streets. Then, large advertisements appeared in newspapers: 'For a national government', 'The failing government must be replaced', 'Let Ben Gurion and Eshkol meet', and these were backed up by readers' letters. This was an innovation; letters published in the Israeli press usually deal with such topics as the postal service or the shortcomings of public transport. Now there were letters with headlines such as 'Chamberlain is still remembered', or 'Make Ben Gurion Prime Minister'. It became the main topic of conversation and signatures were collected for various appeals and manifestoes. Eventually there were even some demonstrations – all this quite unprecedented in a country where political activity had always been the monopoly of party caucuses and secretariats. Eshkol's supporters later claimed that it was a calculated attempt by opposition leaders to sow confusion among the public, to turn the people against its elected leaders, to make political capital out of a grave national crisis. Eshkol's critics said that it was a spontaneous movement and that the Government had no one to blame but itself. The truth, for once, was in the middle: the 'movement' was partly spontaneous, partly organised; the Government's inability to inspire the public with confidence certainly aggravated the crisis. Mr Eban could well argue that he and thousands of other British soldiers waited in the desert for many months. But Jews, he should have known, are more excitable people than the British; nor was the political and military situation comparable. After the war, expert foreign observers argued that Israel's existence was never in danger, and that the Israeli Government, knowing its military strength, never felt that the country was threatened with destruction.[27] The advantages of hindsight are considerable.

During that week of domestic crisis the party leaders displayed feverish activity. Everyone met everyone else and not just once; there were countless proposals and initiatives to broaden the Government. It is nearly impossible to retrace all these moves in detail; nor would it be of great relevance to do so for most suggestions and solutions were discarded after a few hours. The situation changed several times daily. Eshkol had already decided on 23 May to bring in the leaders of the opposition for consultation, but many politicians, both within the Government and outside it, thought that this was not sufficient. Begin, the Herut leader, asked Shimon Peres whether Ben Gurion would be willing to be Prime Minister again with Eshkol as his deputy. Begin and Ben Gurion had been personal enemies, not merely political foes, for many years for reasons well known to all students of Israeli history; but this, Begin realised, was the time to bury the hatchet. Ben Gurion's answer was affirmative, but Begin in meetings with Eshkol and other coalition leaders realised that the scheme was unworkable; these two old war horses would never draw together in one harness (as Eshkol put it). Ben Gurion was keeping up his violent attacks on his former party comrades; the whole idea was hopeless. Moshe Shapira, leader of the National Religious bloc, another key figure in the negotiations behind the scenes, tried a different approach: what if Ben Gurion became Minister of Defence and head of a war council composed of Allon, Dayan, Yadin and Laskov (the latter three former Chiefs of Staff). It was to no avail, Shapira then submitted a proposal for broadening the coalition by bringing both Gahal and Rafi into the Government; Dayan's name was immediately suggested as an obvious choice for the Ministry of Defence. Moshe Dayan, like Allon a native born Israeli, was at 52 one of Israel's most distinguished, and certainly most colourful, political and military figures. Like Allon he had entered politics after leaving the army. Not all his schemes had been brilliant, but he had not been unsuccessful as Minister of Agriculture. He left Mapai to follow Ben Gurion, though with some hesitation. In the eyes of the public he was a man of exceptional fighting spirit and great personal charm – the 'victor of Sinai'. Those who had known him from a closer angle and had worked with him were divided in their opinion, political considerations quite apart. No one doubted his courage, his determination, his intellectual gifts; but there were many who said that he was basically a lone wolf, who had difficulty in working in a team, that he lacked inner harmony and discipline; his political wisdom was not always above suspicion. Some saw him as a potential dictator, perhaps as an Israeli de Gaulle; they had difficulty in envisaging him working under Eshkol. When the crisis broke, Dayan offered Eshkol his services as an army commander under Rabin; he would not be interested, he said, in accepting a political appointment without any clearly defined responsibility. (At one stage it had been suggested that he should become Deputy Prime Minister, another of the many suggestions made in those days.)[28]

Mapai's old guard did not like the idea of Dayan's appointment; Ahdut Avoda and Mapam were even less enthusiastic. The Mapai secretariat met on 25 May and reaffirmed its confidence in Eshkol's leadership. Rafi had suggested that party political differences should be forgotten at this time of national crisis; its members were willing to rejoin the party from which they had seceded several years before. This was very gratifying for Mapai, but would not profound political and personal differences make close cooperation virtually impossible? Wasn't the present leadership perfectly able to cope with the situation? Wasn't the army strong enough to defeat the Egyptians, the Syrians, and all other comers in the Arab world? This, at any rate, was Golda Meir's view; nearly seventy and in indifferent health for many years, she was still one of the main pillars of Mapai and a central figure in the struggle. 'We need no partners for victory,' Mrs Meir is reported to have said; and her confidence was justified –

Israel would have won the war without Dayan, Begin, and the other minister who joined the cabinet on 1 June. But, like Eshkol, she ignored the importance of psychological factors and of the popular image of the Government; and she also overrated the toughness of her own colleagues. Many of them had gradually been persuaded that Eshkol had to be replaced as Minister of Defence. Certain sections of Mapai had long been advocating reunion with Rafi – the influential Haifa branch for instance, and some of the Mapai Kibbutzim. As events during the next few days were to show, some of Eshkol's oldest and closest political friends, too, had lost faith in him.

The movement for a national government was contradictory in character: partly it was born out of a sincere belief that in that hour of crisis all party differences should be forgotten and that the best men in the country should form a new government irrespective of party affiliation and past quarrels; partly it was the result of a sudden wave of emotion which, though short of panic or mass hysteria, was certainly deeply irrational, reflecting an almost mystical belief that only the 'victor of Sinai' could save Israel. It was by no means a straightforward clash between 'hawks' and 'doves'. Among Dayan's main backers were prominent 'doves', such as the leaders of the National Religious bloc. Eshkol, on the other hand, had been in favour of military action, and his chief support came from leading 'hawks' such as Golda Meir, Yigal Allon, and the Ahdut Avoda. All this made the issue very confused. Partly the strange line-up can be explained in terms of the complicated relations between the various Israeli parties and political leaders in the past. But even this does not provide entirely satisfactory answers. What made Shapira and other religious leaders who had voted in the cabinet against military action support Dayan, who, as everyone knew, was a leading 'hawk'? Eshkol asked the question at a cabinet meeting on 27 May. Shapira's answer, though somewhat disingenuous, was no doubt sincere: we trust Dayan's judgment more than yours. They were willing to be persuaded (or to be bullied or cajoled) by Dayan into a course of action they had just rejected. They were willing to cause the downfall of the Government in order to bring in a man in whom they had confidence even though this man advocated a policy about which they had grave doubts. All this, in retrospect, seems difficult to understand;

once the decision to make war is made the military machine takes over and operations are carried out according to plans prepared long in advance. At that stage the decisive word is spoken by the tank brigades and the fighter planes; the personality of the Prime Minister and the Minister of Defence is for a while almost irrelevant. But these are rational considerations; people under stress make their decisions not only on the basis of cold calculations – they need psychological reassurance and a symbol. Dayan was a symbol of military strength and confidence, Eshkol was not. It was easier for the Pentagon with its giant computers to be fully convinced of Israel's victory than for some of those nearer to the scene.

The struggle for a national government continued during the last four days of May. Again there were countless meetings; the Gahal leaders met in Ben Gurion's house and decided that Gahal would join the Government only if Rafi did; Rafi made its entry dependent on Gahal's. Both were firmly resolved to accept nothing less than Dayan's appointment as Minister of Defence. Shapira also made it known that his party would leave the Government unless it became an all-party coalition. Above all, there was a showdown inside Mapai. Late in the evening of 30 May, the Mapai and Ahdut Avoda parliamentary caucus met in the Knesset; Eshkol arrived in a good mood after a full and tiring working day. He was quite unprepared for the scenes that were to follow. One speaker after another mounted the rostrum to demand that Eshkol should resign as Minister of Defence. Some were more emphatic than others, but all agreed that morale was low and could only be restored by the appointment of Dayan or Allon. The people were confused, it was said; the man in the street was getting more and more angry about the hesitation shown by the Government; there was a danger that within a day or two there would be street demonstrations. One after another Eshkol's old comrades came out in favour of a new Minister of Defence: David Hacohen, Kaddish Luz, Reuben Barkat, Akiba Gubrin, Devora Nezer, Moshe Baram, and they spoke in the name of many others who were not members of the Knesset. Eshkol got restive: when they had elected him almost four years before had they not envisaged that one day there might be a major crisis? What had he done wrong? Had he not in the cabinet been on the side of the angels? If there was hesitation, was it not the fault of those who now so urgently desired a national government? Eshkol might have committed mistakes, his public relations had been lamentable, but had his record as Prime Minister in the field of Defence and Foreign Affairs really been all that negative? Not one of his old friends spoke up for him. Eshkol was a very lonely man that evening; he left the meeting in a black mood well after midnight. The idea of resigning occurred to him more than once that evening and during the following days.

The choice was now between Dayan and Yigal Allon. Comparisons are invidious; in this case it is almost impossible to say who was the better candidate. Both had considerable military experience, both were on excellent terms with the army command. Dayan was more flamboyant, more in the public eye; but after a few days in office the public would have been equally accustomed to Allon. Dayan was preferred; partly no doubt because he was thought to be less of a party politician than Allon, less compromised by the record of the Eshkol government. Gahal and the National Religious bloc preferred him to Allon, whom they thought too much of a left-wing doctrinaire. Moreover, Dayan's military experience was more recent than Allon's; he had been Chief of Staff in 1956; his name was better known outside Israel and it would have a tremendous impact in the Arab world. Eshkol and Golda Meir favoured Allon's candidacy; the Mapai secretariat met almost uninterruptedly for three days. During the meeting of 1 June there was a demonstration of Tel Aviv housewives ('women and mothers for national unity'), apparently organised by Rafi in Hayarkon Street under the window of Mrs Meir's office: they were shouting 'We want Dayan'. Estimates put their number at seventy-five, a hundred, or slightly higher. (The Israeli beauty queen was said to be among them.) It emerged that a majority in the Mapai secretariat favoured Dayan, and that several Mapai ministers might secede and make common cause with Rafi and Gahal to establish a new government. In the circumstances, Allon withdrew his candidacy, saying that the discussions must end, they were distracting the public from the war effort and weakening its preparedness.'[29] At 7 p.m. Eshkol informed Rafi that Mapai wanted Dayan as Minister of Defence. Rafi went into session at Ben Gurion's home, to announce after a little while that it accepted the offer.

153

Ben Gurion said that though he had not changed his view of the Government he favoured Dayan's entrance because of the grave crisis. Gahal announced that two of its members would also join the coalition: Menahem Begin, and another to be named the following day. Golda Meir declined to join the cabinet as Minister without Portfolio. A week of bitter recriminations ended in a sudden wave of good will and mutual congratulations. Eshkol praised Allon's gesture as an expression of profound national responsibility, and called Begin 'a true patriot'. The Mapai secretariat, which had almost unanimously opposed Eshkol, now warmly applauded the Prime Minister in a gesture unprecedented in the annals of that austere body. In fact more than a little bitterness was left; the wounds opened during that week would not heal soon.

But this was not the time for nursing personal grudges and settling party political accounts. The new cabinet met at a late hour the same evening. Eshkol welcomed the new ministers: 'I am certain that national unity will be received with sympathy throughout the nation and by the diaspora ... ' Dayan, wearing khaki but without his general's insignia, replied briefly: he was grateful for the trust put in him; he was assuming a heavy burden and would do his best to justify the faith put in him. News was just coming in that the Security Council had adjourned, and was unlikely to accept any resolution on the Middle East crisis. De Gaulle had repeated that France would be actively neutral. More Iraqi troops were on their way to Jordan. There were three more days of uneasy peace to come.

The news of Dayan's appointment spread like wildfire and public relief was immense. It was not merely that the new Government had a majority of 112 out of the 120 Knesset members; confidence in the leadership had been restored; 'At last', people said that evening and toasted each other. Bonfires were lit in the army camps, and the soldiers sang Yerushalayim shel sahav, ve nechoshet ve shel or (Jerusalem the Golden ...), the song which had been heard for the first time at the Annual Song Festival on 16 May, and which was to become within a few weeks both the hymn of Jerusalem, and the 'Tipperary' and Lilli Marlene' of the six-day war. Party politics were not entirely forgotten; Lamerhav attacked Dayan for criticising the Government after his appointment; a Mapam leader, writing in

Ma'ariv, complained about Dayan's boastful statements. But for the man in the street, and especially for the soldier, this appointment symbolised the new spirit that was to prevail; now, at last things were bound to happen.

They were going to happen indeed. Dayan did not lose much time; he had been briefed by the general staff well before his appointment. On the very day he became Minister of Defence, General Bar Lev, who was to succeed Rabin after the war, became Deputy Chief of Staff; General Zur, a former chief of staff and a Rafi supporter, was brought in as special assistant to Dayan. Eshkol asked Dayan not to chop off too many heads in his Ministry, or at least to make changes gradually. But Dayan was clearly in a hurry; Dr Dinstein, the Deputy Minister, left office within a few days. Almost immediately after the war controversy started as to what extent Dayan had really helped to win the war. Had he simply been the man in the limelight, stealing the show from Rabin by his greater flair for public relations? Was the decision to attack already taken when Dayan was co-opted as Minister of Defence, or was it he who pushed it through? There is no unambiguous answer. After Hussain's visit to Cairo and the pact between Egypt and Jordan, most members of the cabinet reached the conclusion that war was inevitable. There was no formal decision, but it would have been taken, in all probability, even if Dayan had not joined the cabinet. Rabin was not in the best of health on the eve of the war and Dayan therefore played a decisive role; the main decisions were his. The efficiency of the army had been brought under Rabin to such a high level, that the personality of the commander-in-chief was not crucial; the war would have been won by any Israeli general. But there was the psychological factor, incalculable and yet of the greatest significance. Morale had been low; it was immediately restored as the result of Dayan's appointment.

There was a fresh wave of volunteering: reservists stationed in the Negev were lending a hand with the harvest; twenty-five residents of Nazareth, headed by the Arab mayor, went to dig fortifications in a nearby Kibbutz; thousands contributed part of their wages; the inmates and wardens of Ramleh Central prison donated blood. It was announced that income tax would go up by 10 per cent for the rest of the fiscal year, capital gains tax from 25 per cent to 30 per cent. Four weeks earlier there would have been a great outcry; now everyone accepted it as the most natural thing in the world. The only question when people met, was 'when?' Civil defence workers were told to be in a state of full preparedness; it was generally assumed that the Arab air force would concentrate on civilian targets. Brigadier Haim Herzog had emerged during these days as chief military commentator; he devoted his radio talk on 1 June to this subject: 'Some civilians imagine an air raid on Israel would resemble the blitz of the Second World War, when hundreds of German aircraft bombed British cities and thousands of British and American aircraft bombed German cities. But I want to state one fact – a fact and not an estimate: in view of the present strength of the Arab air forces in this region, there is no possibility whatsoever of a blitz.' General Herzog's broadcasts were later remembered as one of the main features of those days, almost like 'Jerusalem the Golden'. He openly discussed the military threat facing the country, he did not hide the dangers. The man in the street felt that he was being treated like an adult, taken into the confidence by the army command. On that evening, however, Herzog could not help but conclude his broadcast for the first time with what seemed a little boasting: 'Knowing the facts, I can say that if I had a choice between sitting in an Egyptian aircraft sent to bomb Tel Aviv and sitting in a house in Tel Aviv, then I would prefer for the good of my health to sit in Tel Aviv.'

On Friday night Yigal Allon, in uniform, appeared at a mass meeting in the Habima theatre in Tel Aviv. War was inevitable he said, unless the Gulf of Aqaba was reopened for Israeli shipping, unless there was mutual de-escalation of the forces massed on Israel's frontiers, and unless there was a clear undertaking to stop guerrilla raids. Allon could not tell his listeners that he knew there would be war within three or four days. But he did say: 'There is not the slightest doubt about the outcome of this war, and of each of its stages, and we are not forgetting the Jordanian and the Syrian fronts either.'[30] The next day was the Sabbath; tens of thousands went to the beaches and swimming pools over the weekend; the cinemas again reported full houses. Many soldiers had been given leave; some later said that it was a trick, designed to deceive the enemy; it was Dayan's idea; he had also told several foreign correspondents that nothing of great importance was likely to happen in the next few weeks. On Saturday

Dayan, again dressed in uniform but without insignia, faced batteries of TV cameras and some 300 correspondents in a jovial mood. He preferred a diplomatic solution, he said, but this now seemed doubtful. Diplomatic activity alone would hardly induce the Egyptians to reduce the number of their troops in Sinai, nor would they reopen the Straits of Tiran. But it would be up to the Government to decide whether to take action, and when. Dayan was unhurried, very relaxed: 'We are not a nation of stop-watchers. I do not anticipate any major changes in a month, two months or six months, but I think we can win.' It was too early for him to say anything about the Government's policy; consultations had not yet started; he had not even been sworn in as a minister: 'Whatever can be done in the diplomatic way I would welcome and encourage, but if nevertheless it comes to real fighting I would not like American or British boys to be killed here, and I do not think we need them.' Dayan shared the general feeling that should there be a conflict, it would be costly in terms of casualties. He recalled that British and French troops had fought during the later stages of the Sinai campaign, and that there would be no British planes to bomb Egyptian airfields this time. 'Someone will have to pay.' He was also asked whether he thought that in the event of war the Egyptians would use long distance missiles. He replied in one word: She'yenasu (let them try).[31] It was a remarkable performance. On the same day General Rabin visited military units on the Jerusalem front; he welcomed the suggestion that soldiers should be permitted to receive their children from time to time in their camps. It would be good for the children and it would boost the morale among the reservists.

The cabinet meanwhile continued in session. On Saturday evening Dayan reported on the military preparations. The army had plans for all contingencies, but final decisions had to be made. Dayan was convinced that the Straits of Tiran could not be reopened short of occupying the whole Sinai peninsula. At the same time the army command felt that no decisive result could be attained unless the core of the Egyptian forces massed in Sinai were destroyed. Accordingly, Israeli units in the south were regrouped for a three-pronged attack: against Khan Yunis – Rafah, in the direction of Abu Ageila, and lastly across the sand-dunes in the general direction of Jebel Libni – Bir Lahfan –

Abu Ageila. It was decided to stage for the time being a holding operation against the Syrians in the north, and not to attack Jordan unless Jordan attacked first. It was expected that the Jordanians would at most stage a local attack as a show of solidarity with Nasser. This was to be repelled by the Jerusalem command with its own forces. The main blow was to be directed against the Egyptians.

On Sunday 4 June the cabinet approved these plans. There was no formal vote: the Prime Minister and the Minister of Defence were from now on entitled to give the order to attack at any time they chose, at the slightest Egyptian provocation. By now all ministers had reached the conclusion, some of them reluctantly, that war was inevitable, and that any further waiting would tip the balance against Israel. Eban, as he later said, became a hawk around 1 June; the other ministers came around at the same time. The Mapam ministers wanted to consult their party colleagues; later on they made their approval of military action retroactive.[31a] The declarations of the Arab leaders had become more and more menacing: they were now talking about an immediate invasion: 'Meet you in Tel Aviv ... ' There were not only verbal threats: Egyptian planes had repeatedly violated Israeli airspace in the previous few days, Egyptian patrols had crossed into Israeli territory, settlements in the south had been shelled. More threatening still, the Jordanian troops had been put under the command of the Egyptian General Riadh. An Iraqi division with more than 150 tanks began to cross the Jordan into the West Bank on Sunday. It was clear that Johnson's plan for an international flotilla had come to nothing; no effective action would be taken by the United States or any other power. Israel was on its own.

The cabinet had moved its seat a few days previously from Jerusalem to Tel Aviv to make it easier for Eshkol to be in constant touch with the War Room at army headquarters. As the ministers left the meeting on Sunday they felt that a momentous decision had been taken: the fate of the state of Israel was now in the hands of the army. They were aware of the risks. More anxious hours of waiting were ahead, but the intolerable tension of the last two weeks had been even worse: the waiting, the confusion, the vain hope that the powers or the UN would intervene. They had tried to end the conflict by diplomatic means; it was now clear, beyond any shadow of doubt, that such a solution was not feasible. As they saw it, it was not quite certain whether Nasser and the other Arab countries would attack immediately or whether they would prefer to strangle Israel by stages. Neither prospect appealed to them; they were unwilling to wait any longer.

The swiftness of Israel's subsequent victory distorts, in a way, the historical perspective; it certainly makes it difficult to re-create and to understand the agony of the days before. Since Israel won so easily, since there were relatively few victims, and hardly any among the civilian population, everyone must have been very confident of victory. Confident of victory they were, but at what price? An eyewitness, an English immigrant, wrote about these days:

On 3 June, 1967, I put my chances of survival, optimistically, at 50:50. I had already said goodbye to my parents in England, written my last letters, and was wondering whether I could get my vet to put my pet to sleep (I didn't). The chances were that I would be bombed, shelled, burned, gassed or shot to death. I work in the port area; the school where I teach had no adequate air-raid shelters, and the post office where I do voluntary work is a fire-trap at the best of times. No town could be more of a 'sitting duck' target than Haifa.[32]

The ministers took a more optimistic view of their, and their country's chance of survival. But they, too, believed on 3 June that there would be heavy losses; most of them had sons and daughters in the army; the home of everyone was within reach of heavy Arab guns. The Arabs assumed it would be a walkover; no Israeli thought so.

The army and the air force of 4 June were making their last preparations: as usual there were some snags: not enough small arms were available for the armoured divisions, there was some muddle with transport. Above all, the morning mist over the Nile and the Suez Canal, which would vitally affect the airstrike, caused the planners some difficulties; last minute adjustments were necessary.

Next morning shortly after seven the planes took off from the airfields and at 8.15 a.m. H.Q. Southern Command gave the order of attack to the ground forces.

5

The Impotence of Power

The big powers played a secondary role in a crisis in which the limits of their influence on small countries were clearly demonstrated. It is fashionable to blame diplomats for crises, but given the nature of the conflict, the commitments and the opposed interests of the powers (which coincided only in one point – to prevent a direct confrontation), and the impotence of the United Nations, it is difficult even in retrospect, to suggest alternative policies to prevent war once Nasser had concentrated troops in Sinai and closed the Straits of Tiran. For Syria's actions and Nasser's initial decision the Soviet Union bears a large part of the responsibility. But its intention was not, as many believed during the early days of the crisis, to create a 'second front' in the Middle East. It was, in all probability, more modest in character: to deter Israel, to help Syria in its predicament. Neither Washington nor Moscow thought the conflict would lead to war. When Richard Nolte, the new American ambassador, arrived at Cairo airport on 21 May, and was asked by waiting newspapermen about his thoughts on the crisis he is reported to have exclaimed: 'What crisis?'[1]

The keys to the crisis were in Cairo, Damascus, and Jerusalem; the policies of the powers are of relevance only in so far as they encouraged or inhibited the Arab governments and Israel. The extent of the Soviet commitment to assist Syria and Egypt, and of the American commitment to help Israel if attacked, will remain in doubt for a long time; partly because these were secret undertakings, partly because they were elusive: it is doubtful whether they were ever explicitly discussed and formulated in detail. In Israel the exact nature of the American commitment was heatedly debated for ten days: it was open to various interpretations, and no one was quite sure which was the most authentic. Subsequently it appeared that the Soviet commitment to the Arabs was not clear either; Nasser and the Syrians

160

acted as if they had no doubts, but after the war many Arabs were hurt and disappointed claiming that they had hoped for more substantial Soviet help. The Soviet Union had provided the Arabs with the tools for making war, they had also committed themselves to prevent intervention by any western country on the side of Israel. Many Arabs thought there were Soviet promises beyond these two basic points. Probably this was wishful thinking: there is no good reason to believe the Soviets committed themselves unilaterally or that the Arabs asked them to do so: 'The Arabs were too confident of winning without direct Soviet intervention as long as the Soviets could give them a guarantee against intervention by the United States or any other western power.'[2] America's commitment to Israel was even less clear; hardly anyone in the administration remembered the various promises made in the nineteen-fifties. When Foreign Minister Eban, during his visit to Washington, reminded his hosts of an undertaking made on behalf of the American Government by Mr Dulles ten years earlier, he met with blank stares followed by a good deal of urgent telephoning between the State Department and the office of President Eisenhower: 'The decision making machinery in Washington was busy making decisions unaware of a fundamental decision made ten years ago.'[3]

The first American comment on the crisis was made on 16 May, by a State Department press officer and by Arthur Goldberg in the Security Council: there was cause for concern about the overall Middle East situation. America was urging restraint on all parties, hoping that these efforts would be met with a constructive response. There was not much encouragement for such hopes when the Syrian *chargé d'affaires* met Lucius Battle, Assistant Secretary of State for Near Eastern Affairs. Mr Toumeh denied any complicity on the part of his government in the Arab guerrilla activities, it was impossible, and not incumbent on Syria, to control their activities or to protect the demarcation lines. Mr Toumeh passed immediately to the offensive: the CIA was directing and financing the present crisis; a new Suez was in the offing. U Thant's decision to withdraw UNEF was regarded by the administration as an act of folly; comment in Congress and Senate was even more outspoken: 'A shocking development', 'capitulation'. An emergency session of the Security Council was first mooted. Goldberg told reporters that the

United States would avoid interfering with U Thant's mission to Cairo but considered the Security Council primarily responsible for peacemaking. There were exchanges between Washington and Moscow about the Middle East situation from 19 May, each assuring the other of their desire to preserve peace in the area. It does not seem that any constructive measure was suggested; perhaps these exchanges were thought necessary in view of the movements of the Eastern Mediterranean task force of the Sixth Fleet, and the gradual Soviet naval build up in the Mediterranean (NATO forces were put on alert only on 26 May). On 21 May, Egypt and Israel called up reserves and alarm was reported for the first time in the Cairo diplomatic community. On the next day Nasser proclaimed the closure of the Straits of Tiran; Washington commented on the 'grave danger to peace'. The White House press secretary announced that America was committed to the principle of maintaining peace in the Middle East.[4] On the same day, however, both Britain and France declared that they relied on the UN to preserve the peace. They no longer felt themselves bound by the Tripartite Declaration of 1950 under which the United States, Britain, and France undertook to prevent changes by force on Israel's borders. There was considerable indecision in Washington about the exact nature of the US commitment to Israel. President Eisenhower was called after Nasser closed the Straits and asked for details about the commitment he made in 1957.* He is said to have answered that it was a commitment of honour for the United States Government to live up to his assurance to former Prime Minister Ben Gurion that the Straits would be kept open.[5] As a result President Johnson declared the next day that the blockade was illegal and

---

* The aide memoire by Secretary of State Dulles (dated 11 February 1957) to the Israeli Government had this to say about the Gulf of Aqaba: 'with respect to the Gulf of Aqaba and access thereto, the USA believes that the Gulf constitutes international waters and that no nation has the right to prevent free and innocent passage in the Gulf and through the Straits giving access thereto ... In the absence of some overruling decision to the contrary, e.g. by the International Court of Justice, the United States, on behalf of vessels of US registry, is prepared to exercise the right of free and innocent passage and to join with others to secure general recognition of this right. It is of course clear that the enjoyment of free and innocent passage by Israel would depend upon its prior withdrawal in accordance with the UN resolutions. The United States has no reason to assume that any littoral State would under these circumstances obstruct the right of free and innocent passage. The USA believes that the UN Emergency Force should move into the Straits area as the Israeli forces are withdrawn.

potentially disastrous to the cause of peace. He said that the American Government had urged U Thant to give the highest priority to the Aqaba question in his talks with President Nasser. He condemned the hurried withdrawal of UNEF and the recent build-up of military forces: 'The United States is firmly committed to the support of the political independence and territorial integrity of all the nations in the area.'[6] On the same day Mr Nolte in Cairo called on the Egyptian Foreign Minister, even before he had presented his credentials to President Nasser. According to Egyptian sources, this was the only official contact between Cairo and Washington during the first few days of the crisis. Mr Nolte is said to have made five points: UNEF should remain in Sharm al Shaykh and Gaza until a decision had been reached by the General Assembly. The US regarded the blockade as a matter of far-reaching consequence; any restriction would constitute an act of aggression. No Egyptian forces should enter the Gaza strip, where the UN was to remain responsible for administration until the issue was settled. The Egyptian and the Israeli troops now concentrated in Sinai and the Negev should be withdrawn. When Mahmud Riyad enquired whether these were 'instructions from Washington', Mr Nolte is said to have answered: 'no, only an attempt to think aloud'.[7] Whereupon Riyad explained at considerable length why Egypt felt no inclination to think aloud in America's presence: 'we do not trust your policy'. Israel was planning aggression against Syria, and the UAR could not accept this. As for Sharm al Shaykh no one could question that this was Egyptian national territory – and in any case Israel's very existence was illegitimate, and the question of navigation rights did not therefore arise.

Two days before, Mr Nolte had not believed the crisis was serious. His second in command, David Nes, had been convinced already in January that Nasser was planning a major confrontation with Israel and the West. In a letter to Senator Fulbright, Chairman of the Senate Foreign Relations Committee, he had urged that a top professional diplomat or a well known business executive close to President Johnson be appointed ambassador to Cairo. When Nes complained to Nolte that in his comment at the airport he had seriously underestimated the gravity of the situation, he was reported to have been told that Washington thought Mr Nes an alarmist.[8]

Neither the British nor the French position was quite clear during the early days of the crisis. George Brown, the Foreign Secretary, twice postponed his planned visit to the Soviet Union, the second time to attend a special cabinet meeting. At this meeting the British Government decided to take a leading part in the efforts to reopen the Straits. British officials said that Nasser's decision to close the Gulf to Israeli shipping had brought the Middle East to the brink of war. The primary responsibility for keeping peace in the area rested with the United Nations, but the main maritime nations also had a special obligation. It was decided to send George Thompson, Minister of State, and several high ranking naval officers to Washington for consultations with the United States. There was opposition in the cabinet by some ministers who were concerned about the financial implications of the crisis. According to one observer, in whose view British policy was too much inclined in favour of Israel, the Cabinet adopted its decision only with the greatest reluctance and in great haste, under pressure of the threat that Israel might attack at any moment. ('It is believed in London that the Israelis were in fact preparing to attack at 4 a.m. that day. They were stopped by strong pressure exerted on Mr Eshkol by President Johnson.')[9] Mr Brown's mission to Moscow was largely devoted to talks about the Middle East, but did not produce any results. The Soviet leaders still believed, or pretended to believe at this stage, that there had been merely some Israeli provocations; there was no serious Middle Eastern crisis. As one London newspaper put it: 'The clear meaning of what was said to Mr Brown and at a subsequent press conference in Moscow yesterday, is that the Russians believe that they have little to lose and all to gain from a serious weakening, if not total defeat, of the most Western-orientated nation in the Middle East – short of escalation into a major war.'[10]

Until 24 May, France had taken up no official position on the conflict. At a cabinet meeting on that day, President de Gaulle impressed on somewhat surprised ministers that France should take a strictly neutral line in the dispute. George Gorse, Minister of Information, announced that the 1950 Tripartite Declaration was no longer binding. As for the rights and wrongs of the dispute, there was a conflict between international law and the vagueness of the UN agreements with Egypt after the Sinai campaign.

The Security Council was powerless to act without agreement between America, the Soviet Union, Britain and France, and it was therefore the special responsibility of these four to meet and to take joint action to preserve peace. The next day it was announced that France opposed the idea of sending a test ship through the Straits of Tiran.

Reception of the French proposal was mixed. America and Britain were, with some reluctance, willing to accept the French plan, and the Egyptian Information Minister declared: 'We trust France, and particularly de Gaulle'; but the Soviet Union was not interested. Federenko, the Soviet representative, said at the meeting of the Security Council on the 24th that there was an 'artificially dramatic climate fostered by some Western powers'. This remained *grosso modo* the official Soviet attitude up to the Egyptian military defeat. He thought the Security Council had been too hastily summoned, and that its consultations served no useful purpose. This view had the support of France, India, Bulgaria, Mali, Nigeria and others – and it was not entirely without justification. For those who had sponsored this meeting, Canada and Denmark (and indirectly America and Britain), did not really know what they wanted the Council to do. The three points in their draft resolution were self-evident – full support for U Thant's pacification efforts, inviting him to report, and requesting all member states to refrain from any steps which might worsen the situation. Yet such was the mood of the majority on the Council that it refused to support even a resolution to back U Thant's peace-keeping mission. The Secretary General was reported none too pleased about this meeting during his absence, but some of the Western delegates felt, as the president of the Security Council of that month, Hans Tabor of Denmark, said, that the crisis was deteriorating at an alarming speed, that the stage was set for a major military clash, and that the slightest miscalculation, or misunderstanding, could lead to war.[11] The Council adjourned its debate; it met again on the 29th, to discuss both U Thant's report on his mission, and, somewhat surprisingly, an UAR charge of Israeli aggression. When the Council reconvened, the US proposed that Egypt should allow freedom of navigation through the Straits and that the Council should call on both sides to avoid warlike action, including the announced blockade: if any state wished to change the *status quo*, it should be done by peaceful means. Once this interim resolution was passed the Council should look for a 'reasonable, peaceful and just solution'. Goldberg, referring to U Thant's appeal that all parties concerned exercise special restraint and forgo belligerence, focused in this speech on the words 'forgo belligerence'. He said that he believed 'from the context of the situation that with respect to the particularly sensitive area of Aqaba, forgoing belligerence must mean forgoing any blockade of the Gulf of Aqaba during the breathing spell requested by the Secretary General, and permitting free and innocent passage of all nations and all flags through the Straits of Tiran to continue as it has during the last ten years'.[12] The Arab speakers said in reply that the three Arab states bordering the Gulf – Saudi Arabia, Jordan, and Egypt – were already in a state of war with Israel and therefore had the right to ban the vessels of an enemy. Egypt was at war with Israel – as one baffled observer put it – but Israel had no right to be at war with Egypt. Mohammad Awad el Kony, the Egyptian representative, and other Arab speakers (including the Lebanese and Iraqi foreign ministers) maintained that the Gulf of Aqaba had been Arab territory for a thousand years, that the Israelis had prepared an attack on Syria, that Egypt was determined to blockade the Gulf. Federenko gave them full support. Egypt had exercised its sovereign rights; if Washington and London wanted to relax the tension, they should withdraw their fleets from the Mediterranean. Goldberg had asked the two sides to forgo belligerence so as to give the Council a breathing space. In a counter move, el Kony called on the Council to ensure that Israel rejoined the Egyptian-Israeli Mixed Armistice Commission, which Israel had boycotted since 1956. It is not quite clear in what way such a move would have had a bearing on the situation – it would have affected neither the blockade nor the troop concentrations. The Egyptians probably felt they had to do something to regain the diplomatic initiative. The American resolution, despite its mild wording, was unacceptable to the majority; there were private talks between delegates to reach an agreed resolution, but these, too, failed. The Council met again on 3 June, and listened to an Israeli declaration that 'nothing less than complete non-interference with free and innocent passage through the Gulf of Aqaba was acceptable'. The Syrian delegate answered that if Israel, either alone or with overt US participation, committed aggression in the Gulf of Aqaba (by breaking the blockade) the Arab nations would react strongly and unitedly.

At that stage events had bypassed the Security Council; the world press continued to report its meetings only briefly; the reports usually closed with the routine formula: 'The debate has been adjourned for further private consultations.' At UN Headquarters there was from the beginning confusion and indecision, reflecting the split among the member states. To add a grotesque touch, the General Assembly pursued its ostrich-like tactics, debating in general terms the problem of peace-keeping operations (without any reference to the current conflict).

The proceedings of the Security Council were broadcast and televised at great length; this, to put it cautiously, did not enhance the reputation of the United Nations among viewers and listeners. The endless procedural wrangles, the reluctance to accept any resolution however innocent, above all the unwillingness on the part of the majority to admit that there was a real danger of war, made a most unfortunate impression. Certain delegations no doubt had instructions to procrastinate, based on the belief that if more time passed, Egypt would be able to consolidate its gains. But at least some of the confusion was unrehearsed; while it reflected the stalemate among member countries, it affected, of course, the prestige of the United Nations as such.

America and Britain had agreed on 24 May to reopen the Straits of Tiran to international shipping, not excluding in principle military action. When George Thompson, British Minister of State, visited Washington on 24 May, several blueprints prepared by American and British experts were discussed. One provided for an Aqaba Gulf Users' Conference which would arrange for United Nations' pilots to board each ship passing through the Tiran Straits. Another plan envisaged a flotilla composed of warships of the various maritime powers. A few days later, when it appeared that diplomatic efforts to make Nasser withdraw would not be successful, Washington briefly considered a compromise solution. Under this proposal the UAR would agree to allow foreign flag ships to pass through the Gulf of Aqaba, but would be permitted to block passage to Israeli ships.[13] America and Britain prepared a three point declaration to be signed by the maritime powers which, while not specifically committing them to support Israel flag ships to challenge the blockade, would somehow provide a basis for Israel and other nations to break it by running their ships through the Straits.[14] All this was extremely nebulous: Washington had thrown its support behind the British effort to rally the maritime nations against the blockade; first there had been talk about '40–50' nations, later about '15–20'. It soon appeared that of the countries approached, most were not willing to sign a joint declaration, let alone participate in the task force plan; it could have led to the loss of oil concessions and other complications in their relations with the Arab countries. Eight maritime powers are reported to have agreed initially to consider an operation, on condition that it was carried out under the auspices of the United Nations: Norway, Italy, Japan, Liberia, Argentine, Canada, Australia, and New Zealand. (Press reports also mentioned Portugal, Costa Rica and a few other countries.) It was, however, virtually excluded from the very beginning that the United Nations would endorse any such action: the Soviet veto in the Security Council, and the composition of the General Assembly, were an effective guarantee to bar any such step. A tentative promise did not therefore entail any risk; to dispel any doubt, some of these governments (such as Italy) made it clear after a few days that they would not in any case take part. Apart from the two sponsors, only the Netherlands, and possibly Australia and New Zealand, were prepared if necessary to challenge Cairo's control of the Gulf of Aqaba outside the United Nations.

It is not clear whether the United States and Britain were at any stage seriously considering the use of force. The prevailing view in both State Department and the Pentagon was from the beginning that military action should be avoided. By 29 May it emerged that, in spite of Washington's early pronouncement that it would regard the closure of the Gulf of Aqaba as an aggressive and illegal act, it was not prepared to take or support physical action to enforce freedom of navigation.[15] It was hinted that Washington would be willing to sustain Israel's economy, in particular with regard to oil requirements, if Israel refrained from attempts to break the blockade. Was it really believed that such a solution would be seriously considered by Israel? Diplomatic activities continued nevertheless without interruption: on 31 May, the House of Commons debated the Middle East. The

168

Foreign Secretary said that his government would consider any unilateral closure of the Gulf of Aqaba as an 'act of belligerence'. He urged U Thant to send a personal representative to the Middle East to promote conciliation between Israel and the Arab countries. At the same time he criticised U Thant's decision to comply with Nasser's demand to remove UNEF: 'It cannot be right that when a fire is known to be imminent, the fire brigade should be ordered to depart.'[16] The analogy with the fire brigade had first been drawn by Abba Eban, but it had not been accepted by all; was not UNEF far too weak to deal with a real fire? It could be a fire brigade only so long as there was no fire. It had neither the authority nor the equipment to deal with a real fire but could merely signal by its withdrawal that a real fire was being lit.[17] Brown also said that U Thant's action cast doubt on the credibility of UN forces elsewhere in the world, just as the Egyptian closure of the Gulf of Aqaba could have repercussions on the rights of navigation elsewhere – including some of the maritime exits from the Soviet Union. On that same day the US aircraft carrier *Intrepid* was passing through the Suez Canal, and the Soviet Union sent the first of ten warships scheduled to pass through the Dardanelles to the Mediterranean. This was the *Mahomet Gadzhiev*, an escort vessel built along the lines of a frigate. But the Soviet Union was clearly not worried by the thought that the Turks would close the Dardanelles. Winding up the debate in the House of Commons, Harold Wilson gave warning that the fighting in the Middle East might result in a war whose consequences would engulf the whole world. The confrontation between the Arab states and Israel had all the dangers and characteristics of a 'holy war' that could spread further. He was warmly cheered from both sides of the House when he declared: 'One condition of lasting peace is the recognition that Israel has the right to live.' But the cabinet had failed to reach a decision on the possible use of a naval force to break up the blockade in the event of failure of peaceful means to ensure free passage. The official policy was still to obtain, together with the United States, support from the maritime nations for a declaration upholding the right of free passage. In Washington that day a State Department spokesman said that America supported the British initiative for international pressure on the UAR to end the blockade. But, as Dean Rusk made it clear on another occasion, that day, there was no immediate plan to test the blockade. The *New York Times* gave details of the new State Department compromise plan: free passage for all but Israeli ships during an 'interim period', in the course of which a permanent solution would be sought.[18]

The next day brought further disappointments for Israel: Wilson's campaign for an international declaration supporting freedom of navigation received a setback at the very beginning of his trip to America. The Canadian Government 'seemed lukewarm if not actually cool' towards Britain's campaign for an unambiguous declaration. Lester Pearson, Canadian Prime Minister, told Wilson that Canada would act only through the United Nations, which in the given circumstances meant that it would not act.[19] In Washington Dean Rusk told the Senate Foreign Relations Committee that the US had been compelled to restrict her aims in the organisation of resistance to Nasser's blockade. Since several maritime nations (including Britain) hesitated to take a firm stand on the question of a free passage and to commit themselves to a definite course of action, Rusk proposed to water down the declaration to a mere statement affirming that the Straits were an international waterway, and that therefore their blockade was unlawful.

There was a great deal of wavering among the western powers, but whose fault was it? If Dean Rusk put the blame on Britain, British observers blamed America: Johnson was deliberately letting Wilson make the running in trying to wriggle out of the Middle East crisis, to switch the blame for selling Israel short on to Britain.[20] But the importance of this factor of mutual distrust should not be exaggerated, for the American administration must have known by the time Wilson arrived in Washington that war in the Middle East had come much nearer. Even had the maritime powers agreed among themselves and decided to act, this would not have solved Israel's main problem – the build up of the Arab armies on Israel's border. From Israel's point of view the blockade was now a secondary issue. America's stand was dictated by one overriding consideration: what would the Soviet Union do? The exchanges with Moscow during the crisis were inconclusive and ambiguous. According to official circles in Washington, the Russians advised Nasser to hold to his blockade proclamation, counting upon the western powers to protest only with words and to restrain the Israelis from forcing the issue.[21] Washington tried to impress on Moscow that this would be a serious miscalculation: the campaign for a holy war against Israel and the growing Arab military build-up could force the Israelis to take action even before the blockade controversy was resolved: 'Moscow would face the choice of joining the fight or deserting Cairo at the worst possible moment.'[22] The Soviet leaders thought America was bluffing; Israel would never dare to go it alone. Moscow ignored American appeals that if the Soviet Union wanted to reduce the risk of violence, something more than freezing the present situation was needed. Russia made it clear that it would not intervene so long as America stayed out; this was the only guiding line for Washington and it acted accordingly.

'The focus of American effort to solve the Near East crisis without violence is in the UN,' a State Department Press officer told reporters on 1 June. But meanwhile talks continued on many levels; Dean Rusk saw the Egyptian ambassador, on the same day Foy Kohler and Eugene Rostow, deputy under-secretaries of state, had talks with the Russian *chargé d'affaires* and other diplomats. Both Kohler and Rostow favoured a more active American line during the crisis, but their views did not prevail. The visit of a senior American diplomat to Cairo had been suggested to Rostow by the Egyptian ambassador a few days earlier, and it had been decided to send Charles Yost, a former American ambassador to Damascus. He was in Cairo now but his dispatches were not encouraging; his talks with the Egyptian Foreign Minister had made no progress. Nasser was too busy to see him, and Yost returned to Washington on 4 June. President Johnson had sent a personal message to Nasser on 30 May; Nasser answered on 3 June; his reply apparently dealt with the forthcoming visit of Vice-President Humphrey to Cairo and the dispatch of Zakaria Mohiedin to Washington. But Nasser was in no hurry.

On 2 June Johnson and Wilson had a long meeting in Washington. Wilson said at a press conference that freedom of shipping was still the key to the Middle East crisis; earlier, in Ottawa, he had stated that there were only a few days left to find a solution. He repeated in Washington that 'Time is not on our side – we've got to use every minute of that time to try to avoid the crisis which is in danger of resulting.' Johnson and Wilson studied a four point programme which provided for efforts in the UN to gain time through a Security Council resolution calling for restraint, and with U Thant exerting influence in the same direction. Britain was to try to mobilise the major maritime states in support of the famous 'declaration'. Should this declaration fail of its desired effect, an attempt would be made to get individual maritime states to put political and economic pressure on Egypt to desist from the blockade. If all steps proved fruitless, the two powers would reluctantly agree to consider the establishment of an international naval force to escort merchant ships through the straits. At the end of the meeting it was announced that the two leaders had decided to intensify the efforts to get maximum support of the maritime powers for a common declaration, but at the same time, American officials admitted that all the efforts had so far been in vain.[23] British correspondents reported that America had switched its policy away from the previous tough line towards a compromise solution which would save face for Egypt. Alarm was aroused in London among the numerous ministers and high officials who already had deep misgivings about official British policy: 'It looked as though Britain would be left out on a limb, having appeared to take the initiative in pledging to keep the Gulf of Aqaba open with the implication that, if necessary, this would be done by force.'[24] The American press had gained a different impression. While Mr Wilson was tough in public, 'the impression in American quarters was that, privately, the British were wavering because of Britain's concern that too forceful a line of action on Israel's behalf might endanger valuable oil concessions and revenues in the Arab world'.[25] At his press conference in Washington, Wilson said that it was a fact that no great number of Israeli vessels actually went through the Straits; the vital factor for Israel was, in his view, to get essential cargoes through to Eilat. (Israeli sources said in reply that three Israeli ships had been on regular runs from the Persian Gulf, Africa, and the Far East to Eilat, averaging about one ship a week, not to mention chartered ships and foreign tankers.) Israel expressed its willingness to sign the declaration of the maritime powers; it had been invited by the United States. But, according to press reports this approach did not have the blessing of Britain. The Foreign Office argued that Israeli adherence to the declaration might wreck the whole scheme by bringing the signatories into open conflict with the UAR over the crucial question of ships flying the Israeli flag.[26] After the Washington meeting, official policy was still to establish a common front of maritime powers. The American and British Governments were willing to take only multilateral action, and the fate of Israel seemed to hang on whether a handful of maritime nations would join with the United States and Britain to force Nasser to keep the Gulf open.[27] London and Washington did not say whether a naval force provided by three nations would be needed to qualify genuinely as multilateral, or whether the signatures of four, five or ten were needed. Were they disappointed at their failure to get these signatures? What if a naval task force had been established and Nasser had not been deterred? What if Egyptian shore batteries opened fire on American and British ships? This was exactly the prospect which Washington dreaded most because of the likely political and military repercussions. President Johnson had reiterated, in principle, the decisions taken by the Eisenhower administration in 1957 by insisting that the blockade of the Gulf of Aqaba was illegal and by sending US ships through the Straits and protecting them. Johnson had restated the principle, as one commentator put it, but he had not followed it with the same decision to act unilaterally if necessary.[28] United States policy was motivated by fear of a direct confrontation with the Soviet Union and at the same time it was influenced by the disarray in the western camp. France's position, in particular, had contributed greatly to the general paralysis. De Gaulle had persuaded himself that America had become too powerful in recent years and had to be opposed even if this implied siding with the Soviet Union; Israel hardly counted in his grand design. The Syrian Foreign Minister, who was in Paris for talks with de Gaulle, expressed Arab appreciation of the new French policy, which 'differed conspicuously from the aggressive attitude of the United States'.[29] In a statement made by de Gaulle at a cabinet meeting on 2 June nothing was said at all about the principle of the freedom of shipping; the worst thing would be to open hostilities. Israel, the declaration said *expressis verbis*, had a right to exist. It did not have the right to break Nasser's blockade if this might lead to war. This statement was echoed the next day in the Security

Council by the French delegate, Roger Seydoux: France would oppose which ever side initiated military action.[30]

The United States and Britain continued to go through the motions of diplomacy during the last days before the fighting began, but no one believed that a joint declaration would ever be published or that it would be of any use if it were. Nasser had solemnly declared that he would not recognise such a declaration; it would be regarded as an act of hostility against Egyptian rights and the prelude to war with the Arab world. President Johnson reiterated (in a speech mainly devoted to domestic topics) his determination to preserve peace in the Middle East and the territorial integrity of the nations involved.[31] According to rumours a declaration of sorts was to be published on 5 or 6 June: this would give time for the Security Council to approve (or reject) a resolution calling on both sides to act with restraint. Brazil and the Argentine believed that if the words 'forgo belligerence', which had offended the Arabs and the Soviet bloc, were dropped from the appeal in favour of a more general formula, there would be unanimous support for a call for restraint. Some observers thought that the idea to test the blockade had not been entirely given up, but had merely been delayed for about ten days, and that it would eventually be made by a ship flying a flag of convenience.[32] But on 4 June most officials in Washington expected 'some kind of explosion.[33] This was no more than natural; all the diplomatic moves had been made and had failed. After the war, Arab sources argued that a new round of negotiations was just about to begin; according to Soviet sources, agreement was virtually assured when Israel decided to launch its attack. But the only thing that was certain was Humphrey's proposed trip to Cairo (the news originated in Cairo, the State Department denied any knowledge, the White House did not comment) and Zakaria Mohiedin's visit to Washington. Since no common ground had been discovered in all previous talks, there was no reason to assume that these visits would somehow, miraculously, be crowned by success. Nasser would not retreat and lose all his gains because of vague threats of unspecified political or economic sanctions. Israel had made it clear that it would not put up with the blockade of Eilat. Above all, the issue of the blockade was no longer of paramount importance. No one talked about the real threat to peace – the troop concentrations.

France and Britain announced that the tripartite declaration of 1950, which would have involved their intervention, was dead; Washington felt it could not intervene because of the danger of global war. Washington did not know that Israel would attack on 5 June; it had warned Jerusalem repeatedly against recourse to military action, the last time a week before the fighting broke out. But by 4 June there was no doubt in the minds of most officials in Washington that Israel would not accept this advice, for the simple reason that America was powerless to help the Jewish state against the dangers facing it. Similar views prevailed in most western capitals; there was no longer any hope for a peaceful conclusion to the conflict. A war between Israel and the Arab countries was dangerous, but given Israel's resolution not to accept a Middle Eastern Munich – or worse – it was expected. It was in some ways less risky than a protracted international crisis – provided, of course, the conflict could be localised. President Johnson and his advisers were no doubt worried men when the news about the outbreak of hostilities reached them in the early hours of 5 June, but they cannot have been surprised, and there was perhaps a slight feeling of relief that someone had at last attempted to cut the Gordian knot.

The Soviet Union had given Egypt and Syria full political, military and economic support for over a decade. The Soviet press had warned the Arabs for years, almost without interruption, against American intrigues and Israeli war psychoses. It took a leading part in spreading war scares in the Middle East, including the one in mid-May that played such a central role in unleashing the war. At the same time the Soviet leaders were apparently convinced that neither the great quantities of arms supplied nor the war scares would lead to full scale fighting. Had they believed their own propaganda, they should not have been surprised by the outbreak of war. But the available evidence shows that they were not impressed by their own arguments and that they did not expect a war.

Four separate theories have been advanced by them to explain the origin of the crisis. The earliest version had it that the United States wanted another Vietnam, in accordance with the doctrine of local conflicts and small wars. (This was parallel to the early western theory that Russia had instigated the Middle Eastern conflict to bring pressure on America to withdraw from Vietnam).

According to a second theory, the expansionism of the Israeli ruling circles was mainly to blame. Yet another version claimed that American and British oil companies had prepared the conflict in an attempt to regain their lost positions in the Arab world. Occasionally, this theory was slightly modified: it had been a conspiracy between the oil companies and world Jewry, with Senator Jacob Javits of New York as the link.[34] Lastly, there was the CIA theory; the Israeli attack had been planned and organised in April, as part of a combined action of the CIA, the Israeli Government, King Hussain, and King Faisal of Saudi Arabia. These versions do not necessarily exclude each other, but they were hardly ever employed simultaneously. Nor were any of them necessarily believed; some were clearly propagandist in character, and made no claim to serious political analysis. But even more serious attempts to understand the character of the crisis revealed a great deal of confusion and contradiction. In its early stages, the official Soviet line was that the worsening of the situation in the Middle East was 'linked with the new crimes of the United States agression in Vietnam and with provocations against Cuba.[35] It was part of a global conspiracy, with Israel a mere pawn on the international chessboard. On 22 May, the day Nasser decided to blockade the Straits of Tiran, he received a message from the central committee of the Soviet Communist party and the council of ministers. Its contents have not been revealed; according to news from Cairo, it pledged support to the Egyptian cause. The first public Soviet statement on the situation in the Middle East came the following day: 'He who would venture aggression in the Middle East would encounter not only the united strength of the Arab countries, but also resolute resistance to aggression on the part of the Soviet Union and all peace-loving countries.' The statement expressed the conviction that the peoples were not interested in fanning a military conflict in the Near East: 'Only a handful of colonial oil monopolies and their hangers-on can be interested in such a conflict. Only the forces of imperialism, in the wake of whose policy Israel follows, can be interested in this.' The statement emphasised that the maintenance of peace and security in an area *which directly adjoins the frontiers of the Soviet Union* (our emphasis) was in the vital interest of the peoples of the USSR.[36] What did resolute resistance mean? Armed resistance or political opposition? The statement could be interpreted in various ways. America was not mentioned by name once in this manifesto; a certain effort was made to de-emphasise the conflict. A demonstration by Arab students in Moscow was not given publicity in the domestic Soviet media.[37] There were no solidarity demonstrations with Egypt and Syria throughout the Soviet Union until after the war. The war in Vietnam, even the situation in Cuba, was given more publicity in the Soviet press than the Middle East for the first ten days of the crisis. At a Soviet foreign ministry press conference after George Brown's visit to Moscow, it was stated that in the Russian view the dangers arising from aggression in Vietnam were far greater.[38] Brown's appeal to the Soviet leaders calling for the 'restraint and active imagination' required to discharge the Soviet Union's responsibility as a great power was thought to be misplaced. On 25 May, the Egyptian War Minister Shamsedin Badran flew to Moscow accompanied by a ten-man delegation. There was no official Soviet statement about the outcome of these talks, but Nasser, after the return of Badran to Cairo on 29 May, said that he was greatly encouraged by the results. He told members of the National Assembly that Kosygin had sent him a message saying Russia 'stands with us in the battle'. The Soviet Union would not allow foreign intervention that would prevent a return to the state of affairs before 1956: 'I wish to tell you today that the Soviet Union is a friendly power and stands by us as a friend. In all our dealings with the USSR since 1955 – it has not made a single request from us. The USSR has never interfered in our policy or internal affairs. This is the USSR as we have always known it. Actually it is we that made urgent requests of the USSR. Last year, we asked for wheat and they sent it to us. When I also asked for all kinds of weapons, they gave them to us.'[39] The day Nasser spoke, a high level Syrian delegation including Nuredin Atassi and Ibrahim Makhus, the Foreign Minister, went to Moscow. It had long meetings with Kosygin, Brezhnev and the Soviet defence chiefs. From the subsequent communiqués we learn that it was a 'hasty visit', that it took place in an atmosphere of warm welcome and cordiality, that the Soviet leaders 'showed profound understanding for the reality of the current crisis.'[40] But the Syrian aims were more far-reaching than a return to the conditions prevailing before 1956 and the

177

strict observance of the armistice agreements; Soviet newspaper readers had been told that this was all the Arabs wanted. As a result of the visits, the many letters and notes exchanged during the crisis, and the reports they received from the Arab capitals, the Soviet leaders must have been well informed about Arab war aims. Yet they behaved as if they were not taking the Arab declarations quite seriously and acted as if they thought no one else was either. The press gave prominence to a statement by U Thant, according to which Nasser had assured him that Egypt would not take any offensive action against Israel.[41] The Soviet leaders once again assured the Egyptian war minister and the Syrian leaders of their general support; the Arabs interpreted this as the green light for stepping up military preparations and political warfare, short of firing the first shot.

Only after 26 May did the Soviet leaders gradually recognise that the situation in the Middle East was more serious than they had at first realised. Their Arab allies had started a train of events over which they were about to lose control. Soviet newspapers reacted by attacking 'Israeli extremists and their protectors abroad'; the western powers were clearly inciting Israel to ill-considered action. While Cairo's attitude was constructive, Israel was described as utterly irresponsible. 'The impression is created,' one commentator wrote, 'that someone is ready to take dangerous steps and kindle the fires of war in the Near East to settle the question whether or not two or four ships will sail through the Straits of Tiran.'[42] This was a remark directed against Israel, but it could also be interpreted as criticism of Nasser, who had just said that he would not budge an inch from his stand. Moscow was not altogether happy about the Arab call for a 'holy war'. Part of the evidence for this was revealed only after the war. The Soviet Union was critical of Ahmed Shukairy's slogan to liquidate Israel; Moscow commentators said that some politicians had done considerable harm to the Arab cause by their speeches about the destruction of Israel, about bloodbaths, etc.[43] Great pains were taken to stress that these 'petty-bourgeois ultra-nationalists' had no connection with the Arab governments'; 'the official point of view in Cairo has nothing in common with these hysterical loud mouths'; Shukairy's slogans 'were never taken seriously in Egypt's leading quarters'.[44] This was, of course, nonsense; there was no difference between Shukairy's propaganda, the statements of the Syrian leaders, and the Egyptian press and radio. Everyone in the Arab world knew it; it was the kind of indirect criticism which has been the usage in Soviet relations with friendly countries for a long time. There had been words of warning, albeit in a roundabout way, even before the war broke out. *Novoe Vremia*, the weekly devoted to foreign affairs, wrote on 2 June that the hawks in the imperialist camp were not the only warmongers; the Chinese leaders too, were calling the Arabs to light the flames of war in the Middle East: 'But the real friends of the Arab peoples think not about unleashing military conflicts but about the peace in the Middle East which is needed so much by the young Arab states facing economic development. Nor should it be forgotten that the main focus of international tension is in South East Asia. Every deflection of the attention of international public opinion from the events in Vietnam plays into the hands of the imperialists.* Yet at the same time other Soviet organs published comment which could be interpreted as a hardly veiled threat of Soviet intervention. Obviously, there was no unanimity about how to control the Middle East crisis. It has been argued that the crisis was at least partly the work of a group of Communist leaders, Shelepin, Yegorichev and Semichastny – most of them ex-Komsomol officials. These Soviet 'hawks' reportedly reached the conclusion that a more militant foreign policy was needed; greater risks should be taken in the confrontation with America. As chief of the Soviet internal security and intelligence apparatus Semichastny was certainly in a good position to influence the course of events. The rumour about an impending Israeli attack on Syria in mid-May emanated perhaps from these quarters. But Semichastny was removed from his job on 18 May after the damage was done, well before all the consequences could be foreseen. It is doubtful whether his dismissal had much to do with the Middle Eastern conflict. The demotion of other

---

* Comments in *Novoe Vremia*, generally thought to express the views of the Soviet foreign ministry, were sometimes more moderate in tone than those in the rest of the Soviet press. The most extreme Soviet views were found in *Trud* and *Komsomolskaia Pravda*. *Nedelia*, a weekly supplement of *Izvestia*, also expressed slightly unorthodox views on occasion. For instance, that it was not altogether correct to equate Israel with Hitlerism. *Krasnaia Zvezda*, the army newspaper, took a very hard line, but only after the war; somewhat surprisingly it refrained from publishing substantial comment during the crisis and the war.

members of this group shortly after the end of the war may have been linked with this crisis, though it seems more likely that it was connected with the wider implications of the West–East conflict (Kosygin's meeting with Johnson in Glasboro, etc.). There were differences of opinion among the Soviet leaders; there were 'hawks' and 'doves' in Moscow as well as in Washington, Israel and the Arab world. One can imagine what arguments were used by these two groups or by those on middle ground. Speculation as to who advocated what programme is somewhat risky, and in this specific context not particularly relevant.

After 1 June, Moscow was aware that time was running out. The French ambassador was told that, unfortunately, the Vietnam war made it impossible to hold a four power conference; in the Soviet view it would be preferable to wait for the outcome of the Security Council meeting.[45] But it is unlikely that Moscow had any illusions about the Security Council; the underlying idea must have been that the existing situation could be 'frozen': the western plan for breaking the blockade would be unsuccessful and Israel, alone, would not dare to challenge Nasser and the Syrians. But the news from the capitals of the Middle East was not encouraging: in Israel the 'extremists' were about to enter the Government. The announcement from the Arab countries that Israel would be destroyed, though suppressed in the Soviet press, was noted in Moscow official quarters. The situation was highly explosive; Izvestia noted that the political barometer was fast reaching danger point.[46] The Egyptian-Jordanian pact was welcomed in Moscow because 'it strengthened the position of the Arab countries in the present conflict with the imperialist forces'.[47] The next day a series of resolutions adopted at a conference of the Arab Communist parties was published in Pravda. One of them attacked Jordan for 'aiming to disrupt the progressive conquests of the Syrian people'. But this was clearly an out-of-date comment, harking back to the days when Jordan was still being accused of plotting with the CIA and Israel against the 'progressive' Arab countries. After 2 June, all Soviet criticism of 'reactionary' Arab countries ceased and all attacks were directed against Israel, as well as the United States and Britain, 'trying to organise a Holy Alliance of capitalist countries against the Arab states defending their sovereignty'.[48] (This referred to the abortive attempt to collect signatures for a 'declaration'.)

On the eve of the war Russia's hands were as much tied as America's. Its sympathies were on the side of Egypt and Syria; it had a stake in a conflict which (it was frequently stressed) concerned an area near the Soviet borders, and in which therefore direct Soviet interests were involved. But there was also the understanding with America about non-interference by the super-powers. The conflict between the Arab states and Israel was, from the Soviet point of view, to a large extent a private quarrel, which had only an indirect bearing on the global conflict. Egypt and Syria were not members of the eastern bloc, nor did Israel belong to any western defence treaty. And yet it was not simply a conflict between two neutrals; Syria and Egypt were in Soviet eyes 'progressive' countries, Israel was 'reactionary', an American satellite. Every Egyptian or Syrian achievement was indirectly a Russian success, every setback an indirect defeat for the Soviet Union. There were obvious limits to Soviet support for its clients in the Middle East. Moscow (like America) would envisage military action only if major, direct interests of the Soviet Union were concerned. The Straits of Tiran were a minor issue by any standard and of no direct Soviet concern. The Arab-Israeli conflict, and the outcome of the war, had a major impact on Soviet policy but only in a roundabout way.

According to the Soviet concept, the gradual victory of communism throughout the world is ensured as a result of the growth of the strength of the Soviet Union and other communist countries. There a new society is being built which is not only more affluent, but also freer and more democratic in character than any western society. At the same time more and more non-western countries will choose the non-capitalist road of development, some peacefully, others, directly threatened by imperialism or neo-colonialism, through wars of national liberation. As for this second group of countries, the scheme is not working too well; a sizable number of them have embarked on the 'non-capitalist' road during the last two decades, but some have developed into caricatures of socialism (as the Russians see it), picking on the way a quarrel with Russia for not being radical enough. Others have failed: the 'progressive' leaders of Indonesia and Ghana, to give but two examples, have been overthrown. It has been the tacit assumption of communist strategy that once a progressive leadership prevails in a country there will be no backsliding.

Communism would grow steadily in strength whereas its enemies would weaken. But the nuclear stalemate has frozen the international situation; Soviet capacity to help the smaller countries has been narrowly circumscribed, it is up to them, unaided, to carry out the struggle for liberation. But what if they are unable to cope with this task? Theoretically, this possibility can hardly ever arise because the 'popular forces', however small, always in the end triumph over 'reaction' however powerful. In practice there were complications: the 'progressive' forces in the Middle East, despite the advantage of great numerical strength and material superiority, were defeated by 'reactionary' Israel. In such a situation there was bound to be pressure for direct Soviet intervention. The Soviet Union had therefore a vested interest in the prevention of local conflicts which, while of no immediate concern to Russia, might involve it directly or indirectly. But what if a local conflict occurs after all? The Arab-Israeli war was a perfect illustration. Direct Soviet military interference was unthinkable; it would have meant a confrontation with the other super-power over a non-vital issue. Not to help meant a loss of face, which Russia's enemies would exploit in their propaganda. Coming after the coups in Indonesia, Greece and Ghana the Israeli victory seemed to constitute the culmination of a 'trend': there were bound to be voices claiming that America, not Russia, was the strongest power, and that the tide was running against communism. When Boumedienne visited Moscow after the war, he asked his Soviet hosts to what extent they were willing to support wars of liberation. The Soviets countered with another question: what do you think of nuclear war? This counter question was unlikely to make a great impression on the Algerian leader and his colleagues of the 'progressive' camp: nuclear arms for them are an abstraction; they have no direct knowledge of their effects. Moreover, they assume, perhaps not altogether wrongly, that in a nuclear war New York and Moscow are more likely to be destroyed than Algiers and Damascus. The Soviet dilemma became more acutely painful after the war, but essentially it existed well before: how to help Syria and Egypt without overstepping the line that could mean confrontation with America? How to refrain from giving all-out support without losing credibility and playing into the hands of the Chinese? These were the main issues, and it is only natural that individual

Soviet leaders had different answers: no one wanted to risk war with America over the Straits of Tiran, it is unlikely that anyone suggested that Russia should drop the Arab countries altogether, but between these two extremes there were undoubtedly different accents and degrees of emphasis.

This was the basic Soviet dilemma; all other questions were relatively unimportant. The Soviet Union had supplied Egypt and Syria with great quantities of arms; it had given political support with the intention of strengthening Soviet influence in the Arab world, not with the idea that there should be a war. It had underrated the irrational in the behaviour of its clients; it had misjudged the way Israel would react; and it had not anticipated that, once the conflict had escalated, it would not be able to control it – even with the help of America. There had been irresponsibility, lack of judgment and foresight; perhaps at one stage or another a group in the Kremlin had wanted to intensify the conflict.* But there had been no deliberate warmongering on the part of the Soviet Union in the sense that it wanted a war between Israel and the Arab countries. On the other hand, there was not much resolution and conviction behind the last minute Soviet peace efforts. Did Nasser refuse to listen to the Russians? The Russians had no clear message for him apart from the request not to fire the first shot – which he heeded. Soviet policy throughout the Middle East crisis was torn in various directions; it tried to combine objectives that could not be combined. It was ambiguous, but the ambiguity was inherent in Moscow's relations with the Arab countries in the Middle Eastern imbroglio, and in the world situation in general.

* A report by Dr Zuayen the Syrian Prime Minister about his mission to the Soviet Union is of interest in this context. According to this account the Syrian delegation realised in Moscow that there were differences of opinion between Soviet military and civilian leaders about the policy to be followed in the Middle East. The former argued in closed session that while they agreed with Syrian policy vis-à-vis Israel not all their colleagues shared their view. The Arab leaders would have to pursue a more militant line to show that they were really serious. This report was published in *Al Muntadel*, the internal newsletter of the Ba'ath. The Syrian Prime Minister possibly misinterpreted or distorted the views of his hosts. But he definitely gained the impression that a more aggressive line would meet the approval of some influential circles in the Soviet Capital. See also A. Ben Zur in *Al Hamishmar*, 9 November 1967.

6

Public Opinion and the Crisis

The Israeli-Arab conflict had a profound impact on public opinion throughout Europe and America. Not since the Spanish Civil War had sympathies been so deeply divided. For a while it became a major domestic issue in France and Italy and there were stormy scenes in the Indian parliament. It split the left in many countries and made, temporarily at any rate, philosemites of Austrians and Poles. It induced Spanish communists to support General Franco for the first time in their history. It made for strange bed-fellows in both camps.

It had such an impact because it was the best covered conflict in history.* There was a feeling of immediacy, of direct personal involvement not only in Europe and the United States; even far away Japan had its TV camera crews in Tel Aviv and Cairo ready for instant relay.

In many cases the profound emotional involvement manifested itself in demonstrations, meetings, and other forms of action, such as the collection of money, offers to send blood or to volunteer for work in Israel. For others it was a dramatic contest, something like a big sports event, gripping and tense, but without major political – let alone moral – implications. In Europe and the United States public opinion was overwhelmingly in favour of Israel. According to the polls 55 per cent of all Americans expressed sympathies with Israel, 50 per cent of all Englishmen, 58 per cent of all Frenchmen, and 67 per cent of the Dutch (4 per cent were pro-Arab in America, 5 per cent in Britain, 2 per cent in France, none in Holland). These figures give a certain indication of the general mood, but their significance

---

* From a professional point of view *Le Monde* and French radio stations (Europe I) provided the best coverage throughout the crisis. British and American coverage of the actual fighting was often excellent; the war reporters and photographers showed their usual daring. But they were much weaker on the complicated political ramifications of the crisis. All major newspapers, radio and TV networks had their special correspondents in Israel and in the Arab countries.

should not be overrated.* Sometimes they were contradictory – if a clear majority of Frenchmen supported Israel, an equally high proportion supported de Gaulle's policy, which was not exactly pro-Israeli.

In most European countries there was a conflict between interest and sentiment: state interest favoured (or seemed to favour) the Arab cause – or at least strict neutrality; sentiment favoured David against Goliath. This emerged in the position taken by most governments. The majority of those who sympathised with Israel did not necessarily favour helping the Jewish state in any other way than through the United Nations.

Generalisations about public opinion are dangerous. At a time of rapid change, public opinion is subject to great fluctuations. Before 5 June the Jews were the underdogs, Israel in danger of destruction. After the victory, the picture changed: the television networks no longer showed fanatical crowds shouting 'Death to the Jews', but wretched refugee families, starving women and weeping children. Naturally, public sympathies began to change. Generalisations are difficult, furthermore, because conditions varied so much from one country to another. Pro-Israeli sympathies in Europe and North America have been explained with reference to the holocaust which produced guilt feelings not only in Germany but equally among the other Christian nations. There is some truth in this, but it does not help us to understand, for instance, why sympathies for Israel were strongest in the smaller European countries (such as Holland and Switzerland) nor does it explain the pro-Israeli mood in Latin America or in certain parts of Africa and Asia.

There were some obvious trends: the democratic left in its majority supported Israel. The right was split; the extremists on both wings were violently anti-Israel. The *Rockwell Report* said: 'Watch the Jew-dominated United States Government clobber the Arabs if Israel is really in danger, even if we have to fight a

* Experience has shown that at least half the population is uninformed or has no opinion and tend to accept the position of the mass media. The mass media in America, and France, and to a lesser extent in Britain, were more in sympathy with Israel than with the Arabs. A change in their position would have, and in some instances did, express itself in a swing in public opinion. On the other hand, polls also showed (in America for instance) that sympathies with Israel were more pronounced among the highly educated and better informed sections of the population.

third world war to save these trouble-making Jews, as well we might.' The tenor of other anti-semitic newspapers was similar. The moderate right was split, one part giving Israel demonstrative support, another section advocating neutrality. The communists were basically anti-Israeli but there were considerable differences between the various parties. In France and Italy the foreign policy of the Government came under attack from public opinion, including many supporters of the Government parties, but found unexpected support among the communists. The dilemma of the left-wing, 'progressive' intelligentsia was most painful. Many of them believed that the political regimes in Egypt and Syria were basically socialist and progressive in character, that revolutionary Arab nationalism was part of the general revolt of the wretched of the earth against the arrogance of power, and that they were therefore *a priori* deserving all support. These men and women had grave doubts about Israel and accepted much of the communist line about the colonialist character of Israel and its function as a tool of western imperialism. At the same time most of them found the declared policies of the Arab countries, including the Arab left wing (destruction of Israel, annihilation of its inhabitants) unpalatable. They strongly affected the peace movement in America. One of its young supporters wrote: 'I think it must have been this way for many of my generation, that the Arab-Israeli conflict was a moment of truth ... For the first time I knew what it was to be up against the killers ... I will never again say that if I had been an adult during World War II I might have been for non-intervention or if I had been a man, a conscientious objector. I have lost the purity of the untested' (*Village Voice*, 15 June 1967). Their moral dilemma and their changes of mood will be described in more detail below.

Lastly, the Jews. In their overwhelming majority they supported Israel. Some had reservations, a few, not necessarily all communists, used the opportunity to make it known that Israel meant nothing to them. But the others, including many who had not before shown much interest in Israel or Jewish activities, were profoundly shocked. Raymond Aron in a moving article wrote about the dilemma of the assimilated Jew: 'I am what is usually called an assimilated Jew. As a child I wept about the misfortunes of France at Waterloo and Sedan – not about the

186

destruction of the Temple. No colour but the tricolour, no anthem but the Marseillaise, ever brought tears to my eyes ... yet if the big powers, coldly calculating their interest, let that little state, which is not mine, be destroyed, this crime, a small one by its scale, would not leave me much will to live. And I think that many millions would be ashamed of mankind.' (*Figaro Littéraire*, 12 June 1967.)

The Jews wanted to help Israel, but possibilities were limited. Their political power is usually exaggerated. Individual Jews had positions of influence in government and in the mass media. But Jews in politics, more often than not, have leaned over backwards to dispel all suspicion of dual loyalties. The fact that the Jews, a small and not universally beloved minority, espoused the cause of Israel, did not necessarily help that cause in public opinion. Arab leaders complained bitterly that the world's press, the radio and the television stations were all dominated by the Jews, and as a result gave a one-sided, distorted picture of the conflict. It was an exaggeration – they certainly had not *Pravda* in mind, or the Peking press. Nor All India Radio, nor the press and radio of the East European countries, or of Turkey, Greece or Spain. If the American and the west European press and radio favoured Israel, their support was not remotely as uniform and wholehearted as the official sympathies for the Arab cause expressed in Russia, China, and the other communist countries. But the Arabs wanted not only the assistance of communist governments and mass media, but also the encouragement of that section of world public opinion which was less exposed to government control and manipulation, and carried therefore greater moral weight. And they were hurt because it was not greater.

The United States

The American position on the Middle East conflict was neutral in word and deed, but when the spokesman of the State Department declared that it was neutral also in thought he ran into some trouble. There existed a special relationship between America and Israel. The achievements of the young state had made a profound impression on many Americans; a western-type democracy appealed more to them than did the regimes surrounding it. Israel's pioneering spirit stirred memories of lost American dreams, whereas the violent anti-Americanism of Egypt, Syria or Algeria did not exactly improve American feelings towards the Arab world. One should not perhaps overstate the depth of emotion or the intensity of the commitment, but as far as public opinion was concerned the feeling for Israel certainly outweighed the investments in the Arabian oilfields. Public opinion was not willing to support active intervention in favour of Israel, as had been suggested. There was certainly no enthusiasm for forcing the blockade of the Straits of Tiran, even though it was tacitly assumed that America would not stand idly by if the very existence of Israel were threatened.

The great reluctance to get militarily involved in yet another war had of course to do with Vietnam: 'one war is about all we can manage at a time' was the general feeling among the administration. When the Middle East crisis broke the great Vietnam debate which had raged for years had just gathered new momentum. The new crisis upset the established pattern and caused, in many cases, a sudden reversal of position. 'The doves of Vietnam sprout hawk feathers over Israel', wrote one columnist. And another asked: 'Who else but Israel could have turned our doviest doves into tiger sharks?' (William F. Buckley.) A writer in the *Wall Street Journal* observed: 'The Jews have been among the most dovish about the war in Vietnam. Administration men have almost maliciously enjoyed the way the Mid-east crisis has dulled some of this Jewish dissent' (7 June 1967). This was at best an oversimplification: previous polls had shown no significant difference between the attitude of the American Jews to the war and that of other ethnic and religious groups; there was no 'Jewish position' on Vietnam. According to a Gallup Poll in September 1966, 43 per cent of American Jews approved President Johnson's policy and 40 per cent disapproved. (39 per cent of the Protestants approved and 43 per cent disapproved according to the same poll.) But since the Jews were prominent in the battle against war in Vietnam, and since some of the same men now called for action with 'nerve and firmness of intent', as an advertisement in the *New York Times* put it, the reversal seemed all the more impressive. To the argument that, having opposed the idea of America playing the part of world policemen, it was inconsistent to call for American intervention in the Middle

East, it was said in reply that not all the critics of the administration's policy were doves – some rejected it on practical grounds. Nor did all the 'doves' turn into 'hawks' over Israel. Some of the liberals (Schlesinger, Galbraith, Robert Lowell) did not sign the appeal for intervention on behalf of Israel. Nor did the communists, Trotskyites, or the believers in the third world liberation struggle budge: for them Israel was just another imperialist state, a CIA-sponsored American military base. Israel did not fit into their categories of the international class struggle between the agrarian proletariat and the industrial metropolis, and was therefore rejected. Those critics of the administration's Vietnam policy who demanded American support for Israel saw no inconsistency in their attitude: Israel, Emmet John Hughes wrote, was 'a triumph of moral unity and political creativity', in stunning contrast to the wrecked and primitive political life of South Vietnam. The bond with Israel was essentially moral, not a calculation of self-interest. The commitments were not of matching weight and logical affinity. In short, there was no analogy: 'The historic natures of the two conflicts bear as much similarity as sand and jungle.' The supporters of Israel also argued that their position was by no means 'hawkish': they had urged the use of the influence (and strength) of the United States to secure a lasting peace between Israel and the Arab countries. But since this policy would have involved the use of force, the dispatch of military and naval units, the allegations of double standards were not dropped. There was a curious parallelism in American reactions to the Middle East conflict. The John Birch Society argued that the intention of the war was 'to divert the attention of the American people for a brief interlude from the horror of the far bigger mess in Vietnam' (*Bulletin*, July 1967). This statement would have been accepted without reservation by some progressives who likewise regarded the Middle East conflict as a major nuisance because it split the ranks of the Left. (The American communist newspapers reluctantly followed the Soviet Line, but attempted to put most of the blame not on Israel but on CIA plots and the conspiracies of the oil companies.) The 'respectable' right (Goldwater) supported Israel; the attitude of most churches on the other hand was not on the whole pro-Israeli.

The New Left faced a most acute dilemma. Among trade unionists or Catholics they had never gained much support; the emergence of 'Black Power' had antagonised many erstwhile militants of the civil rights movement. The Middle East conflict threatened to split the New Left altogether. The extremists argued that Israel was a colonial state, that the governments of Levi Eshkol and Marshal Ky were alike in most respects, that Arab socialism, as practised by Nasser and the Syrians, was the wave of the future. Objectively, the destruction of Israel by the Arab revolutionary liberation movement was progressive in character. These views provoked sharp dissent; the New Left had in any case been disappointed by the record of some of their former idols, like Nkrumah and Sukarno, and the performance of their regimes. A growing number of people now voiced doubts about the revolutionary and socialist character of Egypt and Syria. The chauvinist features of Nasserism and some other of its less pleasant aspects provoked the question: 'What kind of revolutionary commitment leads them to misinterpret all this and call it national liberation?' (*Ramparts*, July 1967). Such considerations did not, of course, lead to an espousal of the Israeli cause; there was much criticism of the 'double dealing and malicious role' of US foreign policy, of the 'cold war consensus of the American press with its simple good guy–bad guy expectations'. But the dilemma made it impossible for most members of the New Left to equate, in good conscience, Vietnam and the Middle East. Israel did not fit into their own good guy–bad guy consensus, and there was a great deal of heart-searching in these quarters, the more so as the leaders of the movement refrained from taking a public stand.

Lastly, the role of the American Jews: there were 5·75 million of them, only 3 per cent of the population, but they were concentrated in the big conurbations of the East and West Coasts. They were, on the whole, better educated and politically more active than other ethnic groups. There were only 18 Jewish Senators and Congressmen, but Jews, both in view of their concentration in certain key states and their heavy contributions to both parties, had political influence disproportionate to these figures, and it was suggested that any Democratic president would have to take their views into account and that consequently there might be a real conflict between Jewish sympathies and American political and economic interests in the Middle East. The Jewish emotional tie with Israel, it was implied, might well be harmful to America at a time of crisis. No one knows how powerful the often quoted Jewish vote really was; probably its impact was overrated. Jews had never voted as a bloc; they were always active campaigners, but there is no evidence that they really controlled anything like the 169 votes often mentioned in public discussion. The policy of President Johnson and his administration during the crisis was not more affected by Jewish pressure than President Eisenhower and Dulles had been ten years earlier. American public opinion was, in the majority, on the side of Israel, but the administration certainly played it cool; as a British observer put it, it carried aloofness very far and showed great determination to play fair with the Arab states (*Economist*, 10 June).

But the Arab states never gave it a chance.

Britain

The general trend of public opinion in Britain was similar to that in the United States, though pro-Israeli feeling was less intense. Traditionally there was not much love lost between Israel and the British Foreign Office or the editorial offices of *The Times*. The stand taken by the leading 'quality' newspapers was, on the whole, one of equidistant neutrality, in contrast to America. At the height of the crisis, leading liberal newspapers such as the *Observer*, the *Economist*, and the *Guardian* (a fervent champion of the Zionist cause in the past) suggested that Israel should make concessions to appease the Arab states. This, the *Guardian* wrote on 3 June, was only in accordance with equity. Israel was responsible for the crisis: 'when a chief of staff threatens to overthrow a neighbouring government he must expect an international crisis and ought not to expect automatic international support when it happens'.

The *Observer* also called for Israeli concessions; the analogy with Czechoslovakia in 1938 was misleading, it said; Mr Wilson was criticised for promising to help Israel against the Egyptian blockade. The *Economist*, less moralistic in tone, argued that Israel had been outmanœuvred; no longer occupying a position of strength, it had to make territorial concessions. 'President Nasser has to choose between being a local Arab Bismarck and a statesman with claim to world stature. The Israelis have the unhappier and lesser choice of seizing the ball of peace if, and when, it is thrown towards them' (3 June).

Further to the left there was little comfort for Israel either. *Peace News*, a mouthpiece of British pacifists, had been traditionally pro-Nasser. Nasser, it said, had been a source of stability and moderation in the area; his political survival should be ensured and nothing done to humiliate him publicly. *Tribune*, the organ of the Labour left, put all its hope on U Thant. Lord Russell's Peace Foundation published a manifesto in the name of 'The Israeli Socialist Organisation' and the 'Palestinian Democratic Front', the existence of which had been a secret well hidden even from Middle Eastern experts. The *New Statesman* on 16 June, published a reader's letter which ran: 'After your support of the *blitzkrieg* for the extension of "our borders" – as the Chief Rabbi of England's *Volksisraeliten* called the borders of Zionist occupied Palestine – your paper should be named the *Jew Statesman*, and take for its motto whatever is the Hebrew equivalent of *Sieg Heil*.' And (in *Tribune*, 23 June): 'Scratch a left-wing Jew and you find a Zionist. Paul Rose's hysterical letter shows the ideological abyss into which all socialists plunge when they allow their emotions to do their thinking for them ... If he is now preaching support for a Zionist state ... then he can no longer be classed as an international socialist ... international socialists must give unconditional support to Arab nationalism'.

A Trotskyite spokesman argued that Israel had attacked the Arab countries to save the pound sterling, and the communists predictably denounced the Israeli pawns of imperialism. The impression was created that Israel, mainly, though not exclusively, a cause sponsored by the left in the past, had been deserted by its former well-wishers. There was an element of truth in such allegations: Israel had developed a modern, reasonably efficient, western type of state – not something likely to appeal to those whose sympathies in the world struggle were on the side of Mao and the anti-western forces; Nasser's Egypt, for obvious reasons, was far more likely to attract their sympathy. Yet to argue that the left as a whole had jettisoned Israel would be inaccurate; the line of the *New Statesman* during the crisis was as pro-Israeli as that of the Tory *Daily Telegraph*. 'What should be understood above all is that Arab aims are unlimited ... the West's course therefore is clear. It is to make an unequivocal declaration of support for Israel's right to exist as a state and to be treated like any other internationally recognised state. All this needs to be said in clearer language than we have heard from our ministers ...' (*New Statesman*, 2 June 1967). The Middle Eastern conflict cut across existing party lines and even the (relatively) monolithic *Morning Star* (successor to the *Daily Worker*) published readers' letters criticising the Communist party's anti-Israeli line.

In the Labour Government the Prime Minister and some of his close advisers were believed to have pro-Israeli sympathies. The Foreign Minister, George Brown, was thought to be closer to the Arab point of view. He had met Nasser not long before in Cairo and, in contrast to other western diplomats, thought he could get along with him. The left wing of the Labour party was fairly evenly divided between pro-Israeli and Nasserites. Most, though not all, Jewish M.P.s supported Israel, whereas among non-Jews not a few, though not necessarily pro-Arab, believed in the progressive character of Nasser's regime. The motives behind Conservative attitudes were complex. Traditionally, the Tories have been markedly pro-Arab, but these sympathies had been for statesmen and regimes that had long disappeared. There was no love lost between them and Nasser; for many of them the crisis (and the subsequent Israeli victory) vindicated their stand over Suez twelve years earlier. The leading Liberals supported Israel, whereas the Young Liberals, rebellious as usual, favoured Nasser. The general mood in Britain was on the whole cautiously pro-Israeli; extreme manifestations were thought to be in bad taste. When Emanuel Shinwell, a former Minister of War, suggested in the House of Commons that the Prime Minister congratulate Israel in its hour of triumph, he was shouted down and there was a minor fracas. But the television appearances of Mr Christopher Mayhew and Mr Anthony Nutting (also a former minister), who took a pro-Nasser line, also provoked severe criticism.

Official circles, in particular the Foreign Office, emphasised that Britain was more vulnerable than other western countries because so much of its oil imports came from the Middle East, and the withdrawal of Arab deposits from London would be a blow to the City; from a commercial point of view, too, the Arab countries were more important for Britain than Israel;

hence it was necessary to keep on good terms with the Arabs. There was great eagerness in some sections of the British press, the radio and television, to offer advice on how to solve the crisis. Editorial writers wrote unsolicited memoranda to Mr Johnson as well as to Mr Kosygin, to Nasser and, above all, to Eshkol. This almost compulsive attitude should be seen against the background of Britain's past as a Middle Eastern power, and the firm belief in some circles that although Britain's position in the world was no longer what it used to be, it still had more political wisdom than the powers that had taken its place since – not to mention the Arabs and Israel.

Lastly, the experts – the orientalists, the historians, political scientists, economists specialising in Middle Eastern affairs, and the journalists stationed in the Middle Eastern capitals. Most of them were pro-Arab, like their colleagues in France and other European countries. Area experts often develop a genuine liking for, and identification with, their chosen region (and there were of course more specialists on the Arab countries than on Israel). Concentration on their area and its problems tends to distort the judgment of experts; like diplomats who have been accredited for too long to one specific country, they 'go native'. Personal friendships and a natural feeling of gratitude cloud their critical faculties. They will think up many extenuating circumstances to explain the lack of real progress in their area; for searching criticism of its basic ills one will look to their writings in vain. The reaction is a natural one, and it explains why both the academic expert and the political journalist were more often than not mistaken in their appraisal of – for instance – the balance of strength in the Middle East on the eve of war. This was a general trend among the area experts in Europe, and, to a somewhat lesser extent, America – there was nothing specifically British about it. The general pattern of British reaction to the events in the Middle East was not very different from that in other western countries. There was a little less support for Israel among the Liberals and the non-communist left than in other west European countries.*

---

*To explain this, a minute analysis of the character and development of the non-communist left in Britain over recent years would be necessary. This hardly seems necessary in the present context, since the differences between Britain and other European countries were not very marked.

From the Arab point of view, the British reaction was disappointing; in addition to the traditional supporters of Nasser and the Arab cause, there was, in many circles, great readiness to give publicity to the Arab cause, from a sense of fairness rather than of enthusiasm; there was no spontaneous pro-Arab feeling.

France

No political or moral issue since the Second World War has stirred France as much as the Arab-Israeli conflict in 1967. Thousands demonstrated nightly in the streets of Paris: on the Champs Elysées, before the Israeli Embassy on Avenue Wagram; on the left bank masses shouted 'Nasser Assassin' and 'Nasser au poteau', and there were Arab counter-demonstrations against 'Israeli Racialism'. There were countless meetings, and hordes of volunteers, the circulation of *Le Monde*, the leading quality newspaper, rose on the eve of the war from 385,000 to 533,000, and there were similar increases in the circulation of *Figaro*, *France-Soir*, and other papers. The enemies of the Vietnam war – a numerous class in France – had some weeks before launched a long-term appeal to collect 'a billion' (i.e. ten million new francs); the friends of Israel collected a billion in one day – and not as a result of contributions from a few millionaires either. This enthusiasm was sudden and unexpected; it cut right across party lines both on the left and on the right. While France's leading political forces were either against Israel (the communists), or maintained a neutrality that was, in the circumstances, interpreted as a betrayal (Gaullists), or kept aloof from the conflict (the Catholic Church), public opinion was overwhelmingly in favour of Israel. The communists (about whom more elsewhere), were almost isolated on the left, and found it difficult enough to persuade their own supporters of the correctness of their stand, let alone to make an impact on the broad public. There were no conspicuous defections from the party, but there were heated debates among the rank and file, reflected in the letter columns of *Humanité*. More than one old militant was reported to have said: 'Between the party line and Israel I have chosen ...'.

The Middle East conflict affected communist relations not

only with the left-wing intelligentsia – their political weight was not that great – but with their political allies, the socialists, and the left-of-centre groups. During the last year or two progress had been made towards an Alliance of the Left, if not a new Popular Front. This had been based on the assumption, on the part of the non-communist left, that the communists had become more democratic, less dependent on Moscow. Now, much of this was again put into question. If the French communists could not afford to take a line independent of Moscow on an issue that, from their point of view, was marginal, this seemed to justify the suspicions of those who had claimed all along that basically French communism had not changed since Stalin's day, that it still did not have a will and a policy of its own. The far right was split. Some right-wing extremists, including anti-semitic groups, supported Israel, much to the embarrassment of its left-wing friends. These included Tixier Vignancourt and certain Algerian ultras; men who a few years before had shouted 'Algérie Francaise' now sounded with their claxons 'Israel vain-cra'. Some organs of the extreme right (*Rivarol* and *Aspects de la France*), came out against Nasser, others such as *Défense de l'Occident*, attacked Israel. M. Poujade refused 'to die for Israel'. The journal *Minute*, the 'Rassemblement Européen de la Liberté', stayed neutral. Most ideologists of the extreme right, writers such as Maurice Bardèche and Paul Rassinier, were, as usual, against Israel and favoured a pro-Arab orientation.

The Gaullist camp was uneasy about the political line taken by its leader which, at first strictly neutral, subsequently veered towards open support for the Arabs. The General's motives were complex (they are discussed elsewhere in this study), but they were not shared by many of his supporters, including those who had followed him almost blindly for many years. In the cabinet only a minority stood behind him (Edgar Faure, G. Gorse, Alain Peyrefitte). Messmer, the Minister of Defence, at one stage threatened to resign. Debré, Maurice Schuman and the others were embarrassed. Rank and file Gaullists like Neuwirth, Fautan, Tribonet, Jean Claude Servan Schreiber, Sanguinet, were in open revolt. They did not accept the official party view that France had no obligations *vis-à-vis* Israel; they thought that there was more than a little truth in the criticism of foreign newspapers that 'Israel was to be thrown to the Egyptian sharks' as part of a bargain in which France would regain its political and economic positions in North Africa and the Arab world. Only a few years previously, de Gaulle had talked about the lasting friendship with his Israeli allies; now this was to be sacrificed on the altar of naked self-interest. How could the embargo on arms to Israel be morally justified, while arms continued to be sent to Algeria, one of the most aggressive countries in the Arab bloc?

The moral dilemma of the left-wing intelligentsia was painful: Israel had never been very popular in these circles which, during the late fifties and sixties, had been in the forefront of the struggle for Algerian independence and against American imperialism (Vietnam). To be in favour of the third world and its aspirations, to be anti-American, had been *de rigueur*, and since Israel did not fit into these categories it was not a fashionable cause to support; whereas the attitude towards Nasser was, on the whole, more sympathetic.

The majority of French *progressistes* were convinced that Nasser and the Syrians were 'objectively' progressive, while Israel was not. Yet, no matter how often Professor Rodinson, the leading Marxist anti-Israel expert, proved that Israel was a colonialist country and Israeli socialism a sham, a nagging doubt remained; something in them rebelled against accepting these theories. There were the memories of the Resistance, the fact that hundreds of thousands of Jews, the survivors of the extermination camps, had found a haven in Israel – would their extermination be a progressive achievement too? Nor did the Arab left make it easy for their French well-wishers; they angrily rejected any initiative for a peaceful solution. M. Sartre tried to sponsor a dialogue between Arabs and Jews in his journal, but he had to give up the attempt, since all the left-wing Arabs he approached refused categorically to recognise the existence of Israel. There were disquieting reports about the activities of ex-Nazis who had found an asylum in Cairo and who were employed there as propaganda specialists; there was the flood of anti-semitic (not just anti-Zionist) propaganda emanating from the Arab capitals, ranging from the *Protocols* to ritual murder stories. It could of course be argued that in certain circumstances anti-semitism too was a progressive factor, but many on the French left, including staunch friends of the Soviet Union, had their doubts. When the crisis broke an appeal was signed by Sartre, Schwartz, Claude Roy, Picasso and others which said:

1. That the security and sovereignty of Israel, plainly including free shipping in international waters, are a necessary condition and starting point for peace.
2. That such peace is attainable and must be ensured and affirmed by direct negotiations between sovereign states in the mutual interests of the people involved.

Sartre subsequently affirmed Israel's right to exist (*Al Ahram*, 3 July 1967) despite his criticism of the Israeli Government and its policies. Jean Daniel, another keeper of the conscience of the left, friend of Ben Bella and other North African leaders, wrote at the end of a long and tortuous editorial about Israel in *Le Nouvel Observateur* (31 May 1967) entitled 'Faut-il détruire Israél?': 'Still, today we must take sides. Is Israel ultimately threatened with death? No, not at any price. For each of us, whatever our political convictions, this would be a permanent disgrace.'

Some socialists were more outspoken: Robert Mizrahi, a professor of philosophy and a member of Sartre's circle, said at a meeting that for years he had looked for the Arab left but he had not found it; it did not exist. This was something that had not been good form to mention on the French left. He also spoke of the 'Fascist aspects' of Nasser's rule. Claude Lanzmann, editorial secretary of *Temps Modernes*, likened the Arab leaders preaching the extermination of Israel to General Westmoreland; he, a staunch anti-imperialist of many years' standing, had never thought to find himself in a position which would compel him to applaud President Johnson if he found that the United States was the only country to help Israel.

There were counter-attacks against 'Israeli racialism', against the new 'Union sacrée en faveur d'Israél', from which only the most reactionary elements profited. De Gaulle too had his defenders, not only on the extreme left. François Mauriac indignantly rejected the cartoons depicting de Gaulle as an oriental carpet dealer – and the insults from Israel (We thought we had a friend, we only had a *fournisseur*): he personally found it almost impossible to choose between Israel and Ishmael. He said that de Gaulle's supreme indifference was in the best interests not only of France but of all those involved in the conflict. This appreciation was not shared by many: when Courve de Murville, the Foreign Minister, declared that France had played an important part during the crisis his words were greeted with derisive laughter.

There were in France during the crisis, by and large, two attitudes towards the Arab-Israeli conflict: The one represented by the Government, the other by public opinion. The two had little in common.

Italy

The dichotomy between Government and public opinion in Italy was very similar to that in France; in some ways it showed that the political parties were not all powerful. For the Christian-Democrats and the communists are the strongest forces by far in political life, and a consensus between the two – a rare enough spectacle – would normally ensure peace in the political arena. On this occasion, however, it did not. The policy advocated by Moro and, above all, Foreign Minister Fanfani, was one of strict equidistant neutrality from the hostile camps; '*microgollismo all' Italiana*', the critics called it (*Corriere della Sera*, 8 June 1967). True, the Italian Government had never been as friendly towards Israel as had de Gaulle, and it never went so far in its opposition to the Jewish state during the crisis. Equally, the Italian communists were perhaps marginally less hostile to Israel than their French comrades, but then they had always been considered far more 'liberal' and independent than the French, and the hostile attitude of *Unità* came therefore as a greater shock than the bitter attacks of *Humanité*. Many Italian intellectuals including, for instance, Fellini, de Sica, Latuada, signed appeals in support of Israel. Almost the entire press – including *Avanti, Popolo, Secolo, Voce Repubblicana, Corriere della Sera* – was critical of the Government. The normally pro-communist *Paese Sera* came out in favour of Israel; only after a major administrative shake-up (including the ousting of the editor) was the political line adjusted. There was a split in the left-wing *Espresso*. Even the Communist party was divided. Senator Emilio Sereni declared that though most of his relations lived in Israel he fully supported the just cause of the Arabs. Another senator, Terracini, one of the oldest Italian communists, publicly came out in favour of Israel. There was dissension too within the Government. Fanfani's policy was attacked openly by Nenni, the deputy Prime Minister, and implicitly, by Saragat, Italy's President. At one stage Fanfani demonstratively walked out of a cabinet meeting after having been subjected to searching criticism for many hours. The line taken by Fanfani and other Christian-Democrats in the Government was that Italy had many political and business interests in the Arab world, and that Italian policy would therefore be best served by strict neutrality. The criticism of the socialists, the Liberal party, and public opinion in general was that such a policy was immoral; it did not take into account the merits of the case: To be neutral on the freedom of shipping meant to accept Nasser's point of view. It was suspected that the Fanfani line had at least in part been inspired by the attitude of the Vatican; from the ecumenical point of view the Arab East and North Africa were of course far more important than Israel, but this charge was indignantly rejected. Fanfani, a correspondent in *Avanti* said, wanted to use the crisis for his own ends, to gain the reputation of a peacemaker of international stature. There was uneasiness among Italians about the character of Nasser's regime, which in some vital respects reminded them of the not so distant past of their own country. Would the emergence of a semi-fascist, semi-communist Egypt as the leading force in the Eastern Mediterranean be in the best interest of Italy? As for the Italian loans to Egypt ($120 million), it was to be feared that this money, presumably used to arm Egypt, was lost for good; if so – why send good money after bad? (*Epoca*, 26 June.)

In previous years the Israeli-Arab conflict had hardly ever exercised the minds and emotions of Italian politicians and intellectuals – much less so than in most other European countries. The Italian Jewish community was small and assimilated, and the Zionist issue had never played a part in Italian political life. It was all the more surprising when the Arab-Israeli conflict became almost overnight a major issue in Italy, not only as a foreign political question but also as a moral problem. Who in the city of Bologna would have thought, in April 1967, that the Socialist-Communist municipal coalition in that city would break up as a result of events in the far away Gulf of Aqaba and the Sinai desert? Such were the complexities and ironies of modern history.

Central Europe

European public opinion was with Israel whatever the governments said in their official statements. There were demonstrations in many countries with signs such as 'Hands off Israel' and 'Shall Israel become another Auschwitz?' Individual citizens sent blood and money, thousands volunteered for work in Israel, meetings of solidarity took place in front of the Israel embassies. That most Jews identified themselves with Israel in this hour of crisis was natural, but how to explain that so many non-Jews chose to take sides in a conflict that did not directly concern them?

In Germany there was the feeling that a special responsibility rested upon the people 'as a consequence of our guilt', as a Protestant Church Council put it. But guilt feelings and a special responsibility do not explain the equally strong sympathies and manifestations of goodwill for Israel in countries such as Switzerland, Holland or Scandinavia. In these countries it seemed a struggle between David and Goliath, between a small country threatened with extinction by vastly superior forces; Israel was fighting not only its own struggle but that of all small countries. 'The courageous Israeli victory,' the influential *Neue Zürcher Zeitung* wrote subsequently, 'was a source of inspiration to all small countries because it showed that their fate did not entirely depend on the policies of the powers but that they could shape their destinies themselves, provided only they had the resolution to do so.' Friedrich Dürrenmatt, the Swiss playwright, said in a moving speech in Zürich that the commitment of the intellectual in favour of Israel was an obligation beyond all tactical considerations. Israel was born out of a natural law; for the United Nations to vote against Israel would legalise the murder of Israel (*Weltwoche*, 27 June 1967).

Moral commitment was not of course the decisive factor as far as official attitudes were concerned. The Governments of Greece and Turkey adopted a pro-Egyptian line though they had no particular reason to feel very friendly towards the Arab states. The Greek minority had been expelled from Egypt and its property seized; there had been considerable friction between Turkey, a member of NATO, and the pro-Soviet Arab governments. But both Ankara and Athens felt that in the Middle East Arabs mattered far more than Jews: the thirteen votes of the Arab League in the UN might be needed in a vote on Cyprus. In these circumstances the Greek and Turkish attitude was not surprising; nor was the Spanish stand in favour of Nasser. The Franco regime had no diplomatic relations with Israel, but there were traditional ties of friendship with Egypt and the North African countries. Portugal, on the other hand, had a bitter quarrel with Egypt which supported the terrorist movement in Portuguese Africa, and it refused therefore to side with Nasser. While General Franco's stand was supported for once by his bitterest enemies, the communists, public opinion in Spain did not share this view; many newspapers were cautiously pro-Israeli.

The small countries of west, central and northern Europe had no direct stake in the Middle East. They saw in the conflict analogies with their own problems: in Austria and Switzerland the crisis and the subsequent Israeli victory figured prominently in discussions on national defence. Did not the conflict show that at a time of crisis a small country was entirely on its own? That it was doomed unless it had both the necessary force and the resolution to fight, regardless of consequences? In Holland, where sympathies with Israel were particularly prominent, Christians felt that the call and promise of the Lord bound every believing Christian to the Jewish people; socialists, on the other hand, felt that Israel had given one of the few successful examples of a socialist and democratic society in a part of the world where the plants of freedom and social progress had hardly ever flowered. There was genuine enthusiasm for Israel in Germany, albeit occasionally for the wrong reason. Some German patriots were impressed by the *blitzkrieg*, and there were the inevitable parallels with Rommel and his Desert Foxes. Many a patriotic beer-table strategist was heard to say that all would be fine if only 'our politicians' would show half as much resolution as the Israeli leaders, if only the left-wing attacks on healthy patriotism (as shown by Israel) would cease! There had been a great educational effort in the new Germany to refurbish the image of the Jew, but there is no doubt that there, and elsewhere, the events of the five days in June caused a more profound change in this image than twenty years of well-meaning speeches, movies, and lectures. The Jews were thought to be rich and clever; now they suddenly emerged as a nation of exemplary fighters, a source of inspiration to patriots everywhere. This conviction was not shared by the German extreme right, which continued to denounce Israel as bitterly, and often in the same terms, as the communist Government of East Germany. Israel, said the *Deutsche National Zeitung*, had been created by 'violence, expulsion and murder'; it was guilty of racialism and intolerance, it was perpetrating 'Auschwitz in the desert'. It was led by war criminals: 'We accuse Israel of Mass Murder and Expulsion' (23 June). One issue of the newspaper which featured Dayan's photograph on its front page alongside a picture of Adolf Hitler was eventually seized by the West German authorities. Such views were accepted, however, only by a very few in West Germany outside the fanatical anti-semitic circles, the (illegal) Communist party, and certain ultra-left sects among students. Their anti-Israeli attitude was merely a by-product of their general political philosophy, another attempt to shock society and *épater le bourgeois*. If everyone was in favour of Israel surely the consensus ought to be broken. The consensus did not last anyway; Israel's victory caused elation among its supporters but it was only natural that the wave of sympathy should ebb once the immediate danger to the survival of the state was over. The 20,000 gas masks which had been sent to Israel were now returned. They had been sent despite the doubts of the Defence Minister, and they had also seriously worried Signor Fanfani, who thought that he might compromise Italy's neutral status if he let such war material pass through Rome airport.

European reactions came as a shock to the Arabs. They explained their political isolation as a result of the ignorance of most Europeans of the real issues involved in the Middle East and of the great influence of the Jews on both politics and the means of mass communications. It was not a satisfactory explanation – there were Jews in most European countries but their influence was limited, and their views on Israel (as on any other subject) were not necessarily shared by their fellow citizens.

Individual Jews were in the forefront of the anti-Zionist campaign in France and elsewhere. There was, admittedly, considerable ignorance about the details of the Arab-Israeli conflict; but the Arab belief that those familiar with their case would necessarily share it was a little naïve. The bare essentials of the conflict were known: a number of states had solemnly declared that they were determined to destroy a neighbouring country. Most Europeans thought that this was not the right way to solve a problem, whatever the rights and wrongs of the case. In its essentials it was not after all a complicated dilemma that demanded great knowledge and profound study.

Africa

Unexpectedly, the Arab-Israeli conflict had strong repercussions all over sub-Saharan Africa. The initial odds favoured the Arabs, even though many hundreds of Israeli advisers and technical experts had been active in most African countries. In Tanzania, for instance, both the police and the Labour Service had been trained by Israelis, who had also supervised large development projects. Despite her own financial problems, Israel had given Tanzania a substantial loan. Yet, at the time of the crisis, the Tanzanian press turned against Israel. It wrote about 'arrogant sabre rattling and shameless threats of invasion' when the Israeli Government announced it would not put up with the blockade. Dr Nyerere, while reaffirming Israel's right to exist, came out squarely in favour of the Egyptian point of view; so did the Governments of Mali, Guinea, Burundi, Senegal, Cameroon, Somalia, and one or two others. These countries, in which Soviet and Chinese influence was strong, had links with Egypt and Algeria; the Arab demand for a show of African solidarity against an 'outpost of western imperialism' fell on fertile ground. Dr Nyerere, Modibu Keita and Sekou Touré were impressed by Israel's pioneering achievements, but, ultimately, the charges of 'neo-colonialism' levelled against her outweighed her constructive efforts and the good-will that had been created over many years. Israel was not anti-western and this in the last resort was what mattered. Considerable pressure was exerted by the Soviet Union and, surprisingly, France, which still wielded a certain influence in her former colonies. Occasionally such pressure was counter-productive. The French attempt to line up African states against Israel antagonised more countries than it attracted. President Houphouet Boigny of the Ivory Coast, a former French cabinet minister, for instance, assured Israel of his total support and the Israeli embassy received many offers from volunteers who declared their readiness to fight. President Banda of Malawi told his parliament not to believe the 'lies and propaganda emanating from Cairo' – there was a great lesson for African countries in Israel's stand.

Africa's two youngest nations – Botswana and Lesotho – supported Israel, which provoked violent Soviet attacks on them. Botswana, said the Soviet radio, had taken a disgraceful step and had become an accomplice of the imperialists. The Somali republic promised military aid to the Arabs; more than 8,000 volunteers wanted to leave for Cairo to fight. This made it almost inevitable that Somalia's neighbour (and enemy) Kenya, should take a different attitude. The *East African Standard* wrote (7 June 1967), that President Nasser was the aggressor: if a new world war occurred it would be his fault. In some countries public opinion hardly existed and the personal predilections of a few leaders decided the issue. Gabon, for instance, was pro-Israel, but at one time its president would have been overthrown had it not been for French military intervention. President Leon Mba felt himself under an obligation towards President de Gaulle – it must have occurred to him that if he defied France now, French help might not be forthcoming in the future. Gabon chose accordingly. On the whole, however, the struggle for African support ended in a draw: slightly more than a third of the African states came out against Israel, the rest either opposed Nasser or remained neutral. Both Egypt and Israel were disappointed.

India

Official Indian policy towards Israel had been traditionally hostile: in 1938 Gandhi had advised German Jews not to emigrate to Palestine but to stay in Nazi Germany and practise passive resistance. Nehru had also opposed the formation of a Jewish state, and (with the exception of China) India was the only major country not to give Israel diplomatic recognition. According to the official line, the Indian attitude was not only intrinsically just, it was also in the country's interest to win Arab support against Pakistan (and China). Indian critics attacked these arguments which, they said, made nonsense of the non-alignment policy, and moreover had never been effective. The Arab states had shown no inclination to give India the support it wanted at the time of the crisis in 1962 and again in 1965.

Mrs Indira Gandhi and Mr Chagla, the Foreign Minister, took a strong anti-Israel stand from the beginning of the conflict. In this they had the support of the communists and the Muslim extremists, who, on this occasion, established a common front. A pro-communist paper announced that just as West Germany [*sic*] had become a mass grave for the Jews in the Second World War, so Palestine would be turned into a second burial ground for them (*Blitz*, 15 July 1967). It also denounced the West German Government for seizing the neo-fascist *National Zeitung* for having told the truth about Israel. Official Indian policy was, however, severely criticised throughout the country and it ran into considerable difficulties, not only in the Indian Houses of Parliament; there was resistance even within the Congress party and the Government. It is doubtful whether Mrs Gandhi and Mr Chagla would have carried the day but for the death of several members of the Indian UNEF contingent on the first day of the war – which was represented by the Indian Government as 'deliberate Israeli murder'. An opposition leader said in parliament that Indian official policy had never been so sharply divorced from public opinion as on this issue. The leading newspapers were all critical; some argued that India should have been neutral in the conflict, others maintained that India should have restrained the Arabs and prevented the war rather than give all-out support for President Nasser. An investigation made by the Indian Institute of Public Opinion revealed that 'majority literate opinion in the four metropolitan cities of Bombay, Calcutta, Madras and Delhi was critical of the Government's stand. As many as 95 per cent of the respondents had heard about the war', the *Statesman* reported (14 August 1967), the highest figure ever recorded in surveys on an issue where India was not directly involved. The results of the survey were, briefly, that only one out of four persons thought the UAR had been justified in closing the Straits of Tiran, and only one in four thought that Indian friendship with the Arabs should remain the paramount consideration of the future: 'Nearly double that proportion think we should treat Arabs and Jews at par.' There were interesting regional differences: in Calcutta a larger percentage held Israel responsible for the war than in Delhi; Bombay and Madras were the most critical of the Indian Government's stand. Indian official policy, they argued, had been morally reprehensible and politically self-defeating: it antagonised many of the country's friends and tried to curry favour with those who would not reciprocate anyway when it mattered. In parliament the Government had to face a major storm; there were personal attacks on the Foreign Minister whose policy, it was maintained, was out of touch with the mood of the country. Public opinion did not shake the Government's resolution to persevere in its policy; it certainly did not affect the Indian stand at the United Nations. The Arab-Israel conflict did, however, have an indirect effect on Indian politics; it coincided with major reverses for the Government on the domestic front and it strengthened the feeling among critics that India had an inept government and that a change in Delhi was overdue. In this way, a conflict that would normally have been of limited interest to Indians, made an unexpected impact.

Latin America

Latin American public opinion clearly favoured Israel; while the governments declared themselves neutral, the press and the public demonstrated in various ways their support for the Jewish state. Blood donors flocked to the Jewish hospitals, leading intellectuals signed appeals to stand by Israel in its 'just fight', thousands wanted to volunteer; among the left-wing groups there was disillusion about the Eastern bloc's total support for the Arabs. In Argentina only the fascist Tucuara supported the Arab cause; there were sporadic street fights in Buenos Aires, and the leader of the group, Pueynedon, volunteered to fight for the Arabs. Leaflets to join the 'fight for the liberation of Palestine occupied by international Zionism' were distributed. Tucuara support for the Arabs alienated the Liberals and left-wing groups even more. Considerable efforts had been invested by Egypt in previous years to gain support in countries with strong Arab communities. In the Argentine, for instance, there were 700,000 Arabs as against 450,000 Jews. But these communities were linked by traditional bonds of friendship; in joint appeals thousands of Arabs and Jews in Rio de Janeiro, Parana, and Bella Horizonte appealed for peace in the Middle East. The leading Argentine and Brazil newspapers, such as *Prensa, La Nacion, Jornal do Brazil,* supported Israel. Nasser was accused (by the *Jornal do Brazil*) of plotting a holy war of extermination against a small, beleaguered country, instead of waging holy war against the poverty of his own people. The United Nations were criticised for their weakness in face of a 'dictator's madness'. The Chilean Government declared itself 'physically neutral, but by no means indifferent'. There was much support for Israel in Uruguay, and, as in other Latin American countries, ferment on the left; *Marcha,* a left-wing magazine, wrote that Israel's destruction would destroy all belief in mankind. There was almost universal criticism of the Soviet Union (and of France) for having encouraged Nasser in his 'intransigent position'. The Guatemalan Senate and Congress condemned the blockade, while the Presidents of Mexico and Costa Rica appealed to both sides to abandon their arms and to settle their problems by peaceful means. The only Latin American country which gave full support to the Arab cause was Cuba. Relations between Havana and Jerusalem had been quite friendly, but on this occasion Castro's government was in no doubt that revolutionary Egypt and Syria had to be defended against imperialist Israel. The defence was carried to extreme lengths: one commentator on Havana television said on 7 June 1967:

> The leaders of the Israeli army are very unscrupulous in allowing their army to be commanded in every case by Nazi officers – the same Nazis who murdered more than 10 million [*sic*] Jews during the Second World War.

But this was stretching credulity too far: two days later a statement was read out that Comrade Mendoza had spoken merely as a radio commentator, not as a representative of the Government or of the state party, nor as a military expert.*

Latin American attitudes towards the conflict were thus on the whole not unlike those in Europe, despite the greater

* Cuban attacks on Israel continued; Havana – unlike the Soviet Union – was against the cease-fire proposed by the UN. But the Cubans, unlike the other communist states, did not break off relations with Israel.

receptivity to anti-American propaganda. The extreme left, and the far right, supported the Arabs; the rest were overwhelmingly in favour of Israel.

The Soviet Bloc and the Communist Parties

The great majority of the communist countries and all the important communist parties supported the Arabs in their conflict with Israel. It is impossible to say whether this official position was widely accepted; public opinion in communist countries cannot be gauged as in the West. China's Red Guards acclaimed President Nasser with great enthusiasm, but the Middle East was not exactly one of the problems which occupied them most. The Soviet Government did not encounter serious internal opposition to the party line on the Middle East, but it did not arouse much enthusiasm either. In most East European countries the anti-Israel line was unpopular, and in the case of some western communist parties it caused serious difficulties. It was not sufficiently important to cause a split, but it certainly deepened existing differences of opinion and thus contributed to the general trend towards polycentrism.

It was obvious that the Soviet Union would support the Arabs during the crisis: the intrinsic importance of the Arab world in Soviet global strategy (and the relative unimportance of Israel), the Soviet political, economic, and military investment there, made this a foregone conclusion. Ideologically, too, it could be justified; Israel, though not belonging to the western military or political bloc, was certainly pro-western in sympathy; the Arab countries were not. Nevertheless, all-out support for the Arab cause was bound to create complications; for Soviet policy in the Middle East had to show that it did not follow the traditional pattern of big power imperialism; it had to be rationalised, justified in doctrinal terms. And at this point the difficulties set in.

Under Stalin, a simple order would have been sufficient; fourteen years later the monolith had crumbled, and detailed explanations were necessary. There were many Jews in western communist parties who would raise awkward questions about the Arab threats to exterminate Israel; how could this be justified in terms of proletarian internationalism, let alone the struggle for world peace?

Could the resistance of a small country to much bigger neighbours threatening its very existence be explained in categories of Israeli imperialism, Hitlerism, and quasi-fascism? Why did Moscow break off relations with Israel? Had the Soviet Union throughout its history not kept normal relations with fascist countries? The questions became even more embarrassing after the Arab defeat: if the Arab countries were really progressive and revolutionary, how could they have been defeated by a country so much smaller and weaker, ruled by an 'anti-popular clique'? The defeat of one's allies was bad enough; defeat in such circumstances had an aura of the ridiculous. There were, of course, answers to such criticism. True, the Jews had suffered from nazism, but that did not change the fact that *objectively* they played a reactionary role in the Middle East as an outpost of western imperialism against the rising tide of revolutionary Arab nationalism. Emotions and false sentimentalism were out of place in the appraisal of the situation. The religious-nationalist call for a holy war against the Jews was one element in the Arab cause which the Soviet Union found not easy to digest. The explanation given was that only the reactionary Arab states were in favour of destroying Israel ('the most blood-thirsty sounding slogans came from precisely the most reactionary rulers whom western imperialism most favours and courts' – Palme Dutt in *Labour Monthly*, July 1967, 301). On other occasions it was argued that this extremism was an unfortunate by-product of Chinese propaganda; in the course of time, these elements of confusion in Arab policy and doctrine would disappear. Meanwhile such minor blemishes should not affect the overall estimate.

Progressive and reactionary peoples – not just classes – have always existed in Marxist theory. In Marx's day the Russians, the Czechs, and the South Slavs had been reactionary peoples obstructing the march of history and the progress of socialism. Now it was Israel. These assumptions were hardly ever stated in so many words, but they were largely instrumental in the rationalisation of communist attitudes. It was also argued that the struggle between Israel and its Arab neighbours was really a desperate attempt by the western oil companies to strengthen their hold on the Middle East, or that the whole conflict was merely a smoke screen for the Israeli design to overthrow the revolutionary Arab countries with the help of the reactionary Arab regimes. It is not easy to discuss such arguments seriously; there is no oil in Israel, nor indeed in any significant quantity in Egypt, Jordan or Syria. Oil companies have a vested interest in the preservation of peace, and it was obvious that in a war between Israel and the Arab countries they would be the main losers: the flow of oil would cease, the installations seized, perhaps nationalised. The 'secret alliance between Israel and the reactionary Arab states' was another red herring which played an important role in Soviet propaganda right up to the moment when King Hussain signed his agreement with Nasser, and King Faisal, too, expressed his support for Egypt. Some of these arguments were manifestly absurd and it is not certain that they were believed by those who used them. Putting the blame on conspiratorial forces (CIA, oil companies, etc.) usually goes down well with part of the public, and had the additional advantage of providing a plausible explanation of how a very small reactionary country could successfully resist much larger progressive forces. Communism never referred to the one correct explanation – namely, that it was a clash between two nationalisms. Was this a deliberate omission? There is a temptation to overrate Soviet cynicism and to underrate Russia's ignorance; Moscow's estimate of the balance of power was mistaken, and its political appraisal was equally unsophisticated. Soviet political observers have been trained to think in terms of imperialist intrigues; they may have seriously believed that Mr Eshkol and General Dayan were the local branch managers of Standard Oil of New Jersey. There are some indications that Soviet Foreign Ministry personnel, and a few others who have been exposed to direct contact with western (or Middle Eastern) realities, took a more sophisticated view. Others sincerely believed that monopoly capitalism was the key to the Arab-Israeli conflict and that the plot to attack Syria and Egypt had been hatched in some Wall Street office. The political equivalent of the flat-earth theory has deep roots in Soviet and communist thought; so has the state-of-siege mentality. There have been changes since Stalin's day but Soviet reactions during the Middle Eastern crisis showed that they were less far-reaching than many had believed.

During the first two weeks of the crisis the Soviet media underplayed the importance of the conflict; press and radio devoted little space (or time) to the mounting tension in the Middle East. On 16 May, Israel's (alleged) military build-up on the Syrian border was denounced; on the next day, the journal of the Soviet armed forces demanded an end to the 'provocative intrigues around Syria'. The impression was created (*Izvestia*, 18 May) that there was secret plotting between the American, British and Israeli authorities. On the same day, the Soviet public learned that Nasser had taken 'preventive measures'; on the 19th, that he had demanded the withdrawal of the UN forces; on the 20th that these forces had been withdrawn and replaced by Egyptian forces. So far, the gathering crisis had been relegated to the obscurity of minor paragraphs on the foreign news pages. It was on the 24th that news was given of the blockade of the Gulf of Aqaba. However, all these events were described as of limited importance; even ten days later a Soviet commentator said that the question of free passage for Israeli ships was certainly not the real issue at stake.

What then was the real issue? According to a *Pravda* commentator (22 May), the crisis was part and parcel of the Washington concept of local conflicts and little wars, scheduled to strengthen imperialist positions in various parts of the world: Syria, whose anti-imperialist outlook had displeased Washington, might in the next few days become the object of further provocation. *Izvestia* (23 May) saw a close connection between America's anti-Castro campaign, orgies of police brutality in Greece, the screech of American planes over Hanoi, and the threats from Tel Aviv. 'The CIA and nobody else has instigated the anti-Syrian conspiracy', said the *Pravda* commentator on 25 May. But even then there was a tendency to play down the significance of the crisis. When the British Foreign Secretary, George Brown, visited Moscow, it was reported that at his press conference he had described the situation in the Middle East as serious, but had been advised by his Soviet interlocutors that the Vietnam war was far more dangerous and that America's allies should make this clear to Washington in no uncertain terms. *Pravda* (25 May) said that the Tass correspondent in Cairo had received an assurance from Nasser that all he wanted was a return to the conditions prevailing before 1956; the Security Council was to play a positive role in this by giving its recognition to the blockade; flagrant interference in the rights and encroachments on the sovereignty of the Arabs was to cease.

The Soviet reader and listener who had no other source of information was thus led to believe that this was another minor crisis, part of an overall American blueprint which would blow over if only the peace-loving peoples showed sufficient vigilance and firmness. The crisis had broken not as the result of any decision taken by Nasser, but in consequence of Israeli threats. Israel was the villain of the piece, but not the main villain, for Israel would not dare to take a single step without American agreement. This assumption was based on a genuine misreading of the situation: but then Soviet observers have always underrated the degree of Israel's freedom of manœuvre and independence. The idea that Israel could act without consulting Washington, that it could even embarrass or defy Washington, was dismissed out of hand as unworthy of serious consideration. In the early fifties such simplistic views could be explained as merely transferring the pattern of Eastern Europe's almost total dependence on the USSR to the West. Ten years later such explanations would not do. If little Albania could defy Moscow, or Rumania, why not consider the possibility of similar defiance in the West? But Soviet observers were firmly convinced that Israel was a small and unimportant country even in comparison with the Arab states. They regarded the continued survival of Israel as a minor miracle, especially in view of the well known traditional lack of military virtues among Jews (a deeply-rooted Russian stereotype), and the well known fighting spirit of the Arabs. Seen from Moscow, Israel had a certain nuisance value because of the sentimental attachment of many American Jews and Jewish influence among certain sections of the European left. But Israel *per se* was not taken seriously; it hardly figured at all on the Soviet international chessboard. Chuvakhin, the Soviet ambassador in Israel, made no secret of his conviction that he had been accredited to Lilliput. As late as 30 May, Radio Moscow accused the West of clearly inciting Israel to ill-considered action; the West, needless to say, had done nothing of the sort, but was counselling patience.

From 1 June, the belief gained ground in Moscow that war in the Middle East was a possibility: 'Somebody was ready to light the torch of war to settle the question whether or not two or four ships will sail the Straits of Tiran' (Maevsky, *Pravda*). The irresponsibility of the 'hawks' in Israel was sharply condemned, and put in stark contrast to the constructive proposals made by Cairo. The appointment of General Dayan was reported under the headline 'The situation is fraught with danger' (*Pravda*, 3 June).

According to *Izvestia* of the same day, the political barometer was fast reaching danger point. On the next day, twenty-four hours before the outbreak of war, *Izvestia*, quite rightly, saw black crows circling, and the Soviet reader was told that his country was doing everything possible to prevent the violation of peace and security in the Middle East. The general idea was that if tension had now risen it was all the fault of Israel and its backers. They had provoked a crisis that could have easily been settled by peaceful means. The argument that Soviet policy might have had something to do with the crisis was indignantly rejected, for instance, in an attack on Mrs Golda Meir, the former Israeli Foreign Minister (*Izvestia*, 29 May). Almost all reports about the crisis came from Cairo and other Arab capitals, and all reflected the Arab viewpoint. At the same time, the language of the attacks was not as violent as it became after the war. Soviet policy before 5 June expressed concern about the situation in the Middle East. After the war the undertones of indignation and anger became far stronger. It is impossible to say with any accuracy to what extent all this reflected the mood of the Soviet public. According to reports from western visitors, Soviet Jews were, on the whole, in favour of Israel, while among the Uzbek, the Kazakh, and other Soviet Central Asian peoples there were marked sympathies for the Arabs, going beyond the official party line. Among the population as a whole there was confusion and some resentment against those who were endangering world peace, but at no stage before 5 June was the conflict considered a major threat to peace, nor were emotions deeply stirred. Among the intelligentsia there was uneasiness about the Soviet line. It was difficult to work up much enthusiasm for Nasser or much indignation about Dayan. The Soviet public did not care sufficiently about either.

Once the Soviet leadership had taken a clear stand on the Middle East conflict – and there was never any doubt that it would – this line was consistently pursued. There was no need for long explanations, internal discussions or external polemics, for the line was never challenged. The situation of the communist parties in the West was different: they had to justify their policy to their members (who were often critical), to their sympathisers, and to public opinion in general.

For historical reasons, the Arab-Israeli conflict also played a much more important role in eastern and south-eastern Europe than in the Soviet Union. It was not merely that communist newspapers outside the Soviet Union devoted far more space to news and comments about the crisis; to a much larger extent the subject engaged the minds and heated the emotions of people.

East Germany and Czechoslovakia stuck close to the Soviet line. The Czech Government accused Israel of inciting a war psychosis in the Middle East. This was the country in the Soviet bloc with the closest economic and military ties with Egypt and Syria. On the very eve of the crisis the Czech Chief of Staff was in Cairo together with other high ranking officers, and a treaty of military cooperation had just been concluded. East Germany likewise gave the fullest support to Syria and Egypt; its anti-Israeli propaganda was more extreme than that of any other Eastern bloc country. Of this propaganda the *Guardian* wrote:

So twisted has been the reporting in the East German Press, manipulated with a skill that would have done justice to a Goebbels, that even some of Ulbricht's regime's most loyal followers are said to be embarrassed lest the campaign draws accusations of an unbridled anti-semitism on German soil.

There is no denying that East German attacks on the Israeli criminals, murderers, and torturers, the accusations of 'systematic extermination of Arabs', 'orgies of blood and atrocity', were politically and psychologically revealing. East Germany had never accepted responsibility for the Nazi crimes; in contrast to West Germany it had not indemnified the Jewish victims of Nazism; there was no reason why it should do so, it was argued, because in the East, unlike the West, Nazism had been completely eradicated and this, of course, was far more important. Nevertheless, East Germany had always felt at a disadvantage *vis-à-vis* West Germany on this issue, and the Arab-Israeli conflict offered an opportunity to demonstrate that its policy had been right all along. Israel was a fascist state; even the supply of gas masks by Bonn to Israel was denounced as a 'war crime'. There were other considerations: for many years East Germany had battled against the Hallstein doctrine, trying to gain full diplomatic recognition by countries outside the Soviet bloc. In this it had not been too successful. The Arab-Israeli conflict offered a unique opportunity for a breakthrough; would not full East German support make Arab diplomatic recognition almost inevitable? Lastly, there was the fact that, politically, East Germany had changed less since Stalin's days than the other bloc countries; its propaganda had always been shriller and more mendacious. In comparison with *Neues Deutschland*, *Pravda* was moderate and statesmanlike.

Polish and Hungarian attitudes, up to the outbreak of war, were less extreme. Both Warsaw and Budapest expressed support for Nasser, without however condemning Israel in such terms as the East Germans. The Hungarians denounced 'aggressive endeavours' in general, the Poles wished Nasser success in attaining the UAR's just goals by peaceful means; Israel was not usually mentioned by name. After 5 June this changed: Gomulka accused Polish Jews of fifth column activities (19 June); Hungarian leaders, more in sorrow than in anger, argued that those who, for family reasons or by reason of 'horrible memories' supported Israel, were politically mistaken. 'These decent people forget that the leaders of Israel are the ones who court disaster' (Radio Kossuth, 20 June). However, even after the end of the war, there were occasional references to Israel's right to exist, and great pains were taken to stress that their condemnation had nothing to do with anti-semitism: 'Not a single socialist country wants to put the Israelis (as a whole) on the pillory' (*Nepszabadsag*, 21 June 1967).

Bulgaria followed the Soviet lead; on the eve of the war Todor Zhivkov declared that 'our sympathies are on the side of the Arab countries' (*Rabotnichesko Delo*, 4 June).

Rumania took an independent line; whilst supporting 'the just struggle of the Arab countries', Ceausescu called for rational and fair agreements that would take into account the legitimate rights of the peoples concerned (31 May). In contrast to the other communist governments, Rumania called for direct talks between Israelis and Arabs. Subsequently, while promising economic help to Egypt, Rumania did not sign the statement of the

East European communist regimes, did not threaten Israel with sanctions, and did not break off diplomatic relations.

Yugoslavia, on the other hand, came out squarely behind the Soviet Union. There had been close personal ties between Tito and Nasser from the days of Bandung and the attempts to establish a neutralist bloc; Tito, no doubt, felt a moral as well as a political obligation to support Egypt. He said that in the provocations and incidents on Israel's borders there was probably blame on both sides, but Israel acted provocatively and (in retrospect) there could be no doubt that Israel was fully prepared for aggression: 'Can a country, in the course of a few days, prepare for a mighty blow?' (speech at the seventh plenary session of the CC of the League of Communists of Yugoslavia, 1 July 1967).

Albania, which for several years had played with great consistency the anti-revisionist maverick in the Balkans, was for once in agreement with its East European neighbours in condemning Israel. But it saw the origins of the crisis in an American-Soviet conspiracy against the Arab countries. In this they followed, not surprisingly, the Chinese lead in regarding the Middle Eastern crisis, from the very beginning, as a case of Soviet-American collusion; the Americans were enemy No. 1, the Russians No. 1 assistant. Peking denounced the 'heinous swindle and double dealing of the Soviet revisionists' engaged in 'behind-the-scenes dealings with the USA'. Peking's Middle East policy in the late fifties and sixties had made little headway; its influence was limited to Syria and the Palestine Liberation Army. The most recent declarations of support for the PLO had been made on 16 May, when Shukairy stated that China was offering arms on condition that they should be used for revolution and to regain the homeland. In Syria, some years previously, the Chinese had tried to establish a foothold, but the Syrian leaders, while sympathetic to China's aggressive line, realised that its capacity to give help was limited, that it had become isolated in world affairs, and eventually, Damascus reverted to a policy of neutrality in Sino-Soviet affairs. Peking tried to make good use of the conflict (and subsequently the disappointment in some Arab circles with the Soviet Union) by stressing on every occasion that it was the only true ally of the Arabs, that China recognised its internationalist duty to help the

Arab countries against Israel. Israel as an independent factor was completely ignored by Peking. One of the accusations against Kosygin was that he went so far as to disregard the will of the Arab people by describing Israel, a lackey of US imperialism, as an 'independent national state' (*People's Daily*, 24 June 1967), and a reporter of the New China News Agency cabled from Cairo on 6 June that he had been told by Egyptians that 'the victory in our battle today testifies to the correctness of Chairman Mao's thesis that the reactionaries and imperialists are paper tigers' (*NCNA*, 7 June 1967). China had never been particularly well informed on Middle East policies; just as most westerners did not know the difference between Honan and Hunan, the Middle Eastern imbroglio remained a closed book to the Chinese. In any case, the country was almost totally absorbed in the cultural revolution, and this was not the right moment for a major initiative in a distant part of the globe. The other communist parties of Asia – those of Mongolia, North Korea, North Vietnam, Ceylon and Pakistan – all condemned Israel in their statements and some added that this was an American manœuvre to divert attention from the aggression in Vietnam.

So much then about communist official policy. In Asia there was no violent clash between the communist line and public opinion, nor was there any dissension within the parties.

In Europe affairs were far more complicated. According to western correspondents there was much sympathy for Israel among the population in Czechoslovakia, Poland and Hungary, and there was dissension even in East Germany. Some of this emerged from the East European press; the editor of the Polish *Zycie Literackie*, Machayek, wrote after the end of the war (18 June 1967):

And again, the so called man in the street: Look at those Israelis. Fast, aren't they? Like a different nation. These people, they say, are no sheep driven to the slaughter. They waged a Blitzkrieg ...

The Polish church was on Israel's side. Slonimsky, one of Poland's leading poets, wrote a poem in defence of Israel which made the rounds amongst the intelligentsia. There were conflicting voices in the Yugoslav press, despite Tito's personal engagement. While *Borba* charged Israel with genocide, and said that direct negotiations between Israelis and Arabs were out of question, *Politika* (4 June) criticised the Arab extremists' call for force in order to deny Israel's right to exist. After the war a Yugoslav newspaper (*Vjesnik i Srjedu*) drew attention (not without evident pride or, at least, *Lokalpatriotismus*) to the fact that some of the leading Israeli generals were former partisans, or of Yugoslav origin. According to western correspondents in Prague, the local population, especially the younger generation, identified itself with Israel, some because they remembered Munich, others because they were inveterate sports fans and admired a knockout when they saw one (cf. *Frankfurter Allgemeine Zeitung*, 12 June 1967).

There was a surprising parallelism in the reactions of the communist parties of France and Italy to the conflict. 'Nothing could be more misleading than the western propaganda image of the poor, innocent little state of Israel exposed to the hostility of the whole Arab world', the French communists said. Behind Israel there were the great imperialist powers. The Egyptian decision to close the Straits of Tiran drew the teeth of Israel's anti-Syrian plans. In Syria a socialist revolution was taking place which must be defended; Arab socialism was advancing at breakneck speed, according to the Italian communists. The right-wing extremists in Tel Aviv wanted a limited conflict with the Arab countries but this would set off a chain reaction involving the Great Powers (Yves Moreau in *Humanité*, 23 and 25 May, Alberto Jacoviello in *Unità*, 3 June 1967). The communist parties of France and Italy promised unconditional support to the Arabs. This was their basic attitude throughout the crisis, but it did not evoke much response on the French and Italian left; it was not even wholeheartedly accepted inside the parties. There were many critical readers' letters in *Humanité*; in Italy, the communist evening paper *Paese Sera* prepared a page denouncing Egyptian aggression which was suppressed only under strong pressure by the party executive. Terracini, chairman of the communist group in the Senate, sent a cable to the World Jewish Congress in which he expressed solidarity and sympathy with Israel and observed that the Arabs were denying Israel's right with 'exceptional fanaticism'. The Communist Federation of Rome, in a message to the local Jewish community, stressed the right of Israel to full national independence.

There were many such manifestations and they induced the French and Italian Communist parties to reiterate that, while Israel was an artificially created state, while it was colonialist in character and bore the responsibility for the present crisis, while it played the same role in the Middle East as West Germany played in Europe, communism did not intend to question the existence of Israel (René Andrieu in *Humanité*, 30 May 1967). The communist leaders accepted the Arab viewpoint about the colonialist, imperialist, even fascist character of the Jewish state, but they stopped short of drawing the ultimate conclusion. They attempted to reconcile their 'unconditional support' for the Arabs with their refusal to accept the destruction of the state of Israel. (For a detailed discussion of this dilemma see Roger Paret, '*Humanité*'s Internal Contradictions', and Gino Bianco, 'Italian Communist Attitudes', in *Wiener Library Bulletin*, July 1967.) This was an impossible task, because the Arab position on Israel was perfectly clear and simple; it had been expressed by President Nasser, the Ba'ath leaders and other Arab spokesmen countless times; when *Humanité* now argued that the Arabs were ready to sit down with Israel at the conference table to discuss a peaceful solution (*Humanité*, 2 June 1967) this was an interpretation which Nasser and the Syrians would never have accepted.

The French and Italian communist leaders were embarrassed by the calls for mass destruction and annihilation; they did not go down well with the peace slogans and the traditional ideal of international working class solidarity. The only thing they could do was to ignore or to belittle the Arab declarations about Israel. Responsible Arab leaders, it was argued, had never indulged in such fanaticism; they had been misquoted and misinterpreted; some of their speeches *were* a little wild, but they didn't really mean it. The outbreak of war and the Israeli victory eliminated this dilemma, making it possible to brand Israel as the aggressor and brutal conqueror with more conviction than before.

The crisis had revealed a curious identity of outlook between the French communists and de Gaulle, and the Italian communists and Fanfani. But, in a wider sense, both parties felt isolated; the tide of public opinion was running against them. Both parties had tried very hard in previous months and years to work for an alliance of all left-wing and progressive forces in

France and Italy; they had stressed their independence and democratic character. The Arab-Israeli conflict was a setback for them; even those among the left who favoured collaboration with the communists were now beset with grave doubts. If the communists were unable to afford an independent line on a comparatively unimportant foreign political issue, if they had to revert to a policy that in some respects fatally resembled Stalin's best days, did it not mean that the character of the party had not essentially changed during the last decade? French and Italian communist leaders have never shied from a political fight and their behaviour during this crisis was aggressive enough: yet they were fighting back like a boxer driven into a corner, and they were not too happy about their position. Their dislike of Israel was genuine enough but they were not enthusiastic about the Arabs either. They had to accept responsibility for irresponsible statements made by non-communist leaders, which gravely compromised them. They had to pay lip service to a people's war which they hoped would never come. They were overjoyed when the immediate crisis was over.

The Communist party in Great Britain followed the Soviet line, provoking some protests from the rank and file. Further explanations had to be provided by the leadership: the party supported the Arab liberation movement in its struggle against imperialism, but it did not support extremist Arab demands for a war to destroy the state of Israel (*Morning Star*, 2 June 1967). When war broke out, the anti-Israeli line hardened despite more criticism which was reflected, for instance, by readers' comments in the *Morning Star*. In the United States the pattern was similar: support for the Arabs, dissociation from the appeals for war and destruction. Most of the blame for the crisis was put on President Johnson, and the CIA and Wall Street rather than on Israeli policy. The Jewish section of the party found this explanation disingenuous and was subsequently dissolved. Among the communist parties in the smaller European countries there was a great deal of uneasiness: a few followed the Soviet lead unquestioningly but most had their reservations. These included the Scandinavian parties, those of Holland, Switzerland and Austria. While the Soviet Union recognised only the pro-Arab Communist party (Rakah) of Israel, several European parties continued to back the pro-Israeli party (Maki).

The Trotskyites

Trotskyism had been, traditionally, even more severe than communism in its condemnation of Israel, calling at the same time for a more revolutionary policy on the part of the Arab countries: 'We stand on the side of the Arab masses and the Arab countries against the Zionist state.' They left open the question whether the state of Israel had a right to exist. One of them wrote during the crisis that the only solution was the workers and peasant revolution aimed at the establishment of a socialist republic, with full rights for the Jews, Kurds and other minorities (Tony Cliff, 'The Struggle in the Middle East', *International Socialism* pamphlet). Other Trotskyites said that the Arab movement would not deny the elementary rights of the Jewish masses, provided that the Jewish masses in Israel did not identify their fate with that of Zionism: 'At some future date there must be coexistence and collaboration between the Arab states, including a Palestinian Arab state, and the Jewish national community now in Palestine' (*World Outlook*, 14 July 1967 – Resolution on the Middle East conflict by the United Secretariat of the Fourth International, adopted 28 June 1967). Within the Trotskyite movement there were, as usual, half a dozen different approaches; to the outside observer these doctrinal differences may seem minute but they are sources of bitter strife between the various sects that constitute this movement. Politically, of course, none of this mattered, but their declarations were not devoid of interest for a student of politics specialising in sectarian attitudes and the fossilisation of ideas. Nowhere could this be found as pure as amongst the Trotskyites; parties in power or mass movement in opposition have sooner or later to make concessions to reality however strong their ideological commitment. Sects are more fortunate; they can afford to think and to move in the rarefied atmosphere of pure doctrine, however outdated.

'World Jewry'

The May crisis made a deep impact on Jews all over the world, including many who had not in the past identified themselves with Jewish activities or the state of Israel. Jews have the reputation of being an excited (and easily excitable) people – characteristics that are not difficult to explain with reference to recent Jewish history. Many of them talked of another Auschwitz and a new holocaust, but then they were neither Middle East specialists nor military experts. The news in the papers and on the radio sounded very bad in late May, and the experts were not markedly optimistic about the survival of Israel either. Many Jews had friends and relations in Israel and were therefore directly concerned, but even those who had no such ties felt, often for the first time in their lives, that a Jew, however remote from organised Jewish life, had some special relationship toward the state of Israel, regardless of whether he was a Zionist, had supported the establishment of a Jewish state in 1948, or felt himself in accord with its policies. In the past such ties might have been denied, but when the very existence of the state was threatened they felt they had been mistaken. There had been a wave of enthusiasm among Jewish communities in 1947–8 but this had gradually ebbed away, and most assimilated Jews – and the process of assimilation was making constant progress in almost all western countries – followed events in the Jewish state with diminishing interest. They might perhaps visit Israel once or twice, but they certainly did not regard it as their own country. The average Jewish college student in the United States, the biggest Jewish centre in the world, was far more interested in the Civil Rights movement than in the Kibbutzim. The young men and women of this generation did not think of themselves primarily as Jews but as citizens of the world. They shared a common origin and, usually, some characteristics, but their Jewish origin had little positive meaning in their lives. Their knowledge of, and interest in, things Jewish was by and large negligible. The younger generation was far removed from things Jewish, and it was moving further away all the time.

The crisis was for them a moment of truth. Most of them rallied spontaneously; it was an atavistic reflex, the critics said, but a natural one: they sensed that their group, or at any rate a vital part of it, was in danger of extinction. And since this danger came only two decades after the greatest catastrophe in Jewish history they felt a sense of special obligation to help.

The big demonstrations all over the world have been noted; even in the communist countries there were semi-public manifestations of support despite the risks involved. Mr Gomulka spoke about a 'fifth column' in Poland, the Hungarian communist leaders put it more delicately – but meant the same. Jews had, traditionally, played a large part in left-wing organisations; now they faced a special dilemma in view of the total support given by the Soviet Union and the communist parties to the forces threatening Israel with annihilation. Many dissociated themselves from the party line.

A great deal of money was collected within a few days. American Jews were urged 'to give as you never gave before'. Fifty families in Boston contributed two and a half million dollars in one night; the Jewish community in Britain collected more than £10 million. Much of this did not come from a handful of millionaires; there were collections in the streets and in homes. Many gave a week's or a month's salary. In Queens, NY, a teenager pounded the pavements with a Manishewitz borscht bottle and returned with $72·60. An elderly lady in Paris gave five Napoleon gold coins which she had been saving for her funeral, children gave their savings, teenagers the money they had saved for their holidays. The response was amazing, even for a community renowned for its willingness to give in time of need. Volunteers for Israel numbered 9,000 in Britain alone, many thousands more in America, Canada, France, South Africa, Latin America. More than a thousand volunteers registered in the Israeli consulates in Switzerland. About 5,000 volunteers from 38 countries had arrived in Israel by June, some for a month or two, others for longer. They had come despite the official ban on travel that was in force in America and in many other countries. They included physicians, accountants, engineers, students, people from all walks of life. Many more failed to reach Israel, for communications were interrupted when war broke out; there were angry scenes at the airports, a rush for seats in the few planes leaving for Lydda. Within the much embattled Jewish communities the disputes ceased; even the ultra-orthodox 'Neturei Karta', who did not recognise the existence of the Jewish state, called off its demonstrations and campaigns. This spontaneous upsurge had a great indirect effect on Jewish life, though it was by no means clear that it would be a lasting one. Those who now expressed their solidarity with Israel had no intention of joining the official Jewish and Zionist organisations. These organisations, especially in Europe, but also in the

United States, had never had much appeal for the intelligentsia, certainly not for the younger generation. Emergency committees of various sorts were now created to absorb all these new energies. Small groups of writers got together, scientists and businessmen met on private initiative to decide how they could most effectively help Israel. Much of this enthusiasm was to disappear once the immediate danger was over, but it was an interesting phenomenon and, from the Jewish point of view, an encouraging one. Who could have believed that Jews all over the world were still capable of so much common feeling and action, such a demonstration of solidarity?

There were some dissidents who asked, as a writer in a British daily did: 'What is this dangerous talk about Jews *shirking* their duty?' and answered 'What is my duty where Israel is concerned? The answer is that I have none, feel none and will accept none.' The American Council of Judaism, a small body of wealthy and highly respectable citizens, protested against the pro-Israel 'hysteria'. It was no great surprise that Jewish communists in France, who fifteen years earlier had justified Stalin's anti-Jewish policy, would now defend with equal zest the party line on Israel. The most violent attack against Israel in Britain came from the late Isaac Deutscher. Some Jewish intellectuals refused the invitation to sign open letters in defence of Israel, and the playwright, Peter Weiss, published an article (*Aftonbladet*, Stockholm, 17 June) in which he accused Israel of threatening the peace, charged certain Israeli leaders with fascist tendencies, and complained that, as a result, the struggle against the war in Vietnam had suffered. Such attacks caused much bitterness among Jews and there was talk of traitors and Quislings. But there has never been complete unity among any people in history, not even in England after Dunkerque. Was it not inevitable that among a group like the Jews, dispersed all over the globe, with far less internal cohesion, there would be some dissenting voices?

The final word on the subject was said by a French Jew who wrote a letter to *Le Monde* in response to some distinguished left-wing professors who had dissociated themselves from pro-Israeli manifestations and had incidentally stressed their rank and titles: 'I am glad to see that the Jews are at last an ethnic group like all others with their "ultras" and their renegades.

This reassures me. It is true that I am only Charles Ajenstat – worker on the E.D.F.'

Some Tentative Conclusions

A thorough analysis of public opinion during the crisis in various parts of the globe could be provided only in a separate book – probably only in a series of books: a monograph would be needed to study public opinion in France alone during the three weeks preceding the war. But the general attitudes clearly emerge even from a cursory survey. Nasser and the Syrian leaders received great, often enthusiastic support throughout the Arab world and North Africa, and to a lesser extent in other Muslim countries. Outside this area they had the official blessing of the Soviet bloc, China, and some Asian and African countries; whether there was much spontaneous enthusiasm is doubtful. Israel had many sympathisers in Europe, the Americas, and to a lesser degree in parts of Asia and Africa, on a non-official level also in the communist world. This feeling stemmed from various sources. Natural sympathy for a country facing vastly superior forces, a residue of guilt feeling *vis-à-vis* the Jews, dating from the Second World War, abhorrence of the threats of destruction and mass murder against Israel. These popular sympathies were not necessarily shared by governments and foreign ministries, which, in view of the greater political and economic importance of the Arab countries, thought such identification with Israel unwise. There was in many countries a real conflict between the government and public opinion; it emerged that, not surprisingly, in most cases the impact of public opinion on official policy was strictly limited. In some countries public opinion made a greater dent in *raison d'état* than in others: a comparison between the United States and France would provide interesting insights for the student of politics – and not only for him.

The present study deals only with the events leading up to 5 June; after the outbreak of war the picture changed. Israel was no longer the underdog; hundreds of thousands of Arabs had been displaced as the result of the war. Israel found itself in the unaccustomed and unpopular role of a conqueror and occupying power. These factors worked in favour of the Arabs. On the other hand, great prestige and credit accrued to Israel from its victory; the Arab governments had to work hard to refurbish their image in the world. There were conflicting trends even in the communist world: the war and its consequences made it much easier to depict Israel as an aggressor and a colonialist power. On the other hand, its victory against forces that, in the communist view, were not only more progressive but so much stronger and better armed, put the Russians and the other communist powers into an awkward, even a ridiculous position. The outcome of the war did not produce much self-criticism in the Arab world; in the communist countries, on the other hand, explanations of the defeat had to be provided for domestic consumption.

Most Jews, all over the world, identified themselves with the fate of Israel, however faint their ties with the Jewish state or with Judaism in general. On the whole the conflict affected public opinion more deeply than could have been expected. Television gave this war a greater immediacy and brought it (literally) home to a greater number of people than any other conflict in history. For a little while it appeared that the big powers might interfere and that a local conflict could turn into a world war.

For a great many people it was a moral issue: whatever the rights and the wrongs of the Arab-Israeli conflict, the threat of annihilation was inhuman. The Arabs bitterly resented this kind of reaction: if the claims of Zionism were unethical, why was it taboo to reopen the Palestine issue, why was 'Israel there to stay?' Arab spokesmen explained their defeat in the battle for world public opinion by reference to the ruthless efficiency of Israeli propaganda. But Israeli propaganda was by no means very efficient, nor would many Israelis agree that they were the winners in this struggle. Israel is a small country with distinct priorities and limited resources. Its 'Information Services' never had high priority. There was a spontaneous wave of sympathy for Israel before 5 June, quite irrespective of Israeli propaganda. There were also many disappointments. Throughout the crisis both sides always hoped for total support by public opinion, and both were therefore never quite satisfied.

Conclusion

A great victory is a great danger. For human nature
it is more difficult to bear than a defeat.

F. NIETZSCHE: *Unzeitgemässe Betrachtungen*

This account of the crisis ends with the morning of 5 June. The
roar of the Mystères and the Mirages rising from the tarmacs of
the Israeli airports would provide a dramatic finale for a movie
director; to the historian it is a somewhat unsatisfactory ending.
But it is obviously the conclusive date for the present study: for
on that day a new train of events was set into motion, the end of
which is not in sight. The war and the rapid Israeli victory immediately overshadowed the pre-history of the conflict: the
fears, doubts and hesitations, but also the confusion and the
grim resolution of the *Konenut* period were quickly forgotten.
The result of the war has altered everyone's outlook on the crisis
that preceded it: it threw such a flattering light upon the policy
of the Israeli Government that hesitation now appeared purposeful; even mistakes assumed the aspect of prudent manœuvres. In fact, accident played a certain role, and so did luck;
but basically, as we now know, the outcome of the war was
never in question. The result would not have been very different
had it broken out on 25 May, or 15 June.

On the Arab side, the news of defeat changed a mood of
exhilaration and patriotic enthusiasm, first to incredulity and
then to dejection; and this with converse effects upon judgment
of the preceding events. Nasser's brilliant policy during the
second half of May, Hussain's visit to Cairo and the signing of
the pact, the Syrian intransigence and Shukairy's speeches – all
these things have since been seen in a different light, as distorting
as revealing. The dust raised by a decisive conflict is apt to
obscure and falsify our view of previous efforts to prevent or
profit by it. It is helpful to know what happened after 5 June, but
hindsight does not necessarily help one to understand why the

228

Russians and the Syrians, the Egyptians and the Israelis acted as they did during the three weeks' crisis.

As for the historical importance of this third Arab-Israeli war, whether it was an episode in a long-drawn-out conflict, or a decisive turning-point, speculation would be premature. Perhaps it was the last war before the conflict turned nuclear, perhaps it will be followed in a number of years by another conventional military campaign. These questions will be more profitably discussed from the vantage point of the year 2000; the chain of events that began on 5 June is likely to continue for a long time. The present study has been devoted to a less ambitious subject – the origins of this war. Upon this, too, it will be a long time before historians can assemble all the evidence and reconstruct the whole from fully detailed documentation. Surprises, no doubt, will be in store, but I doubt whether these will decisively affect the general picture. There are, in our day and age, military, scientific and technical secrets, but political secrets seldom remain hidden for long. Nor is it likely that documents will shed much light on the deeper causes; they will tell us about certain events and actions, but only rarely about the underlying motives.

Future historians are quite likely to make the origins of the war of 1967 appear more complicated than they were. A temptation to see hidden purpose and detailed planning where there were mainly accidents and contingencies is always present – and nowhere is it stronger than in the Middle East, with its inbuilt belief in the conspiracy theory of history. Indeed, the truth about the third Arab-Israeli war seems too uncomplicated to be given wide credence. The facts, that Nasser stumbled into it, that Israel was unprepared and confused, that Russian intelligence was incompetent and Russian judgment poor, that America was powerless to do anything – all this sounds too banal to be generally accepted. Yet, on the basis of what we now know, it seems that only the Fatah and perhaps the Syrian leaders wanted the war. They were impatient with the many anti-Israeli resolutions that had been adopted over the last ten years and had not brought the liberation of the homeland any nearer. They were genuinely convinced that a 'people's war' would do the trick; it would harass the Israelis, compel them to engage in massive retaliation and thus, sooner or later, involve the regular armies of the Arab countries. Their general assumption was that the combined might of the Arab states was superior to Israel. At worst the war would end in a stalemate – to be repeated again after a few years. The Arabs could afford these campaigns, Israel could not. Israel would disappear as a result of this escalation of harassment just as the French colons had vanished from Algeria. The Arabs genuinely believed that Zionism regarded Israel not as a homeland to be defended to the last against all enemies, but as a territory for financial investment, speculations and exploitation. They believed that the Jews, lacking patriotism and roots in the country, would lose their nerve and eventually give up Israel, if they were exposed to this treatment long enough.

The Kremlin had been consistently pro-Arab since the middle fifties; and this policy was strengthened by the emergence of a radical left-wing government in Syria in February 1966. Moscow had a low opinion of the military capacity of Israel, partly owing to traditional patterns of thought ('Jews do not fight'), and partly from weakness in its political and military intelligence. Nor did the Soviet leadership realise how difficult it would be at a time of crisis to control its allies in the Arab world. The irrational motivation, of the Syrian Government in particular, was under-rated. It may never be fully established whether the rumour that started it all, about troop concentrations and an impending Israeli attack, was a deliberate lie, or was really believed by the parties concerned. On the available evidence, it is unlikely that the Russians and Syrians could have believed it. But Middle Eastern rumours should be seen in their natural context, the propensity of Arab and Communist regimes to see plots and conspiracies everywhere, and their siege mentality. Moscow definitely intended to mobilise Nasser to save Syria and to control it, but this was to be a limited exercise in brinkmanship, not a war. Russia wanted an Egyptian show of strength; it is not certain to what extent it had advance knowledge of Nasser's subsequent actions. At this stage, however, the initiative passed into Nasser's hands and the Russians lost whatever control they had before. They had to continue to support Nasser, unless they were willing to sacrifice all their prestige and influence in the Arab world. They tried to minimise the risks involved by making a halfhearted attempt to restrain Nasser and the Syrians – unsuccessfully, as it appeared.

When Nasser was alarmed by the Russians and the Syrians in early May, he could not possibly have attributed more urgency and importance to the crisis than on many such occasions in the past. But he was now, under the defence treaty, bound by a formal obligation to come to Syria's help. Above all, there was the growing feeling that he ought to regain the initiative, and ultimately the leadership of the Arab world. He was faced by a mounting crisis in Egypt, the continuing provocations by Jordan and Saudi Arabia, and the taunts that he was hiding behind the UNEF. Thus, in the end, Nasser was provoked to act in a way that he himself had often deprecated. For a long while he had resisted this pressure, but eventually he must have concluded that he stood to lose more from inaction than from brinkmanship. Of Israel's power he did not think too highly; he was convinced that its successes of 1956 were the result of collusion with Britain and France; without such help (and he assumed correctly that Israel would now have to act alone), he believed that Israel had no chance of success against the combined might of the Arab armies. Egyptian intelligence had assured him that there was a political crisis in Israel – economic difficulties, dissatisfaction with the Government, a split among the leadership. And, his political experience being limited to non-democratic countries, he gravely underestimated the strength and moral resources of Israel. Democratic regimes are permanently in a state of crisis, dictatorships never – officially. That is why democracies always appear weaker than they are, and dictatorships stronger.

Not that Nasser's decision was based on a rational calculation of the risks. He acted in a fit of anger and annoyance. In the beginning his ambitions were limited, and whether U Thant's quick surrender was of decisive importance will remain in doubt. Nasser may have wanted only a partial withdrawal of UNEF, and perhaps U Thant's reply: 'All or nothing' made it impossible for him to retreat. But was this really the main turning point in the prehistory of the war? Nasser had set his mind upon gaining control of Sharm al Shaykh, and once his army was deployed there, he had no excuse not to impose the blockade. War was not yet inevitable at this point. Israel would have reacted somehow sooner or later, but there was marked reluctance in Israel 'to die for Sharm al Shaykh'. This was a major political defeat for Israel but it was not a question of life and death. Yet escalation continued: the Egyptian troop concentrations in Sinai provoked a general call-up in Israel. The Arab leaders countered by further military measures, by the pact between Nasser and Hussain, the dispatch of Iraqi units to Jordan, and by intensifying their threats. And then, the real issue was no longer the Straits of Tiran, but the very existence of the state of Israel.

The Israeli Government had been certain that there would be no war in 1967, nor in the next few years. Nasser's moves came as a total surprise. The Government was confused – so was the public. The army, after recovering from its initial shock, favoured military action at the earliest possible stage, arguing that delay would mean only a mounting toll of victims. But at first there was reluctance to accept their view, not from any doubt that Israel would ultimately win the war, but from a fear of heavy civilian casualties. It was decided to make an all out diplomatic effort against the blockade and the threats of invasion. But America and Britain were unwilling to act alone, and among the other Western countries there was marked lack of enthusiasm for concerted action. The statesmen continued to go through the motions, but, by the first days of June, it was clear that no one was going to reopen the Straits of Tiran for Israel.

Meanwhile it had been realised in Tel Aviv and Jerusalem that the gravest danger was that of the troop concentrations. Against the Egyptian military preparations, diplomatic action could not be of much help. The Eshkol administration was now under increasing criticism for inactivity and the demand for a national government became stronger every day. In part this was an agitation stirred up by groups who had old political scores to settle with Eshkol and the Mapai. But the rapid response it found was due to a growing belief, both among civilians and in the army, that the Government was incompetent. This view was only partly justified by the hesitation and weakness shown by some members of the Government: it was mainly due to a breakdown in communication. The Government was stronger than its image and Mr Eshkol's actions were more forceful than his speeches, but the psychological factor can be of great importance in such a situation. It was not so much as a strategist that Dayan became necessary, but as a symbol to restore confidence

232

in the leadership. This cost Israel a week of internal haggling, in which domestic passions almost eclipsed the menace from without, before agreement was reached about the inclusion of the new ministers. And by that time, Hussain's visit to Cairo, and Nasser's rash declarations of intent to destroy the state of Israel itself, left the Government no more room for manœuvre. Israel was bound to act – whatever the risks involved. By the first of June, public opinion both in the Arab countries and in Israel was convinced that war was inevitable. Was it really, though, on a longer and wider view? All the decisive motives were present – the Arab refusal to put up with the existence of Israel, the arms race, guerrilla warfare and Israel's retaliatory policy. But, for Nasser, the destruction of Israel was a long term objective, not a plan for early realisation. It was only the Fatah and the Syrian leaders who demanded a war of liberation at the earliest possible date. Nasser had great reservations, but since he was basically committed to the same policy, he could not now refuse to go to the aid of a sister Arab country against the common Zionist enemy. Moreover, Israel's policy of retaliation had lately exacerbated the conflict. But for Samu and the battle of 7 April, there would not have been a war in 1967 – which is not to say that it might not have come a year or two later. Had Israel refrained from major raids, the storm might have passed it by, and left the Arab leaders entirely absorbed in their own bitter conflicts. Then, in a few years time, some Arab governments might be readier to resign themselves to Israel's existence. Still, this was no more than a faint hope. Given the arms race, and, above all, the persistent anti-Israeli indoctrination, there was no good reason to assume that the resort to arms could be postponed indefinitely. Expectations had been raised far too high, and a whole generation had been brought up to believe in Israel's imminent destruction.

Neither America nor the Soviet Union wanted this war. The Americans, like the Israelis, did not expect it in 1967; the warnings of the few who did had been ignored. From the American point of view, preservation of the *status quo*, however unsatisfactory, was preferable to any violent upheaval with its unpredictable consequences. Besides the innate conservatism of American foreign policy, there were specific reasons to fear that a war between Israel and the Arabs would adversely affect American interests in the Middle East. Direct Soviet intervention was thought unlikely in Washington, but it was a possibility that could not be ruled out altogether. American policy, therefore, was to come to an understanding with the Soviet Union that the two superpowers should not directly interfere. The danger of a confrontation between America and Russia was thus averted without difficulty, for the stakes involved were small compared with the risks of a third world war. The two powers even made a concerted effort to restrain both Israel and the Arab countries. But when the Soviet ambassador asked Nasser not to fire the first shot, things had already gone too far. The Soviet leaders thought that Washington would be more successful in bringing pressure on Israel, but the Americans were less optimistic: they knew from recent experience that there are limits to big-power influence over small countries, especially when vital questions of their national security are involved. The USA could have restrained Israel only by taking the initiative in reopening the Straits of Tiran and by somehow inducing Nasser to withdraw his threats. Unilateral action by America was ruled out from the beginning; no one in Washington wanted American involvement in yet another war, and while the other maritime powers were reluctant to join in breaking the blockade, America hesitated to take the initiative. Thus, the plans that had been worked out by American and British experts were abandoned. By 1 June, it was clear that no workable plan was possible, and Washington resigned itself to the idea that Israel might have to act alone. According to the Pentagon's assessment, Israel was sure to prevail, not only against Egypt but against any coalition of Arab countries. Nevertheless, war remained a grave risk in the eyes of most Washington officials. An Israeli victory (it was thought) would even further weaken the position of the West in the Arab world. It was generally thought that an Israeli defeat would make American intervention unavoidable, if the Arab leaders tried to carry out their threats to destroy Israel. Whether America would, in fact, have intervened remains an open question. The possibility of an Israeli defeat had been briefly discussed in Washington, and on this occasion, too, it became palpably obvious that there was very little America could do other than send the navy and evacuate the Israelis to Ellis Island, as some highly placed officials put it. So America was inactive during this critical stage; and what policy might have served American interest better is an open question. The understanding with the Soviet Union removed the danger of a world war, but at the same time made a local conflict more likely. It tied American hands, and put any further work for a positive settlement out of the question. Inactivity, too, was a gamble, and it would have ended in disaster.

The Soviet Union had an enormous political, military and economic investment in the Middle East. Since 1955 it had established strong positions in Egypt and Syria, and subsequently in Algeria and the Yemen. Gradually it was drawn into inter-Arab politics and intrigues. The 'progressive' Arab governments were grateful for sympathy and economic aid; but they welcomed political support and armaments with even more enthusiasm. Arms had become the leading line of Soviet exports to the Middle East; the Western powers also supplied tanks and aircraft, but usually in reply to Soviet shipments – and at the insistence of its allies in the Middle East, both Arab and Israeli, who felt threatened by their neighbours' Russian weapons.

The Soviet leaders did not worry unduly about the consequences of this arms race; they had supplied plenty of arms to other parts of the world and no major armed conflict had ensued. Evidently they thought that in the Middle East, too, the arms were to be used mainly as status symbols by their clients.

In view of its great investments in Egypt and Syria, the Soviet Union had long felt a special concern for the fortunes of those countries: and by the spring of 1967 Moscow had anxieties about Syria which were not altogether unfounded. For even after the Syrians had suffered a severe punitive raid by Israel, Damascus was unwilling to desist from its guerrilla warfare or from lobbing occasional shells over the border: it was only a question of time before Israel would again retaliate: the Syrian Government was in a far from healthy condition and it might collapse under another military defeat. To avert this danger, and also to teach Israel a lesson, the Soviet Government called upon Egypt for assistance. This may have seemed the obvious thing to do, but in fact it lit the fuse that led to an explosion they did not at all intend. They expected at most some limited affrays, bigger perhaps than the previous skirmishes, but a long way short of all-out war.

Soviet policy towards Israel is always far less emotional than that of the Arabs. In Soviet eyes, Israel is only a minor pawn in the big-power struggle, objectionably aligned on the enemy's side. This Soviet attitude is not, indeed, quite free from emotional undertones: for Israel and the Jews in general have given Soviet politicians a good many headaches ever since the Revolution, in domestic as well as foreign affairs. Anti-semitism had been rampant in Russia for a long time before 1917, and Zionism has always been regarded as an enemy. The Jews could never be fitted into the pattern of Soviet nationalities, nor into the Soviet plans in the Middle East. Even 'progressive' Jews complained and protested about Soviet policies and some of them were prominent in the anti-Soviet camp. And on all the Soviets' reactions to Israel or to Jewish organisations there is a cutting edge that cannot be accounted for in terms of Marxist-Leninist doctrine.

The exact nature of the Soviet undertaking to Egypt and Syria is not known. While Moscow had promised full support, it was understood that this did not extend to Soviet military intervention. But the Soviet leaders failed to foresee that the Arab governments would expect more than they had been promised as soon as they felt they were losing the battle. The Arabs had been satisfied with Soviet promises because they were confident they would defeat Israel. When the fortune of war turned against them they looked for more than verbal declarations. They never made it quite clear exactly what it was that they expected, but they were bitterly disappointed not to get it.

The United Nations played only a minor role in the crisis. It was paralysed by conflicting interests between the various member nations; many of them opposed United Nations intervention until the war had broken out.

U Thant acted precipitately in withdrawing the UNEF immediately, but it is doubtful whether temporisation on his part would have decisively affected the net result. He tried to mediate, but there was no room for an independent United Nations policy, even had there been one – and the lack of any consensus among the member nations made that impossible from the beginning.

There still remain a great many question marks. Some are upon question of detail – such as, for instance, Mr Gromyko's visit to Cairo on 30 March 1967, and whether Syria, Russia and Egypt all believed in the war scare of 17 May, whether some believed, while others did not, or whether it was a unanimous lie. It is not clear whether Nasser had Soviet support for imposing the blockade. Nor do we know how soon or how clearly the Americans made it known that they had given up all hope of a diplomatic solution – or to what extent Israel's decision was influenced by this.*

We can only guess what was going on in Nasser's mind during mid-May; even the documentation that will some day be available may not shed much light on this. There are unsolved problems concerning Israeli policy between the middle of May and 5 June. Abba Eban's policy for instance; and how far the demand for a national government was spontaneous. The military were confident of winning a war quickly, and for this they must have had good reasons. I have in most instances tried to provide answers to these questions and I shall be surprised if the interpretations given prove altogether wrong through future disclosures. But many problems will continue to intrigue students of the origins of this war for a long time to come, and much will remain forever in the realm of speculation.

For eighteen years, a state of almost permanent crisis, involving countless *coups d'état* and a war, had left the political map of the Middle East virtually unchanged. Then, in a few hours of fighting on 5 June 1967 it was suddenly and spectacularly redrawn. It is true that many of the old landmarks remain: so do the region's dominant economic, political and social forces – the oil, Arab nationalism, and Israel's will to survive in a hostile environment. Most of the leading actors are still present, too, though for some of these the prospects of political survival are not brilliant. Before 5 June, Middle Eastern affairs resembled a game of chess (or a war game) that had often been played before and allowed but a limited amount of variation in the moves.

* According to some Israeli observers, the administration was above all worried by the charge of collusion; hence Johnson's initial hesitation to see Eban, which was interpreted at first as a lack of sympathy. Later on, it was argued that the President simply wanted to make it known that he had not much to offer; but that the administration would not be too offended if Israel decided to solve the problem alone. During the crisis, Israeli leaders had to engage in both Kremlinology and in Washingtonology; Abba Eban reported one thing, General Amit another. There were some straws in the wind, but apparently not enough for an unequivocal estimate.

The game has become less predictable, for it is now being played on a different board and with a number of new pieces.

Predictions about future moves are therefore much more hazardous than they were. Even so, we ought not wholly to rule out speculation – be it only speculation about the past. The question: 'What would have happened if ...' is not altogether an idle one, for what has happened assumes a meaning only in the context of the alternatives that existed. Could the war have been prevented? The answer is obvious. The Syrians and Nasser should have known that making threats from a position of weakness is a dangerous policy. Nor should they have underrated the strength and the resolution of the adversary. The threats, the blockade and the troop concentrations could have but one affect on the Israelis. It has been claimed after the event that the threats were not meant literally. Perhaps they were not. But in the modern world one has to start from the assumption that one's statements are taken seriously, and that one's adversaries will act accordingly. And if the Arab objective really was to destroy Israel, or only 'to teach it a lesson', 1967 was not a good time for trying. Militarily, the Arab states were not ready to follow up their threats. Also several alternatives were open to them: If Nasser and Syria were genuinely afraid of a full-scale Israeli attack in May, they could have taken counter-measures on a limited scale. They might not know whether these would be successful, but the risk would have been smaller from the Arab point of view.

Similarly, the Russians could have threatened political sanctions against Israel instead of managing the crisis in such a way that they were bound to lose control over it. Admittedly, their policy towards Israel up to May 1967 had been so unfriendly that they had not left much leeway for manœuvring; in retrospect this also looks like a mistake.

As for Nasser, if he wanted to interfere with Israeli shipping, he might well have waited for six or twelve months. The British had already announced that they would withdraw from Aden; the establishment of nationalist governments in South Arabia would have made a blockade on Israeli shipping possible, in conditions much less risky than in the Gulf of Aqaba. The policy of harassing Israel through guerrilla warfare could have been pursued, even though the prospects were not brilliant. The

Syrian leaders claimed to have studied the works of Mao and Che Guevara, but obviously they had not digested them. For Mao attributed decisive importance to factors that did not exist in Israel, such as the existence of an extensive territory, with its corollary, a lack of means of communication in the hinterland; the numerical insufficiency of enemy troops, the absence of airborne units, etc. Guevara and Regis Debray insisted that the first objective of a guerrilla war is to destroy enemy forces. The Fatah never attacked the Israeli army units; they could not even have dreamt about the further stages of guerrilla warfare such as the establishment of 'foci' or the 'descent to the city', without succeeding in that first objective. Arab guerrillas were not dealing with the Kuomintang, nor with Algerian colons, nor a banana republic ruled by haciendeuros. They were challenging a modern state, with an army and a people solidly behind them. They ought to have realised that hit and run raids from across the border could at most be only a source of harassment to the Jews and a possible encouragement to sections of the Arab minority in Israel. But there was no chance of any decisive success by means of guerrilla tactics. Israel could be defeated only by the regular armies of the Arab states, who would not be ready to do it for years to come.

This had been the underlying assumption of Arab strategy, that in the long run time was against Israel: that $2\frac{1}{2}$ million Jews could not hold out forever against 100 million Arabs; the state of Israel like that of the Crusaders would inevitably be destroyed in the end. But there was great impatience in the Arab capitals and, at the same time, belief in the inevitable course of history was not so strong as it used to be. Whether big populations are a blessing or a curse to modern states is by no means certain; but there is no doubt that, militarily as well as technologically, it is quality and not quantity that matters. Nor is it certain that time was working against Israel: between 1947 and 1967 it certainly was not. Leaders among the Arab refugees had begun to murmur doubts that they or even their grandchildren would ever return to the homeland, unless something was done quickly. It is obvious that, given an equal speed of modernisation on both sides, the Arab power must sooner or later be much greater than that of Israel. But modernisation was not yet making such rapid progress as had been expected. There was moreover the fear that a future generation of Arabs might 'get soft' – and forget Palestine; similar fears may have crossed Mao's mind when he decided that his country needed a cultural revolution. Above all, Arab leaders were afraid of a nuclear stalemate in the Middle East: once that happened the frontiers would, as in Europe, be frozen for a long time to come. Perhaps the danger was even more immediate. Within a year or two the Aswan Dam would be completed, and Egypt would become vulnerable even to high explosive bombs. We know from their literature that the Palestinian refugee leaders were worried by these considerations – and perhaps not they alone. If so, the solution of the Palestine problem was getting more urgent than ever before. One had to choose between a policy likely to bring about the destruction of Israel as quickly as possible, or at least to deliver a blow to the Jewish state that would cripple its further progress. Alternatively, one had to accept the fact, however unpleasant, that Israel had come to stay.

The Arab leaders were neither ready for a full-scale war, nor willing to think about peace with Israel. Only a very few Arabs in responsible positions felt that the 'dull and endless strife' with Israel was unprofitable; that the unsuccessful attempt to defeat Israel was sapping the Arab countries' strength and energy; or that it was gradually making the Middle East a backwater of history, and preventing the general development of the Arab world. The Arab countries had to devote a very high share of their gross national product to expensive armaments and pre-parations for the hoped-for day of conquest. This is a main reason why the real growth of most Arab countries has been small – in the region of 2·5 per cent per annum; Israeli growth over the last decade has been almost three times as high. Admittedly, the fact of Israel's continuing existence was a constant injury to Arab pride; but the nursing of a moral injury might blind one to a concrete danger. Disasters worse than Palestine might await the Arab cause unless its human energies could be directed into different and more profitable channels. This was the ineluctable dilemma that confronted the Arab world before the war of 1967, though it was only dimly realised. Since then, it has in most respects become more acute. The price to be paid for an armament race has risen; the date of achieving a decisive victory over Israel is receding even further into the future.

Could Israel have prevented a war in 1967?

Yes, but not for very long. For the struggle between Israel and the Arabs was not about the refugees, or the Jordan waters, or the Straits of Tiran – or even about Israel's frontiers. All these factors played important parts, but the essential issue – reduced to the simplest possible formula – was between Israel's survival and the Arabs' pride and dignity. The destruction of the state of Israel was official Arab policy, for the Arab governments were not reconciled to that state's existence. They felt that their prestige depended upon a military victory that would revenge the defeats of 1948 and 1956.

Israeli restraint alone would therefore have been insufficient to avert a war. There are some who say, and have said so all along, that Israel ought to have pursued a radically different policy from its foundation as a state. Israel should have realised that in the long run it could not survive as an eastern 'outpost of the West', its only hope of acceptance by its neighbours was to become truly Middle East in character, and become an integral part of the Afro-Asian world to which it really belonged. In other words, Israel should have joined the 'third world', body, soul and spirit. Within a big Arab federation (it was argued) Israel would play an important role. The Arabs would demand the cessation of immigration – but not so many immigrants would be coming, in any case. Half of Jewish Israel is now of Middle Eastern origin; and in Israel itself there have been advocates of integration. The only realistic policy therefore would be, to recognise that revolutionary Arab nationalism is the wave of the future, and that Israeli victories can be no more than transitory episodes in an irreversible historical movement – that is in the rise to political consciousness of the Arab masses, as personified by Nasser and the Syrian leaders.

There are some valid points in this line of argument. Radical Arab nationalism may well prevail in more countries during the coming years. The long-term survival of Israel is not yet assured. Gestures play an inordinate role in Middle Eastern politics; a few chilly remarks by de Gaulle during the crisis made the Arabs forget that it was France, not America or England, that had equipped the Israeli army. Some Israeli gestures of good will and one or two unilateral concessions would have had a beneficial effect. It is a matter of regret that they have not been made.

On a closer scrutiny, however, it is clear that a general reorientation towards the third world was never a feasible alternative.

Geographically and historically, Israel is closer to the Mediterranean world – to Italy, Greece, Turkey, than to the Afro-Asian bloc. The third world is passing through a profound crisis, politically, socially and economically; and nowhere is this more palpable than in the Arab countries. There has been little advance towards political stability and economic progress, or towards unity. In recent years most of these countries have fallen further back both in comparison with the West and with the Eastern bloc. This has produced a profound malaise, sometimes bordering upon collective hysteria. Until recent times, most of their ills could be laid at the door of colonialism or neo-colonialism; but with every year that passes such explanations become less convincing. Israel has a great many unresolved problems, it faces serious internal crises. But it has tackled modernisation fairly successfully, though in some respects it is lamentably far from perfection. But in the world as it is, Israel is a reasonably democratic and effective state. It could have tried to cut its ties with the Jews in the West (which are anyway growing weaker year by year); it could have attempted to copy Egypt's and Syria's anti-neo-colonialist style; and such behaviour might have warmed the hearts of certain observers in the West. In the eyes of most Arabs it would, quite rightly, have carried little conviction. For however hard they tried, the results of efforts by Israelis to adopt the third-world mentality in general, and current Arab attitudes in particular, would be more curious than convincing. The political psychology of backwardness is an organic growth, it cannot be artificially simulated. Hate, envy and resentment against the West are historical products of certain mechanisms that do not exist in Israel. Israel was not a colony, and does not suffer from post-colonial hangover. If it pretended to be part of the 'wretched of the earth' – who would believe it? Countries like Egypt and Syria are at present in a disturbed frame of mind; one may sympathise with them in their plight and hope for a change in the not too distant future. But those who recommend Israeli integration say in fact that Israel could gain the friendship and the confidence of the Arabs by behaving like them. Such recommendations not only seem impractical, they are less than honest. Friendship and confidence can perhaps be acquired in the long run by willingness to work for a genuine *modus vivendi*, by candour, by realising that the Arab states have some legitimate grievances against Israel and against the West. They could certainly not be gained by deliberate adaptation to a political psychosis.

The assumption, then, that peace between Israel and the Arab countries could have been won by a different foreign political orientation on the part of Israel seems ill founded. It was not for pursuing any specific policy that Israel was attacked, but for existing. This does not necessarily mean that fighting between the Arabs and Israel is inevitable for an indefinite future. Much will depend on the general world situation. In 1967 the crisis developed, it appears, irrespective of events in other parts of the globe. But intrinsically the Middle East is not one of the principal centres of world politics. What happens in China or India, in the Soviet Union, Europe or America is of greater importance for the future of mankind. To realise this does not necessarily bring peace in the Middle East any nearer; that is more likely to happen as the result of certain trends within Israel and the Arab countries.

Israel will not remain what it is. The Zionist phase of Israel is about to end or is already over; the Arab fears of mass immigration into Israel are misplaced. The Zionist mystique born out of the suffering and longing of East European Jewry is gradually replaced by a different concept of modern statehood as the first native born generation takes over the political and the military leadership. The implications of statehood are dawning only gradually upon Israel: The Jewish Agency was Zionist in character, a modern state containing a substantial minority needs a different basis. There is resistance against change such as the inevitable separation between state and religion. But it will be a rearguard action, the present uneasy compromise cannot last. The new country will offer, one hopes, much of interest and value to the outside world. But it will not be necessarily *Or Legoyim* – a spiritual light to the non-Jews. A normal state does not mean an end to tribulations and danger, but it is the end of the idea of a Jewish mission as it was preached by the prophets.

The Arab countries in their endeavour to become modern

industrial societies will have to undergo profound changes. Trying to catch up with the twentieth century, they face an uphill struggle. For it is not simply a matter of introducing modern methods of production; they will have to shed cherished beliefs, deeply ingrained characteristics and mental habits. To understand Arab political behaviour it is not sufficient to study Arab social, economic and political life as it is usually done. For the political behaviour of the Arabs (like that of any other nation) is also formed by their general behaviour, and this, in turn is shaped by family structure, internalised values and beliefs that are carried forward from generation to generation. Arab political behaviour in 1967 could, of course, be explained with reference to 'foolish speeches' and 'miscalculations'. But in a deeper sense this policy followed a long established pattern, it was by no means altogether accidental. Just as Nasser and the Syrian leaders can only be understood when one considers their personalities, Arab political behaviour in general makes sense only in the wider context of Arab national character, to use a somewhat unsatisfactory abbreviation. Equally, modernisation in the Arab world means not merely the change of political institutions but a far more profound change in values and beliefs established over many centuries. This is, to put it cautiously, not an easy process, nor does one know what will be at the end of it.

On the present basis it is illusory to hope for a meeting of minds between Arabs and Israel. But one should not be hypnotised by the current state of affairs: Neither the Arabs nor Israel will stay what they now are. It is at least conceivable that some of the more developed Arab countries and Israel will become more alike in coming generations. Affinity in outlook does not necessarily make friends of individuals or nations. But it will make at least rational discussion of common problems possible.

The crisis of 1967 is instructive upon many points besides those I have mentioned: One is that small nations in critical situations cannot rely on the big powers for help.

Big powers may be preoccupied elsewhere, or their intervention may be ruled out by some other factor in the delicate global balance of power. The crisis also confirmed that, with all their tremendous military strength, Russia and America may be quite unable to control a relatively small crisis. For where vital questions of national security are at stake, even the smallest countries will disregard advice, requests, or even threats from the super-powers. The lessons of 1967 will be studied for a long time but should not be studied too hard, for fear of overrating their general validity. The situation in May 1967 was unique; nothing quite like it had ever existed; nor is just such a constellation of forces likely to recur.

It began like a standard scene in a Western: A game of poker in a sleazy saloon. I have compared the moves in the conflict between 1948 and 1967 to gambits in chess; but the escalation crisis in 1967 was of course much more like a game of poker. As the games theorists would put it this was a play of imperfect information: and from the start the bluffing was overdone. Israel could not afford to lose a single game. The Arabs did not have enough money for the stakes and should never have played, still less issued a challenge, in the first place. Indeed, this game should never have taken place, but no one could withdraw once the play had started.

REFERENCES

References

Chapter 3

1. Nasser's speech on 22 May 1967; *Le Nouvel Observateur*, 31 May 1967.
2. *Le Monde*, 6 June 1967 and Eric Rouleau et al., *Israel et Les Arabes*, p. 54. According to Rouleau the news reached Cairo on 8 May.
3. *Unità*, 25 May 1967.
4. *Le Figaro*, 17 May 1967. There was also a Soviet statement, distributed by Tass, that the security subcommittee of the Knesset had in a meeting in early May empowered the Israeli Government to take major retaliatory action against the Syrians.
5. *Jerusalem Post*, 14 May 1967.
6. *Guardian*, 13 May 1967.
7. *Guardian*, Beirut Correspondent, 15 May 1967.
8. *Al Kifah*, Beirut, 11 May 1967.
9. Speech of 22 May 1967.
10. Damascus Radio, 13 May 1967.
11. 21 April 1967.
12. *Al Huriya*, 24 April 1967.
13. *Al Anwar*, Beirut, 12 May 1967.
14. *Novoe Vremia*, 28 April 1967.
15. Damascus Radio, 9 May 1967.
16. *Al Nahar*, Beirut, 10 May 1967.
17. *Al Muharar*, 12 August 1966.
18. *Falastin*, 17 November 1966; *Al Muharar*, 17 May 1967.
19. *Al Anwar*, 7 May 1967.
20. *Al Kuds*, 10 May 1967.
21. *Izvestia*, 18 May 1967.
21a. 'Makor Musmakh' in *Bamahane*, July 1967.
22. *Al Ahram*, 26 May 1967.
23. Cairo Radio, 17 May 1967.
23a. Haim Herzog in *Ha'aretz*, 2 June; 'Makor Musmakh' in *Bamahane*, July 1967.
24. *New York Times*, 28 June 1967.
25. Voice of the Arabs, 18 May 1967, Ahmad Said was demoted in September 1967.

26. Voice of the Arabs, 19 May 1967.
27. Voice of the Arabs, 20 May 1967.
28. *Al Thawra al Arabiya*, 18 May quoted by Baghdad Radio.
29. Radio Amman, 19 May 1967.
30. *Al Thawra*, Damascus, 20 May 1967.
31. Prof. D. Johnson: Rights of Sea Passage, *Sunday Times*, London, 4 June 1967.
32. Belayev and Primakov in *Pravda*, 31 July 1967.
33. Claire Sterling, *Reporter*, 29 June 1967.
34. *Economist*, 3 June 1967.
35. *Al Ahram*, 25 May 1967.
36. Baghdad Radio, 1 June 1967.
37. *Al Ahram*, 2 June 1967.
38. *Al Mussawar*, 25 May 1967.
39. *Observer*, London, 4 June 1967.
40. *Le Monde*, 2 June 1967.
41. Damascus Radio, 11 June 1967.
42. Cairo Radio, 6 June 1967.
43. Cairo Radio, 8 June 1967.
44. *Al Anwar*, 28 May 1967.
45. *Al Nahar*, 25 May 1967.
46. *Al Gumhuriya*, 25 May 1967.
47. *Al Nahar*, 26 May 1967.
48. *Al Gumhuriya*, 23 May 1967.
49. Amman Radio, 5 June 1967.
50. Prime Minister Atassi, Damascus Radio, 14 June 1967.
51. Nasser's speech on 23 July 1967.
52. Ibid.

Chapter 4

1. *Jerusalem Post*, 16 May 1967; Amos Eilon in *Commentary*, August 1967, p. 60 et. seq.
2. *Ha'aretz*, 16 May 1967.
2a. *Ogonyok*, 25 June 1967.
3. A. Zimuki in *Yediot Ahronot*, 16 June 1967.
4. *U.S. News and World Report*, 17 April 1967.
5. *Davar*, 17 May, *Jerusalem Post*, 16 May 1967.
6. *Ha'aretz*, 17 May 1967, military correspondent.
7. *Al Ahram*, 18 May 1967.
8. Z. Shiff, *Ha'aretz*, 19 May 1967.
9. Amos Eilon, 'Mi ohev et Abba Eban?', *Ha'aretz*, 28 July 1967.
9a. *Mabat Hadash*, 24 May 1967.

9b. *Ma'ariv*, 4 October 1967.
10. *Jerusalem Post*, weekly edition, 26 May 1967.
11. A. Schweitzer in *Ha'aretz*, 22 May 1967.
12. *Jerusalem Post*, 23 May 1967.
13. *Ha'aretz, Ma'ariv*, 23 May; *Ha'aretz*, 4 October 1967.
14. *Jerusalem Post*, weekly edition, 26 May 1967.
15. *Ma'ariv*, 24 May 1967.
16. *Jerusalem Post*, 26 May 1967.
17. *New York Times*, 10 July 1967.
18. F. Ofner in *Jerusalem Post*, 6 July 1967.
19. Ibid.
20. A. Eilon, 'Mi ohev et Abba Eban?', *Ha'aretz*, 28 July 1967.
21. Israeli Broadcasting Service, 30 May 1967.
22. Hanna Semer in *Davar*, 29 May, and in *Davar*, 31 May 1967.
23. Yigal Allon, 'Le 'acher sheshet hayamim halalu', *Lamerhav*, 14 August 1967.
24. *Ha'aretz*, 29 May 1967.
25. *Ha'aretz*, 30 May 1967.
26. S. Segev, *Sadin Adom*, Tel Aviv, 1967, pp. 70–1.
27. A. Hourani, *Observer*, 3 September 1967.
28. M. Meisels in *Ma'ariv* 2 June; A. Zimuki in *Yediot Ahronot*, 25 June 1967; S. Naqdimon in *Yediot Ahronot* 6–20 October 1967.
29. *Jerusalem Post*, 2 June 1967.
30. *Ha'aretz*, 4 June 1967.
31. *Jerusalem Post, Ha'aretz*, 4 June 1967.
31a. Z. Schiff, *Ha'aretz*, 4 October 1967.
32. *Economist*, 1 July 1967.

Chapter 5

1. *Washington Star, Baltimore Sun*, 15 June 1967.
2. Theodore Draper, 'Israel and World Politics', *Commentary*, August 1967.
3. Louis Heron in *The Times*, 30 May 1967.
4. *New York Times*, 21 May 1967.
5. T. Draper, loc. cit., p. 38.
6. *Washington Post*, 24 May 1967.
7. *Al Ahram*, 26 May 1967.
8. T. Draper, loc. cit., p. 39, *Baltimore Sun*, 14 June 1967. But see also Nolte's interview in *The International Herald Tribune*, 13 September.
9. R. Stephens, *Observer*, 4 June 1967.
10. *Daily Telegraph*, 27 May 1967.

11. *New York Times*, 25 May 1967.
12. United Nations, Security Council, Provisional Verbatim Record, 29 May 1967 (S/PV1343) p. 16.
13. *New York Times*, 29 May 1967.
14. *New York Times*, 2 June 1967.
15. *Guardian*, 30 May 1967.
16. *Times*, 1 June 1967.
17. T. Draper, loc. cit., p. 43.
18. *New York Times*, 31 May 1967.
19. *Daily Telegraph*, 2 June 1967.
20. *Sunday Telegraph*, 3 June 1967.
21. Max Frankel, *New York Times*, 3 June 1967.
22. Ibid.
23. *Jerusalem Post*, 4 June 1967.
24. *Observer*, 4 June 1967.
25. *International Herald Tribune* (Paris), 5 June 1967.
26. *Times*, 3 June 1967.
27. *Guardian*, 5 June 1967.
28. James Reston in *International Herald Tribune* (Paris), 30 May 1967.
29. *Jerusalem Post*, 2 June 1967.
30. *International Herald Tribune* (Paris), 5 June 1967.
31. Ibid.
32. *Jerusalem Post*, 5 June 1967.
33. *Arab Report and Record*, 24 June, p. 168.
34. *Kommunist*, 14 (August) 1967, pp. 115–16.
35. V. Maevsky, *Pravda*, 21 May 1967.
36. *Pravda*, 24 May 1967.
37. Tass in English, 22 May 1967.
38. *Pravda*, 27 May 1967.
39. Cairo Radio, 28 May 1967.
40. Damascus Radio, 30 May 1967.
41. *Pravda*, Tass, 28 May 1967.
42. Maevsky in *Pravda*, 1 June; also *Pravda*, 29 May 1967.
43. I. Belaev and E. Primakov in *Pravda*, 29 July, 3 August 1967.
44. Ibid.
45. Reuter dispatch from Moscow, 31 May 1967.
46. *Izvestia*, 3 June 1967.
47. *Pravda*, 1 June 1967.
48. V. Maevsky, *Pravda*, 4 June 1967.

BIBLIOGRAPHY

Bibliographical Note

The contemporary press and the radio broadcasts are for the time being the most important sources. I have made use both of the American (FBIS – Daily Report) and the British monitoring (Summary of World Broadcasts, part IV, published by the BBC). In a few cases I have used the Israeli monitoring.

Valuable information for this account has been gathered through interviews. But since almost all of those interviewed are in official positions I could not directly quote them. Since it is not very illuminating to quote unnamed ministers, officials, advisers or commanders, I have reluctantly refrained from quoting them altogether.

Of the many books about Egypt, Nasser, Syria, Israel, and the Arab-Israeli conflict only a few published in recent years are listed.

On Egypt's economy and social problems:

CHARLES ISSAWI: *Egypt in Revolution* (London, 1963 new ed.), still the standard work on the subject.

B. HANSEN and G. A. MAZOUK: *Development and Economic Policy in the UAR* (Egypt), (Amsterdam, 1965).

D. WEISS: *Wirtschaftliche Entwicklungsplanung in der VAR* (Cologne, 1964).

Egyptian politics under Nasser:

ANWAR ABDUL MALEK: *Égypte, Société militaire* (Paris, 1962), is still of certain interest since it contains much factual material about the Egyptian left.

PETER MANSFIELD: *Nasser's Egypt* (London, 1965), is a brief survey from a pro-Nasser point of view.

Also of some interest are Ahmad Abu al Fath: *Gamal Abd al Nasser* (Beirut, 1961. French translation: Paris, 1962), and PETER MEIER-RANKE: *Der rote Pharao* (Hamburg, 1964).

Syria and the Ba'ath:

PATRICK SEALE: *The Struggle for Syria* (London, 1965).
G. H. TORREY: *Syrian Politics and the Military* (Ohio, 1964).
MICHEL AFLAQ: *Fi sabil al-Ba'ath* (Beirut, 1959) (about the Ba'ath).
CLOVIS MAQSUD: *Azamad al yasar al-arabi* (Beirut, 1960) (about Arab socialism).
All these books were written before the *coup d'état* of February 1966.

The Army and Politics in the Middle East:

ELIEZER BE'ERI: *Hakezuna vehashilton be ulam ha'aravi* (Merhavia, 1966). (The officer class in Politics and Society of the Arab East.)
Also B. VERNIER: Le role Politique de l'Armée en Syrie. (*Revue de la Politique Etrangère*, 5, 1965).
P. J. VATIKIOTIS: *The Egyptian Army in Politics* (Bloomington, 1966), and *Politics and the Military in Jordan* (London, 1967).

Israel:

No study of Israeli domestic or foreign policy has been published in recent years. The following provide some background information:

SHIMON PERES: *Hashlav haba* (Tel Aviv, 1965) (on defence problems).
YIGAL ALLON: 'Habitakhon hashotef be'aspaklariat ha'istrategia', in *Ot*, February 1967 (on current political and military problems).
'Ma akhare ha' shalom' (a symposium), in *Keshet*, 31, 1966.
'Mediniut hakhuz ve' habitakhon' (a symposium on foreign and defence politics), in *Ot*, September 1966, pp. 19–44.

General background:

B. LEWIS: *The Middle East and the West* (London, 1964).
Les Temps Modernes: Le conflit Judéo-Arabe (Paris, 1967).
MALCOLM KERR: *The Arab Cold War, 1958–64* (London, 1965).
WALTER LAQUEUR: *Communism and Nationalism in the Middle East* (second edition London, 1957), and *The Soviet Union and the Middle East* (London, 1959), are now out of date, but there are no more recent studies on these subjects.

Books on the Arab-Israeli war:

Of those so far published only a few deal briefly with the origins of the war:
RANDOLPH S. and WINSTON S. CHURCHILL: *The six days' war* (London, 1967).

SHMUEL SEGEV: *Sadin Adom* (Tel Aviv, 1967).

ERIC ROULEAU et al.: *Israel et les Arabes* (Paris, 1967).

THEODORE DRAPER: 'Israel and World Politics' in *Commentary*, August, 1967 (the diplomatic prehistory of the war). An extended version was subsequently published in book form (New York, 1968).

Hayamim hagedolim. Shidure Ha'aluf Haim Herzog (Tel Aviv, 1967). (The broadcasts of Brigadier Haim Herzog.)

Skira hodshit, 5–7, 1967. (Monthly survey for officers published by the Chief Education Officer of the Israeli Defence Forces.)

Yeme Juni (Tel Aviv, 1967). (Collection of essays and documents on the war published by the Israeli Ministry of Defence.)

CECIL HOURANI: 'An Arab speaks to the Arab world' in *Encounter*, November 1967.

The Eshkol interview in *Ma'ariv* (4 October 1967) is of considerable interest; Ze'ev Shiff (*Ha'aretz*, 4 October 1967) has given a fairly detailed, day-by-day, account of the three weeks before 5 June. The establishment of the national government is described in great detail in a series of articles by Shlomo Nagdimon in *Yediot Ahronot* (6–20 October 1967).

Ot (November 1967) featured an article by Yigal Allon in which it was argued that it had been a mistake to send the Foreign Minister to the Western Capitals in late May 1967.

Ma'ariv (1 December 1967) published an interview with Abba Eban in which some details about his interview with de Gaulle were disclosed.

Al Kateb (August 1967) and *Al Tali'a* (August 1967) the two leading Egyptian periodicals included several essays about the origins and the character of the Six Days War. Dr Gamal Hamadan maintained that 'the enemy acted according to a doctrine which we ourselves had propagated for years'.

ELIAHU BEN ELISSAR and ZE'EV SCHIFF:

La guerre Israelo-Arabe (Paris, 1967) is an account by two Israeli military correspondents of both the pre-war period and the military operations.

APPENDICES

Appendix 1

by U Thant

Report on the withdrawal of the United Nations
Emergency Force 27 June 1967.

Introduction

1. This report on the withdrawal of the United Nations Emergency
Force (U.N.E.F.) is submitted because, as indicated in my statement
on 20 June 1967 to the fifth emergency session of the General Assembly (1527th plenary meeting), important questions have been
raised concerning the actions taken on the withdrawal of U.N.E.F.
These questions merit careful consideration and comment. It is in the
interest of the United Nations, I believe, that this report should be
full and frank, in view of the questions involved and the numerous
statements that have been made, both public and private, which continue to be very damaging to the United Nations and to its peace-
keeping role in particular. Despite the explanations already given in
the several reports on the subject which have been submitted to the
General Assembly and to the Security Council, misunderstandings
and what, I fear, are misrepresentations, persist, in official as well as
unofficial circles, publicly and behind the scenes.

2. A report of this kind is not the place to try to explain why there
has been so much and such persistent and grossly mistaken judgment
about the withdrawal of U.N.E.F. It suffices to say here that the shat-
tering crisis in the Near East inevitably caused intense shock in many
capitals and countries of the world, together with deep frustration
over the inability to cope with it. It is, of course, not unusual in such
situations to seek easy explanations and excuses. When, however, this
tactic involves imputing responsibility for the unleashing of major
hostilities, it is, and must be, a cause for sober concern. The objective
of this report is to establish an authentic, factual record of actions
and their causes.

3. It follows, therefore, that the emphasis here, therefore, will be
upon facts. The report is intended to be neither a polemic nor an apo-
logia. Its sole purpose is to present a factually accurate picture of
what happened and why. It will serve well the interests of the United

261

Nations, as well as of historic integrity, if this presentation of facts can help to dissipate some of the distortions of the record which, in some places, apparently have emanated from panic, emotion and political bias.

Chronology of Relevant Actions

4. Not only events, but dates, and even the time of day, have an important bearing on this exposition. The significant events and actions and their dates and times are therefore set forth below.

16 May 1967

5. 2000 hours G.M.T. (2200 hours Gaza local time). A message from General Fawzy, Chief of Staff of the United Arab Republic Armed Forces, was received by the Commander of U.N.E.F. Major General Rikhye, requesting withdrawal of 'all U.N. troops which install O.P.'s along our borders.' (A-6730, para. 6, sub-para. 3 (a).) Brigadier Mokhtar, who handed General Fawzy's letter to the Commander of U.N.E.F., told General Rikhye at the time that he must order the immediate withdrawal of United Nations troops from El Sabha and Sharm el Sheikh on the night of 16 May since United Arab Republic armed forces must gain control of these two places that very night. The U.N.E.F. Commander correctly replied that he did not have authority to withdraw his troops from these positions on such an order and could do so only on instructions from the Secretary General; therefore, he must continue with U.N.E.F. operations in Sinai as hitherto. Brigadier Mokhtar told the Commander of U.N.E.F. that this might lead to conflict on that night (16 May) between United Arab Republic and U.N.E.F. troops, and insisted that the Commander issue orders to U.N.E.F. troops to remain confined to their camps at El Sabha and Sharm el Sheikh. General Rikhye replied that he could not comply with this request. He did, of course, inform the contingent commanders concerned of these developments. He also informed United Nations Headquarters that he proposed to continue with U.N.E.F. activities as established until he received fresh instructions from the Secretary General.

6. 2130 hours G.M.T. (1730 hours New York time). The Secretary General received at this time the U.N.E.F. Commander's cable informing him of the above-mentioned message from General Fawzy. The U.N.E.F. Commander was immediately instructed to await further instructions from the Secretary General and pending this later word from him, to 'be firm in maintaining U.N.E.F. position while being as understanding and as diplomatic as possible in your relations with local U.A.R. officials.'

7. 2245 G.M.T. (1845 hours New York time). The permanent

representative of the United Arab Republic visited the Secretary General at this time at the latter's urgent request. The Secretary General requested the permanent representative to communicate with his Government with the utmost urgency and to transmit to it his views (A–6730, para. 6, sub-para. 3 (c)). In particular, the Secretary General requested the permanent representative to obtain his Government's clarification of the situation, pointing out that any request for the withdrawal of U.N.E.F. must come directly to the Secretary General from the Government of the United Arab Republic.

8. 2344 hours G.M.T. The U.N.E.F. Commander further reported at this time that considerable military activity had been observed in the El Arish area since the afternoon of 16 May 1967.

17 May 1967

9. 0800 hours G.M.T. (0400 hours New York time). The Commander of U.N.E.F. reported then that on the morning of 17 May, thirty soldiers of the Army of the United Arab Republic had occupied El Sabha in Sinai and that United Arab Republic troops were deployed in the immediate vicinity of the U.N.E.F. observation post there. Three armoured cars of the United Arab Republic were located near the Yugoslav U.N.E.F. camp at El Sabha and detachments of fifteen soldiers each had taken up positions north and south of the Yugoslav contingent's camp at El Amr. All U.N.E.F. observation posts along the armistice demarcation line and the international frontier were manned as usual, but in some places United Arab Republic troops were also at the line.

10. 1030 hours G.M.T. (0630 hours New York time). The Commander of U.N.E.F. reported then that troops of the United Arab Republic had occupied the U.N.E.F. observation post at El Sabha and that the Yugoslav U.N.E.F. camps at El Quseima and El Sabha were now behind the positions of the army of the United Arab Republic. The Commander of U.N.E.F. informed the Chief of the United Arab Republic Liaison Staff of these developments, expressing his serious concern at them. The Chief of the United Arab Republic Liaison Staff agreed to request the immediate evacuation of the observation post at El Sabha by United Arab Republic troops and shortly thereafter reported that orders to this effect had been given by the United Arab Republic military authorities. He requested, however, that to avoid any further misunderstandings, the Yugoslav observation post at El Sabha should be withdrawn immediately to El Quseima camp. The Commander replied that any such withdrawal would require the authorization of the Secretary General.

11. 1200 hours G.M.T. (0800 hours New York time). The Chief of

the United Arab Republic Liaison Staff at this time conveyed to the Commander of U.N.E.F. a request from General Mohd Fawzy, Chief of Staff of the Armed Forces of the United Arab Republic, for the withdrawal of the Yugoslav detachments of U.N.E.F. in the Sinai within twenty-four hours. He added that the U.N.E.F. Commander might take '48 hours or so' to withdraw the U.N.E.F. detachment from Sharm el Sheikh. The Commander of U.N.E.F. replied that any such move required instructions from the Secretary General.

12. 0930 hours G.M.T. (1600 hours New York time). The Secretary General at this date held an informal meeting in his office with the representatives of countries providing contingents to U.N.E.F. to inform them of the situation as then known. There was an exchange of views. The Secretary General gave his opinion on how he should and how he intended to proceed, observing that if a formal request for the withdrawal of U.N.E.F. were to be made by the Government of the United Arab Republic, the Secretary General, in his view, would have to comply with it, since the Force was on United Arab Republic territory only with the consent of the Government and could not remain there without it. Two representatives expressed serious doubts about the consequences of agreeing to a peremptory request for the withdrawal of U.N.E.F. and raised the questions of consideration of such a request by the General Assembly and an appeal to the United Arab Republic not to request the withdrawal of U.N.E.F. Two other representatives stated the view that the United Arab Republic was entitled to request the removal of U.N.E.F. at any moment and that that request would have to be respected regardless of what the General Assembly might have to say in the matter, since the agreement for U.N.E.F.'s presence had been concluded between the then Secretary General and the Government of Egypt. A clarification of the situation from the United Arab Republic should therefore be awaited.

14. 2150 hours G.M.T. (1750 hours New York time). The Secretary General at this time saw the Permanent Representative of the United Arab Republic and handed to him an aide-mémoire, the text of which is contained in paragraph 6 of document A–6730. The Secretary General also gave to the Permanent Representative of the United Arab Republic an aide-mémoire calling to the attention of his Government the 'good faith' accord, the text of which is contained in paragraph 7 of document A–6730.

18 May 1967
15. 1321 hours G.M.T. (0921 hours New York time). The Commander of U.N.E.F. reported at this time that his liaison officer in

Cairo had been informed by an ambassador of one of the countries providing contingents to U.N.E.F. that the Foreign Minister of the United Arab Republic had summoned the representatives of nations with troops in U.N.E.F. to the Ministry of Foreign Affairs and informed them that U.N.E.F. had terminated its tasks in the United Arab Republic and in the Gaza Strip and must depart from the above territory forthwith. This information was confirmed by representatives of some of these countries at the United Nations.

16. Early on 18 May the U.N.E.F. sentries proceeding to man the normal observation post at El Sabha in Sinai were prevented from entering the post and from remaining in the area by United Arab Republic soldiers. The sentries were then forced to withdraw. They did not resist by use of force since they had no mandate to do so.

17. 1100 hours G.M.T. United Arab Republic soldiers at this time forced Yugoslav U.N.E.F. sentries out of their observation post on the international frontier in front of El Kuntilla Camp. One hour later, United Arab Republic officers arrived at the water point and asked U.N.E.F. soldiers to withdraw the guard.

18. 1220 hours G.M.T. At this hour United Arab Republic soldiers entered the U.N.E.F. observation post on the international frontier in front of El Amr Camp and forced the Yugoslav soldiers to withdraw. Later two United Arab Republic officers visited El Amr Camp and asked the U.N.E.F. platoon to withdraw within fifteen minutes.

19. 1210 hours G.M.T. United Arab Republic officers then visited the Yugoslav camp at Sharm el Sheikh and informed the Commanding Officer that they had come to take over the camp and the U.N.E.F. observation post at Ras Nasrani, demanding a reply within 15 minutes. The contingent commander replied that he had no instructions to hand over the positions.

20. 1430 hours G.M.T. The U.N.E.F. Yugoslav detachment at El Quseima Camp reported that two artillery shells, apparently ranging rounds from the United Arab Republic artillery, had burst between the U.N.E.F. Yugoslav camps at El Quseima and El Sabha.

21. 1030 hours New York time. The Secretary General met at this time with the permanent representative of Israel who gave his Government's views on the situation, emphasizing that the U.N.E.F. withdrawal should not be achieved by a unilateral United Arab Republic request alone and asserting Israel's right to a voice in the matter. The question of stationing U.N.E.F. on the Israel side of the line was raised by the Secretary General and this was declared by the permanent representative of Israel to be entirely unacceptable to his Government.

22. 1600 hours G.M.T. (12 noon New York time). At this hour the Secretary General received through the permanent representative of the United Arab Republic the following message from Mr. Mahmoud Riad, Minister of Foreign Affairs of the United Arab Republic:

'The Government of the United Arab Republic has the honor to inform Your Excellency that it has decided to terminate the presence of the United Nations Emergency Force from the territory of the United Arab Republic and Gaza Strip.

'Therefore, I request that the necessary steps be taken for the withdrawal of the the force as soon as possible.

'I avail myself of this opportunity to express to Your Excellency my gratitude and warm regards.

At the same meeting the permanent representative of the United Arab Republic informed the Secretary General of the strong feeling of resentment in Cairo at what was there considered to be attempts to exert pressure and to make U.N.E.F. an 'occupation force'.

The Secretary General expressed deep misgivings about the likely disastrous consequences of the withdrawal of U.N.E.F. and indicated his intention to appeal urgently to President Nasser to reconsider the decision. Later in the day, the representative of the United Arab Republic informed the Secretary General that the Foreign Minister had asked the permanent representative by telephone from Cairo to convey to the Secretary General his urgent advice that the Secretary General should not make an appeal to President Nasser to reconsider the request for withdrawal of U.N.E.F. and that, if he did so, such a request would be sternly rebuffed. The Secretary General raised the question of a possible visit by him to Cairo and was shortly thereafter informed that such a visit as soon as possible would be welcomed by the Government of the United Arab Republic.

23. 1700 hours New York time. The Secretary General met with the U.N.E.F. Advisory Committee, set up under the terms of paragraphs 6, 8 and 9 of resolution 1001 (ES-I) of 7/8 November 1956, and the representatives of three countries not members of the Advisory Committee but providing contingents to U.N.E.F. to inform them of developments and particularly the United Arab Republic's request for U.N.E.F.'s withdrawal, and to consult them for their views on the situation. At this meeting, one of the views expressed was that the United Arab Republic's demand for the immediate withdrawal of U.N.E.F. from United Arab Republic territory was not acceptable and that the ultimate responsibility for the decision to withdraw rested with the United Nations acting through the Security Council or the General Assembly. The holder of this view therefore urged further discussion with the Government of the

266

United Arab Republic as well as with other Governments involved. Another position was that the Secretary General had no choice but to comply with the request of the Government of the United Arab Republic, one representative stating that the moment the request for the withdrawal of U.N.E.F. was known his Government would comply with it and withdraw its contingent. A similar position had been taken in Cairo by another Government providing a contingent. No proposal was made that the Advisory Committee should exercise the right vested in it by General Assembly resolution 1001 (ES-I) to request the convening of the General Assembly to take up the situation arising from the United Arab Republic communication. At the conclusion of the meeting, it was understood that the Secretary General had no alternative other than to comply with the United Arab Republic's demand, although some representatives felt the Secretary General should previously clarify with that Government the meaning in its request that withdrawal should take place 'as soon as possible'. The Secretary General informed the Advisory Committee that he intended to reply promptly to the United Arab Republic, and to report to the General Assembly and to the Security Council on the action he had taken. It was for the member states to decide whether the competent organs should or could take up the matter and to pursue it accordingly.

24. After the meeting of the Advisory Committee, at approximately 1900 hours New York time on 18 May, the Secretary General replied to the message from the Minister for Foreign Affairs of the United Arab Republic through that Government's permanent representative as follows:

I have the honor to acknowledge your letter to me of 18 May conveying the message from the Minister of Foreign Affairs of the United Arab Republic concerning the United Nations Emergency Force. Please be so kind as to transmit to the Foreign Minister the following message in reply:
Dear Mr. Minister,
Your message informing me that your Government no longer consents to the presence of the United Nations Emergency Force on the territory of the United Arab Republic, that is to say in Sinai, and in the Gaza Strip, and requesting that the necessary steps be taken for its withdrawal as soon as possible, was delivered to me by the permanent representative of the United Arab Republic at noon on 18 May.
As I have indicated to your permanent representative on 16 May, the United Nations Emergency Force entered Egyptian territory with the consent of your Government and in fact can remain there only so long as that consent continues. In view of the message now received from you, therefore, your Government's request will be complied with and I am proceeding to issue instructions for the necessary arrangements to be put in train

without delay for the orderly withdrawal of the force, its vehicles and equipment and for the disposal of all properties pertaining to it. I am, of course, also bringing this development and my actions and intentions to the attention of the U.N.E.F. Advisory Committee and to all Governments providing contingents for the force. A full report covering this development will be submitted promptly by me to the General Assembly, and I consider it necessary to report also to the Security Council about some aspects of the current situation in the area.

Irrespective of the reasons for the action you have taken, in all frankness, may I advise you that I have serious misgivings about it for, as I have said each year in my annual reports to the General Assembly on U.N.E.F., I believe that this force has been an important factor in maintaining relative quiet in the area of its deployment during the past 10 years and that its withdrawal may have grave implications for peace.

With warm personal regards,

U Thant

It is to be noted that the decision notified to the Government of the United Arab Republic in this letter was in compliance with the request to withdraw the force. It did not, however, signify the actual withdrawal of the force which, in fact, was to remain in the area for several more weeks.

25. Formal instructions relating to the withdrawal of U.N.E.F. were sent to the U.N.E.F. Commander by the Secretary General on the night of 18 May (see Annex).

26. Also on the evening of 18 May the Secretary General submitted his special report to the General Assembly (A–6730).

27. On 19 May the Secretary General issued his report to the Security Council on recent developments in the Near East.

19 May 1967

28. 1130 hours New York time. The Secretary General again received the permanent (S–7896) representative of Israel who gave him a statement from his Government concerning the withdrawal of U.N.E.F., strongly urging the Secretary General to avoid condoning any changes in the *status quo* pending the fullest and broadest international consultation.

29. On the afternoon of 22 May, the Secretary General departed from New York, arriving in Cairo on the afternoon of 23 May. He left Cairo on the afternoon of 25 May, arriving back in New York on 26 May (see S–7906). While en route to Cairo during a stop in Paris, the Secretary General learned that on this day President Nasser had announced his intention to reinstitute the blockade against Israel in the Straits of Tiran.

17 June 1967

30. The withdrawal of U.N.E.F. was completed. Details of the actual withdrawal and evacuation of U.N.E.F. are given in document A/6730/Add. 2.

Main Points at Issue

31. Comment is called for on some of the main points at issue even prior to the consideration of the background and basis for the stationing of U.N.E.F. on United Arab Republic territory.

The Causes of the Present Crisis

32. It has been said rather often in one way or another that the withdrawal of U.N.E.F. is a primary cause of the present crisis in the Near East. This is, of course, a superficial and oversimplified approach. As the Secretary General pointed out in his report of 26 May 1967 to the Security Council (S–7906), this view 'ignores the fact that the underlying basis for this and other crisis situations in the Near East is the continuing Arab-Israel conflict which has been present all along and of which the crisis situation created by the unexpected withdrawal of U.N.E.F. is the latest expression'. The Secretary General's report to the Security Council of 19 May 1967 (S–7896) described the various elements of the increasingly dangerous situation in the Near East prior to the decision of the Government of the United Arab Republic to terminate its consent for the presence of U.N.E.F. on its territory.

33. The United Nations Emergency Force served for more than 10 years as a highly valuable instrument in helping to maintain quiet along the line between Israel and the United Arab Republic. Its withdrawal revealed in all its depth and danger the undiminishing conflict between Israel and her Arab neighbours. The withdrawal also made immediately acute the problem of access for Israel to the Gulf of Aqaba through the Straits of Tiran – a problem which had been dormant for over ten years only because of the presence of U.N.E.F. But the presence of U.N.E.F. did not touch the basic problem of the Arab-Israel conflict – it merely isolated, immobilized and covered up certain aspects of that conflict. At any time in the last ten years either of the parties could have reactivated the conflict and if they had been determined to do so U.N.E.F.'s effectiveness would automatically have disappeared. When, in the context of the whole relationship of Israel with her Arab neighbours, the direct confrontation between Israel and the United Arab Republic was revived after a decade by the decision of the United Arab Republic to move its forces up to the line, U.N.E.F. at once lost all usefulness. In fact, its effectiveness as a buffer and as a presence had already vanished as can be seen from the

chronology given above, even before the request for its withdrawal had been received by the Secretary General from the Government of the United Arab Republic. In recognizing the extreme seriousness of the situation thus created, its true cause, the continuing Arab-Israel conflict, must also be recognized. It is entirely unrealistic to maintain that that conflict could have been solved, or its consequences prevented, if a greater effort had been made to maintain U.N.E.F.'s presence in the area against the will of the Government of the United Arab Republic.

The Decision on U.N.E.F.'s Withdrawal

34. The decision to withdraw U.N.E.F. has been frequently characterized in various quarters as 'hasty', 'precipitous', and the like, even, indeed, to the extent of suggesting that it took President Nasser by surprise. The question of the withdrawal of U.N.E.F. is by no means a new one. In fact, it was the negotiations on this very question with the Government of Egypt which, after the establishment of U.N.E.F. by the General Assembly, delayed its arrival while it waited in a staging area at Capodichino airbase, Naples, Italy, for several days in November, 1956. The Government of Egypt, understandably, did not wish to give permission for the arrival on its soil of an international force, unless it was assured that its sovereignty would be respected and a request for withdrawal of the force would be honoured. Over the years, in discussions with representatives of the United Arab Republic, the subject of the continued presence of U.N.E.F. has occasionally come up, and it was invariably taken for granted by United Arab Republic representatives that if their Government officially requested the withdrawal of U.N.E.F. the request would be honoured by the Secretary General. There is no record to indicate that this assumption was ever questioned. Thus, although the request came as a surprise, there was nothing new about the question of principle nor about the procedure to be followed by the Secretary General. It follows that the decision taken by him on 18 May 1967 to comply with the request for the withdrawal of the force was seen by him as the only reasonable and sound action that could be taken. The actual withdrawal itself, it should be recalled, was to be carried out in an orderly, dignified, deliberate and not precipitate manner over a period of several weeks. The first troops in fact left the area only on 29 May.

The Possibility of Delay

35. Opinions have also been frequently expressed that the decision to withdraw U.N.E.F. should have been delayed pending consultations of various kinds, or that efforts should have been made to resist

the United Arab Republic's request for U.N.E.F.'s withdrawal, or to bring pressure to bear on the Government of the United Arab Republic to reconsider its decision in this matter. In fact, as the chronology given above makes clear, the effectiveness of U.N.E.F. in the light of the movement of United Arab Republic troops up to the line and into Sharm el Sheik, had already vanished before the request for withdrawal was received. Furthermore, the Government of the United Arab Republic had made it entirely clear to the Secretary General that an appeal for reconsideration of the withdrawal decision would encounter a firm rebuff and would be considered as an attempt to impose U.N.E.F. as an 'army of occupation'. Such a reaction, combined with the fact that U.N.E.F. positions on the line had already been effectively taken over by United Arab Republic troops in pursuit of their full right to move up to the line in their own territory, and a deep anxiety for the security of U.N.E.F. personnel should an effort be made to keep U.N.E.F. in position after its withdrawal had been requested, were powerful arguments in favour of complying with the United Arab Republic request even supposing there had not been other overriding reasons for accepting it.

36. It has been said that the decision to withdraw U.N.E.F. precipitated other consequences such as the reinstitution of the blockade against Israel in the Straits of Tiran. As can be seen from the chronology, the U.N.E.F. positions at Sharm el Sheikh on the Straits of Tiran (manned by 32 men in all) were in fact rendered ineffective by United Arab Republic troops before the request for withdrawal was received. It is also pertinent to note that in response to a query from the Secretary General as to why the United Arab Republic had announced its reinstitution of the blockade in the Straits of Tiran while the Secretary General was actually en route to Cairo on 22 May, President Nasser explained that his Government's decision to resume the blockade had been taken some time before U Thant's departure and it was considered preferable to make the announcement before rather than after the Secretary General's visit to Cairo.

The Question of Consultations

37. It has been said also that there was not adequate consultation with the organs of the United Nations concerned or with the members before the decision was taken to withdraw the Force. The Secretary General was, and is, firmly of the opinion that the decision for withdrawal of the force, on the request of the host Government, rested with the Secretary General after consultation with the Advisory Committee on U.N.E.F., which is the organ established by the General Assembly for consultation regarding such matters. This was

made clear by Secretary General Hammarskjold, who took the following position on 26 February 1957 in reply to a question about the withdrawal of the force from Sharm el Sheik:

'An indicated procedure would be for the Secretary General to inform the Advisory Committee on the United Nations Emergency Force, which would determine whether the matter should be brought to the attention of the Assembly.' (Official Records of the General Assembly, Eleventh Session, annexes, agenda item 66, document A–3563, annex I, B, 2.)

The Secretary General consulted the Advisory Committee before replying to the letter of 18 May 1967 from the United Arab Republic requesting withdrawal. This consultation took place within a few hours after receipt of the United Arab Republic request, and the Advisory Committee was thus quickly informed of the decision which the Secretary General had in mind to convey in his reply to the Foreign Minister of the United Arab Republic. As indicated in the report to the Security Council of 26 May 1967;

'The Committee did not move, as it was its right to do under the terms of paragraph 9 of General Assembly resolution 1001 (ES–I) to request the convening of the General Assembly on the situation which had arisen.' (S–7906, para. 4.)

38. Before consulting the Advisory Committee on U.N.E.F., the Secretary General had also consulted the permanent representatives of the seven countries providing the contingents of U.N.E.F., and informed them of his intentions. This, in fact, was more than was formally required of the Secretary General in the way of consultation.

39. Obviously, many Governments were concerned about the presence and functioning of U.N.E.F. and about the general situation in the area, but it would have been physically impossible to consult all of the interested representatives within any reasonable time. This was an emergency situation requiring urgent action. Moreover, it was perfectly clear that such consultations were sure to produce sharply divided counsel, even if they were limited to the permanent members of the Security Council. Such sharply divided advice would have complicated and exacerbated the situation, and, far from relieving the Secretary General of the responsibility for the decision to be taken, would have made the decision much more difficult to take.

40. It has been said that the final decision on the withdrawal of U.N.E.F. should have been taken only after consideration by the General Assembly. This position is not only incorrect but also unrealistic. In resolution 1000 (ES–I) the General Assembly established

a United Nations command for an emergency international force. On the basis of that resolution the force was quickly recruited and its forward elements flown to the staging area at Naples. Thus, though established, it had to await the permission of the Government of Egypt to enter Egyptian territory. That permission was subsequently given by the Government of Egypt as a result of direct discussions between Secretary General Hammarskjold and President Nasser of Egypt. There is no official United Nations document on the basis of which any case could be made that there was any limitation on the authority of the Government of Egypt to rescind that consent at its pleasure, or which would indicate that the United Arab Republic had in any way surrendered its right to ask for and obtain at any time the removal of U.N.E.F. from its territory. This point is elaborated later in this report (see paras. 71–80 below).

41. As a practical matter, there would be little point in any case in taking such an issue to the General Assembly unless there would be reasonable certainty that that body could be expected expeditiously to reach a substantive decision. In the prevailing circumstances, the question could have been validly raised as to what decision other than the withdrawal of U.N.E.F. could have been reached by the Assembly once United Arab Republic consent for the continued presence of U.N.E.F. was withdrawn.

42. As regards the practical possibility of the Assembly considering the request for U.N.E.F.'s withdrawal, it is relevant to observe that the next regular session of the General Assembly was some four months off at the time the withdrawal request was made. The special session of the General Assembly which was meeting at the time could have considered the question, according to rule 19 of the Assembly's rules of procedure, only if two-thirds or 82 members voted for the inclusion of the item in the agenda. It is questionable, to say the least, whether the necessary support could have been mustered for such a controversial item. There could have been no emergency special session since the issue was not then before the Security Council, and therefore the condition of lack of unanimity did not exist.

43. As far as consultation with or action by the Security Council was concerned, the Secretary General reported to the Council on the situation leading up to and created by the withdrawal of U.N.E.F. on 19 May 1967 (S-7896). In that report he characterized the situation in the Near East as 'extremely menacing.' The Council met for the first time after this report on 24 May 1967, but took no action.

44. As has already been stated, the Advisory Committee did not make any move to bring the matter before the General Assembly, and no representative of any Member Government requested a meeting of

either the Security Council or the General Assembly immediately following the Secretary General's reports (A-6730 and S-7896). In this situation, the Secretary General himself did not believe that any useful purpose would be served by his seeking a meeting of either organ, nor did he consider that there was basis for him to do so at that time. Furthermore, the information available to the Secretary General did not lead him to believe that either the General Assembly or the Security Council would have decided that U.N.E.F. should remain on United Arab Republic territory, by force if necessary, despite the request of the Government of the United Arab Republic that it should leave.

Practical Factors Influencing the Decision

45. Since it is still contended in some quarters that the U.N.E.F. operation should somehow have continued after the consent of the Government of the United Arab Republic to its presence was withdrawn, it is necessary to consider the factors, quite apart from constitutional and legal considerations, which would have made such a course of action entirely impracticable.

46. The consent and active cooperation of the host country is essential to the effective operation and indeed, to the very existence, of any United Nations peace-keeping operation of the nature of U.N.E.F. The fact is that U.N.E.F. had been deployed on Egyptian and Egyptian-controlled territory for over $10\frac{1}{2}$ years with the consent and cooperation of the Government of the United Arab Republic. Although it was envisaged in pursuance of General Assembly Resolution 1125 (XI) of 2 February 1957 that the force would be stationed on both sides of the line, Israel exercised its sovereign rights to refuse the stationing of U.N.E.F. on its side, and the force throughout its existence was stationed on the United Arab Republic side of the line only.

47. In these circumstances, the true basis for U.N.E.F.'s effectiveness as a buffer and deterrent to infiltration was, throughout its existence, a voluntary undertaking by local United Arab Republic authorities with U.N.E.F., that United Arab Republic troops would respect a defined buffer zone along the entire length of the line in which only U.N.E.F. would operate and from which United Arab Republic troops would be excluded. This undertaking was honoured although U.N.E.F. had no authority to challenge the right of United Arab Republic troops to be present anywhere on their own territory.

48. It may be pointed out in passing that over the years U.N.E.F. dealt with numerous infiltrators coming from the Israel as well as from the United Arab Republic side of the line. It would hardly be logical to take the position that because U.N.E.F. has successfully

maintained quiet along the line for more than 10 years, owing in large measure to the cooperation of the United Arab Republic authorities, that this Government should then be told that it could not unilaterally seek the removal of the force and thus in effect be penalized for the long cooperation with the international community it had extended in the interest of peace.

49. There are other practical factors relating to the above-mentioned arrangement which are highly relevant to the withdrawal of U.N.E.F. First, once the United Arab Republic troops moved up to the line to place themselves in direct confrontation with the military forces of Israel, U.N.E.F. had, in fact, no further useful function. Secondly, if the force was no longer welcome, it could not as a practical matter remain in the United Arab Republic, since the friction which would almost inevitably have arisen with that Government, its armed forces and with the local population would have made the situation of the force both humiliating and untenable. It would even have been impossible to supply it. U.N.E.F. clearly had no mandate to try to stop United Arab Republic troops from moving freely about on their own territory. This was a peace-keeping force, not an enforcement action. Its effectiveness was based entirely on voluntary cooperation.

50. Quite apart from its position in the United Arab Republic, the request of that Government for U.N.E.F.'s withdrawal automatically set off a disintegration of the force, since two of the Governments providing contingents quickly let the Secretary General know that their contingents would be withdrawn, and there can be little doubt that other such notifications would not have been slow in coming if friction had been generated through an unwillingness to comply with the request for withdrawal.

51. For all the foregoing reasons, the operation, and even the continued existence of U.N.E.F. on United Arab Republic territory, after the withdrawal of United Arab Republic consent, would have been impossible, and any attempt to maintain the force there would without question have had disastrous consequences.

Legal and Constitutional Considerations and the Question of Consent for the Stationing of U.N.E.F. on United Arab Republic Territory

52. Legal and constitutional considerations were, of course, of great importance in determining the Secretary General's actions in relation to the request of the Government of the United Arab Republic for the withdrawal of U.N.E.F. Here again, a chronology of the relevant actions in 1956 and 1957 may be helpful.

53. 4 November 1956. The General Assembly, at its first emergency special session in Resolution 998 (ES-I), requested 'the Secretary General to submit to it within 48 hours a plan for the setting up, with the consent of the nations concerned, of an emergency international United Nations Force to secure and supervise the cessation of hostilities ...'

54. 5 November 1956. The General Assembly, in its Resolution 1000 (ES-I), established a United Nations Command for an emergency international force, and, *inter alia*, invited the Secretary General 'to take such administrative measures as may be necessary for the prompt execution of the actions envisaged in the present resolution.'

55. 7 November 1956. The General Assembly, by its Resolution 1001 (ES-I), *inter alia*, approved the guiding principles for the organization and functioning of the emergency international United Nations Force and authorized the Secretary General 'to take all other necessary administrative and executive action'.

56. 10 November 1956. Arrival of advance elements of U.N.E.F. at staging area in Naples.

57. 8–12 November 1956. Negotiations between Secretary General Hammarskjold and the Government of Egypt on entry of U.N.E.F. into Egypt.

58. 12 November 1956. Agreement on U.N.E.F. entry into Egypt announced and then postponed, pending clarification, until 14 November.

59. 15 November 1956. Arrival of advance elements of U.N.E.F. in Abu Suweir, Egypt.

60. 16 November to 18 November 1956. Negotiations between Secretary General Hammarskjold and President Nasser in Cairo on the presence and functioning of U.N.E.F. in Egypt and cooperation with Egyptian authorities, and conclusion of an 'aide-mémoire on the basis for the presence and functioning of U.N.E.F. in Egypt' (the so-called 'good faith accord'). (Ibid., document A–3375, annex.)

61. 24 January 1957. The Secretary General in a report to the General Assembly (Ibid., Document A–3512) suggested that the force should have units stationed on both sides of the armistice demarcation line and that certain measures should be taken in relation to Sharm el Sheik. On 2 February 1957, the General Assembly, by its resolution 1125 (XI), noted with appreciation the Secretary General's report and considered that 'after full withdrawal of Israel from the Sharm el Sheikh and Gaza areas, the scrupulous maintenance of the armistice agreement required the placing of the United Nations Emergency Force on the Egyptian-Israel armistice demarcation line and the implementation of other measures as proposed in the

Secretary General's report, with due regard to the considerations set out therein with a view to assist in achieving situations conducive to the maintenance of peaceful conditions in the area.'

62. 7 March 1957. Arrival of U.N.E.F. in Gaza.

63. 8 March 1957. Arrival of U.N.E.F. elements at Sharm el Sheikh.

64. In general terms the consent of the host country to the presence of peace-keeping machinery is a basic prerequisite of all the United Nations peace-keeping operations. The question has been raised whether the United Arab Republic had the right to request unilaterally the withdrawal 'as soon as possible' of U.N.E.F. from its territory or whether there were limitations on its rights in this respect. An examination of the records of the first emergency special session and the eleventh session of the General Assembly is relevant to this question.

65. It is clear that the General Assembly and the Secretary General from the very beginning recognized, and in fact emphasized, the need for Egyptian consent in order that U.N.E.F. be stationed or operate on Egyptian territory. Thus, the initial Resolution 998 (ES-I) of 4 November 1956 requested the Secretary General to submit a plan for the setting up of an emergency force, 'with the consent of the nations concerned'. The 'nations concerned' obviously included Egypt (now the United Arab Republic), the three countries (France, Israel and the United Kingdom) whose armies were on Egyptian soil and the states contributing contingents to the force.

66. The Secretary General, in his report to the General Assembly of 6 November 1956, stated, *inter alia*:

'9. Functioning, as it would, on the basis of a decision reached under the terms of the Resolution 337 (V) "Uniting for peace", the force, if established, would be limited in its operations to the extent that consent of the parties concerned is required under generally recognized international law. While the General Assembly is enabled to establish the force with the consent of those parties which contribute units to the force, it could not request the force to be stationed or operate on the territory of a given country without the consent of the Government of that country.' (Ibid., First Emergency Special Session, Annexes, agenda item 5, Document A/3302, para. 9.)

67. He noted that the foregoing did not exclude the possibility that the Security Council could use such a force within the wider margins provided under Chapter VII of the United Nations Charter. He pointed out, however, that it would not be necessary to elaborate this point further, since no use of the force under Chapter VII, with the rights in relation to member states that this would entail, had been envisaged.

68. The General Assembly in its Resolution 1001 (ES-I) of 7 November 1956 expressed its approval of the guiding principles for the organization and functioning of the emergency international United Nations Force as expounded in paragraphs 6 to 9 of the Secretary General's report. This included the principle of consent embodied in paragraph 9.

69. The need for Egypt's consent was also stated as a condition or 'understanding' by some of the states offering to contribute contingents to the force.

70. It was thus a basic legal principle arising from the nature of the force, and clearly understood by all concerned, that the consent of Egypt was a prerequisite to the stationing of U.N.E.F. on Egyptian territory, and it was a practical necessity as well in acquiring contingents for the force.

The 'Good Faith' Aide-Memoire of 20 November 1956

71. There remains to be examined whether any commitments were made by Egypt which would limit its pre-existing right to withdraw its consent at any time that it chose to do so. The only basis for asserting such limitation could be the so-called 'good faith' aide-mémoire which was set out as an annex to a report of the Secretary General submitted to the General Assembly on 20 November 1956.

72. The Secretary General himself did not offer any interpretation of the 'good faith' aide-mémoire to the General Assembly or make any statement questioning the remarks made by the Foreign Minister of Egypt in the General Assembly the following week (see paragraph 74 below). It would appear, however, that in an exchange of cables he had sought to obtain the express acknowledgement from Egypt that its consent to the presence of the Force would not be withdrawn before the Force had completed its task. Egypt did not accept this interpretation but held to the view that if its consent was no longer maintained the force should be withdrawn. Subsequent discussions between Mr. Hammarskjold and President Nasser resulted in the 'good faith' aide-mémoire.

73. An interpretative account of these negotiations made by Mr. Hammarskjold in a personal and private paper entitled 'aide-mémoire,' dated 5 August 1957, some eight and a half months after the discussions, has recently been made public by a private person who has a copy. It is understood that Mr. Hammarskjold often prepared private notes concerning significant events under the heading 'aide-mémoire.' This memorandum is not in any official record of the United Nations nor is it in any of the official files. The General Assembly, the Advisory Committee on U.N.E.F. and the Government

of Egypt were not informed of its contents or existence. It is not an official paper and has no standing beyond being a purely private memorandum of unknown purpose or value, in which Secretary General Hammarskjold seems to record his own impressions and interpretations of his discussions with President Nasser. This paper, therefore, cannot affect in any way the basis for the presence of U.N.E.F. on the soil of the United Arab Republic as set out in the official documents, much less supersede those documents.

Position of Egypt

74. It seems clear that Egypt did not understand the 'good faith' aide-mémoire to involve any limitation on its right to withdraw its consent to the continued stationing and operation of U.N.E.F. on its territory. The Foreign Minister of Egypt, speaking in the General Assembly on 27 November 1956, one week after the publication of the 'good faith' aide-mémoire and three days following its approval by the General Assembly said:

'We still believe that the General Assembly resolution of 7 November 1956 still stands, together with its endorsement of the principle that the General Assembly could not request the United Nations Emergency Force to be stationed or to operate on the territory of a given country without the consent of the Government of the country. This is the proper basis on which we believe, together with the overwhelming majority of this Assembly, that the United Nations Emergency Force could be stationed or could operate in Egypt. It is the only basis on which Egypt has given its consent in this respect.' (Official Records of the General Assembly, Eleventh Session, Plenary Meetings, 597th meeting, para. 48.)

He then added:

'... as must be abundantly clear, this force has gone to Egypt to help Egypt, with Egypt's consent; and no one here or elsewhere can reasonably or fairly say that a fire brigade, after putting out a fire, would be entitled or expected to claim the right of deciding not to leave the house.' (Ibid., para. 50.)

Analysis of the 'Task' of the Force

75. In the 'good faith' aide-mémoire the Government of Egypt declared that, 'when exercising its sovereign rights on any matters concerning the presence and functioning of U.N.E.F., it will be guided, in good faith, by its acceptance of General Assembly resolution 1000 (ES-I) of 5 November 1956.'

76. The United Nations in turn declared 'that the activities of U.N.E.F. will be guided, in good faith, by the task established for the

force in the aforementioned resolutions (1000 (ES-I) and 997 (ES-I));
in particular, the United Nations, understanding this to correspond
to the wishes of the Government of Egypt, reaffirms its willingness to
maintain U.N.E.F. until its task is completed.'

77. It must be noted that, while Egypt undertook to be guided in
good faith by its acceptance of General Assembly resolution 1000
(ES-I), the United Nations also undertook to be guided in *good faith*
by the task established for the force in resolution 1000 (ES-I) and 997
(ES-I). Resolution 1000 (ES-I), to which the declaration of Egypt
referred, established a United Nations Command for the force 'to
secure and supervise the cessation of hostilities in accordance with all
the terms' of resolution 997 (ES-I). It must be recalled that at this
time Israel forces had penetrated deeply into Egyptian territory and
that forces of France and the United Kingdom were conducting military operations on Egyptian territory. Resolution 997 (ES-I) urged as
a matter of priority that all parties agree to an immediate cease-fire,
and halt the movement of military forces and arms into the area. It
also urged the parties to the armistice agreements promptly to withdraw all forces behind the armistice lines, to desist from raids across
the armistice lines, and to observe scrupulously the provisions of the
armistice agreements. It further urged that, upon the cease-fire being
effective, steps be taken to reopen the Suez Canal and restore secure
freedom of navigation.

78. While the terms of resolution 997 (ES-I) cover a considerable
area, the emphasis in resolution 1000 (ES-I) is on *securing and supervising the cessation of hostilities*. Moreover, on 6 November 1956 the
Secretary General, in his second and final report on the plan for an
emergency international United Nations Force, noted that 'the Assembly intends that the Force should be of a temporary nature, the
length of its assignment being determined by the needs arising out of
the present conflict.' (Ibid., First Emergency Special Session, Annexes, agenda item 5, document A–3302, para. 8.) Noting further the
terms of resolution 997 (ES-I) he added that 'the functions of the
United Nations Force would be, when a cease-fire is being established, to enter Egyptian territory with the consent of the Egyptian
Government, in order to help maintain quiet during and after the
withdrawal of non-Egyptian troops, and to secure compliance with
the other terms established in the resolution of 2 November 1956'
(997 (ES-I)). (Ibid., para. 12.)

79. In a cable delivered to Foreign Minister Fawzi on 9 or 10
November 1956, in reply to a request for clarification as to how long
it was contemplated that the force should stay in the demarcation line
area, the Secretary General stated: 'A definite reply is at present

impossible but the emergency character of the Force links it to the immediate crises envisaged in resolution 2 November (997 (ES-I)) and its liquidation.' This point was confirmed in a further exchange of cables between the Secretary General and Dr. Fawzi on 14 November 1956.

80. The Foreign Minister of Egypt (Dr. Fawzi) gave his understanding of the task of the Force in a statement to the General Assembly on 27 November 1956:

'Our clear understanding – and I am sure it is the clear understanding of the Assembly – is that this force is in Egypt only in relation to the present attack against Egypt by the United Kingdom, France and Israel, and for the purposes directly connected with the incursion of the invading forces into Egyptian territory. The United Nations Emergency Force is in Egypt, not as an occupation force, not as a replacement for the invaders, not to clear the Canal of obstructions, not to resolve any question or settle any problem, be it in relation to the Suez Canal, to Palestine or to any other matter; it is not there to infringe upon Egyptian sovereignty in any fashion or to any extent, but on the contrary, to give expression to the determination of the United Nations to put an end to the aggression committed against Egypt and to the presence of the invading forces in Egyptian territory.' (Ibid., Eleventh Session, Plenary Meetings, 597th meeting, para. 49.)

81. In letters dated 3 November 1956 addressed to the Secretary General, the representatives of both France and the United Kingdom had proposed very broad functions for U.N.E.F., stating on behalf of their Governments that military action could be stopped if the following conditions were met:

(a) Both the Egyptian and Israel Governments agree to accept a United Nations Force to keep the peace.
(b) The United Nations decides to constitute and maintain such a Force until an Arab-Israel peace settlement is reached and until satisfactory arrangements have been agreed in regard to the Suez Canal, both agreements to be guaranteed by the United Nations.
(c) In the meantime, until the United Nations Force is constituted, both combatants agree to accept forthwith limited detachments of Anglo-French troops to be stationed between the combatants. (Ibid., First Emergency Special Session, Annexes, documents A–3268 and A–3269.)

These broad functions for the force were not acceptable to the General Assembly, however, as was pointed out in telegrams dated 4 November 1956 from Secretary General Dag Hammarskjold to the Minister for Foreign Affairs of France and the Secretary of State for Foreign Affairs of the United Kingdom. (Ibid., document A–3284, Annexes 2 and 4.)

82. Finally, it is obvious that the task referred to in the 'good

faith' aide-mémoire could only be the task of the Force as it had been defined in November 1956 when the understanding was concluded. The 'good faith' undertaking by the United Nations would preclude it from claiming that the Egyptian agreement was relevant or applicable to functions which the force was given at a much later date. The stationing of the Force on the armistice demarcation line and at Sharm el Sheikh was only determined in pursuance of General Assembly resolution 1125 (XI) of 2 February 1957. The Secretary General, in his reports relating to this decision, made it clear that the further consent of Egypt was essential with respect to these new functions. (Ibid., Eleventh Session, Annexes, agenda item 66, documents A-3512, para. 20, and A-3527, para. 5.) Consequently the understanding recorded in the 'good faith' aide-mémoire of 20 November 1956 could not have been itself, a commitment with respect to functions only determined in February and March, 1957. It is only these later tasks that the force had been performing during the last 10 years – tasks of serving as a buffer and deterring infiltrators which went considerably beyond those of securing and supervising the cessation of hostilities provided in the General Assembly resolutions and referred to in the 'good faith' aide-mémoire.

The Stationing of U.N.E.F. on the Armistice Demarcation Line and at Sharm el Sheikh

83. There remains to examine whether Egypt made further commitments with respect to the stationing of the Force on the armistice demarcation line and at Sharm el Sheikh. Israel, of course, sought to obtain such commitments, particularly with respect to the area around Sharm el Sheikh.

84. For example, in an aide-mémoire of 4 February 1957 (Ibid., document A-3527, annex I), Israel sought clarification as to whether units of the United Nations Emergency force would be stationed along the western shore of the Gulf of Aqaba in order to act as a restraint against hostile acts, and would remain so deployed until another effective means was agreed upon between the parties concerned for ensuring permanent freedom of navigation and the absence of belligerent acts in the Straits of Tiran and the Gulf of Aqaba. The Secretary General pointed out that such 'clarification' would require 'Egyptian consent.' He stated:

'The second of the points in the Israel aide-mémoire requests a "clarification" which, in view of the position of the General Assembly, could go beyond what was stated in the last report only after negotiation with Egypt. This follows from the statements in the debate in the General Assembly, and the report on which it was based, which makes it clear that the stationing of the Force at Sharm el Sheikh, under such terms as those mentioned in the question posed by Israel, would require Egyptian consent.' (Ibid., document A-3527, para. 5.)

85. It is clear from the record that Egypt did not give its consent to Israel's proposition. The Secretary General's report of 8 March 1957 (Ibid., document A-3568) recorded 'arrangements for the complete and unconditional withdrawal of Israel in accordance with the decision of the General Assembly'. There is no agreement on the part of Egypt to forgo its rights with respect to the granting or withdrawing of its consent to the continued stationing of the force on its territory. On the contrary, at the 667th plenary meeting of the General Assembly on 4 March 1957, the Foreign Minister of Egypt stated:

'At our previous meeting I stated that the Assembly was unanimous in expecting full and honest implementation of its resolutions calling for immediate and unconditional withdrawal by Israel. I continue to submit to the Assembly that this position – which is the only position the Assembly can possibly take – remains intact and entire. Nothing said by anyone here or elsewhere could shake this fact or detract from its reality and its validity, nor could it affect the fullness and the lawfulness of Egypt's rights and those of the Arab people of the Gaza Strip.' (Ibid., Eleventh Session, Plenary Meetings, 667th meeting, para. 240.)

86. The Foreign Minister of Israel in her statement at the 666th meeting of the General Assembly, on 1 March 1957, asserted that an assurance had been given that any proposal for the withdrawal of U.N.E.F. from the Gulf of Aqaba area would come first to the Advisory Committee on U.N.E.F. (see paragraphs 95–98 below).

Question of the Stationing of U.N.E.F. on Both Sides of the Armistice Demarcation Line

87. Another point having significance with respect to the undertakings of Egypt is the question of the stationing of U.N.E.F. on both sides of the armistice demarcation line. The Secretary General, in his report on 24 January 1957 to the General Assembly (Ibid., Eleventh Session, Annexes, agenda item 66, document A-3512) suggested that the force should have units stationed also on the Israel side of the armistice demarcation line. In particular, he suggested that units of the force should at least be stationed in the El Auja demilitarized zone. (Article VIII of the Egyptian-Israel General Armistice Agreement provides, *inter alia*, that an area comprising the village of El Auja and vicinity, as defined in the article, shall be demilitarized and that both Egyptian and Israel armed forces shall be totally excluded therefrom. The article further provides that on the Egyptian side of

the frontier, facing the El Auja area, no Egyptian defensive positions shall be closer to El Auja than El Qouseima and Abou Aoueigila which had been occupied by the armed forces of Israel.) He indicated that if El Auja were demilitarized in accordance with the Armistice Agreement and units of U.N.E.F. were stationed there, a condition of reciprocity would be the Egyptian assurance that Egyptian forces would not take up positions in the area in contravention of the Armistice Agreement. (Official Records of the General Assembly, Eleventh Session, Annexes, agenda item 66, document A–3512, paras. 15–22.) However, Israel forces were never withdrawn from El Auja and U.N.E.F. was not accepted at any point on the Israel side of the line.

88. Following the Secretary General's report, the General Assembly on 2 February 1957 adopted resolution 1125 (XI), in which it noted the report with appreciation and considered:

'... that, after withdrawal of Israel from the Sharm el Sheikh and Gaza areas, the scrupulous maintenance of the Armistice Agreement requires the placing of the United Nations Emergency Force on the Egyptian-Israel armistice demarcation line and the implementation of other measures as proposed in the Secretary General's report, with due regard to the considerations set out therein with a view to assist in achieving situations conducive to the maintenance of peaceful conditions in the area.'

89. On 11 February 1957 the Secretary General stated in a report to the General Assembly that, in the light of the implication of Israel's question concerning the stationing of U.N.E.F. at Sharm el Sheik (see paragraph 84 above), he 'considered it important ... to learn whether Israel itself, in principle, consents to a stationing of U.N.E.F. units on its territory in implementation of the functions established for the force in the basic decisions and noted in resolutions 1125 (XI) where it was indicated that the force should be placed "on the Egyptian-Israel armistice demarcation line." ' (Ibid., document A–3527, para. 5.) No affirmative response was ever received from Israel. In fact, already on 7 November 1956 the Prime Minister of Israel, Mr. Ben-Gurion, in a speech to the Knesset, stated, *inter alia*, 'On no account will Israel agree to the stationing of a foreign force, no matter how called, in her territory or in any of the territories occupied by her.' In a note to correspondents of 12 April 1957 a 'United Nations spokesman' stated:

'Final arrangements for the U.N.E.F. will have to wait for the response of the Government of Israel to the request by the General Assembly that the force be deployed also on the Israeli side of the armistice demarcation line.'

90. In a report dated 9 October 1957 to the 12th session of the

General Assembly (Ibid., Twelfth Session, Annexes, agenda item 65, document A-3694, para. 15), the Secretary General stated:

'Resolution 1125 (XI) calls for placing the Force "on the Egyptian-Israel armistice demarcation line", but no stationing of U.N.E.F. on the Israel side has occurred to date through lack of consent by Israel.'

91. In the light of Israel's persistent refusal to consent to the stationing and operation of U.N.E.F. on its side of the line in spite of General Assembly resolution 1125 (XI) of 2 February 1957 and the efforts of the Secretary General, it is even less possible to consider that Egypt's 'good faith' declaration made in November 1956, could constitute a limitation of its rights with respect to the continued stationing and operation of U.N.E.F. on Egyptian territory in accordance with the resolution of 2 February 1957.

92. The representative of Israel stated at the 592nd meeting of the General Assembly, on 23 November 1956:

'If we were to accept one of the proposals made here – namely that the Force should separate Egyptian and Israel troops for as long as Egypt thought it convenient and should then be withdrawn on Egypt's unilateral request – we would reach a reduction to absurdity. Egypt would then be in a position to build up, behind the screen of this Force, its full military preparations and, when it felt that those military preparations had reached their desired climax, to dismiss the United Nations Emergency Force and to stand again in close contact and proximity with the territory of Israel. This reduction to absurdity proves how impossible it is to accept in any matter affecting the composition or the functions of the Force the policies of the Egyptian Government as the sole or even the decisive criterion.' (Ibid., Eleventh Session, Plenary Meetings, 592nd meeting, para. 131.)

93. The answer to this problem which is to be found in resolution 1125 (XI) of 2 February 1957 is not in the form of a binding commitment by Egypt which the record shows was never given, but in the proposal that the force should be stationed on both sides of the line. Israel in the exercise of its sovereign right did not give its consent to the stationing of U.N.E.F. on its territory and Egypt did not forgo its sovereign right to withdraw its consent at any time.

Role of the U.N.E.F. Advisory Committee

94. General Assembly resolution 1001 (ES-I) of 7 November 1956, by which the Assembly approved the guiding principles for the organization and functioning of U.N.E.F., established an Advisory Committee on U.N.E.F. under the chairmanship of the Secretary General. The Assembly decided that the Advisory Committee, in the performance of its duties, should be empowered to request, through the usual procedures, the convening of the General Assembly and to

report to the Assembly whenever matters arose which, in its opinion, were of such urgency and importance as to require consideration by the General Assembly itself.

95. The memorandum of important points in the discussion between the representative of Israel and the Secretary General on 25 February 1957 recorded the following question raised by the representative of Israel:

'In connection with the duration of U.N.E.F.'s deployment in the Sharm el Sheikh area, would the Secretary General give notice to the General Assembly of the United Nations before U.N.E.F. would be withdrawn from the area, with or without Egyptian insistence, or before the Secretary General would agree to its withdrawal?' (Ibid., Eleventh Session, Annexes, agenda item 66, document A–3563, annex I, A, 2.)

96. The response of the Secretary General was recorded as follows:

'On the question of notification to the General Assembly, the Secretary General wanted to state his view at a later meeting. An indicated procedure would be for the Secretary General to inform the Advisory Committee on the United Nations Emergency Force, which would determine whether the matter should be brought to the attention of the Assembly.' (Ibid., annex I, B. 2.)

97. On 1 March 1957 the Foreign Minister of Israel stated at the 666th plenary meeting of the General Assembly:

'My Government has noted the assurance embodied in the Secretary General's note of 26 February 1957 (A–3363, annex) that any proposal for the withdrawal of the United Nations Emergency Force from the Gulf of Aqaba area would first come to the Advisory Committee on the United Nations Emergency Force, which represents the General Assembly in the implementation of its resolution 997 (ES-I) of 2 November 1956. This procedure will give the General Assembly an opportunity to ensure that no precipitate changes are made which would have the effect of increasing the possibility of belligerent acts.' (Ibid., Eleventh Session, Plenary Meetings, 666th meeting, para. 8.)

98. In fact, the 25 February 1957 memorandum does not go as far as the interpretation given by the Foreign Minister of Israel. In any event, however, it gives no indication of any commitment by Egypt, and so far as the Secretary General is concerned it only indicates that a procedure would be for the Secretary General to inform the Advisory Committee which would determine whether the matter should be brought to the attention of the General Assembly. This was also the procedure provided in General Assembly resolution 1001 (ES-I). It was, furthermore, the procedure followed by the Secretary General on the withdrawal of U.N.E.F.

Observations

99. A partial explanation of the misunderstanding about the withdrawal of U.N.E.F. is an evident failure to appreciate the essentially fragile nature of the basis for U.N.E.F.'s operation throughout its existence. U.N.E.F. in functioning depended completely on the voluntary cooperation of the host Government. Its basis of existence was the willingness of governments to provide contingents to serve under an international command and at a minimum of cost to the United Nations. It was a symbolic force, small in size, with only 3,400 men, of whom 1,800 were available to police a line of 295 miles at the time of its withdrawal. It was equipped with light weapons only. It had no mandate of any kind to open fire except in the last resort in self-defence. It had no formal mandate to exercise any authority in the area in which it was stationed. In recent years it experienced an increasingly uncertain basis of financial support, which in turn gave rise to strong annual pressures for reduction in its strength. Its remarkable success for more than a decade, despite these practical weaknesses, may have led to wrong conclusions about its nature, but it has also pointed the way to a unique means of contributing significantly to international peace-keeping.

Annex

Cable Containing Instructions for the Withdrawal of U.N.E.F. Sent by the Secretary General to the Commander of the U.N.E.F. on 18 May 1967, at 2230 Hours New York Time

The following instructions are to be put in effect by you as of date and time of their receipt and shall remain operative until and unless new instructions are sent by me.

1. U.N.E.F. is being withdrawn because the consent of the Government of the United Arab Republic for its continued deployment on United Arab Republic territory and United Arab Republic-controlled territory has been rescinded.

2. Date of the commencement of the withdrawal of U.N.E.F. will be 19 May when the Secretary General's response to the request for withdrawal will be received in Cairo by the Government of the United Arab Republic, when also the General Assembly will be informed of the action taken and the action will become public knowledge.

3. The withdrawal of U.N.E.F. is to be orderly and must be carried

out with dignity befitting a force which has contributed greatly to the maintenance of quiet and peace in the area of its deployment and has earned widespread admiration.

4. The force does not cease to exist or to lose its status or any of its entitlements, privileges and immunities until all of its elements have departed from the area of its operation.

5. It will be a practical fact that must be reckoned with by the Commander that as of the date of the announcement of its withdrawal the force will no longer be able to carry out its established function as a buffer and as a deterrent to infiltration. Its duties, therefore, after 19 May and until all elements have been withdrawn, will be entirely nominal and concerned primarily with devising arrangements and implementation of arrangements for withdrawal and the morale of the personnel.

6. The force, of course, will remain under the exclusive command of its United Nations Commander and is to take no orders from any other source, whether United Arab Republic or national.

7. The Commander, his headquarters staff and the contingent commanders shall take every reasonable precaution to ensure the continuance of good relations with the local authorities and the local population.

8. In this regard, it should be made entirely clear by the Commander to the officers and other ranks in the force that there is no discredit of the force in this withdrawal and no humiliation involved for the reason that the force has operated very successfully and with, on the whole, cooperation from the Government on the territory of an independent sovereign State for over 10 years, which is a very long time; and, moreover, the reasons for the termination of the operation are of an overriding political nature, having no relation whatsoever to the performance of the force in the discharge of its duties.

9. The Commander and subordinate officers must do their utmost to avoid any resort to the use of arms and any clash with the forces of the United Arab Republic or with the local civilian population.

10. A small working team will be sent from headquarters by the Secretary General to assist in the arrangements for, and effectuation of, the withdrawal.

11. The Commander shall take all necessary steps to protect United Nations installations, properties and stores during the period of withdrawal.

12. If necessary, a small detail of personnel of the force or preferably of United Nations security officers will be maintained as long as necessary for the protection of United Nations properties pending their ultimate disposition.

13. U.N.E.F. aircraft will continue flights as necessary in connection with the withdrawal arrangements but observation flights will be discontinued immediately.

14. Elements of the force now deployed along the line will be first removed from the line, the IF and ADL, including Sharm el Sheikh, to their camps and progressively to central staging.

15. The pace of the withdrawal will of course depend upon the availability of transport by air, sea and ground to Port Said. The priority in withdrawal should of course be personnel and their personal arms and equipment first, followed by contingent stores and equipment.

16. We must proceed on the assumption that U.N.E.F. will have full cooperation of United Arab Republic authorities on all aspects of evacuation, and to this end a request will be made by me to the United Arab Republic Government through their Mission here.

17. As early as possible the Commander of U.N.E.F. should prepare and transmit to the Secretary General a plan and schedule for the evacuation of troops and their equipment.

18. Preparation of the draft of the sections of the annual report by the Secretary General to the General Assembly should be undertaken and, to the extent possible, completed during the period of the withdrawal.

19. In the interests of the force itself and the United Nations, every possible measure should be taken to insure against public comments or comments likely to become public on the withdrawal, the reasons for it and reactions to it.

Appendix 2

The Hammarskjold Memorandum on a Middle East Peace Force

The following is the text of an aide-mémoire prepared on Aug 5, 1957, by Dag Hammarskjold, then Secretary General, for his files on negotiations covering the presence of United Nations troops in the United Arab Republic. Before his death, Mr Hammarskjold gave a copy of the memorandum to a friend, Ernest A. Gross, former United States representative at the United Nations.

As the decision on the U.N.E.F. (United Nations Emergency Force) was taken under Chapter VI (of the Charter) it was obvious from the beginning that the resolution did in no way limit the sovereignty of the host state. This was clear both from the resolution of the General Assembly and from the second and final report on the emergency force. Thus, neither the General Assembly nor the Secretary General, acting for the General Assembly, created any right for Egypt, or gave any right to Egypt, in accepting consent as a condition for the presence and functioning of the U.N.E.F. on Egyptian territory. Egypt had the right, and the only problem was whether that right in this context should and could in some way be limited.

Cable from Burns

My starting point in the consideration of this last-mentioned problem – the limitation of Egypt's sovereign right in the interest of political balance and stability in the U.N.E.F. operation – was the fact that Egypt had spontaneously endorsed the General Assembly resolution of November 5 (creating the force) and by endorsing that resolution had consented to the presence of the U.N.E.F. for certain tasks. They could thus not ask the U.N.E.F. to withdraw before the completion of the tasks without running up against their own acceptance of the resolution on the force and its tasks.

The question arose in relation to Egypt first in a cable received 9 November from Burns (E. L. M. Burns, Canadian lieutenant general who was chief of staff of the United Nations Truce Supervision Organization in Palestine and who became in November, 1956, commander of the United Nations Emergency Force and is now adviser on disarmament to the Canadian Government) covering an interview

290

. the same day with Fawzi (Mahmoud Fawzi, Egyptian Foreign Minister in 1956 and now Deputy Premier for Foreign Affairs of the United Arab Republic). In that interview Egypt had requested clarification of the question how long it was contemplated that the force would stay in the demarcation line area. To this I replied the same day:

'A definite reply is at present impossible, but the emergency character of the force links it to the immediate crisis envisaged in the resolution of 2 November (calling for truce) and its liquidation. In case of different views as to when the crisis does not any longer warrant the presence of the troops, the matter will have to be negotiated with the parties.' In a further cable to Burns the same day I said, however, also that 'as the United Nations force would come with Egypt's consent, they cannot stay nor operate unless Egypt continues to consent'.

On 10 November Ambassador Loutfi (Omar Loutfi, chief Egyptian delegate at the United Nations in 1956, later an Under Secretary of the United Nations, who died in 1963), under instruction, asked me, 'whether it was recognized that an agreement is necessary for their (U.N.E.F.'s) remaining in the canal area' once their task in the area had been completed. I replied that it was my view that such an agreement would then be necessary.

On 11 November Ambassador Loutfi saw me again. He then said that it must be agreed that when the Egyptian consent is no more valid, the U.N. force should withdraw. To this I replied that I did not find that a withdrawal of consent could be made before the tasks which had justified the entry, had been completed; if, as might happen, different views on the degree of completion of the tasks prescribed proved to exist, the matter should be negotiated.

The view expressed by Loutfi was later embodied in an aide-mémoire, dated the same day, where it was said: 'The Egyptian Government takes note of the following:

A. It being agreed that consent of Egypt is indispensable for entry and presence of the U.N. forces in any part of its territory, if such consent no longer persists, these forces shall withdraw.'

I replied to this in a memo dated 12 November in which I said: 'I have received your aide-mémoire setting out the understanding on the basis of which the Egyptian Government accepts my announcing today that agreement on the arrival in Egypt of the United Nations force has been reached. I wish to put on record my interpretation of two of these points.' Regarding the point quoted above in the Egyptian aide-mémoire, I then continued:

'I want to put on record that the conditions which motivate the consent to entry and presence, are the very conditions to which the tasks established for the force in the General Assembly resolution (requesting preparations for establishment of the force), 4 November, are directed. Therefore, I assume it to be recognized that as long as the task, thus prescribed, is not completed, the reasons for the consent of the government remain valid, and that withdrawal of this consent before completion of the task would run counter to the acceptance by Egypt of the decision of the General Assembly, I read the statement quoted in the light of these considerations. If a difference should develop, whether or not the reasons for the arrangements are still valid, the matter should be brought up for negotiation with the United Nations.'

Message from Fawzi

This explanation of mine was sent to the Egyptian mission after my telephone conversation in the morning of the 12th with Dr. Fawzi where we agreed on publication of our agreement on the entry of the U.N.E.F. into Egypt. In view of the previous exchanges, I had no reason to believe that my statement would introduce any new difficulty. I also counted on the fact that Egypt probably by then was as committed as to be rather anxious not to reopen the discussion. However, I recognized to myself that there was an element of gambling involved which I felt I simply had to take in view of the danger that further delays might cause Egypt to change its mind, accept volunteers and throw our approaches overboard.

However, the next morning, 13 November, I received a message from Dr. Fawzi to the effect that the Government of Egypt could not subscribe to my interpretation of the question of consent and withdrawal, as set out on 12 November, and therefore, in the light of my communication of that date, 'felt impelled to consider that the announced agreements should remain inoperative until all misunderstandings were cleared up.' The Government reiterated in this context its view that if its consent no longer persisted, the U.N.E.F. should withdraw.

I replied to this communication – which caused a further delay of the transportation of troops to Egypt by at least 24 hours – in a cable sent immediately on receipt of the communication. In drafting my reply I had a feeling that it now was a must to get the troops in and that I would be in a position to find a formula, saving the face of Egypt while protecting the U.N. stand, once I would discuss the matter personally with President Nasser.

In the official reply 13 November I said that my previous statements had put forward my personal opinion that 'the reasons' for consent remained valid as long as the task was not completed. I also said that for that reason a withdrawal of consent leading to the withdrawal of the force before the task was completed (as previously stated) in my view, 'although within the rights of the Egyptian Government would go against its acceptance of the basic resolution of the General Assembly'. I continued by saying that my reference to negotiation was intended to indicate only that the question of withdrawal should be a matter of discussion to the extent that different views were held as to whether the task of the General Assembly was fulfilled or not. I referred in this respect to my stand as explained already in my message of 9 November, as quoted above.

'Freedom of Action'

I commented upon the official reply in a special personal message to Fawzi, sent at the same time, where I said that we 'both had to reserve our freedom of action, but that, all the same, we could go ahead, hoping that a controversial situation would not arise'. 'If arrangements would break down on this issue' (withdrawal only on completion of the tasks), 'I could not avoid going to the General Assembly' (with the conflict between us on this question of principle) 'putting it to their judgment to decide what could or could not be accepted as an understanding. This situation would be a most embarrassing one for all but I would fear the political repercussions, as obviously very few would find it reasonable that recognition of your freedom of action should mean that you, after having permitted the force to come, might ask it to withdraw at a time when the very reasons which had previously prompted you to accept were still obviously valid.' I ended by saying that I trusted that Fawzi on the basis of this personal message could help me by 'putting the stand I had to take on my own rights in the right perspective'. The letter to Fawzi thus made it clear that if the Government did not accept my stand on withdrawal as a precondition for further steps, the matter would be raised in the Assembly.

On the basis of these two final communications from me, Egypt gave green lights for the arrival of the troops, thus, in fact, accepting my stand and letting it supersede their own communication 13 November.

In my effort to follow up the situation, which prevailed after the exchange in which different stands had been maintained by Egypt and by me, I was guided by the consideration that Egypt constitutionally had an undisputed right to request the withdrawal of the troops, even if initial consent had been given, but that, on the other hand, it should be possible on the basis of my own stand as finally tacitly accepted, to force them into an agreement in which they limited their freedom of action as to withdrawal by making a request for withdrawal dependent upon the completion of the task – a question which, in the U.N., obviously would have to be submitted to interpretation by the General Assembly.

Obstacles to Solution

The most desirable thing, of course, would have been to tie Egypt by an agreement in which they declared that withdrawal should take place only if so decided by the General Assembly. But in this naked form, however, the problem could never have been settled. I felt that the same was true of an agreement to the effect that withdrawal should take place upon 'agreement on withdrawal' between the U.N. and the Egyptian Government. However, I found it worthwhile to try a line, very close to the second one, according to which Egypt would declare to the United Nations that it would exert all its sovereign rights with regard to the troops on the basis of a good faith interpretation of the tasks of the force. The United Nations should make a reciprocal commitment to maintain the force as long as the task was not completed. If such a dual statement was introduced in an agreement between the parties, it would be obvious that the procedure in case of a request from Egypt for the withdrawal of U.N.E.F. would be as follows. The matter would at once be brought before the General Assembly. If the General Assembly found that the task was completed, everything would be all right. If they found that the task was not completed and Egypt, all the same, maintained its stand and enforced the withdrawal, Egypt would break the agreement with the United Nations. Of course Egypt's freedom of action could under no circumstances be limited but by some kind of agreement. The device I used meant only that instead of limiting their rights by a basic understanding requesting an agreement *directly concerning withdrawal*, we created an obligation to reach agreement on the fact that the tasks were completed, and thus, *the conditions for a withdrawal established*.

I elaborated a draft text for an agreement along the lines I had in mind during the night between 15 and 16 November in Capodichino (Italy). I showed the text to Fawzi at our first talk on 16 November and I discussed practically only this issue with Nasser for seven hours in the evening and night of 17 November. Nasser, in this final discussion, where the text I had proposed was approved with some amendments, showed that he very fully understood that, by limiting their freedom of action in the way I proposed, they would take a very serious step, as it would mean that the question of the extent of the task would become decisive for the relations between Egypt and the

United Nations and would determine Egypt's political freedom of action. He felt, not without justification, that the definition given of the task in the U.N. texts was very loose and that, tying the freedom of action of Egypt to the concept of the task – which had to be interpreted also by the General Assembly – and doing so in a written agreement, meant that he accepted a far-reaching and unpredictable restriction. To shoot the text through in spite of Nasser's strong wish to avoid this, and his strong suspicion of the legal construction – especially of the possible consequences of differences of views regarding the task – I felt obliged, in the course of the discussion, to threaten three times, that unless an agreement of this type was made, I would have to propose the immediate withdrawal of the troops. If any proof would be necessary for how the text of the agreement was judged by President Nasser, this last mentioned fact tells the story.

It is obvious that, with a text of the content mentioned approved by Egypt, the whole previous exchange of views was superseded by a formal and explicit recognition by Egypt of the stand I had taken all through, in particular on 9 and 12 November. The previous exchange of cables cannot any longer have any interpretative value as only the text of the agreement was put before the General Assembly and approved by it with the concurrence of Egypt and as its text was self-contained and conclusive. All further discussion, therefore, has to start from the text of the agreement, which is to be found in document A/3375. The interpretation of the text must be the one set out above.

Appendix 3

Nasser's speech at UAR Advanced Air Headquarters,
25 May 1967

The entire country looks up to you today. The entire Arab nation
supports you. It is clear that in these circumstances the entire people
support you completely and consider the armed forces as their hope
today. It is also a fact that the entire Arab nation supports our armed
forces in the current situation through which the entire Arab nation
is passing.

What I wish to say is that we are now in 1967 and not in 1956 after
the tripartite aggression. A great deal was said then and all the secrets
revealed had a double interpretation. Israel, its commanders and
rulers, boasted a great deal after 1956. I have read every word written
about the 1956 events and I also know exactly what happened in 1956.

On the night of 29th October 1956 the Israeli aggression against us
began. Fighting began on 30th October. We received the Anglo-
French ultimatum which asked us to withdraw several miles west of
the Suez Canal. On 31st October the Anglo-French attack on us
began. The air raids began at sunset on 31st October. At the same
time all our forces in Sinai were withdrawn completely to inside
Egypt.

Thus in 1956 we did not have an opportunity to fight Israel. We
decided to withdraw before the actual fighting with Israel began.
Despite our decision to withdraw Israel was unable to occupy any of
our positions except after we left them. Yet Israel created a major uproar, boasted and said a great deal about the Sinai campaign and the
Sinai battle. Everyone of you knows all the rubbish that was said.
They probably believed what they said themselves.

Today, more than 10 years after Suez all the secrets have been
exposed. The most important secret concerns when they brought Ben
Gurion to France to employ him as a dog for imperialism, to begin
the operation. Ben Gurion refused to undertake anything unless he
was given a written guarantee that they would protect him from the
Egyptian bombers and the Egyptian Air Force. All this is now no
longer secret. The entire world knows. It was on this basis that France

sent fighter aircraft to Ben Gurion, and it was also on this basis that Britain pledged to Ben Gurion to bomb Egyptian airfields within 24 hours after the aggression began.

This goes to show how much they took into account the Egyptian forces. Ben Gurion himself said he had to think about the Haifa-Jerusalem-Tel Aviv triangle, which holds one-third of Israel's population. He could not attack Egypt out of fear of the Egyptian air force and bombers. At that time we had a few Ilyushin bombers. We had just acquired them to arm ourselves. Today we have many Ilyushins and other aircraft. There is a great difference between yesterday and today, between 1956 and 1967. Why do I say all this? I say it because we are in a confrontation with Israel. Israel today is not backed by Britain and France as was the case in 1956. It has the United States supporting it and supplying it with arms. But the world cannot again accept the plotting which took place in 1956.

Israel has been clamouring since 1956. They spoke of Israel's competence and high standard of training. It was backed in this by the West and the Western press. They capitalised on the Sinai campaign where no fighting actually took place because we withdrew to confront Britain and France.

Today we have a chance to prove the fact. We have, indeed, a chance to make the world see matters in their true perspective. We are now face to face with Israel. In recent days Israel has been making aggressive threats and boasting. On 12th May a very impertinent statement was made. Anyone reading this statement must believe that these people are so boastful and deceitful that one simply cannot remain silent. The statement said that the Israeli commanders announced they would carry out military operations against Syria in order to occupy Damascus and overthrow the Syrian Government. On the same day the Israeli Premier, Eshkol, made a very threatening statement against Syria. At the same time the commentaries said that Israel believed that Egypt could not make a move because it was bogged down in Yemen.

Of course they say that we are bogged down in Yemen and have problems there. We are in Yemen but they seem to have believed the lies they have been saying all these years about our being in Yemen. It is very possible that the Israelis themselves believed such lies. We are capable of carrying out our duties in Yemen and at the same time doing our national duty here in Egypt, both in defending our borders and in attacking if Israel attacks any Arab country.

On 13th May we received accurate information that Israel was concentrating on the Syrian border huge armed forces of about 11 to 13 brigades. These forces were divided into two fronts, one south of

Lake Tiberias and the other north of the Lake. The decision made by Israel at this time was to carry out an attack against Syria starting on 17th May. On 14th May we took action, discussed the matter and contacted our Syrian brothers. The Syrians also had this information. Based on the information Lt-Gen. Mahmud Fawzi left for Syria to co-ordinate matters. We told them that we had decided that if Syria was attacked Egypt would enter the battle right from the start. This was the situation on 14th May; forces began to move in the direction of Sinai to take up their normal positions.

News agencies reported yesterday that these military movements must have been the result of a previously well laid plan. I say that the sequence of events determined the plan. We had no plan prior to 13th May because we believed that Israel would not have dared to make such an impertinent statement.

On 16th May we requested the withdrawal of the United Nations Emergency Force [UNEF] in a letter from Lt-Gen. Mahmud Fawzi. We requested the complete withdrawal of the UNEF. A major world wide campaign, led by the United States, Britain and Canada, began opposing the withdrawal of the UNEF from Egypt. Thus we felt that attempts were being made to turn the UNEF into a force serving neo-imperialism. It is obvious that the UNEF entered Egypt with our approval and therefore cannot continue to stay in Egypt except with our approval. Until yesterday a great deal was said about the UNEF. A campaign is also being mounted against the UN Secretary-General because he made a faithful and honest decision and could not surrender to the pressure brought to bear upon him by the United States, Britain and Canada to make the UNEF an instrument for implementing imperialism's plans.

It is quite natural, and I say this quite frankly, that had the UNEF ignored its basic task and turned to working for the aims of imperialism we would have regarded it as a hostile force and forcibly disarmed it. We are definitely capable of doing such a job. I say this now not to discredit the UNEF but to those who have neo-imperialist ideas and who want the UN to achieve their neo-imperialist aims – that there is not a single nation which respects itself and enjoys full sovereignty which could accept these methods in any shape or form. At the same time I say that the UNEF has honourably and faithfully carried out its duties. The UN Secretary-General refused to succumb to pressure. He issued immediate orders to the UNEF to withdraw. Consequently we praise the UNEF which has stayed 10 years in our country serving peace. And when they left – at a time when we found that the neo-imperialist force wanted to divert them from their basic task – we gave them a cheerful send-off and saluted them.

298

Our forces are now in Sinai and we are fully mobilised both in Gaza and Sinai. We notice that there is a great deal to talk about peace these days. Peace, peace, international peace, international security, UN intervention, and so on and so forth, all appears daily in the press. Why is it that no one spoke about peace, the UN and security when on 12th May the Israeli premier and the Israeli commanders made their statements that they would occupy Damascus, overthrow the Syrian region, strike vigorously at Syria, and occupy a part of Syria? It was obvious that the press approved of the statements made by the Israeli premier and commanders.

There is talk about peace now. What is peace? If there is a true desire for peace we say that we also work for peace. But does peace mean ignoring the rights of the Palestinian people because of the passage of time? Does peace mean that we should concede our rights because of the passage of time? Nowadays they speak about a UN presence in the region for the sake of peace. Does a UN presence in the region for peace mean that we should close our eyes to everything? The UN has adopted a number of resolutions in favour of the Palestinian people. Israel has implemented none of these resolutions. This brought no reaction from the UN.

Today US Senators, members of the House Representatives, the press and the entire world speak in favour of Israel, of the Jews. But nothing is said in the Arabs' favour. The UN resolutions which favour the Arabs have not been implemented. What does this mean? No one is speaking in the Arabs' favour. How does the UN stand with regard to the Palestinian people? How does it stand with regard to the rights of the Palestinian people? How does it stand with regard to the tragedy which has continued since 1948? Talk of peace is heard only when Israel is in danger. But when Arab rights and the rights of the Palestinian people are lost, no one speaks about peace, rights, or anything like this.

It is clear, therefore, than an alliance exists between the Western powers, chiefly represented by the United States and Britain, with Israel. There is a political alliance. This political alliance prompts the Western powers to give military equipment to Israel. Yesterday and the day before yesterday the entire world was speaking about Sharm al Shaykh, navigation in the Gulf of Aqabah, and Eilat Port. This morning I heard the BBC say that in 1956 Abd an-Nasir promised to open the Gulf of Aqabah.

Of course, this is not true. It was copied from a British paper called the 'Daily Mail'. No such thing happened. Abd an-Nasir would never forfeit any UAR right. As I said, we would never give away a grain of sand from our soil or our country.

The armed forces' responsibility is now yours. The armed forces yesterday occupied Sharm al Shaykh. What does this mean? It is affirmation of our rights and our sovereignty over the Gulf of Aqabah which constitutes Egyptian territorial waters. Under no circumstances will we allow the Israeli flag to pass through the Gulf of Aqabah.

The Jews threaten war. We tell them you are welcome, we are ready for war. Our armed forces and all our people are ready for war, but under no circumstances will we abandon any of our rights. This water is ours. War might be an opportunity for the Jews, for Israel and Rabin, to test their forces against ours and to see that what they wrote about the 1956 battle and the occupation of Sinai was all a lot of nonsense.

With all this there is imperialism, Israel and reaction. Reaction casts doubt on everything and so does the Islamic alliance. We all know that the Islamic alliance is now represented by three states: the Kingdom of Saudi Arabia, the Kingdom of Jordan and Iran. They are saying that the purpose of the Islamic alliance is to unite the Muslim against Israel. I would like the Islamic alliance to serve the Palestine question in only one way – by preventing the supply of oil to Israel. The oil which now reaches Israel, which reaches Eilat, comes from some of the Islamic alliance states. It goes to Eilat from Iran. Who then is supplying Israel with oil? The Islamic alliance – Iran, an Islamic alliance state. Such is the Islamic alliance. It is an imperialist alliance and this means it sides with Zionism because Zionism is the main ally of imperialism.

The Arab world, which is now mobilised to the highest degree, knows all this. It knows how to deal with the imperialist agents, the allies of Zionism and the fifth column.

They say they want to co-ordinate their plans with us. We cannot co-ordinate our plans in any way with Islamic alliance members because it would mean giving our plans to the Jews and to Israel. This is a vital battle. When we said that we were ready for the battle we meant that we would surely fight if Syria or any other Arab state was subjected to aggression.

The armed forces are now everywhere. The army and all the forces are now mobilised and so are the people. They are all behind you, praying for you day and night and believing that you are the pride of their nation, of the Arab nation. This is the feeling of the Arab people in Egypt and outside Egypt. We are confident that you will honour the trust. Everyone of us is ready to die and not give away a grain of his country's sand. This for us is the greatest honour. It is the greatest honour for us to defend our country. We are not scared by the imperialist, Zionist or reactionary campaigns. We are independent and we know the taste of freedom. We have built a strong national army and achieved our aims. We are building our country. There is currently a propaganda campaign, a psychological campaign, and a campaign of doubt against us. We leave all this behind us and follow the course of duty and victory. May God be with you.

Appendix 4

Nasser's speech of 26 May 1967 to Arab Trade Unionists

Thank you for this initiative. You have provided me with an opportunity to see you. I have actually heard your speeches and resolutions, there is nothing to add during this meeting to what you have already said. You, the Arab workers' federation, represent the biggest force in the Arab world.

We can achieve much by Arab actions, which is a main part of our battle. We must develop and build our countries to face the challenge of our enemies. The Arab world now is very different from what it was 10 days ago. Israel is also different from what it was 10 days ago. Despair has never found its way into Arab hearts and never will. The Arabs insist on their rights and are determined to regain the rights of the Palestinian people. The Arabs must accomplish this set intention and this aim. The first elements of this aim appeared in the test of Syria and Egypt in facing the Israeli threat. I believe that this test was a major starting point and basis from which to achieve complete cohesion in the Arab world. What we see today in the masses of the Arab people everywhere is their desire to fight. The Arab people want to regain the rights of the people of Palestine.

For several years, many people have raised doubts about our intentions towards Palestine. But talk is easy and action is difficult, very difficult. We emerged wounded from the 1956 battle. Britain, Israel and France attacked us then. We sustained heavy losses in 1956. Later, union was achieved. The 1961 secession occurred when we had only just got completely together and had barely begun to stand firmly on our feet.

Later the Yemeni revolution broke out. We considered it our duty to rescue our brothers, simply because of the principles and ideals which we advocated and still advocate.

We were waiting for the day when we would be fully prepared and confident of being able to adopt strong measures if we were to enter the battle with Israel. I say nothing aimlessly. One day two years ago, I stood up to say that we have no plan to liberate Palestine and that revolutionary action is our only course to liberate Palestine. I spoke at the summit conferences. The summit conferences were meant to prepare the Arab states to defend themselves.

Recently we felt we are strong enough, that if we were to enter a battle with Israel, with God's help, we could triumph. On this basis, we decided to take actual steps.

A great deal has been said in the past about the UN Emergency Force (UNEF). Many people blamed us for UNEF's presence. We were not strong enough. Should we have listened to them, or rather built and trained our Army while UNEF still existed? I said once that we could tell UNEF to leave within half an hour. Once we were fully prepared we could ask UNEF to leave. And this is what actually happened.

The same thing happened with regard to Sharm al Shaykh. We were also attacked on this score by some Arabs. Taking over Sharm al Shaykh meant confrontation with Israel. Taking such action also meant that we were ready to enter a general war with Israel. It was not a separate operation. Therefore we had to take this fact into consideration when moving to Sharm al Shaykh. The present operation was mounted on this basis.

Actually I was authorised by the [Arab Socialist Union's] Supreme Executive Committee to implement this plan at the right time. The right time came when Syria was threatened with aggression. We sent reconnaissance aircraft over Israel. Not a single brigade was stationed opposite us on the Israeli side of the border. All Israeli brigades were confronting Syria. All but four brigades have now moved south to confront Egypt. Those four are still on the border with Syria. We are confident that once we have entered the battle we will triumph, God willing.

With regard to military plans, there is complete co-ordination of military action between us and Syria. We will operate as one army fighting a single battle for the sake of a common objective – the objective of the Arab nation.

The problem today is not just Israel, but also those behind it. If Israel embarks on an aggression against Syria or Egypt the battle against Israel will be a general one and not confined to one spot on the Syrian or Egyptian borders. The battle will be a general one and our basic objective will be to destroy Israel. I probably could not have said such things five or even three years ago. If I had said such things and had been unable to carry them out my words would have been empty and worthless.

Today, some 11 years after 1956, I say such things because I am confident. I know what we have here in Egypt and what Syria has. I also know that other states – Iraq, for instance, has sent its troops to Syria; Algeria will send troops; Kuwait also will send troops. They will send armoured and infantry units. This is Arab power. This is the true resurrection of the Arab nation, which at one time was probably in despair.

Today people must know the reality of the Arab world. What is Israel? Israel today is the United States. The United States is the chief defender of Israel. As for Britain, I consider it America's lackey. Britain does not have an independent policy. Wilson always follows Johnson's steps and says what he wants him to say. All Western countries take Israel's view.

The Gulf of Aqabah was a closed waterway prior to 1956. We used to search British, US, French and all other ships. After the tripartite aggression – and we all know the tripartite plot – we left the area to UNEF which came here under a UN resolution to make possible the withdrawal of Britain, France and Israel. The Israelis say they opened the maritime route. I say they told lies and believed their own lies. We withdrew because the British and the French attacked us. This battle was never between us and Israel alone.

I have recently been with the armed forces. All the armed forces are ready for a battle face to face between the Arabs and Israel. Those behind Israel are also welcome.

We must know and learn a big lesson today. We must actually see that in its hypocrisy and in its talks with the Arabs, the United States sides with Israel 100 per cent and is partial in favour of Israel. Why is Britain biased towards Israel? The West is on Israel's side. Gen. de Gaulle's personality caused him to remain impartial on this question and not to toe the US or the British line; France therefore did not take sides with Israel.

The Soviet Union's attitude was great and splendid. It supported the Arabs and the Arab nation. It went to the extent of stating that, together with the Arabs and the Arab nation, it would resist any interference or aggression.

Today every Arab knows foes and friends. If we do not learn who our enemies and our friends are, Israel will always be able to benefit from this behaviour. It is clear that the United States is an enemy of the Arab because it is completely biased in favour of Israel. It is also clear that Britain is an enemy of the Arabs because she, too, is completely biased in favour of Israel. On this basis we must treat our enemies and those who side with our enemies as our actual enemies. We can accord them such treatment. In fact we are not states without status. We are states of status, occupying an important place in the world. Our states have thousands of years of civilisation behind them

– 7,000 years of civilisation. Indeed, we can do much; we can expose the hypocrisy – the hypocrisy of our enemies if they try to persuade us that they wish to serve our interests. The United States seeks to serve only Israel's interests. Britain also seeks to serve only Israel's interests.

The question is not one of international law. Why all this uproar because of the closure of the Gulf of Aqabah? When Eshkol and Rabin threatened Syria, nobody spoke about peace or threats to peace. They actually hate the progressive regime in Syria. The United States, Britain and reaction – which is the friend of the United States and Britain – do not favour the national progressive regime in Syria. Israel, of course, shares their feelings. Israel is an ally of the United States and Britain. When Israel threatened Syria, they kept quiet and accepted what it said. But when we exercise one of our legitimate rights, as we always do, they turn the world upside down and speak about threats to peace and about a crisis in the Middle East. They fabricate these matters and threaten us with war.

We shall not relinquish our rights. We shall not concede our right in the Gulf of Aqabah. Today, the people of Egypt, the Syrian Army, and the Egyptian Army comprise one front. We want the entire front surrounding Israel to become one front. We want this. Naturally there are obstacles at present. Of course, Wasfi at-Tall is a spy for the Americans and the British. We cannot co-operate with these spies in any form, because the battle is one of destiny and the spies have no place in this battle. We want the front to become one united front around Israel. We will not relinquish the rights of the people of Palestine, as I have said before. I was told at the time that I might have to wait 70 years. During the crusader's occupation, the Arabs waited 70 years before a suitable opportunity arose and they drove away the crusaders. Some people commented that Abd an-Nasir said we should shelve the Palestinian question for 70 years. I do not mean exactly 70 years, but I say that as a people with an ancient civilisation, as an Arab people, we are determined that the Palestine question will not be liquidated or forgotten. The whole question then, is the proper time to achieve our aims. We are preparing ourselves constantly.

You are the hope of the Arab nation and its vanguard. As workers, you are actually building the Arab nation. The quicker we build, the quicker we will be able to achieve our aim. I thank you for your visit and wish you every success. Please convey my greetings and best wishes to the Arab workers in every Arab country.

Appendix 5

An armed clash with Israel is inevitable – why?
HASANAYN HAYKAL, *Al Ahram*, 26 May 1967

It is extremely difficult to write about current events, particularly when such events are as swift and violent as a hurricane. But it is easy to write about what has already happened, to give an account and analysis of facts. It is also safe to write about what could take place in the future, because the future is boundless. Tomorrow never comes because every day has a tomorrow. The real problem is to speak about what is taking place while it happens. Then every interpretation may endure only a few minutes or even seconds.

There are two considerations which make the problem even more difficult: the topic is one of destiny and life, and there is the need for rational, intelligent writing without indulging in a long composition or platitudes.

What I am going to say after this introduction will in fact be no more than a collection of observations which I think are important at present. The first observation is that I believe an armed clash between the UAR and Israel is inevitable. This armed clash could occur at any moment, at any place along the line of confrontation between the Egyptians forces and the enemy Israeli forces – on land, air or sea along the area extending from Gaza in the North to the Gulf of Aqabah at Sharm al Shaykh in the South. But why do I emphasise this in such a manner? There are many reasons, particularly the psychological factor and its effect on the balance of power in the Middle East.

Passage through the Gulf of Aqabah is economically important to Israel at a time when it is suffering from the symptoms a man has on waking up after a long, boisterous and drunken party. The fountains of German reparations are drying up. Israel has also drained the sources of contributions and gifts. Although emergency sources will emerge as a result of the present crisis, particularly with the help of Western propaganda trumpets, people in the West, at least many of them, are getting tired of an entity which has been unable to lead a normal life, like a child who does not want to grow up, who cannot

306

depend on himself and does not want to take on any responsibility. Israel is suffering from an economic crisis. There are over 100,000 unemployed, nearly one quarter of Israel's manpower. The new blow has added to the economic plight. Israel attached great importance to its trade with East Africa and Asia. This trade depended on one route: the Red Sea via the Gulf of Aqabah, to Eilat. There were many projects for enlarging the port of Eilat, which at present can handle 400,000 tons a year. In addition, there were the oil lines. Israel has built two pipelines to carry Iranian oil from Eilat to the Haifa oil refinery. Israel has also dreamed of digging a canal from Eilat to Ashdod to compete with or replace the Suez Canal.

In my personal opinion all these important economic matters and questions are not the decisive factor which will influence or dictate the Israeli reaction to the closure of the Gulf of Aqabah. The decisive factor in my opinion is the psychological factor. The economic aspect swings back and forth between yes and no. From this aspect the challenge of war can be either accepted or put off. But the psychological factor cannot swing back and forth. From this aspect there is one answer: Yes. It is in the light of the compelling psychological factor that the needs of security, of survival itself, make acceptance of the challenge of war inevitable.

One thing is clear: The closure of the Gulf of Aqabah to Israeli navigation and the ban on the import of strategic goods, even when carried by non-Israeli ships, means first and last that the Arab nation represented by the UAR has succeeded for the first time, *vis-à-vis* Israel, in changing by force a fait accompli imposed on it by force. This is the essence of the problem, regardless of the complications surrounding it and future contingencies.

As for the complications, we can find in the past ample justification for Arab resistance. We could say that the British mandate in Palestine had sold Palestine to Zionism in accordance with a resolution adopted by the League of Nations. This is true. We could say that the UN betrayed Palestine, and this is true. We could say Arab reaction from the Jordanian King Abdullah to the Saudi King Faysal connived at the plot against Palestine, and this is true. We could say about the Gulf of Aqabah that in 1956 imperialism, represented by the British and French forces, imposed a fait accompli during this period from autumn 1956 to spring 1967. It was imperialist not Israeli arms which imposed this fait accompli. We could say all this is seeking to justify Arab resistance. But the naked and rocky truth which remains after all this is that the accomplished fact was aggressively imposed by force. The Arabs did not have the force to resist the accomplished fact, let alone to change it by force and to impose a substitite consistent with their rights and interests.

As for the contingencies which may be precipitated by this new development, I do not think I need go into detail.

Israel has built its existence, security and future on force. The prevalent philosophy of its rulers has been that the Arab quakes before the forbidding glance, and that nothing deters him but fear. Thus Israeli intimidation reached its peak. Provocation went beyond tolerable bounds. But all of this, from the Israeli point of view, had the psychological aim of convincing the Arabs that Israel could do anything and that the Arabs could do nothing; that Israel was omnipotent and could impose any accomplished fact, while the Arabs were weak and had to accept any accomplished fact. Despite the error and danger in this Israeli philosophy – because two or even three million Israelis cannot by military force or by myth dominate a sea of 80 million Arabs – this philosophy remained a conviction deeply embedded in Israeli thinking, planning and action for many disturbing years, without any Arab challenge capable of restoring matters to their proper perspective.

Now this is the first time the Arabs have challenged Israel in an attempt to change an accomplished fact by force and to replace it by force with an alternative accomplished fact consistent with their rights and interests. The opening of the Gulf of Aqabah to Israel was an accomplished fact imposed by the force of imperialist arms. This week the closure of the Gulf of Aqabah to Israel was an alternative accomplished fact imposed and now being protected by the force of Arab arms. To Israel this is the most dangerous aspect of the current situation ... Therefore it is not a matter of the Gulf of Aqabah but of something bigger. It is the whole philosophy of Israeli security. It is the philosophy on which Israeli existence has pivoted since its birth and on which it will pivot in the future.

Hence I say that Israel must resort to arms. Therefore I say that an armed clash between the UAR and the Israeli enemy is inevitable.

As from now, we must expect the enemy to deal us the first blow in the battle. But as we wait for that first blow, we should try to minimise its effect as much as possible. The second blow will then follow. But this will be the blow we will deliver against the enemy in retaliation and deterrence. It will be the most effective blow we can possibly deal. Why do I say this now? My point of view is as follows:

When one studies the strategy of the Egyptian action of the 10 great days from 14th to 23rd May in which the positions and balance in the Middle East changed, one will immediately perceive two factors which at first sight may appear contradictory: The first factor: Egypt was ready and prepared. The second factor: the Egyptian action was a complete surprise, even to Egypt in so far as it was a reaction to a specific situation, namely, Israel's threat to and readiness to invade Syria.

By analysing the first factor in the strategy of the Egyptian action during the 10 great days which changed the positions and balance in the Middle East we find that there are roots extending from the spring of 1967 back to the time when the UAR called for the Arab summit conferences. The first summit conference was convened in January 1964. The first item submitted by the UAR to that conference was the Jordan headwaters. At that time the anti-Egyptian Western propaganda which was backed by the reactionary elements sought, discreetly at times but most of the time shamelessly, to hamper Egyptian policy at that time by two propaganda themes: (1) that Egypt's whole aim in the summit conferences policy was to settle the Yemeni issue with Saudi Arabia; (2) that when Egypt called for the summit conferences it wanted to abandon the responsibility of action for Palestine, in accordance with the traditional method which says that when you face a problem for which you cannot find a solution the only way to bury and get rid of it is to form a commission to discuss and study it. All this, of course, was untrue, since Egypt at the time imagined that the Arab summit conferences could draw up the policy of the liberation battle and could prepare for it. Egypt wanted unified action to be the front of a broad movement which might have world-wide political influence serving the strategy of battle. Besides, unified Arab action might be beneficial in providing possibilities for defending Arab countries which at that time did not have reassuring defences. At the same time Egypt believed that when the time came for earnest action, loyalty and fidelity to the trust dictated that it should primarily depend on itself.

Accordingly the summit conferences were a broad front suitable for world-wide political influence. It was also possible for them to help strengthen the defence of Arab countries surrounding Israel. Behind this broad front and the consolidation of the other Arab countries surrounding Israel Egypt could prepare and mobilise its own effective forces.

The remainder of the story of the summit conferences is known and I do not propose to repeat it. It ended in utter failure because of Arab reactionary rancour, and because reaction had greater hatred for Arab social progress than for the Israeli enemy, which wants to humiliate all the Arabs whatever their social views. The broad front for unified Arab action therefore collapsed with the failure of the summit conferences. The possibilities of strengthening the defence of the other Arab countries surrounding Israel did not sufficiently materialise as they should have done. Egypt was unable to control all those circumstances but it was able to control the third objective, namely, to prepare and mobilise its effective forces.

Anti-Egyptian Western propaganda, backed by the Arab reactionary elements, continued to attack Egypt fiercely. The attack went to the length of spreading the belief that the entire Egyptian Army had perished in Yemen, had been scattered into aimless groups, and that the remainder had been killed, wounded or captured. Similarly it was said that the Egyptian economy was collapsing and could not stand on its feet, let alone bear the weight of any bold venture and carry on with it. But Egypt knew the truth and was confident that the truth would appear to the entire Arab nation one day when the time was ripe for serious action.

Egypt, then, was prepared and ready. This is the first fact about the strategy of Egyptian action during the 10 great days.

I will now come to the second factor in the crisis. This factor is that the Egyptian action was a complete surprise. It appears, and it is now almost certain, that the forces hostile to Egypt, that is imperialism, Arab reaction and Israel, had come in the end to believe their own propaganda. People sometimes fall prey to the lies they themselves fabricate. Something of that sort must certainly have happened, otherwise Israel would not have persisted in its threats against Syria and gone to the length of the cry of 'march on Damascus'. It must have felt certain that there would be no decisive Egyptian reaction, because there were insufficient forces for any initiative or retaliatory action.

It was this Israeli threat to Syria and information confirming it concerning intentions and plans that precipitated the emergency situation to which Egypt had to react immediately, even though it came as a surprise to it. There was preparation and mobilisation of the effective Egyptian forces. There was national consciousness and abidance by its principles. There was creative leadership. What I mean to say is that Egypt was not prepared for this specific contingency but was prepared for all contingencies including such a one.

Now, to turn to the march of events during the 10 great days which changed the situation and the balance in the Middle East. Events began to move. One calculated and effective step followed another: the decision was taken to implement the joint defence agreement with Syria – this is the decision which Lt-Gen. Muhammad Fawzi, the Chief of Staff of the Egyptian Armed Forces, carried on the five-hour visit to Damascus. Then followed the message addressed by Lt-Gen. Muhammad Fawzi to the Commander of the UN Emergency Force to withdraw his forces from the Egyptian borders with Israel. The Egyptian Armed Forces then, without waiting, actually began occupying all the border positions. The Foreign Minister Mahmud Riyad then sent his message to the UN Secretary-General U Thant on the withdrawal and evacuation of the Emergency Forces in the UAR and Gaza. Then followed the advance on Sharm al Shaykh, the entrance to the Gulf of Aqabah; the order was issued to close the Gulf of Aqabah to Israeli shipping and to strategic goods for Israel even if transported aboard non-Israeli ships; and all the US initiatives were rejected. All these actions were backed by a massive, ready force enjoying a morale brimming over with a fighting spirit the like of which the Middle East has never seen.

Two results were thus achieved, that is to say: (1) The plan against Syria collapsed; the invasion of Syria became impossible because all of the enemy forces streamed into the South to confront the Egyptian concentration. (2) The accomplished fact which the British-French invasion, and not the Israeli Army, had imposed in 1956 to the benefit of Israel, was changed.

In other words the strategy of this stage achieved its first objective by frustrating the plot to invade Syria, and moreover, it achieved another longed-for and precious objective: the return of the armed forces to direct confrontation with Israel and the closing once again of the door to the Gulf of Aqabah in Israel's face.

Is this, then, the end of the matter? I would answer that I have explained – or rather tried to explain – with the first observation in this inquiry that the problem has not ended but rather has hardly begun. This is because I am confident that for many reasons, chiefly the psychological, Israel cannot accept or remain indifferent to what has taken place. In my opinion it simply cannot do so. This means, and that is what I intend to say in the second observation of this inquiry that the next move is up to Israel. Israel has to reply now. It has to deal a blow. We have to be ready for it, as I said, to minimise its effect as much as possible. Then it will be our turn to deal the second blow, which we will deliver with the utmost possible effectiveness.

In short, Egypt has exercised its power and achieved the objectives of this stage without resorting to arms so far. But Israel has no alternative but to use arms if it wants to exercise power. This means that the logic of the fearful confrontation now taking place between Egypt, which is fortified by the might of the masses of the Arab nation, and Israel, which is fortified by the illusion of American might, dictates that Egypt, after all it has now succeeded in achieving must wait, even though it has to wait for a blow. This is necessitated also by the sound conduct of the battle, particularly from the international point of view. Let Israel begin. Let our second blow then be ready. Let it be a knockout.

Appendix 6

Nasser's Press statement of 28 May 1967 at
the Presidential Palace, Heliopolis

I am pleased to meet today the representatives of the world and Arab
press who are making great efforts to cover the important events
which are preoccupying us all. As you all know, the press does not
only cover events: it also participates in creating them. I am referring
here to a valuable aspect of the press. If the authenticity of reports on
any event is important, the form in which we present those reports to
the people is no less important. In other words, there is the topic and
there is the form in which we present it to others. I feel it is our duty
to present to you a picture of reality as we see it. This is part of our
responsibility with regard to a situation which may mean peace or
war to the entire Arab world and whose effects and repercussions
may be felt even beyond the Arab world.

On the other hand, I feel that you who are here on a sacred
mission, namely, the freedom of the press, which also has its serious
side, namely, influencing world sentiment on certain problems – have
the right to ask me to meet you and to answer your questions in person.

I tell you frankly that we are not asking you for anything or trying
to keep anything from you. We want to tell you the truth on anything
that interests you and to give you details on events as we see them. I
have already told you that this is our duty especially in regard to a
question concerning peace or war. We are not concerned about
the rest. It depends on your professional conscience and your
responsibility to the multitudes you serve in all the countries of the
world.

I want to add to this preamble before answering your questions. I
wish to draw your attention to an important point. The problem all
of us are experiencing now and are concerned about – all of us, statesmen, journalists and the multitudes of peoples – is neither the problem of the Straits of Tiran nor the withdrawal of the UNEF. All these
are side issues of a bigger and more serious problem – the problem of
the aggression which has taken place and continues to take place on
the Arab homeland of Palestine and the continuous threat posed

by that aggression against all Arab countries. This is the original problem.

Those who think that the crucial issues of nations and peoples can die and succumb to the symptoms of old age with the passage of time are grossly mistaken. Individuals may succumb to the symptoms of old age, including forgetfulness, but peoples are immortal, rejuvenescent and eternally young. This is specially true in this case, as aggression is not over. It continues to take place and in fact tries to affect and dominate a wider area.

We completely refuse to confine our concern to the subject of the Straits of Tiran or the withdrawal of the UNEF. In our opinion neither topic is open to question. The Straits of Tiran are Egyptian territorial waters, and Egypt has the right of sovereignty over them. No power, no matter how strong – and I am saying this quite clearly so that every side will know its position – can affect or circumvent the rights of Egyptian sovereignty. Any attempt of this kind will be an aggression against the Egyptian people and the entire Arab nation and will result in unimaginable damage to the aggressors.

The subject of the withdrawal of the UNEF is also not open to question. The UNEF came to our territory in the circumstances of the tripartite aggression, the disgraceful collusion which destroyed the moral and material reputation of all the perpetrators. All the secrets of the collusion have been unearthed. They condemn the plotters and brand them with contempt. As I have already said, the UNEF came to our territory with our approval, and its continued existence here depended on this approval. We have now withdrawn our approval and the UN Secretary-General responded faithfully, honestly and honourably to our request. The question of the UNEF is now completely over and is no longer open to discussion.

The circumstances in which we requested the withdrawal of the UNEF are also known to all of you. Syria was threatened. There was a plan to invade Syria. Measures had been taken and a date set for the implementation of this plan. In the meantime, the voices of Israeli officials were heard openly calling for an advance on Damascus. Naturally, we could not stand idly by when Syria was being threatened with invasion. We could not allow this to be done to Syria or to any Arab country. The UAR armed forces, however, had to move to positions from which they could effectively deter aggression. Many natural developments followed our action. These developments were a surprise to everyone except those who had spread biased propaganda against the Arab nation. They were now caught in the trap they had laid for others. They lied and lied until they believed themselves. Reality therefore took them by surprise.

313

We do not believe that any sincere man can describe any measure we have taken in the past two weeks as an aggression or even find in it any trace of aggression. Our forces went to Sinai to deter aggression. In the Straits of Tiran we have exercised the rights of Egyptian sovereignty. Any interference with these rights will itself be an aggression. Why? This takes us back to the source, origin, reality and core of the problem. Israel was created by imperialism and by the forces seeking to dominate the Arab nation. We are not the only ones to say this. It is said by others who are today defending the Israeli aggression. They say it on every occasion. Nearly word for word, they say: They have created Israel and are responsible for its security. They have given Israel the biggest part of Arab Palestine. After this first and biggest aggression, they continued to support its aggressive line.

We must now ask ourselves many questions. What has Israel done with the UN resolutions of 1947, 1948 and 1949? The answer: Israel threw them away. What has Israel done with the Security Council's armistice resolutions? The answer: Israel occupied more Palestinian territory after these resolutions. The best example is the port of Eilat, which Israel built on Arab soil at Umm ar-Rashrash. Israel occupied this area after the armistice resolutions. The armistice agreements were signed in February 1949. In March of that year Israel occupied this area, thus trampling on all the Security Council resolutions and the armistice agreements when the ink with which they were signed had hardly dried.

What has Israel done with the rights of Arab refugees and the UN resolutions concerning them? The answer: The refugees are still displaced from their usurped homeland. What has Israel done with the armistice commissions themselves and their members who, in their mission, represented the UN? The answer: When it decided to occupy the demilitarised zone of Al-Auja in 1955 Israel did not hesitate to arrest the truce observers to keep them away from the zone. In any case this was not strange. Israeli aggression went so far as to assassinate the chief truce observer Count Bernadotte, whose report was not favourable to Israeli designs.

What did Israel do in 1956? What does all that Israel did in 1956 mean? The answer: Israel played its role as an imperialist tool. Its role was disgraceful as is now clear from all that has been published about the Suez secrets. Yet Israel claimed victory. In addition to that it tried – and this was obvious – to annex a part of Egyptian territory, namely, Sinai. Ben Gurion announced it. After Suez, Israel's aggressive record continued until the recent threat to Syria, which set off the present crisis. This is the source of the problem. Any attempt to ignore or condone this problem is unacceptable. This is the matter on which the entire Arab nation stands. It is ready to take it up to the last with Israeli aggression and with the United States, which is continuing to back this aggression politically, economically and militarily.

Appendix 7

Nasser's speech to National Assembly members on 29 May 1967

Brothers, when Brother Anwar al Sadat informed me of your decision to meet me I told him that I myself was prepared to call on you at the National Assembly, but he said you were determined to come. I therefore responded to this and I thank you heartily for your consideration.

I was naturally not surprised by the law which Brother Anwar al Sadat read because I was notified of it before I came here. However, I wish to thank you very much for your feelings and for the powers given me. I did not ask for such powers because I felt that you and I were as one, that we could co-operate and work for the sublime interest of this country giving a great example of unselfishness and of work for the welfare of all. Thanks be to God, for four years now the National Assembly has been working and has given great examples. We have given great examples in co-operation and unselfishness and in placing before us the sublime and highest objective – the interest of this nation.

I am proud of this resolution and law. I promise you that I will use it only when necessary. I will, however, send all the laws to you. Thank you once again. The great gesture of moral support represented by this law is very valuable to my spirit and heart. I heartily thank you for this feeling and this initiative.

The circumstances through which we are now passing are in fact difficult ones because we are not only confronting Israel but also those who created Israel and who are behind Israel. We are confronting Israel and the West as well – the West, which created Israel and which despised us Arabs and which ignored us before and since 1948. They had no regard whatsoever for our feelings, our hopes in life, or our rights. The West completely ignored us, and the Arab nation was unable to check the West's course.

Then came the events of 1956 – the Suez battle. We all know what happened in 1956. When we rose to demand our rights, Britain, France and Israel opposed us, and we were faced with the tripartite

316

aggression. We resisted, however, and proclaimed that we would fight to the last drop of our blood. God gave us success and God's victory was great.

Subsequently we were able to rise and to build. Now, 11 years after 1956, we are restoring things to what they were in 1956. This is from the material aspect. In my opinion this material aspect is only a small part, whereas the spiritual aspect is the great side of the issue. The spiritual aspect involves the renaissance of the Arab nation, the revival of the Palestine question, and the restoration of confidence to every Arab and to every Palestinian. This is on the basis that if we are able to restore conditions to what they were before 1956 God will surely help and urge us to restore the situation to what it was in 1948.

Brothers, the revolt, upheaval and commotion which we now see taking place in every Arab country are not only because we have returned to the Gulf of Aqabah or rid ourselves of the UNEF, but because we have restored Arab honour and renewed Arab hopes.

Israel used to boast a great deal, and the Western powers, headed by the United States and Britain, used to ignore and even despise us and consider us of no value. But now that the time has come – and I have already said in the past that we will decide the time and place and not allow them to decide – we must be ready for triumph and not for a recurrence of the 1948 comedies. We shall triumph, God willing.

Preparations have already been made. We are now ready to confront Israel. They have claimed many things about the 1956 Suez war, but no one believed them after the secrets of the 1956 collusion were uncovered – that mean collusion in which Israel took part. Now we are ready for the confrontation. We are now ready to deal with the entire Palestine question.

The issue now at hand is not the Gulf of Aqabah, the Straits of Tiran, or the withdrawal of the UNEF, but the rights of the Palestine people. It is the aggression which took place in Palestine in 1948 with the collaboration of Britain and the United States. It is the expulsion of the Arabs from Palestine, the usurpation of their rights, and the plunder of their property. It is the disavowal of all the UN resolutions in favour of the Palestinian people.

The issue today is far more serious than they say. They want to confine the issue to the Straits of Tiran, the UNEF and the right of passage. We demand the full rights of the Palestinian people. We say this out of our belief that Arab rights cannot be squandered because the Arabs throughout the Arab world are demanding these Arab rights.

We are not afraid of the United States and its threats, of Britain and her threats, or of the entire Western world and its partiality to Israel. The United States and Britain are partial to Israel and give no consideration to the Arabs, to the entire Arab nation. Why? Because we have made them believe that we cannot distinguish between friend and foe. We must make them know that we know who our foes are and who our friends are and treat them accordingly.

If the United States and Britain are partial to Israel, we must say that our enemy is not only Israel but also the United States and Britain and treat them as such. If the Western Powers disavow our rights and ridicule and despise us, we Arabs must teach them to respect us and take us seriously. Otherwise all our talk about Palestine, the Palestine people, and Palestinian rights will be null and void and of no consequence. We must treat enemies as enemies and friends as friends.

I said yesterday that the States that champion freedom and peace have supported us. I spoke of the support given us by India, Pakistan, Afghanistan, Yugoslavia, Malaysia, the Chinese People's Republic and the Asian and African States.

After my statements yesterday I met the War Minister Shams Badran and learned from him what took place in Moscow. I wish to tell you today that the Soviet Union is a friendly Power and stands by us as a friend. In all our dealings with the Soviet Union – and I have been dealing with the USSR since 1955 – it has not made a single request of us. The USSR has never interfered in our policy or internal affairs. This is the USSR as we have always known it. In fact, it is we who have made urgent requests of the USSR. Last year we asked for wheat and they sent it to us. When I also asked for all kinds of arms they gave them to us. When I met Shams Badran yesterday he handed me a message from the Soviet Premier Kosygin saying that the USSR supported us in this battle and would not allow any Power to intervene until matters were restored to what they were in 1956.

Brothers, we must distinguish between friend and foe, friend and hypocrite. We must be able to tell who is making requests, who has ulterior motives, and who is applying economic pressure. We must also know those who offer their friendship to us for no other reason than a desire for freedom and peace.

In the name of the UAR people, I thank the people of the USSR for their great attitude, which is the attitude of a real friend. This is the kind of attitude we expect. I said yesterday that we had not requested the USSR or any other state to intervene, because we really want to avoid any confrontation which might lead to a world war and also because we really work for peace and advocate world peace. When we voiced the policy of non-alignment, our chief aim was world peace.

Brothers, we will work for world peace with all the power at our disposal, but we will also hold tenaciously to our rights with all the power at our disposal. This is our course. On this occasion, I address myself to our brothers in Aden and say: Although occupied with this battle, we have not forgotten you. We are with you. We have not forgotten the struggle of Aden and the occupied South for liberation. Aden and the occupied South must be liberated and colonialism must end. We are with them; present matters have not taken our minds from Aden.

I thank you for taking the trouble to pay this visit. Moreover, your presence is an honour to the Qubbah Palace, and I am pleased to have met you. Peace be with you.

Appendix 8

Nasser's resignation broadcast of 9 June 1967

Brothers, at times of triumph and tribulation, in the sweet hours and bitter hours, we have become accustomed to sit together to discuss things, to speak frankly of facts, believing that only in this way can we always find the right path however difficult circumstances may be.

We cannot hide from ourselves the fact that we have met with a grave setback in the last few days, but I am confident that we all can and, in a short time will, overcome our difficult situation, although this calls for much patience and wisdom as well as moral courage and ability to work on our part. Before that, brothers, we need to cast a glance back over past events so that we shall be able to follow developments and the line of our march leading to the present conditions.

All of us know how the crisis started in the Middle East. At the beginning of last May there was an enemy plan for the invasion of Syria and the statements by his politicians and all his military leaders openly said so. There was plenty of evidence concerning the plan. Sources of our Syrian brothers were categorical on this and our own reliable information confirmed it. Add to this the fact that our friends in the Soviet Union warned the parliamentary delegation, which was on a visit to Moscow, at the beginning of last month, that there was a premeditated plan against Syria. We considered it our duty not to accept this silently. This was the duty of Arab brotherhood, it was also the duty of national security. Whoever starts with Syria will finish with Egypt.

Our armed forces moved to our frontiers with a competence which the enemy acknowledged even before our friends. Several steps followed. There was the withdrawal of the United Nations Emergency Force and the return of our forces to the Sharm al Shaykh post, the controlling point in the Straits of Tiran, which had been used by the Israeli enemy as one of the after-effects of the tripartite aggression against us in 1956. The enemy's flag passing in front of our forces was intolerable, apart from other reasons connected with the dearest aspirations of the Arab nation.

320

Accurate calculations were made of the enemy's strength and showed us that our armed forces, at the level of equipment and training which they had reached, were capable of repelling the enemy and deterring him. We realised that the possibility of an armed clash existed and accepted the risk.

Before us were several factors – national, Arab and international. A message from the US President Lyndon Johnson was handed to our Ambassador in Washington on 26th May asking us to show self-restraint and not to be the first to fire, or else we should have to face grave consequences. On the very same night, the Soviet Ambassador asked to have an urgent meeting with me at 05.30 [as broadcast] after midnight. He informed me of an urgent request from the Soviet Government not to be the first to open fire.

In the morning of last Monday, 5th June, the enemy struck. If we say now it was a stronger blow than we had expected, we must say at the same time, and with complete certainty that it was bigger than the potential at his disposal. It became very clear from the first moment that there were other powers behind the enemy – they came to settle their accounts with the Arab national movement. Indeed, there were surprises worthy of note:

(1) The enemy, whom we were expecting from the east and north, came from the west – a fact which clearly showed that facilities exceeding his own capacity and his calculated strength had been made available to him.

(2) The enemy covered at one go all military and civilian airfields in the UAR. This means that he was relying on some force other than his own normal strength to protect his skies against any retaliatory action from our side. The enemy was also leaving other Arab fronts to be tackled with outside assistance which he had been able to obtain.

(3) There is clear evidence of imperialist collusion with the enemy – an imperialist collusion, trying to benefit from the lesson of the open collusion of 1956, by resorting this time to abject and wicked concealment. Nevertheless, what is now established is that American and British aircraft carriers were off the shores of the enemy helping his war effort. Also, British aircraft raided, in broad daylight, positions on the Syrian and Egyptian fronts, in addition to operations by a number of American aircraft reconnoitring some of our positions. The inevitable result of this was that our land forces, fighting most violent and brave battles in the open desert, found themselves at that difficult time without adequate air cover in face of the decisive superiority of the enemy air forces. Indeed it can be said without emotion or exaggeration, that the enemy was operating with an air force three times stronger than his normal force.

The same conditions were faced by the forces of the Jordanian Army, fighting a brave battle under the leadership of King Husayn who – let me say for the sake of truth and honesty – adopted an excellent stand; and I admit that my heart was bleeding while I was following the battles of his heroic Arab Army in Jerusalem and other parts of the West Bank on the night when the enemy and his plotting forces massed no less than 400 aircraft over the Jordanian front.

There were other honourable and marvellous efforts. The Algerian people, under their great leader Hawwari Bumedien, gave without reservation and without stinting for the battle. The people of Iraq and their faithful leader Abd ar-Rahman Arif gave without reservation or stinting for the battle. The Syrian Army fought heroically, consolidated by the forces of the great Syrian people and under the leadership of their national Government. The peoples and governments of Sudan, Kuwait, Yemen, Lebanon, Tunisia and Morocco adopted honourable stands. All the peoples of the Arab nation, without exception, adopted a stand of manhood and dignity all along the Arab homeland; a stand of resolution and determination that Arab right shall not be lost, shall not be humiliated, and that the war in its defence is advancing, regardless of sacrifice and setbacks, on the road of the sure and inevitable victory. There were also great nations outside the Arab homeland who gave us invaluable moral support.

But the plot, and we must say this with the courage of men, was bigger and fiercer. The enemy's main concentration was on the Egyptian front which he attacked with all his main force of armoured vehicles and infantry, supported by air supremacy the dimensions of which I have outlined for you. The nature of the desert did not permit a full defence especially, in face of the enemy's air supremacy. I realised that the armed battle might not go in our favour. I, with others, tried to use all sources of Arab strength. Arab oil came in to play its part. The Suez Canal came in to play its part. A great role is still reserved for general Arab action. I am fully confident that it will measure up to its task. Our Armed Forces in Sinai were obliged to evacuate the first line of defence. They fought fearful tank and air battles on the second line of defence.

We then responded to the cease-fire resolution, in view of assurances contained in the latest Soviet draft resolution, to the Security Council, as well as French statements to the effect that no one must reap any territorial expansion from the recent aggression, and in view of world public opinion, especially in Asia and Africa, which appreciates our position and feels the ugliness of the forces of international domination which pounced on us.

We now have several urgent tasks before us. The first is to remove the traces of this aggression against us and to stand by the Arab nation resolutely and firmly; despite the setback, the Arab nation, with all its potential and resources, is in a position to insist on the removal of the traces of the aggression.

The second task is to learn the lesson of the setback. In this connection there are three vital facts, (1) The elimination of imperialism in the Arab world will leave Israel with its own intrinsic power; yet, whatever the circumstances, however long it may take the Arab intrinsic power is greater and more effective. (2) Redirecting Arab interests in the service of Arab rights is an essential safeguard: the American Sixth Fleet moved with Arab oil, and there are Arab bases, placed forcibly and against the will of the peoples, in the service of aggression. (3) The situation now demands a united word from the entire Arab nation; this, in the present circumstances, is irreplacable guarantee.

Now we arrive at an important point in this heartsearching by asking ourselves: does this mean that we do not bear responsibility for the consequences of the setback? I tell you truthfully and despite any factors on which I might have based my attitude during the crisis, that I am ready to bear the whole responsibility. I have taken a decision in which I want you all to help me. I have decided to give up completely and finally every official post and every political role and return to the ranks of the masses and do my duty with them like every other citizen.

The forces of imperialism imagine that Jamal Abd al-Nasser is their enemy. I want it to be clear to them that their enemy is the entire Arab nation, not just Jamal Abd al Nasser. The forces hostile to the Arab national movement try to portray this movement as an empire of Abd al-Nasser. This is not true, because the aspiration for Arab unity began before Abd al-Nasser and will remain after Abd al-Nasser. I always used to tell you that the nation remains, and that the individual – whatever his role and however great his contribution to the causes of his homeland – is only a tool of the popular will, and not its creator.

In accordance with Article 110 of the Provisional Constitution promulgated in March 1964 I have entrusted my colleague, friend and brother Zakariya Muhiedin with taking over the post of President and carrying out the constitutional provisions on this point. After this decision, I place all I have at his disposal in dealing with the grave situation through which our people are passing.

In doing this I am not liquidating the revolution – indeed the revolution is not the monopoly of any one generation of revolutionaries. I take pride in the brothers of this generation of revolutionaries. It has brought to pass the evacuation of British imperialism, has won the independence of Egypt and defined its Arab personality, and has combated the policy of spheres of influence in the Arab world; it has led the social revolution and created a deep transformation in the Egyptian reality by establishing the people's control over the sources of their wealth and the result of Arab action; it recovered the Suez Canal and laid down the foundation of industrial upsurge in Egypt; it built the High Dam to bring fertile greenness to the barren desert; it laid down a power network over the whole of the north of the Nile Valley; it made oil resources gush out after a long wait. More important still, it gave the leadership of political action to the alliance of the people's working forces, the constant source of renewed leaderships carrying the banners of Egyptian and Arab struggle through its successive stages, building socialism, succeeding and triumphing.

I have unlimited faith in this alliance as the leader of national action: the peasants, the workers, the soldiers, the intellectuals and national capital. Its unity and cohesion and creative response within the framework of this unity are capable of creating – through work, serious work, difficult work, as I have said more than once – colossal miracles for this country in order to be a strength for itself, for its Arab nation, for the movement of national revolution and for world peace based on justice.

The sacrifices made by our people and their burning spirit during the crisis and the glorious pages of heroism written by the officers and soldiers of our armed forces with their blood will remain an unquenchable torch in our history and a great inspiration for the future and its great hopes. The people were splendid as usual, noble as their nature, believing, sincere and loyal. The members of our armed forces were an honourable example of Arab man in every age and every place. They defended the grains of sand in the desert to the last drop of their blood. In the air, they were, despite enemy supremacy, legends of dedication and sacrifice, of courage and willingness to perform the duty in the best way.

This is an hour for action; not an hour for sorrow. It is a situation calling for ideals and not for selfishness or personal feelings. All my heart is with you, and I want all your hearts to be with me. May God be with us all, a hope in our hearts, a light and guidance. Peace and the blessing of God be with you.

Appendix 9

Nasser's Revolution Anniversary speech at
Cairo University, 23 July 1967

Brother compatriots, the 15th anniversary of the revolution of 23rd
July 1952 comes while we are living through a crisis. We will not be
exaggerating if we say that this is the most severe crisis we have faced
in the history of our revolutionary work.

At no time has our work been easy. We have always had to face all
kinds of political, economic, and military dangers. Every victory we
have achieved came after difficulties and hardships which we bore
patiently.

To carry out the revolution of 23rd July was not an easy job for our
people after 70 years of British occupation. For 70 years the British,
in collaboration with the feudalists and the capitalists, ruled this
country with the backing of 80,000 British soldiers in the Suez Canal
zone. Nor was our people's resistance to the policy of pacts and zones
of influence which others tried to impose on us an easy job at a time
when the national liberation movement had not attained the present
level of independence and non-subservience.

Moreover, our people's acceptance of the challenge to build the
High Dam was not an easy job in the face of the arrogance of the
United States, which thought that by withdrawing a Western offer to
finance the High Dam it could harm the Egyptian economy and
reveal our people as incapable of assuming the responsibility of
executing such a project, which is unequalled anywhere in the world.
In fact by its arrogance the United States wanted our people to lose
confidence in themselves and to overthrow our revolutionary regime.

Nor was our people's endurance of the horrors of the Suez war an
easy job. In 1956 our people were attacked by three states, two of
which were big Powers. The aggression has utilised the base that
imperialism had established in the heart of the Arab homeland to
threaten and terrorise this homeland, once overtly and the second
time covertly.

Our people's progress in the field of socialist reconstruction, self-
reliance and justice and their attempt to increase national wealth

through the enormous process of industrialisation; reclamation of vast lands; electrification of the entire country; restoration of all foreign interests; elimination of monopolism, capitalism, and feudalism; redistribution of land; provision for education, health and social security services; and the participation of the workers in the profits and administration of firms – all this, brothers, was not an easy job in this country where foreign and feudalist interests once dominated the national resources. It was not an easy job in the heart of this Arab world which was dominated by foreign and feudalist interests. Whatever happens in our country has its repercussions in our entire Arab world whether we like it or not.

Our people's acceptance of the responsibilities of Arab solidarity, the common struggle and of destiny was not an easy job. In exercising these responsibilities we resisted the attempt to invade Syria in 1957, accepted the consequences of unity and secession, supported the revolution in Iraq in 1958, supported the Algerian revolution from 1954 to 1962, and backed the Yemeni revolution and the revolution in South Arabia. The latest problem we have confronted and are still confronting is the attempt to invade Syria.

Brothers, our work has never been easy. The road of the struggle is strewn with dangers, the way to glory with sacrifices, and the way to great hopes with great sacrifices. Should the peoples fail to take this course they would face rigidity and backwardness. They would take no chances and would not face life – the sweet and bitter. Those who do not shoulder responsibilities have no right to entertain hopes. Those who do not take chances become the prisoner of fear itself because of their fear. This is not the quality of vigorous peoples; it is not their nature or their course.

I have said that the crisis we now face is one of the severest we have faced in the history of our revolutionary action for more than one reason. For one thing, this crisis which we are confronting, although it is not the gravest and most difficult we have faced, certainly marks the highest degree of hypocrisy and meanness we have encountered. Imperialism – we must admit this – has benefited from all its encounters with us and with the other peoples who have frequently been exposed to its assaults. This time imperialism did not face us overtly as it did in 1956. But imperialism made an effort – and we must admit that it was skilful – to conceal its role and hide its collusion. In the end perhaps imperialism left nothing to incriminate it but its fingerprints. But this is one thing and catching imperialism redhanded as we did in 1956 is something else.

For another thing, this is perhaps the first revolution anniversary that has found our homeland in the midst of a savage conspiracy.

Despite their courage and insistence on confronting it, our people undoubtedly at the same time are experiencing deep sorrow and severe pain.

Brothers, perhaps Almighty God wanted to test us to judge whether we deserve what we have achieved, whether we are able to protect our achievements, and whether we have the courage to be patient and stand firm against affliction. Brothers, perhaps Almighty God also wanted to give us a lesson to teach us what we had not learned, to remind us of some things we might have forgotten, and to cleanse our souls of the blemishes that have affected us and the shortcomings that we must avoid [applause] as we build our new society. Whatever the Almighty's will may be, we accept His test as our destiny. We are fully confident that He is with us: He will protect our struggle should we set out to struggle; grant us victory if we be determined to triumph and open the road to justice to us; endow us with victory if we be determined to be the victor; and open the road of justice to us if we be able to place ourselves on His right path.

Brother compatriots, I do not want to take you back to the circumstances which paved the way to this crisis. I explained some of these circumstances to you in my address to the nation on 9th June right after the setback. Also I realise, and we must all realise, that what happened has happened and there is no use wailing over the debris. Now it is more important to learn the lesson, overcome the setback, rise above it, and proceed triumphantly on our road towards the achievement of our aspirations.

But I do believe that we must ponder certain important matters so that we may all be able to achieve the highest degree of clarity. The first thing which should be clear to us all is that it was not we who started the crisis in the Middle East. We all know that this crisis began with Israel's attempt to invade Syria. It is quite clear to us all that in that attempt Israel was not working for itself alone but also for the forces which had got impatient with the Arab revolutionary movement.

The information we received about the invasion of Syria came from many sources. Our Syrian brothers had information that Israel had mobilised 18 brigades on their front. We confirmed this information. It became evident to us that Israel had mobilised no less than 13 brigades on the Syrian front. Our parliamentary delegation headed by Anwar as-Sadat was on a visit to Moscow, and our Soviet friends informed Anwar as-Sadat at that time that the invasion of Syria was imminent.

What were we to do? We could have remained silent, we could have waited, or we could have just issued statements and cables of

327

support. But if this homeland had accepted such behaviour it would have meant that it was deserting its mission, its role and even its personality. There was a joint defence agreement between us and Syria. We do not consider our agreements with the peoples of our Arab nation or others merely ink on paper. To us these agreements are sacred, an honour and an obligation. Between us and Syria, between us and all Arab peoples there was and always will be something far greater and more lasting than agreements and treaties: faith in the common struggle and the common fate. Therefore it was imperative that we take concrete steps to face the danger threatening Syria, especially since the statements of Israeli political and military leaders at the time and their open threats to Syria – as reported in the press and frankly noted at the UN – left no room for anyone to doubt any information or to wait or hesitate.

The second question: when we decided to move, our actions led to certain practical results. First we asked for the withdrawal of the UN Emergency Force. Then we restored Egyptian sovereignty rights in the Gulf of Aqabah. This was one of the things our Arab brothers had always insisted on. It was natural that such steps had a great impact on the area and the world.

The third question: by moving and taking the initiative to repel the danger to Syria, we realised – particularly from an international point of view – that the question was whether we should strike first in an armed battle. Had we done this we would have exposed ourselves to very serious consequences, greater than we would have been able to tolerate. First we would have faced direct US military action against us on the pretext that we had fired the first bullet in the battle.

Here I should like to draw your attention to certain important points. The first is the US warnings. Perhaps you have read about these US warnings. President Johnson's adviser summoned our Ambassador in Washington at a late hour at night and told him that Israel had information that we were going to attack. The adviser said this would put us in a serious situation and urged us to exercise self-restraint. They also said they were telling Israel the same thing so that it would also exercise self-restraint. We also received messages from President Johnson referring to the UN and urging us to exercise self-restraint.

The second point – which perhaps I have discussed before – is that on the following day the Russian Ambassador asked to see me and conveyed to me a message from the Soviet Premier urging self-restraint. He informed me about a message he had sent to the Israeli Premier and said that any action on our part would expose the world to great danger.

The third point is that the entire international community was against the outbreak of war. President de Gaulle was clear when he said France would define its attitude on the basis of who fired the first shot.

The fourth point is that we were the victims of a diplomatic trick, a political deception in which we had not imagined a major Power would involve itself. This political trick was played by the United States. It was represented in the US President's speech, his appeals, his request that we co-operate with the UN Secretary-General, and his offer to send the Vice-President to discuss with us ways to save the entire world from this crisis. The UN Secretary-General came here and we co-operated with him to the maximum. The Secretary-General asked for a breathing-space with regard to the Gulf of Aqabah and we agreed to this. He said he wanted this breathing-space so that all concerned would have time to pause and deal with matters. The first thing we pointed out to him was that no Israeli ships would be allowed to pass through the Canal [sic], that no strategic shipments would be allowed to pass, and, in the meantime, we would not search any ships. We accepted this and considered it a proposal by the Secretary-General of the UN, providing a breathing-space for all to discuss the matter.

After that an envoy of the US President arrived here. The emissary suggested that a Vice-President go to the United States. I approved the idea on the understanding that the Vice-President would meet President Johnson and explain our attitude to him. Then I sent a letter to the US President telling him: We welcome the visit of the US Vice-President but at the same time I am prepared to send Vice-President Zakariya Muhiedin to Washington to meet you and explain the Arab view to you. Naturally, the next day I received the reply that they welcomed Zakariya Muhiedin's trip to Washington to meet the American President and they requested that we set a date. We set it for Tuesday 6th June, and we all know that the aggression began on 5th June.

What does this mean? It means that large-scale political and diplomatic activities were going on and it was our right in the light of these activities to think that the explosion would not occur soon.

The fifth point: in spite of all this, we were not reassured about all these things. We knew that something was in the making and that it would not be long in coming. It was obvious that something was being planned against us. In fact, I had felt for two years that something would be prepared against us, since the cessation of US aid and America's warnings to us not to arm or enlarge our army, nor to follow a course of technical development, nor to seek military development.

When we concentrated our forces I estimated that the likelihood of war breaking out was 20 per cent. Before we closed the Gulf of Aqabah, we convened a meeting of the Higher Executive Committee at my home. We discussed the closure of the Gulf of Aqabah. That meeting took place on 22nd May. At that meeting I told them that the possibility of war was 50 per cent. At another meeting I said that the likelihood of war was 80 per cent. At our meeting of the Higher Executive Committee it was obvious that our action would be defensive, that we would attack only if aggression was launched against Syria, and that we would be on the alert. At that meeting no one spoke at all of attacking Israel. There was no intention at all that we would launch an offensive against Israel. As I explained earlier it was clear from all our analyses that any attack on Israel would expose us to great dangers. The foremost of these dangers would be an American attack on us in view of the statements America made saying that it guaranteed the borders of the states in this area. It was obvious to us that when America said it guaranteed the borders of the states in this area and would not tolerate any changes in this area, America did not at all mean the Arab states, but by this it meant Israel. It meant that if an aggression was carried out against Israel, America would implement the statement made by President Kennedy that America guaranteed all the borders in this area.

On these grounds there was no discussion at all of launching an attack on Israel. But our entire operation at the Joint Command was defensive. As we estimated at that time, our concentrations were a deterrent action so that Israel would not commit aggression against Syria.

On 23rd May we announced the closure of the Gulf of Aqabah to Israeli ships. Then came the political changes in Israel at the beginning of June. As we followed what was going on there, the probability of war became 100 per cent.

What does this mean? It means that we did not trust in the least all the political and diplomatic activities of the United States. We realised that something was being planned and that it would not take long.

On Friday 2nd June I personally went to the Armed Forces Supreme Command HQ. I participated at a meeting which was attended by all senior officers of the armed forces. At that meeting I gave my view before listening to theirs. I said at that meeting on Friday 2nd June that we must expect the enemy to strike a blow within 48 to 72 hours and no later on the basis of the indications of events and developments. I also said at that meeting that I expected the aggression to take place on Monday 5th June and the first blow to be struck at our Air Force. The Air Force commander was present at the meeting.

What does this mean? It means that we did not underestimate the situation as a result of all the diplomatic contacts, the dispatch of the UN Secretary-General, and Johnson's approval of a visit by Zakariya Muhiedin. It was quite clear on any political calculation that Israel was bound to take military action, especially after Iraqi forces had moved and Jordan had joined the joint defence agreements.

Question No. 6: After what has happened, we must faithfully and honourably admit that the military battle did not go as we had expected and hoped. It confirmed the proverb that precaution does not deter fate.

I do not wish now to talk about the causes, nor will I permit myself or this people, while the battle continues, to apportion blame. This is a matter for history and the struggle of our people. But I can say with satisfaction, good will and a conscience ready to give an account at any time that first and last the responsibility was mine. I said this in my address to the nation on 9th June, and I say it now and will continue to say it, bearing all the consequences and accepting any judgement of it. Actually this was why I decided to resign on 9th June. I wanted to take the responsibility and step down, and I wanted the enemies of the Egyptian people and the Arab nation to know that the issue is not Abd al Nasser or Abd al Nasser's ambitions, as they said. The Egyptian people's struggle began before Abd al Nasser and will go on after Abd al Nasser. The Arab nation sought its unity before Abd al Nasser. I have said and will always say that I am not the leader of this people. The greatest honour I desire is to be their representative at a particular stage in their continuous struggle, a stuggle not dependent of any individual.

Question No. 7, concerns the US role. A large part of the part played by the United States is still vague. We know only a little about this part. The secrets of the 1956 Suez war became known only last year – exactly 10 years after the war. Therefore, we shall not know the secrets of the 1967 war now. It will be some years before we know everything.

A large part of the US role in the recent aggression is still vague. But we already know a few things. We have already found the answers to several questions. What was behind the political and diplomatic part which the United States played before the battle? This role included the call for self-restraint, the threat that any action taken by us would expose the entire region to dangers, the proposal to send the US Vice-President to confer with us on the subject, the approval of Zakariya Muhiedin's trip to Washington to meet Johnson to confer on the subject and to try to reach a solution. All this took place before the aggression, before the battle.

It was a deception. We must ask: in whose interest was this deception? Certainly, it was in the interest of the imperialist-Israeli aggression. The deception was part of a US plan drawn up two years ago. The aim of this plan was to overthrow the free revolutionary regimes, which do not heed the words of the big Powers and refuse to be under anyone's influence.

What was behind the part played by the Sixth Fleet near our shores a few days before the war? How many arms were transported to Israel in the period from the outset of the crisis to the day of the aggression? How many aircraft reached Israel? How many volunteer pilots? How do we explain the huge air power which the enemy used on all Arab fronts? They attacked the Egyptian, Jordanian and Syrian fronts simultaneously. They also sent aircraft to attack Iraqi airports. On the evening of 7th June just before dawn, King Husayn contacted me by telephone saying that 400 aircraft were attacking the Jordanian front and were seen on his radar equipment. Where did these aircraft come from?

How do we explain the role of the US espionage ship Liberty? You have all read in the papers that an American ship named Liberty was near our territorial waters – probably in these waters – and that the Israelis thought it was an Egyptian warship and attacked it with torpedo boats. Some 34 officers and crew of this US ship were killed in this incident. For whom was this US ship with all its scientific equipment working? It was said that the ship was there to decode operational messages. It was also said that those messages were sent to the United States. Later it was said that the messages were sent to Israel. Messages can be radioed very rapidly. It was also said that those messages were sent to US Embassies in the area. What did the Americans do? When the Israelis hit them they pulled themselves together, hushed up the story, and went to Malta to repair the ship. Had we attacked the US ship, the Americans would have given us an ultimatum because we are neither an American colony nor an imperialist bridgehead. Nor are we in the US sphere of influence.

There is another question: why were there US aircraft over our front lines? On Wednesday 7th June two aircraft bearing US markings were seen over our lines. At first I did not believe it, but the information was certain. We then issued a statement saying that American aircraft had flown over our lines and over the front. We also said that we, therefore, believed the Americans were participating in the operation. We also spoke of the aircraft that were attacking Jordan and said that there had been a non-Israeli air attack on Jordan. We broadcast a statement including details about the two aircraft we had observed in flight.

In the evening I received a letter from President Johnson. He contacted the Soviet Head of State and requested him to send us a letter because at that time we did not have relations with him. He said it was true that there were two US aircraft over our lines, but they were going to the aid of the USS Liberty the spy ship.

The question arises: were there other US aircraft? A second question is: would they have made their admission had we not broadcast the statement? In fact, one asks oneself such questions about the things one knows.

What is the explanation of the US attitude at the UN and after the end of the operations? The US attitude at the UN after the operations was fully to endorse Israel's point of view. The US position at the UN was for unconditional surrender by the Arabs. This was the US position at the UN after the operations had ended. What does this mean?

There is an appalling difference between the two US attitudes – the attitude in 1956 when America was surprised by the tripartite aggression against us and the attitude in 1967 when America was not taken by surprise. In 1956 America was surprised by the tripartite aggression against us. In 1967, despite the letters and the agreement to send Zakariya Muhiedin, America was not surprised by the Israeli aggression against us. When America was surprised it stood steadfast against the aggression and demanded that it be halted and that the aggressive forces withdraw. But when America was not taken by surprise, it supported the aggression and brought pressure to bear on any State which America could influence in any way. The result was the failure of the UN as we have seen.

It is certain that America was not taken by surprise. Stories began to be told. These days American papers abound in news reports saying that the issue has provoked discussions at the highest levels in America. US papers and the American 'Life' magazine said that Israel submitted to the US President the view that it should launch an attack, saying that it felt superior. US newspapers also say that the US President sought the views of the US Chief of Staff and the US Intelligence Director and that they agreed. Accordingly, Israel was allowed to launch the offensive and to perpetrate aggression. At the same time Israel obtained guarantees from the United States that should the Arabs enter Israel, the Sixth Fleet would intercept them and if Israel entered the Arab countries, America would support Israel. These stories were published in newspapers. The Israeli Premier Eshkol has thanked the US President for telling him: The

Sixth Fleet is there for you and to help you. Eshkol replied in a sooth-
ing manner to the US President and told him: I am afraid that when
we become exposed to danger, you will be busy with Vietnam or you
may be spending the weekend at your Texas ranch. But the US
President emphatically assured him that the Sixth Fleet would protect
him should the Arabs cross the borders into Israel. These articles,
statements and all these stories were published in the papers. Therefore, the USA was not surprised by the aggression.

Therefore there was collusion between the USA and Israel. One
must ask oneself questions about these subjects. Of course the only
convincing answer is that the USA colluded with Israel. When the
USA declared before the war that it adhered to Kennedy's declaration guaranteeing borders in this area, it meant Israel's borders. The
USA reassured Israel about its borders but allowed it to violate Arab
territory. The USA asked us to exercise self-restraint, to permit a
breathing-space; at the same time it allowed Israel to commit
aggression.

I said before the fighting that we did not want to go to war with the
USA. Some people may have criticised me for saying and repeating
at the press conference I held before the fighting that the USA was the
strongest and richest power in the world. This is an undeniable fact.
Political policies cannot be founded on delusions or self-deception,
but on facts. When we say that we do not want to go to war with the
USA and cannot do so, I do not find this shameful or harmful. We do
not want to fight the USA and cannot do so. But this does not mean
that we are ready to forsake our freedom and revolutionary willpower
or our aspiration to build our own future in accordance with our own
desire and in the interest of our people, no matter what the circumstances and pressure, no matter how tyrannical the USA is towards
the national liberation movement and the national revolution.

Two years ago I met the US Under-Secretary of State, who brought
a message from Johnson. He said to me: Since you have not met our
requirements, the right of inspection – I have already told you the
story. They asked for the right of inspection with regard to atomic
activities and rockets in our country and the need to limit the power
of the Egyptian Army. We rejected all these requirements. We said
the USA had no right of inspection. The Under-Secretary of State,
Talbot, came to me saying: Since you have refused these requirements, we feel that we are free to supply Israel with all the arms it
requires. If you publicly announce that we are supplying arms to
Israel, we will supply it with even more arms.

I told him: If you supply arms to Israel, we will purchase arms. We
cannot possibly allow matters to proceed in this manner. At that time

the USA decided to supply Israel with a number of tanks and air-craft. It is quite possible that the number they announced did not tally with the actual number they gave to Israel.

This was the US threat. It was a clear threat that they would supply arms to Israel and support it in every way if we did not accept the right of inspection and their demand that we limit the power of the Egyptian Army.

Brothers, these were the sum of the circumstances and implications of what happened. A great deal about these circumstances and implications will be revealed in the future, but as I have already said, what is most important is that what has been done cannot be undone or denied. At the same time, we cannot remain stunned by the shock. As I have already said, the most important thing is that we should draw lessons from the setback. We should surmount the setback and continue the victorious march toward our objectives.

(In the last part of his speech President Nasser commented on domestic affairs.)

Appendix 10

Abba Eban's speech at the Special Assembly
of the United Nations, 19 June 1967

Our Watchword is 'Forward to Peace'
The subject of our discussion is the Middle East, its past agony and
its future hope. We speak of a region whose destiny has profoundly
affected the entire human experience. In the heart of that region, at
the very centre of its geography and history, lives a very small nation
called Israel. This nation gave birth to the currents of thought which
have fashioned the life of the Mediterranean world and of vast regions
beyond. It has now been re-established as the home and sanctuary of
a people which has seen six million of its sons exterminated in the
greatest catastrophe ever endured by a family of the human race.

In recent weeks the Middle East has passed through a crisis whose
shadows darken the world. This crisis has many consequences but
only one cause. Israel's rights to peace, security, sovereignty, economic development and maritime freedom – indeed its very right to
exist – has been forcibly denied and aggressively attacked. This is the
true origin of the tension which torments the Middle East. All the
other elements of the conflict are the consequences of this single
cause. There has been danger, there is still peril in the Middle East
because Israel's existence, sovereignty and vital interests have been
and are violently assailed.

The threat to Israel's existence, its peace, security, sovereignty and
development has been directed against her in the first instance by the
neighbouring Arab states. But all the conditions of tension, all the
impulses of aggression in the Middle East have been aggravated by
the policy of one of the Great Powers which under our Charter bear
primary responsibilities for the maintenance of international peace
and security. I shall show how the Soviet Union has been unfaithful
to that trust. The burden of responsibility lies heavy upon her.

I come to this rostrum to speak for a united people which, having
faced danger to the national survival, is unshakably resolved ot
resist any course which would renew the perils from which it has
emerged.

The General Assembly is chiefly preoccupied by the situation
against which Israel defended itself on the morning of June 5. I shall
invite every peace-loving state represented here to ask itself how it

would have acted on that day if it faced similar dangers. But if our discussion is to have any weight or depth, we must understand that great events are not born in a single instant of time. It is beyond all honest doubt that between May 14 and June 5, Arab governments led and directed by President Nasser, methodically prepared and mounted an aggressive assault designed to bring about Israel's immediate and total destruction. My authority for that conviction rests on the statements and actions of Arab governments themselves. There is every reason to believe what they say and to observe what they do.

The Pattern of Aggression, 1957–1967

During Israel's first decade, the intention to work for her destruction by physical violence has always been part of the official doctrine and policy of Arab states. But many members of the United Nations hoped and believed that relative stability would ensure from the arrangements discussed in the General Assembly in March 1957. An attempt has been made to inaugurate a period of non-belligerency and co-existence in the relations between the UAR and Israel. A United Nations emergency force was to separate the armies in Sinai and Gaza. The Maritime Powers were to exercise free and innocent passage in the Gulf of Akaba and the Straits of Tiran. Terrorist attacks against Israel were to cease. The Suez Canal was to be opened to Israel shipping, as the Security Council had decided six years before.

In March 1957, these hopes and expectations were endorsed in the General Assembly by the United States, France, the United Kingdom, Canada and other states in Europe, the Americas, Africa, Asia and Australia. These assurances, expressed with special solemnity by the four governments which I have mentioned, induced Israel to give up positions which she then held at Gaza and at the entrance to the Straits of Tiran and in Sinai. Non-belligerency, maritime freedom and immunity from terrorist attack were henceforth to be secured, not by Israel's own pressure but by the concerted will of the international community. Egypt expressed no opposition to these arrangements. Bright hopes for the future illuminated this hall ten years ago.

There were times during the past decade when it really seemed that a certain stability had been achieved. As we look back it becomes plain that the Arab governments regarded the 1957 arrangements merely as a breathing space enabling them to gather strength for a later assault. At the end of 1962, President Nasser began to prepare Arab opinion for an armed attack that was to take place within a few brief years. As his armaments grew his aggressive designs came more into light. On December 23, 1962, Nasser said:

337

'We feel that the soil of Palestine is the soil of Egypt, and of the whole Arab world. Why do we all mobilize? Because we feel that the land of Palestine is part of our land, and are ready to sacrifice ourselves for it.'

The present Foreign Minister of Egypt, Mahmoud Riad, echoed his master's voice:

'The sacred Arab struggle will not come to an end until Palestine is restored to its owners.'

In March 1963, the official Cairo radio continued the campaign of menace:

'Arab unity is taking shape towards the great goal – i.e. the triumphant return to Palestine with the banner of unity flying high in front of the holy Arab march.'

The newspaper Al-Gumhuriya published an official announcement on the same day:

'The noose around Israel's neck is tightening gradually ... Israel is mightier than the empires which were vanquished in the Arab East and West ... The Arab people will take possession of their full rights in their united homeland.'

Egypt is not a country in which the press utters views and opinions independently of the official will. There is thus significance in the statement of Al-Akhbar on April 4, 1963:

'The liquidation of Israel will not be realized through a declaration of war against Israel by Arab states, but *Arab unity and inter-Arab understanding will serve as a hangman's rope for Israel.*'

The Assembly will note that the imagery of a hangman's rope or of a tightening noose occurs frequently in the macabre vocabulary of Nasserism. He sees himself perpetually presiding over a scaffold. In June 1967 the metaphor of encirclement and strangulation was to come vividly to life, in Israel's hour of solitude and danger.

In February 1964 Nasser enunciated in simple terms what was to become his country's policy during the period of preparation:

'The possibilities of the future will be war with Israel. It is we who will dictate the time. It is we who will dictate the place.'

A similar chorus of threats arose during this period from other Arab capitals. President Aref of Iraq and President Ben-Bella of Algeria were especially emphatic and repetitive in their threat to liquidate Israel. The Syrian attitude was more ominous because it affected a neighbouring frontier. Syrian war propaganda has been particularly intense in the past few years. In 1964 the Syrian Defence Minister, General Abdulla Ziada, announced:

'The Syrian army stands as a mountain to crush Israel and demolish her. This army knows how to crush its enemies.'

Early last year Syria began to proclaim and carry out what it called a 'popular war' against Israel. The Syrian concept of 'popular war' expressed itself in the dispatch of trained terrorist groups into Israel territory to blow up installations and communication centres, to kill, maim, cripple and terrorise civilians in peaceful homes and farms. Sometimes the terrorists, trained in Syria, were dispatched through Jordan or Lebanon. The terrorist war was formally declared by President Al-Atassi on May 22, 1966, when he addressed soldiers on the Israel-Syrian front:

'We raise the slogan of the people's liberation war. We want total war with no limits, a war that will destroy the Zionist base.'

The Syrian Defence Minister, Hafiz Asad, said two days later:

'We say: We shall never call for, nor accept peace. We shall only accept war and the restoration of the usurped land. We have resolved to drench this land with our blood, to oust you, aggressors, and throw you into the sea for good. We must meet as soon as possible and fight a single liberation war on the level of the whole area against Israel, Imperialism and all the enemies of the people.'

Mr. President, from that day to this, not a week passed without Syrian officials adding to this turgid stream of invective and hate. From that day to this, there has not been a single month without terrorist acts, offensive to every impulse of human compassion and international civility, being directed from Syria against Israel citizens and territory. I would have no difficulty in filling the General Assembly's records with a thousand official statements by Arab leaders in the past two years announcing their intention to destroy Israel by diverse forms of organized physical violence. The Arab populations have been conditioned by their leaders to the anticipation of a total war, preceded by the constant harassment of the prospective victim.

Israel's Policy, 1957–1967

From 1948 to this very day there has not been one statement by any Arab representative of a neighbouring Arab state indicating readiness to respect existing agreements or the permanent renunciation of force to recognize Israel's sovereign right of existence or to apply to Israel any of the central provisions of the United Nations Charter.

For some time Israel showed a stoic patience in her reaction to these words of menace. This was because the threats were not accompanied by a capacity to carry them into effect. But the inevitable result of this campaign of menace was the burden of a heavy race of arms. We strove to maintain an adequate deterrent strength and the decade beginning in March 1957 was not monopolized by security considerations alone. Behind the wall of a strong defence, with eyes vigilantly fixed on dangerous borders, we embarked on a constructive era in the national enterprise. These were years of swift expansion in our agriculture and industry, of intensive progress in the sciences and arts, of a widening international vocation, symbolized in the growth of strong links with the developing world. At the end of this first decade, Israel had established relations of commerce and culture with all the Americas, and with most of the countries of Western, Central and Eastern Europe. In her second decade she built constructive links with the emerging countries of the developing world with whom we are tied by a common aspiration to translate national freedom into creative economic growth and progress.

Fortified by friendships in all five continents, inspired by its role in the great drama of developments, intensely preoccupied by tasks of spiritual cooperation with kindred communities in various parts of the world, and in the efforts to assure the Jewish survival after the disastrous blows of Nazi oppressions, tenaciously involved in the development of original social ideas, Israel went on with its work. We could not concern ourselves exclusively with the torrent of hatred pouring in upon us from Arab governments. In the era of modern communication a nation is not entirely dependent on its regional context. The wide world is open to the voice of friendship. Arab hostility towards Israel became increasingly isolated, while our position in the international family became more deeply entrenched. Many in the world drew confidence from the fact that a very small nation could, by its exertion and example, rise to respected levels in social progress, scientific progress and the human arts, and so our policy was to deter the aggression of our neighbours so long as it was endurable, to resist it only when failure to resist would have invited its intensified renewal, to withstand Arab violence without being obsessed by it, and even to search patiently here and there for any glimmer of moderation and realism in the Arab mind. We also pursued the hope of bringing all the great powers to a harmonious policy in support of the security and sovereignty of Middle Eastern states. It was not easy to take this course. The sacrifice imposed upon our population by Arab violence was cumulative in its effects, but as it piled up month by month the toll of death and bereavement was heavy and in the last few years it was evident that this organized murder was directed by a central hand.

We were able to limit our response to this aggression so long as its own scope appeared to be limited. President Nasser seemed for some years to be accumulating inflammable material without an immediate desire to set it alight. He was heavily engaged in domination and conquest elsewhere. His speeches were strong against Israel, but his bullets, guns and poison gases were for the time being used to intimidate other Arab states and to maintain a colonial war against the villagers of the Yemen and the peoples of the Arabian Peninsula.

But Israel's danger was great. The military build-up in Egypt proceeded at an intensive rate. It was designed to enable Egypt to press its war plans against Israel while maintaining its violent adventures elsewhere. In the face of these developments, Israel was forced to devote an increasing part of its resources to self-defence. With the declaration by Syria of the doctrine of a 'day by day military confrontation', the situation in the Middle East grew darker. The Palestine Liberation Organization, the Palestine Liberation Army, the Unified Arab Command, the intensified expansion of military forces and equipment in Egypt, Syria, Lebanon, Jordan and more remote parts of the Arab continent – these were the signals of a growing danger to which we sought to alert the mind and conscience of the world.

The War Design, 1967
In three tense weeks between May 14, and June 5, Egypt, Syria and Jordan, assisted and incited by more distant Arab states, embarked on a policy of immediate and total aggression.

June 1967 was to be the month of decision. The 'final solution' was at hand.

There was no convincing motive for the aggressive design which was now unfolded. Egyptian and Soviet sources had claimed that a concentrated Israeli invasion of Syria was expected during the second or third week in May. No claim could be more frivolous or farfetched. It is true that Syria was sending terrorists into Israel to lay mines on public roads and, on one occasion, to bombard the Israeli settlement at Manara from the Lebanese border. The accumulation of such actions had sometimes evoked Israeli responses always limited in scope and time. All that Syria had to do to ensure perfect tranquillity on her frontier with Israel was to discourage the terrorist war. Not only did she not discourage these actions – she encouraged them, she gave them every moral and practical support. But the picture of Israeli troop concentrations in strength for an invasion of

Syria was a monstrous fiction. Twice Syria refused to cooperate with suggestions by the UN authorities, and accepted by Israel, for a simultaneous and reciprocal inspection of the Israel-Syrian frontier. On one occasion the Soviet Ambassador complained to my Prime Minister of heavy troop concentrations in the North of Israel. When invited to join the Prime Minister that very moment in a visit to any part of Israel which he would like to see, the distinguished envoy brusquely refused. The prospect of finding out the truth at first hand seemed to fill him with a profound disquiet. But by May 9, the Secretary-General of the United Nations from his own sources on the ground had ascertained that no Israeli troop concentration existed. This fact had been directly communicated to the Syrian and Egyptian Governments. The excuse had been shattered, but the allegations still remained. The steps which I now describe could not possibly have any motive or justification if an Israeli troop concentration which both Egypt and Syria knew, did not exist. Indeed the Egyptian build-up ceased to be described by its authors as the result of any threat to Syria.

On May 14, Egyptian forces began to move into Sinai.

On May 16, the Egyptian Command ordered the United Nations Emergency Force to leave the border. The following morning the reason became clear. For on May 17, 1967, at 6 in the morning, Radio Cairo broadcast that Field-Marshal Amer had issued alert orders to the Egyptian armed forces. Nor did he mention Syria as the excuse. This announcement reads:

'1. The state of preparedness of the Egyptian armed forces will increase to the full level of preparedness for war, beginning 14.30 hours last Sunday.

'2. Formations and units allocated in accordance with the operational plans will advance from their present locations to the designated positions.

'3. The armed forces are to be in full preparedness to carry out any combat tasks on the Israel front in accordance with developments.'

On May 18, Egypt called for the total removal of the United Nations Emergency Force. The Secretary-General of the United Nations acceded to this request and moved to carry out, without reference to the Security Council or the General Assembly, without carrying out the procedures indicated by Secretary-General Hammerskjold in the event of a request for a withdrawal being made, without heeding the protesting voices of some of the permanent members of the Security Council and of the government at whose initiative the force had been established, without consulting Israel on the consequent prejudice to her military security and her vital maritime freedom, and without seeking such delay as would enable alternative measures to be concerted for preventing belligerency by sea and a dangerous confrontation of forces by land.

It is often said that United Nations procedures are painfully slow. This decision was disastrously swift. Its effect was to make Sinai safe for belligerency from North to South, to create a sudden disruption of the local security balance, and to leave an international maritime interest exposed to almost certain threat. I have already said that Israel's attitude to the peace-keeping functions of the United Nations has been traumatically affected by its experience. What is the use of a fire brigade which vanishes from the scene as soon as the first smoke and flames appear? Is it surprising that we are firmly resolved never again to allow a vital Israel interest and our very security to rest on such a fragile foundation?

The clouds now gathered thick and fast. Between May 14 and May 23, Egyptian concentrations in Sinai increased day by day. Israel took corresponding measures. In the absence of an agreement to the contrary it is, of course, legal for any state to place its armies wherever it chooses in its territory. It is equally true that nothing could be more uncongenial to the prospect of peace than to have large armies facing each other across a narrow space, with one of them clearly bent on an early assault. For the purpose of the concentration was not in doubt. On May 18, at 2400 hours, the Cairo radio, Saut el-Arab, published the following order of the day by Abdul Mushin Murtagi, the General then commanding Sinai:

'The Egyptian forces have taken up positions in accordance with a definite plan.

'Our forces are definitely ready to carry the battle beyond the borders of Egypt.

'Morale is very high among the members of our armed forces because this is the day for which they have been waiting – to make a holy war in order to return the plundered land to its owners.

'In many meetings with army personnel they asked when the holy war would begin – the time has come to give them their wish.'

On May 21 General Amer gave the order to mobilize reserves. Now came the decisive step. All doubt that Egypt had decided upon immediate or early war was now dispelled. Appearing at an Air Force Base at 6 o'clock in the morning, President Nasser announced that he would blockade the Gulf of Akaba to Israeli ships, adding: 'The Jews threaten war and we say: by all means, we are ready for war.'

But the Jews were not threatening war. Prime Minister Eshkol was calling for a de-escalation of forces. Nasser treated this as a sign of weakness.

On May 25, Cairo Radio announced:

'The Arab people is firmly resolved to wipe Israel off the map and to restore the honour of the Arabs of Palestine.'

On the following day, May 26, Nasser spoke again:

'The Arab people wants to fight. We have been waiting for the right time when we will be completely ready. Recently we have felt that our strength has been sufficient and that if we make battle with Israel we shall be able, with the help of God, to conquer. Sharm e-Sheikh implies a confrontation with Israel. Taking this step makes it imperative that we be ready to undertake a total war with Israel.'

Writing in Al-Ahram, on May 26, Nasser's mouthpiece, Hasanein Heikal, wrote, with engaging realism:

'I consider that there is no alternative to armed conflict between the United Arab Republic and the Israeli enemy. This is the first time that the Arab challenge to Israel attempts to change an existing fact in order to impose a different fact in its place.'

On May 28, Nasser had a press conference. He was having them every day. He said:

'We will not accept any possibility of co-existence with Israel.'

And on the following day:

'If we have succeeded to restore the situation to what it was before 1956, there is no doubt that God will help us and will inspire us to restore the situation to what it was prior to 1948.'

There are various ways of threatening Israel's liquidation. Few ways could be clearer than this.

The troop concentrations and blockade were now to be accompanied by encirclement. The noose was to be fitted around the victim's neck. Other Arab states were closing the ring. On May 30 Nasser signed the Defence Agreement with Jordan, and described its purpose in these terms:

'The armies of Egypt, Jordan, Syria and Lebanon are stationed on the borders of Israel in order to face the challenge. Behind them stand the armies of Iraq, Algeria, Kuwait, Sudan and the whole of the Arab nation.

'This deed will astound the world. Today they will know that the Arabs are ready for the fray. The hour of decision has arrived.'

On June 4 Nasser made a statement on Cairo Radio after signing the protocol associating Iraq with the Egyptian-Jordanian Defence Pact. Here are his words:

'... We are facing you in the battle and are burning with desire for it to start, in order to obtain revenge. This will make the world realize what the Arabs are and what Israel is ... '

Mr. President, nothing has been more startling in recent weeks than to read discussions about who planned, who organized, who initiated, who wanted and who launched this war. Here we have a series of statements, mounting in crescendo from vague warning through open threat, to precise intention.

Here we have the vast mass of the Egyptian armies in Sinai with seven infantry and two armoured divisions, the greatest force ever assembled in that Peninsula in all its history. Here we have 40,000 regular Syrian troops poised to strike at the Jordan Valley from advantageous positions in the hills. Here we have the mobilized forces of Jordan, with their artillery and mortars trained on Israel's population centres in Jerusalem and along the vulnerable narrow coastal plain. Troops from Iraq, Kuwait and Algeria converge towards the battle-front at Egypt's behest. 900 tanks face Israel on the Sinai border, while 200 more are poised to strike the isolated town of Eilat at Israel's southern tip. The military dispositions tell their own story. The Northern Negev was to be invaded by armour and bombarded from the Gaza Strip. From May 27 onward, Egyptian air squadrons in Sinai were equipped with operation orders instructing them in detail on the manner in which Israeli airfields, pathetically few in number, were to be bombarded, thus exposing Israel's crowded cities to easy and merciless assault. Egyptian air sorties came in and out of Israel's southern desert to reconnoitre, inspect and prepare for the assault. An illicit blockade had cut Israel off from all her commerce with the eastern half of the world.

Blockade on Tiran Straits

Those who write this story in years to come will give a special place in their narrative to Nasser's blatant decision to close the Straits of Tiran in Israel's face. It is not difficult to understand why this outrage had a drastic impact. In 1957 the maritime nations, within the framework of the United Nations General Assembly, correctly enunciated the doctrine of free and innocent passage to the Straits. When that doctrine was proclaimed – and incidentally, not challenged by the Egyptian Representative at that time – it was little more than an abstract principle for the maritime world. For Israel it was a great but still unfulfilled prospect, it was not yet a reality. But during the ten years in which we and the other states of the maritime community have relied upon that doctrine and upon established usage, the principle has become a reality consecrated by hundreds of sailings under dozens of flags and the establishment of a whole complex of commerce and industry and communication. A new dimension has been added to the map of the world's communication. And on that dimension we have constructed Israel's bridge towards the friendly states of Asia and Africa, a network of relationships which is the chief pride of Israel in the second decade of its independence and on which its economic future depends.

All this, then, had grown up as an effective usage under the United Nations' flag. Does Mr. Nasser really think that he can come upon the scene in ten minutes and cancel the established legal usage and interests of ten years?

There was in his wanton act a quality of malice. For surely the closing of the Straits of Tiran gave no benefit whatever to Egypt except the perverse joy of inflicting injury on others. It was an anarchic act, because it showed a total disregard for the law of nations, the application of which in this specific case had not been challenged for ten years. And it was, in the literal sense, an act of arrogance, because there are other nations in Asia and East Africa that trade with the port of Eilat, as they have every right to do, through the Straits of Tiran and across the Gulf of Akaba. Other sovereign states from Japan to Ethiopia, from Thailand to Uganda, from Cambodia to Madagascar, have a sovereign right to decide for themselves whether they wish or do not wish to trade with Israel. These countries are not colonies of Cairo. They can trade with Israel or not trade with Israel as they wish, and President Nasser is not the policeman of other African and Asian States.

Here then was a wanton intervention in the sovereign rights of other states in the eastern half of the world to decide for themselves whether or not they wish to establish trade relations with either or both of the two ports at the head of the Gulf of Akaba.

An Act of War

When we examine, then, the implications of this act, we have no cause to wonder that the international shock was great. There was another reason, too, for that shock. Blockades have traditionally been regarded, in the pre-Charter parlance, as acts of war. To blockade, after all, is to attempt strangulation – and sovereign states are entitled not to have their State strangled.

The blockade is by definition an act of war, imposed and enforced through violence.

Never in history have blockade and peace existed side by side. From May 24 onward, the question of who started the war or who fired the first shot became momentously irrelevant. There is no difference in civil law between murdering a man by slow strangulation or killing him by a shot in the head. From the moment at which the blockade was imposed, active hostilities had commenced and Israel owed Egypt nothing of her Charter rights. If a foreign power sought to close Odessa, or Copenhagen or Marseilles or New York Harbour by the use of force, what would happen? Would there be any discussion about who had fired the first shot? Would anyone ask whether aggression had begun? Less than a decade ago the Soviet Union proposed a draft resolution in the General Assembly on the question of defining aggression. The resolution reads:

'In an international conflict, that State shall be declared an attacker which first commits one of the following acts:
a. Naval blockade of the coastal ports of another State.'

This act constituted in the Soviet view direct aggression as distinguished from other specified acts designated in the Soviet draft as indirect aggression. In this particular case the consequences of Nasser's action had been fully announced in advance. On March 1, 1967, my predecessor announced that:

'Interference, by armed force, with ships of the Israel flag exercising free and innocent passage in the Gulf of Akaba and through the Straits of Tiran, will be regarded by Israel as an attack entitling it to exercise its inherent right of self-defence under Article 51 of the United Nations Charter and to take all such measures as are necessary to ensure the free and innocent passage of its ships in the Gulf and in the Straits.'

The representative of France declared that any obstruction of free passage in the Straits or Gulf was contrary to international law 'entailing a possible resort to the measures authorized by Article 51 of the Charter.'

The United States, inside and outside of the United Nations, gave specific endorsement to Israel's right to invoke her inherent right of self-defence against any attempt to blockade the Gulf. Nasser was speaking with acute precision when he stated that Israel now faced the choice either between being choked to death in her southern maritime approaches or to awaiting the death blow from Northern Sinai.

Nobody who lived through those days in Israel, between May 23 and June 5, will ever forget the air of doom that hovered over our country. Hemmed in by hostile armies ready to strike, affronted and beset by a flagrant act of war, bombarded day and night by predictions of her approaching extinction, forced into a total mobilization of all her manpower, her economy and commerce beating with feeble pulse, her main supplies of vital fuel choked by a belligerent act, Israel faced the greatest peril to her existence that she had known since her resistance against aggression 19 years before, at the hour of her birth. There was peril wherever she looked and she faced it in deepening solitude. On May 24 and on succeeding days, the Security Council conducted a desultory debate which sometimes reached a point of levity. The Soviet Representative asserted that he saw no reason for discussing the Middle Eastern situation at all. The Bulgarian delegate uttered these unbelievable words:

'At the present moment there is really no need for an urgent meeting of the Security Council.'

A crushing siege bore down upon us. Multitudes throughout the world trembled for Israel's fate. The single consolation lay in the surge of public opinion which rose up in Israel's defence. From Paris to Montevideo, from New York to Amsterdam, tens of thousands of persons of all ages, peoples and affiliations marched in horrified protest at the approaching stage of genocide. Writers and scientists, religious leaders, trade union movements and even the Communist parties in France, Holland, Switzerland, Norway, Austria and Finland asserted their view that Israel was a peace-loving State, whose peace was being wantonly denied. In the history of our generation it is difficult to think of any other hour in which progressive world opinion rallied in such tension and agony of spirit.

To understand the full depth of pain and shock, it is necessary to grasp the full significance of what Israel's danger meant. A small sovereign State had its existence threatened by lawless violence. The threat to Israel was a menace to the very foundations of the international order. The State thus threatened bore a name which stirred the deepest memories of civilized mankind and the people of the remnant of millions, who, in living memory had been wiped out by a dictatorship more powerful, though scarcely more malicious, than Nasser's Egypt. What Nasser had predicted, what he had worked for with undeflecting purpose, had come to pass – the noose was tightly drawn.

On the fateful morning of June 5, when Egyptian forces moved by air and land against Israel's western coast and southern territory, our country's choice was plain. The choice was to live or perish, to defend the national existence or to forfeit it for all time.

From these dire moments Israel emerged in five heroic days from awful peril to successful and glorious resistance. Alone, unaided, neither seeking nor receiving help, our nation rose in self-defence. So long as men cherish freedom, so long as small states strive for the dignity of existence, the exploits of Israel's armies will be told from one generation to another with the deepest pride. The Soviet Union has described our resistance as aggression and sought to have it condemned. We reject this accusation with all our might. Here was armed force employed in a just and righteous cause, as righteous as the defenders at Valley Forge, as just as the expulsion of Hitler's bombers from the British skies, as noble as the protection of Stalingrad against the Nazi hordes, so was the defence of Israel's security and existence against those who sought our nation's destruction.

What should be condemned is not Israel's action, but the attempt to condemn it. Never have freedom, honour, justice, national interest and international morality been so righteously protected. While fighting raged on the Egyptian-Israel frontier and on the Syrian front, we still hoped to contain the conflict. Jordan was given every chance to remain outside the struggle. Even after Jordan had bombarded and bombed Israel territory at several points we still proposed to the Jordanian monarch that he abstain from general hostilities. A message to this effect reached him several hours after the outbreak of hostilities on the southern front on June 5.

Jordan answered not with words but with shells. Artillery opened fire fiercely along the whole front with special emphasis on the Jerusalem area. Thus Jordan's responsibility for the second phase of the concerted aggression is established beyond doubt. This responsibility cannot fail to have its consequences in the peace settlement. As death and injury rained on the city, Jordan had become the source and origin of Jerusalem's fierce ordeal. The inhabitants of the city can never forget this fact, or fail to draw its conclusions.

Soviet Role in the Middle East Crisis

Mr. President, I have spoken of Israel's defence against the assaults of neighbouring states. This is not the entire story. Whatever happens in the Middle East for good or ill, for peace or conflict, is powerfully affected by what the Great Powers do or omit to do. When the Soviet Union initiates a discussion here, our gaze is inexorably drawn to the story of its role in recent Middle Eastern history. It is a sad and shocking story, it must be frankly told.

Since 1955 the Soviet Union has supplied the Arab States with 2,000 tanks, of which more than 1,000 have gone to Egypt. The Soviet Union has supplied the Arab States with 700 modern fighter aircraft and bombers, more recently with ground missiles, and Egypt alone has received from the USSR 540 field guns, 130 medium guns, 200 120 mm mortars, anti-aircraft guns, 175 rocket launchers, 650 anti-tank guns, seven destroyers, a number of Luna M and SPKA 2 ground-to-ground missiles, 14 submarines and 46 torpedo boats of various types including missile-carrying boats. The Egyptian Army has been trained by Soviet experts. This has been attested to by

Egyptian officers captured by Israel. Most of this equipment was supplied to the Arab States after the Cairo Summit Conference of Arab leaders in January 1964 had agreed on a specific programme for the destruction of Israel, after they had announced and hastened to fulfil this plan by accelerating their arms purchases from the Soviet Union. The proportions of Soviet assistance are attested to by the startling fact that in Sinai alone the Egyptians abandoned equipment and offensive weapons of Soviet manufacture whose value is estimated at two billion dollars.

Together with the supply of offensive weapons, the Soviet Union has encouraged the military preparations of the Arab States.

Since 1961, the Soviet Union has assisted Egypt in its desire to conquer Israel. The great amount of offensive equipment supplied to the Arab States strengthens this assessment.

A Great Power which professes its devotion to peaceful settlement and the rights of states has for 14 years afflicted the Middle East with a headlong armaments race, with the paralysis of the United Nations as an instrument of security and against those who defend it.

The constant increase and escalation of Soviet armaments in Arab countries has driven Israel to a corresponding, though far smaller, procurement programme. Israel's arms purchases were precisely geared to the successive phases of Arab, and especially Egyptian, re-armament. On many occasions in recent months we and others have vainly sought to secure Soviet agreement for a reciprocal reduction of arms supplies in our region. These efforts have borne no fruit. The expenditure on social and economic progress of one half of what has been put into the purchase of Soviet arms would have been sufficient to redeem Egypt from its social and economic ills. A corresponding diversion of resources from military to social expenditure would have taken place in Israel. A viable balance of forces could have been achieved at a lower level of armaments, while our region could have moved forward to higher standards of human and social welfare. For Israel's attitude is clear. We should like to see the arms race slowed down. But if the race is joined, we are determined not to lose it. A fearful waste of economic energy in the Middle East is the direct result of the Soviet role in the constant stimulation of the race in arms.

It is clear from Arab sources that the Soviet Union has played a provocative role in spreading alarmist and incendiary reports of Israel intentions amongst Arab Governments.

On June 9 President Nasser said:

'Our friends in the U.S.S.R. warned the visiting parliamentary delegation in Moscow at the beginning of last month, that there exists a plan of attack against Syria.'

Similarly an announcement by Tass of May 23 states:

'The Foreign Affairs and Security Committee of the Knesset have accorded the Cabinet special powers to carry out war operations against Syria. Israeli forces concentrating on the Syrian border have been put in a state of alert for war. General mobilization has also been proclaimed in the country...'

There was not one word of truth in this story. But its diffusion in the Arab countries could only have an incendiary result.

Cairo Radio broadcast on May 28 (0500 hours) an address by Marshal Gretchko at a farewell party in honour of the former Egyptian Minister of Defence, Shams ed-Din Badran:

'The U.S.S.R., her armed forces, her people and Government will stand by the Arabs and will continue to encourage and support them. We are your faithful friends and we shall continue aiding you because this is the policy of the Soviet nation, its Party and Government. On behalf of the Ministry of Defence and in the name of the Soviet nation we wish you success and victory.'

This promise of military support came less than a week after the illicit closing of the Tiran Straits, an act which the U.S.S.R. has done nothing to condemn.

USSR Attitudes at the UN

The USSR has exercised her veto right in the Security Council five times. Each time a just and constructive judgment has been frustrated. On January 22, 1964, France, the United Kingdom and the United States presented a Draft Resolution to facilitate work on the West Bank of the River Jordan in the B'not Ya'akov Canal Project. The Soviet veto held up regional water development for several years. On March 29, 1964, a New Zealand resolution simply reiterating UN policy on blockade along the Suez Canal was frustrated by Soviet dissent. On August 19, 1963, a United Kingdom and United States Resolution on the murder of two Israelis at Almagor was denied adoption by Soviet opposition. On December 21, 1964, the USSR vetoed a United Kingdom and United States Resolution on incidents at Tel Dan, including the shelling of Dan, Dafna and Sha'ar Yashuv. On November 2, 1966, Argentina, Japan, the Netherlands, New Zealand and Nigeria joined to express regret at 'infiltration from Syria and loss of human life caused by the incidents in October and November 1966'. This was one of the few resolutions sponsored by member-States from five continents.

The Soviet use of veto has had a dual effect. First, it prevented any resolution which an Arab State has opposed, from being adopted by the Council. Secondly, it has inhibited the Security Council from taking constructive action in disputes between an Arab State and Israel because of the certain knowledge that the veto would be applied in what was deemed to be the Arab interest. The consequences of the Soviet veto policy have been to deny Israel any possibility of just and equitable treatment in the Security Council, and to nullify the Council as a constructive factor in the affairs of the Middle East.

Does all this really add up to a constructive intervention by the USSR in the Arab-Israel tension? The position becomes graver when we recall the unbridled invective against the Permanent Representative of Israel in the Security Council. In its words and in the letter to the Israel Government, the USSR has formulated an obscene comparison between the Israel Defence Forces and the Hitlerite hordes which overran Europe in the Second World War. There is a flagrant breach of international morality and human decency in this comparison. Our nation never compromised with Hitler Germany. It never signed a pact with it as did the USSR in 1939.

To associate the name of Israel with the accursed tyrant who engulfed the Jewish people in a tidal wave of slaughter is to violate every canon of elementary taste and fundamental truth.

In the light of this history, the General Assembly will easily understand Israel's reaction to the Soviet initiative in convening this Special Session for the purpose of condemning our country and recommending a withdrawal to the position that existed before June 5.

Your (the Soviet) Government's record in the stimulation of the arms race, in the paralysis of the Security Council, in the encouragement throughout the Arab World of unfounded suspicion concerning Israel's intentions, your constant refusal to say a single word of criticism at any time of declarations threatening the violent overthrow of Israel's sovereignty and existence – all this gravely undermines your claims to objectivity. You come here in our eyes not as a judge or as a prosecutor, but rather as a legitimate object of international criticism for the part that you have played in the sombre events which have brought our region to a point of explosive tension.

If the Soviet Union had made an equal distribution of the friendship amongst the peoples of the Middle East, if it had refrained from exploiting regional rancours and tensions for the purpose of its own global policy, if it had stood in even-handed devotion to the legitimate interests of all states, the crisis which now commands our attention and anxiety would never have occurred. To the charge of aggression I answer that Israel's resistance at the lowest ebb of its fortunes will resound across history, together with the uprising of our battered remnants in the Warsaw Ghetto, as a triumphant assertion of human freedom. From the dawn of its history the people now rebuilding a State in Israel has struggled often in desperate conditions against tyranny and aggression. Our action on June 5 falls nobly within that tradition. We have tried to show that even a small state and a small people have the right to live. I believe that we shall not be found alone in the assertion of that right, which is the very essence of the Charter of the United Nations. Similarly, the suggestion that everything goes back to where it was before the 5th of June is totally unacceptable. The General Assembly cannot ignore the fact that the Security Council, where the primary responsibility lay, has emphatically rejected such a course. It was not Israel, but Syria, Egypt and Jordan, who violently shattered the previous situation to smithereens. It cannot be recaptured. It is a fact of technology that it is easier to fly to the moon than to reconstruct a broken egg. The Security Council acted wisely in rejecting the backward step, advocated by the Soviet Union. To go back to the situation out of which the conflict arose would mean that all the conditions for renewed hostilities would be brought together again. I repeat what I said to the Security Council. Our watchword is not 'backward to belligerency' but 'forward to peace'.

What the Assembly should prescribe is not a formula for renewed hostilities, but a series of principles for the construction of a new future in the Middle East. With the cease-fire established, our progress must be not backward to an armistice regime which has collapsed under the weight of years and the brunt of hostility. History summons us forward to permanent peace and the peace that we envisage can only be elaborated in frank and lucid dialogue between Israel and each of the states which have participated in the attempt to overthrow her sovereignty and undermine her existence. We dare not be satisfied with intermediate arrangements which are neither war nor peace. Such patchwork ideas carry within themselves the seeds of future tragedy. Free from external pressures and interventions, imbued with a common love for a region which they are destined to share, the Arab and Jewish nations must now transcend their conflicts in dedication to a new Mediterranean future in concert with a renascent Europe and an Africa and Asia which have emerged at last to their independent role on the stage of history.

The Vision of Peace

In free negotiation with each of our neighbours we shall offer durable and just solutions redounding to our mutual advantage and honour. The Arab states can no longer be permitted to recognize Israel's existence only for the purpose of plotting its elimination. They have come face to face with us in conflict. Let them now come face to face with us in peace.

In peaceful conditions we could imagine communications running from Haifa to Beirut and Damascus in the north, to Amman and beyond in the east, and to Cairo in the south. The opening of these blocked arteries would stimulate the life, thought and commerce in the region beyond any level otherwise conceivable. Across the southern Negev, communication between the Nile Valley and the fertile crescent could be resumed without any change in political jurisdiction. What is now often described as a wedge between Arab lands would become a bridge. The Kingdom of Jordan, now cut off from its maritime outlet, could freely import and export its goods on the Israeli coast. On the Red Sea, cooperative action could expedite the port developments at Eilat and Akaba, which give Israel and Jordan their contact with a resurgent East Africa and a developing Asia.

The Middle East, lying athwart three continents, could become a busy centre of air communications, which are now impeded by boycotts and the necessity to take circuitous routes. Radio, telephone and postal communications, which now end abruptly in mid-air, would unite a divided region. The Middle East, with its historic monuments and scenic beauty, could attract a vast movement of travellers and pilgrims if existing impediments were removed. Resources which lie across national frontiers – the minerals of the Dead Sea and the phosphates of the Negev and the Arava – could be developed in mutual interchange of technical knowledge. Economic cooperation in agricultural and industrial development could lead to supranational arrangements like those which mark the European community. The United Nations could establish an economic commission for the Middle East, similar to the commissions now at work in Europe, Latin America and the Far East. The specialized agencies could intensify their support of health and educational development with greater efficiency if a regional harmony were attained. The development of arid zones, the desalination of water and the conquest of tropical disease are common interests of the entire region, congenial to a sharing of knowledge and experience.

In the institutions of scientific research and higher education of both sides of the frontiers, young Israelis and Arabs could join in a mutual discourse of learning. The old prejudices could be replaced by a new comprehension and respect, born of a reciprocal dialogue in the intellectual domain. In such a Middle East, military budgets would spontaneously find a less exacting point of equilibrium. Excessive sums devoted to security could be diverted to development projects.

Thus, in full respect of the region's diversity, an entirely new story, never known or told before, would unfold across the Eastern Mediterranean. For the first time in history, no Mediterranean nation is in subjection. All are endowed with sovereign freedom. The challenge now is to use this freedom for creative growth. There is only one road to that end. It is the road of recognition, of direct contact, of true cooperation. It is the road of peaceful co-existence. This road, as the ancient prophets of Israel foretold, leads to Jerusalem.

Jerusalem, now united after her tragic division, is no longer an arena for gun emplacements and barbed wire. In our nation's long history there have been few hours more intensely moving than the hour of our reunion with the Western Wall. A people had come back to the cradle of its birth. It has renewed its link with the memories which that reunion evokes. For 20 years there has not been free access by men of all faiths to the shrines which they hold in unique reverence. This access now exists. Israel is resolved to give effective expression, in cooperation with the world's great religions, to the immunity and sanctity of all the Holy Places. The prospect of a negotiated peace is less remote than it may seem. Israel waged her defensive struggle in pursuit of two objectives – security and peace. Peace and security, with their territorial, economic and demographic implications, can only be built by the free negotiation which is the true essence of sovereign responsibility. A call to the recent combatants to negotiate the conditions of their future co-existence is the only constructive course which this Assembly could take.

We ask the great powers to remove our tormented region from the scope of global rivalries, to summon its governments to build their common future themselves, to assist it, if they will, to develop social and cultural levels worthy of its past.

We ask the developing countries to support a dynamic and forward-looking policy and not to drag the new future back into the out-worn past.

To the small nations, which form the bulk of the international family, we offer the experience which teaches us that small communities can best secure their interests by maximal self-reliance. Nobody will help those who will not help themselves; we ask the small nations in the solidarity of our smallness, to help us stand firm against intimidation and threat such as those by which we are now assailed. We ask world opinion, which rallied to us in our plight, to accompany us faithfully in our new opportunity. We ask the United Nations, which was prevented from offering us security in our recent peril, to respect our independent quest for the peace and security which are the Charter's higher ends. We shall do what the Security Council decided should be done – and reject the course which the Security Council emphatically and wisely rejected. It may seem that Israel stands alone against numerous and powerful adversaries. But we have faith in the undying forces in our nation's history which have so often given the final victory to spirit over matter, to inner truth over mere quantity. We believe in the vigilance of history which has guarded our steps. The Guardian of Israel neither slumbers nor sleeps.

The Middle East, tired of wars, is ripe for a new emergence of human vitality. Let the opportunity not fall again from our hands.

Appendix 11

Yizhak Rabin, Address upon receiving
an honorary doctorate from the Hebrew
University, 28 June 1967

Your Excellency, President of the State, Mr Prime Minister, President of the Hebrew University, Rector of the University, Governors, Teachers, Ladies and Gentlemen:

I stand in awe before you, leaders of the generation, here in this venerable and impressive place overlooking Israel's eternal capital and the birth-place of our Nation's earliest history.

Together with other distinguished personalities who are no doubt worthy of this honour, you have chosen to do me great honour in conferring upon me the title of Doctor of Philosophy. Permit me to express to you here my feelings on this occasion. I regard myself, at this time, as a representative of the entire Israel Forces, of its thousands of officers and ten of thousands of soldiers who brought the State of Israel its victory in the six-day war. It may be asked why the University saw fit to grant the title of Honorary Doctor of Philosophy to a soldier in recognition of his martial activities. What is there in common to military activity and the academic world which represents civilisation and culture? What is there in common between those whose profession is violence and spiritual values? I, however, am honoured that through me you are expressing such deep appreciation to my comrades in arms and to the uniqueness of the Israel Defence Forces, which is no more than extension of the unique spirit of the entire Jewish People.

The world has recognised the fact that the Israel Defence Forces are different from other armies. Although its first task is the military task of ensuring security, the Israel Defence Forces undertakes numerous tasks of peace, tasks not of destruction but of construction and of the strengthening of the Nation's cultural and moral resources.

Our educational work has been praised widely and was given national recognition, when in 1966 it was granted the Israel Prize for Education, The Nahal, which combines military training and agricultural settlement, teachers in border villages contributing to social and cultural enrichment, these are but a few small examples of the Israel Defence Forces' uniqueness in this sphere.

However, today, the University has conferred this honorary title on

357

us in recognition of our Army's superiority of spirit and morale as it was revealed in the heat of war, for we are standing in this place by virtue of battle which though forced upon us was forged into a victory astounding the world.

War is intrinsically harsh and cruel, bloody and tear-stained, but particularly this war, which we have just undergone, brought forth rare and magnificent instances of heroism and courage, together with humane expressions of brotherhood, comradeship, and spiritual greatness.

Whoever has not seen a tank crew continue its attack with its commander killed and its vehicle badly damaged, whoever has not seen sappers endangering their lives to extricate wounded comrades from a minefield, whoever has not seen the anxiety and the effort of the entire Air Force devoted to rescuing a pilot who has fallen in enemy territory, cannot know the meaning of devotion between comrades in arms.

The entire Nation was exalted and many wept upon hearing the news of the capture of the Old City. Our Sabra Youth and most certainly our soldiers do not tend to sentimentality and shy away from revealing it in public, however, the strain of battle, the anxiety which preceded it, and the sense of salvation and of direct participation of every soldier in the forging of the heart of Jewish history cracked the shell of hardness and shyness and released well-springs of excitement and spiritual emotion. The paratroopers, who conquered the Wailing Wall, leaned on its stones and wept, and as a symbol this was a rare occasion, almost unparalleled in human history. Such phrases and clichés are not generally used in our Army but this scene on the Temple Mount beyond the power of verbal description revealed as though by a lightning flash deep truths. And more than this, the joy of triumph seized the whole nation. Nevertheless we find more and more and more a strange phenomenon among our fighters. Their joy is incomplete, and more than a small portion of sorrow and shock prevails in their festivities. And there are those who abstain from all celebration. The warriors in the front lines saw with their own eyes not only the glory of victory but the price of victory. Their comrades who fell beside them bleeding. And I know that even the terrible price which our enemies paid touched the hearts of many of our men. It may be that the Jewish People never learned and never accustomed itself to feel the triumph of conquest and victory and therefore we receive it with mixed feelings.

The six-day war revealed many instances of heroism far beyond the single attack which dashes unthinkingly forward. In many places desperate and lengthy battles raged. In Rafiah, in El Arish, in Um

Kataf, in Jerusalem, and in Ramat Hagollan, there, and in many other places, the soldiers of Israel were revealed as heroic in spirit, in courage, and in persistence which cannot leave anyone indifferent once he has seen this great and exalting human revelation. We speak a great deal of the few against the many. In this war perhaps for the first time since the Arab invasions of the spring of 1948 and the battles of Negba and Degania, units of the Israel Forces stood in all sectors, few against many. This means that relatively small units of our soldiers, often entered seemingly endless networks of fortification, surrounded by hundreds and thousands of enemy troops and faced with the task of forcing their way, hour after hour, in this jungle of dangers, even after the momentum of the first attack has passed and all that remains is the necessity of belief in our strength, the lack of alternative and the goal for which we are fighting, to summon up every spiritual resource in order to continue the fight to its very end.

Thus our armoured Forces broke through on all fronts, our paratroopers fought their way into Rafiah and Jerusalem, our sappers cleared minefields under enemy fire. The units which broke the enemy lines and came to their objectives after hours upon hours of struggle continuing on and on, while their comrades fell right and left and they continued forward, only forward. These soldiers were carried forward by spiritual values, by deep spiritual resources, far more than by their weapons or the technique of warfare.

We have always demanded the cream of our youth for the Israel Defence Forces when we coined the slogan 'Hatovim l'Tayis' – The Best to Flying, and this was a phrase which became a value. We meant not only technical and manual skills. We meant that if our airmen were to be capable of defeating the forces of four enemy countries within a few short hours, they must have moral values and human values.

Our airmen, who struck the enemies' planes so accurately that no one in the world understands how it was done and people seek technological explanations of secret weapons; our armoured troops who stood and beat the enemy even when their equipment was inferior to his; our soldiers in all various branches of the Israel Defence Forces who overcame our enemies everywhere, despite their superior numbers and fortifications; all these revealed not only coolness and courage in battle but a burning faith in their righteousness, an understanding that only their personal stand against the greatest of dangers could bring to their country and to their families victory, and that if the victory was not theirs the alternative was destruction.

Furthermore, in every sector our Forces' commanders, of all ranks far outshone the enemies' commanders. Their understanding, their will, their ability to improvise, their care for soldiers and above all, their leading troops into battle, these are not matters of material or of technique. They have no rational explanation, except in terms of a deep consciousness of the moral justice of their fight.

All of this springs from the soul and leads back to the spirit. Our warriors prevailed not by their weapons but by the consciousness of a mission, by a consciousness of righteousness, by a deep love for their homeland and an understanding of the difficult task laid upon them; to ensure the existence of our people in its homeland, to protect, even at the price of their lives, the right of the Nation of Israel to live in its own State, free, independent and peaceful.

This Army, which I had the privilege of commanding through these battles, came from the people and returns to the people, to the people which rises in its hour of crisis and overcomes all enemies by virtue of its moral values, its spiritual readiness in the hour of need.

As the representative of the Israel Defence Forces, and in the name of every one of its soldiers, I accept with pride your recognition.

INDEX

Index

363